ALEXANDER THE GREAT

GREAT COMMANDERS
In Action

FROM THE PUBLISHER OF
MILITARY HISTORY

NHS
THE NATIONAL HISTORICAL SOCIETY

★★★
★ ★
★
NHS ═══
★
★★
THE NATIONAL HISTORICAL SOCIETY

Cowles Enthusiast Media/History Group
Jon Guttman - Editor
Roger L. Vance - Editorial Director
Carl von Wodtke - Managing Editor
Nan Siegel - Senior Editor
Gregory Lalire - Senior Editor
Ann Thompson - Copy Editor
Alan Webber - Copy Editor
Barbara Sutliff - Creative Director

Thomas G. O'Keefe - History Group Vice President
Gail Ehresmann-Dryer - Associate Group Publisher
John Stanchak - Editorial Director of New Product Development

Cowles Enthusiast Media/Creative Publishing
Melissa Erickson - Senior Project Manager
Linda Schloegel - Production

COWLES
Enthusiast Media

Library of Congress Cataloging-in-Publication Data
Great commanders in action.p. cm.
ISBN 0-86573-860-2 1. Military history. 2. Generals –Biography.
3. Command of troops. I. Cowles Creative Publishing.
D25.G68 1996   355'.0092'2–dc21   96-36890
                                                                                    CIP

To order additional copies of this book, call
(800) 358-6327.
To subscribe to *Military History* Magazine, call
(800) 829-3340 or outside U.S. (904) 446-6914.

Image p.2 courtesy Library of Congress

Contents

Introduction

Human conflict is older than the Bible, but the first record of brilliant leadership dates to 1469 BC, when King Thutmose III led part of his Egyptian army north through Megiddo Pass (probably at night) to strike a rebel army in flank while it was engaged with his main, southern force. The resulting slaughter was impressive enough for its time to make the battle's Biblical name—Armageddon—a metaphor for annihilation, and the name of Thutmose III synonymous with military brilliance. He would soon have plenty of company.

Since its first issue in August 1984, *Military History* magazine has presented a multitude of famous and lesser-known battles and campaigns—and there seems to be no end to the tales yet to be told. Presented chronologically, the entries in this anthology were selected primarily to exemplify outstanding military leadership throughout the world's history.

Characteristic of the magazine, however, not all of the examples presented herein are necessarily what one might expect. In addition to such familiar names as Alexander the Great, Hannibal Barca, Gaius Julius Caesar, the Duke of Marlborough, Napoleon Bonaparte and Sir Edmund Allenby, there are military geniuses who have been unfairly overlooked, like the great Chinese campaigner Cao Cao; Otto the Great, the Saxon king who decisively defeated the Magyars at Lechfeld and laid the foundation for a united Germany; Miami Chief Michikiniqua (Little Turtle), victor in the worst defeat inflicted on the U.S. Army by American Indians; and Jozef Pilsudski, the Polish marshal who outmaneuvered a brilliant Bolshevik opponent to turn back Communism's first armed incursion into Western Europe.

There are also cases of famous commanders operating in other-than-classic circumstances. At Alesia, Julius Caesar had to prosecute a siege while fending off a large Gallic relief force. At Prague, the costly failure of a Prussian assault compelled an ailing Frederick the Great to take charge. At Marengo, First Consul Napoleon Bonaparte was beaten by the Austrians, but by fighting a second battle that same day, he was able to retrieve a decisive victory from the jaws of imminent defeat—with more than a little help from his gallant lieutenant, Charles Decaix. Arthur Wellesley considered his most memorable victory to have been won years before he became the Duke of Wellington—not at Salamanca or Waterloo, but an Indian town called Assaye. At Chancellorsville, Confederate cavalier Maj. Gen. J.E.B. Stuart suddenly found himself thrust into the role of infantry commander—and filling the shoes of the wounded Lt. Gen. T.J. "Stonewall" Jackson, at that—in what arguably might be Stuart's finest hour.

In addition to the "great captains," we give some of the limelight to subordinate commanders and even junior officers whose exploits deserve their

6

share of credit. Some did attract attention, like Brig. Gen. Anthony McAuliffe, whose defiant reply of "Nuts" to a German ultimatum at Bastogne (which may not have been what he really said) earned him more fame than the defense of the town itself. The same cannot be said of Maj. Gen. John Huston Church, the 24th Infantry Division commander whose little-remembered defense of the Naktong Bulge contributed significantly to Lt. Gen. Walton H. Walker's preservation of the Korean city of Pusan—and stands alongside Jeb Stuart's actions at Chancellorsville as an exemplary case of a subordinate understanding and carrying out his commander's intent. Largely forgotten, too, are the achievements of the Finns during their 1939-40 Winter War with the Soviet Union, which represented in the main the collective product of small-unit actions, of which the most notable, Suomossalmi, was won by a division commander, Colonel H.J. Siilasvuo.

Arguably, the most intriguing commanders highlighted in these pages are those who win—or, in the case of Ramses II at Kadesh, at least stave off disaster—by their ability to think on their feet. Alexander's foiling Persian King Darius III's move to cut off his logistics route at Issus; Duke William of Normandy's overcoming a wall of Saxon shields at Hastings; Prince Bayazid Yilderim's leading his Turks across the front line of battle to save a deteriorating situation at Kosovo; the *Duc* d'Enghien's carrying out a similar maneuver around the Spanish rear at Rocroi; George Washington's striking back at his British and Hessian pursuers at Trenton…these are but a few examples of those moments of brilliance whose consequences—for better or worse—would be felt for centuries to come.

Longtime readers of *Military History* will find a bonus in this eclectic selection of episodes from past issues. Inevitably, mistakes popped up in some of the old articles, which were soon brought to our attention by sharp-eyed readers. Their comments were not dismissed by the editors, who saved a lot of the "nit-picker letters" in the event of future reprints. Consequently, numerous corrections and additions have been incorporated into the chapters that make up this volume. To those many pundits whose feedback has contributed to the accuracy of this book, we'd like to express our heartfelt thanks—and our hopes that with your help, we've got it all right this time around!

Jon Guttman
Editor, *Military History*

NHS
THE NATIONAL
HISTORICAL SOCIETY

The National Historical Society was formed in 1996 as a membership organization dedicated to widespread and easy access to nonpartisan history-related information, products and services. Through its grants program, the NHS supports nonprofit programs and organizations active in efforts to preserve and interpret America's heritage and to further interest in, and study of, history among the general public and students.

The NHS, through its affiliation with the History Group of Cowles Enthusiast Media, seeks to offer its members a wide variety of opportunities to participate in communities of interest. In addition to magazines, books, videos, tours and television programming, the NHS offers members and nonmembers a global gateway to historical information and forums for interaction with history enthusiasts around the world on the Internet via TheHistoryNet (http://www.thehistorynet.com).

Other NHS member benefits include discounts at hundreds of historic sites and museums; Travel Club discounts on airfares and accommodations; special NHS-hosted tour opportunities; a subscription to *Historic Traveler* Magazine; the NHS Newsletter and NHS Collection Catalog; and voting privileges on the annual NHS grants.

For more information about the National Historical Society, call 1-800-849-6148.

Ambush at Kadesh

*Emulating Thutmose III, young Ramses II led his
Egyptian host deep into Syria—blissfully ignorant that he was
doing exactly what Hittite King Muwutallis wanted him to do.*

By Robert Collins Suhr

Thirty-three centuries ago, below the sun-drenched walls of Kadesh, the Egyptian and Hittite empires fought for control of the land now known as Syria in the first battle about which modern man has detailed contemporary accounts.

In the first 100 generations of its recorded history, the kingdom of Egypt had experienced little military action, apart from the occasional civil war or skirmishing for control of Nubia. At one point during the Middle Kingdom, the king (who was identified by his palace, the "High House" or *Peron*, which evolved into the term "pharaoh") felt so secure that he sent his personal bodyguard to Nubia on semipermanent garrison duty. Egypt had no need for a strong military because the deserts to the east and west, and the Mediterranean to the north, protected her from invasion. To the south, the Egyptians ruled Nubia as a conquered province. The Egyptians believed they already possessed the richest lands in the known world, so they had no desire for further conquest.

That era of peace and tranquility ended with what historians call the "Second Intermediate Period." By 1700 BC the Hyksos ("Rulers from Foreign Lands") had conquered Lower Egypt and extended their influence up the Nile from their capital at Avaris in the eastern delta. A vassal prince ruled Nubia, while the kings of Upper Egypt at Thebes paid tribute to the Hyksos.

The rise of Egyptian militarism coincided with the advent of the New Kingdom. Around 1650 BC, Queen Kamose defeated the Hyksos, driving them down the Nile toward the delta. Her grandson Ahmose completed the task of driving the Hyksos from Egypt when he took Avaris in 1590 BC, then pursued them to Sharuhen, in Palestine, which he besieged and destroyed.

The war against the Hyksos whetted the Egyptian appetite for battle. Around 1500 BC, Thutmose I marched as far north as Syria. Later, after winning a resounding victory at the Battle of Megiddo in 1483, Thutmose III established the Egyptian empire with a border in southern Syria.

Thutmose III was ancient Egypt's greatest military leader. His immediate successors, though less brilliant, were capable enough to maintain the borders of the empire. During the reigns of the succeeding kings, Egypt's enemies either seized lands adjacent to those borders or weakened the bonds between the Egyptian king and his vassal rulers.

Historians tout the reign of Akhenaten (1372-1354 BC) for the advances made in the concept of monotheism. For the Egyptian empire, however, his reign was a disaster. At the same time that Akhenaten was concentrating on religious reform—and virtually ignoring international affairs—a threat to Egypt's empire arose from the Anatolian plateau of modern Turkey.

About 1740 BC Tudhaliyas I had re-established the city of Hattusas (near modern Böghazköy, Turkey). Despite the fact that King Anittas of Kussara had destroyed the town about 1900 BC and had placed a curse on the site, the Hittite kings traced their ancestry back to him.

Less than 100 years later, King Labarnas united neighboring city-states to form the Hittite empire. At first the king was answerable to a council of nobles, the *Pankus*, but civil war later led to the concentration of power in the king's hands.

Early in the 14th century BC, Suppiluliumas I (1375-1355 BC) created a new Hittite empire by defeating Kaska and Arxawa and eventually absorbing the Mitanni, an Asiatic people of whom little is known, save that they had constituted the backbone of resistance to Egyptians during the reigns of Thutmose I and III. As the Mitanni fought the Egyptians to the south, the Hittites advanced against the Mitanni from the north. The Mitanni threw back the initial Hittite advance, but increasing pressure from the north eventually pushed the Mitanni into an alliance with the Egyptians. A daughter of the Mitanni king even became one of Thutmose III's wives.

The Egyptian-Mitanni alliance maintained the balance of power in Asia Minor for 30 years, but all that changed during the reign of Akhenaten. The assassination of Mitanni King Tushratta resulted in civil war among aspirants to his throne. Hittite King Suppiluliumas quickly took advantage of the situation when the Mitanni crown prince, Mattiwaza, fled to the Hittites for protection. Suppiluliumas married his daughter to Mattiwaza, then forced the remainder of the Mitanni kingdom to accept him as king. That change put the Mitanni into the Hittite sphere of influence and tilted the balance of power.

With Hittite influence in the area growing, other vassal states of Egypt revolted, forcing the second king of the 19th Dynasty, Seti I, to make a foray into Syria to try to re-establish Egyptian influence. His success was only temporary. As soon as Seti returned to Egypt, the Hittite king, Mursilis II, marched south to take the town of Kadesh on the Orontes River. Once taken, Kadesh became the strongpoint of the Hittite defenses in Syria, although the Hittites ruled through a viceroy in Carchemish.

In spite of their aggressive activities in expanding their political influence in Asia Minor, the Hittite kings actually tried to avoid a direct confrontation

10

with the Egyptians. They paid tribute to the Egyptian king and avoided attacking Egyptians lands. Nevertheless, the two powers were on a collision course, and war finally erupted as the result of the political maneuvering of Ramses II, who succeeded his father, Seti, in 1301 BC, at age 20. Early in his reign, Ramses convinced Prince Bentesina of Amurru to switch alliances. To protect (and to expand) that new influence, Ramses planned to invade Syria. As those plans were being implemented, both Ramses and the Hittite king, Muwutallis, began raising large armies.

The bulk of the Egyptian army was infantry, raised by press gangs that roamed the Nile River valley. The principal infantry weapons were the javelin and the short sword. Every fifth man (probably an officer) carried a baton. For protection, the Egyptians wore close-fitting helmets and mailed tunics made from matting. Each man carried a shield of oxhide over a wooden frame, square at the bottom and rounded at the top. While it protected him, this heavy shield also limited the infantryman's mobility on the battlefield.

Although Ramses' infantrymen were mostly Egyptian—supplemented by Sardian mercenaries hired specifically for this campaign—his bowmen were almost exclusively Nubian, armed with composite bows made of laminated layers of bone and wood.

The most powerful weapon of the Bronze Age was the chariot, and the Egyptians had a small, permanent chariot force. The chariots were relatively small and light, each carrying two men—a driver and a warrior. The Egyptians viewed the chariot as a mobile firing platform; the driver would maneuver it about on the battlefield, while the warrior showered the enemy formation with arrows.

While the bulk of the Egyptian army was infantry, the Hittite strength lay in its own chariotry. The Hittites' acumen in battle was the result of their rigorous training, plus their success in horse breeding and horse training. Those factors combined to give the Hittite commander more maneuverability with which to exploit opportunities as they arose on the battlefield.

The regular Hittite army was small—just a king's bodyguard and a small force to patrol the frontiers and to put down rebellions. In time of a major conflict, however, the king was able to draw upon troops from the local population and from his vassals. Suppiluliumas I began the policy of turning conquered lands into vassal states. That practice precluded the need for large Hittite garrisons, and at the same time it allowed the king to call upon the native population for troops.

As Ramses had done, Muwutallis also filled out his ranks with mercenaries, including a group of Lycian pirates. The Hittite king organized his army into groups of 10. One officer commanded a 10-man unit, 10 of those units formed a group, and then 10 groups formed an even larger group, and so on. The Hittite warriors wore pointed helmets and long robes.

The Hittite chariot had a body made of leather mounted on a wooden frame. That frame in turn was mounted between two spoked wheels, with the axle positioned farther forward than on an Egyptian chariot in order to support the weight of three men: a driver, a warrior and a shield-bearer. Although the warrior carried a curved sword, his principal weapon was the spear. The Hittites used their chariots in mass formation as a shock force to break the enemy's infantry lines, after which the chariots, joined by the infantry, would exploit the resulting confusion to rout the enemy force.

Ramses opened his campaign in the summer of 1296 BC by seizing a port in southern Lebanon. A small Hittite army under Muwutallis advanced on the town, but Ramses drove it off.

Ramses, the arrogantly self-confident 25-year-old heir to a 1,000-year-old empire, intended to strike east from the Mediterranean to the Orontes River, which he would then follow north into Syria (in effect, emulating the successful strategy pursued by Thutmose III 100 years before). That was exactly what Muwutallis wanted Ramses to do, however. An experienced campaigner then into the 20th year of his reign, the Hittite king planned to draw the Egyptians as deep into his territory as he could before engaging them in battle.

Ramses organized his army into six distinct units. The majority of the men were in four divisions, each named after an Egyptian god: Amon, Re, Ptah and Set. Each division was a combined arms unit of 9,000 men—chariots, infantry and bowmen. The fifth unit was made up of Ramses' personal bodyguard. The last unit was a group of Canaanites (the *Na'arum*). Little is known about them, but they apparently were an auxiliary or reserve force.

The two armies were almost equal in size. Ramses had more than 35,000 men in his various units. Muwutallis had 3,500 chariots (10,500 men) and 17,000 infantry, for a total of 27,500. If the Egyptians had more men, the Hittites had many times more chariots.

Ramses sent the *Na'arum* up the coast to seize Sumura on the Mediterranean, to give him a better line of communications with his navy. With the remainder of his army, he marched east to the Orontes. Less than one day's march from Kadesh, Ramses camped at the high (i.e., southern) end of the Buka'a Valley. At that point, the Orontes flowed through a narrow rocky gorge several hundred feet deep. The river was not crossable until it reached Shabtuna, several miles to the north. At dawn, Ramses could see Kadesh in the distance through the haze. With his bodyguard in the van, the Egyptian monarch led his army north along the east bank of the river.

Before he reached Shabtuna, Ramses' men brought in two *Shosu* (Bedouins) who claimed to have been loyal vassals of Egypt conscripted into the Hittite army. They told Ramses what he wanted to hear—that Muwutallis was afraid of him and had retreated with his army toward Aleppo, far to the north.

Without bothering to put scouts out in front, Ramses pressed on ahead with just his bodyguard. In his haste to besiege Kadesh, he left his army spread out behind him through the Buka'a Valley.

The Egyptians crossed the Orontes at Shabtuna, then passed through the forest of Robaui and the clearing that lay between it and Kadesh. West of the town, they crossed a brook, el-Mukadiyek, to reach the clear ground northwest of the city. When Ramses arrived there at about 2:30 p.m., the Division of Amon was still south of Kadesh, struggling to catch up. Once that division arrived, the Egyptians erected a fortified camp, its perimeter marked by a palisade formed with the shields of the infantry.

Ramses' confidence was shaken when a liaison squadron then brought in a pair of Hittite spies it had captured. The Egyptians forced the two to talk by beating them with sticks. They told Ramses that he had just walked into a trap: "Behold, the prince...has many people with him, that he has victoriously brought with him from all the countries. They are armed. They have infantry, and chariots, and weapons, and are more in number than the sands of the sea. Behold, they are in fighting order hidden behind the town of Kadesh."

Muwutallis had indeed lured Ramses into a trap. The two *Shosu* who had reported the Hittites to be far away actually had been sent by the Hittite king for the purpose of lulling Ramses into a false sense of security. Ramses then compounded his problem by allowing his army to become spread out.

Instead of being far to the north, the Hittites were within striking distance, just east of Kadesh. Only a few hours earlier, in fact, the entire Hittite force had been camped on the very ground where Ramses' army now camped. Why the Egyptians had not noticed evidence of that encampment is not clear today.

Although Ramses called his princes together and berated them for failing to provide him with accurate intelligence, he still was not overly concerned about the situation. The Division of Amon had arrived and was going into camp. The Division of Re was just south of Kadesh, emerging from the Forest of Robaui. Ramses had half his army present. He ordered his vizier (chief of staff) to send a messenger to bring up the Division of Ptah. With three-quarters of his army at or within marching distance of Kadesh, he was confident there was little to worry about. What Ramses did not realize was that his divided army was, in fact, teetering on the brink of disaster.

Earlier in the day, the Hittites had withdrawn out of sight east of Kadesh. Then as Ramses arrived at the town, Muwutallis advanced in two sections. The Hittite king's main force, including the majority of his chariots, swung left to cross the Orontes River south of Kadesh, to strike at the rear of the Egyptian army. Muwutallis himself, with the infantry and a reserve force of 1,000 three-man chariots, swung right—intending to block the Egyptian retreat across the Orontes to the north.

As the Egyptian Division of Re marched on Kadesh, there was no sense of urgency—the king's orders had not reached it yet, and would not arrive until it was too late. The Egyptian officers were behind the troops, still in the Forest of Robaui, as the division slowly crawled across the plain, the infantrymen trudging along with their heavy shields slung across their backs.

West of the Orontes, meanwhile, the Hittite chariots quickly spread out into attack formation, then charged. Twenty-five hundred chariots ripped into the rear of the division. Some Egyptians were killed there; others were captured. Some of the survivors fled back into the forest, but most simply ran north toward Kadesh, spreading panic through the rest of the division and making it impossible for anyone to rally it. Within minutes, the Division of Re had ceased to exist as a fighting unit.

Ramses was still berating his officers when the first refugees (including two of his sons) arrived by chariot. At last the Egyptian king realized that he faced disaster. Turning to his vizier, Ramses ordered him to go after the Division of Ptah himself; the Division of Set was so far back that Ramses ignored it.

As the refugees from the Division of Re poured into Ramses' camp, their panic spread among the Division of Amon. Its soldiers, too, joined the flight from the Hittites, leaving Ramses and his bodyguard cut off. "Then the infantry and chariotry fled before them, northward, to the place where his majesty was," wrote Ramses' poet-historian Penator. "Lo, the foe…surrounded the attendants of his majesty, who were by his side."

The vanguard of Hittite chariots crashed through the wall of Egyptian shields, but the royal bodyguard proved to be more than a match for them. Throwing themselves at the horses, some of the bodyguard dragged the chariots to a stop. That allowed other Egyptians to swarm over them, killing many Hittites.

As the Hittite assault reached its high tide, however, only one chariot in the Egyptian camp had its horses in harness for a counterattack—Ramses' own war chariot, drawn by horses named Victory in Thebes and Mut is Satisfied. Ramses summoned his driver, Mennu, but the man was too afraid to come.

At that point, according to Penator, a humbled Ramses prayed to the god Amon for the strength and courage to save his army, and perhaps the empire, from destruction. Then, wrapping the reins about his waist to control the horses so his hands were free, Ramses single-handedly charged the Hittites, grimly determined to restore his fortunes or die trying.

The Egyptian account says Ramses managed to ride completely around the Hittite host, returning to his own camp unharmed. The account—which was written not as an objective work of history but as a flattering tribute to Ramses' prowess as a leader and a warrior—neglected to mention that the Hittites, who understandably believed their enemies to be totally routed, had stopped to loot the Egyptian camp. Only two groups of Hittites remained in their chariots, one on the east flank and another on the west flank of the main force.

By the time Ramses returned to his camp, a small group of Egyptian chariotry had formed, made up of his personal bodyguard and some of the chariots recovered from the broken Divisions of Amon and Re. Ramses rallied them to charge against the Hittite force to the west. The Egyptian king quickly decided the number of chariots there was too great, however, and chose to avoid a direct engagement. Retiring back to his camp, he immediately launched an attack against the Hittite force to the east. This time his counterstroke was successful, driving the Hittites back across the Orontes. In the first few minutes of battle, the Egyptian army had all but been destroyed. Now it was the Hittites' turn to suffer a major disaster.

The main Hittite force was still on foot, looting the Egyptian camp, when the *Na'arum* arrived from the west—apparently the Hittite force on the western flank had fled at their approach. Although the *Na'arum* had chariots, the bulk of their force was infantry. They were equipped and trained to fight on foot, whereas the Hittites were not. With swinging swords and flying spears, the *Na'arum* poured into the Egyptian camp, overwhelming the Hittites. The surviving Hittites fled toward Kadesh.

Muwutallis, who up to that point had seen the battle go entirely his way, suffered a staggering setback, but he still had his reserve chariotry and his infantry. For some reason, though, Muwutallis chose to dispatch only his 1,000 chariots against Ramses' relative handful, while he and his infantry remained on the other side of the river, an action the Egyptians attributed to cowardice.

As the Hittite chariots crossed the Orontes, Ramses changed tactics. Instead of maintaining his distance, he decided to close with the enemy, a form of battle seemingly favorable to the Hittites.

Actually, Ramses wanted to use the terrain as an ally. The Hittite chariots had to cross the river and mount the riverbank to reach the plain where the Egyptians were. The Hittite chariots were most effective at battle speed. Ramses wanted to close with them before they could reach that speed. Also, by fighting them close to the river, he kept the Hittites from deploying into formation. That protected Ramses' flanks and allowed him to fight only a fraction of the Hittite force at one time.

The Hittite chariots splashed through the river and had started up the far bank when the Egyptians descended on them. The impact drove them back into the water. Muwutallis ordered another charge. Again, the Egyptians waited until the Hittite chariots forded the river, then charged them on the bank and once again drove them back. Muwutallis reorganized his ranks before sending his chariots across the river a third time, but with the same, unsuccessful result.

For almost three hours Muwutallis threw his chariots across the river, and for three hours the Egyptians, led by Ramses, drove them back. "Then his majesty advanced swiftly and charged into the foe of the vanquished," said the Egyptian chronicle. "At the sixth charge among them, being like Baal [the Cannite equivalent of Set, the Egyptian god of war] behind them in the hour of his might, I made slaughter among them, and there was none that escaped me." (It is interesting to note that while most of the Egyptian account of the battle was written in the third person, the narrative abruptly changed to the first person in the description of the last Hittite attack.)

On the Hittite side, the casualties included high-ranking figures. Soldiers pulled the half-drowned prince of Charbu from the Orontes and had to revive him by holding him upside down. Less fortunate was Muwutallis' brother Metarema, who was killed by an Egyptian arrow before he could reach the river. Also dead were Cherpaser, the royal scribe; Tergannasa and Pays, Muwutallis' charioteers; Teedura, chief of the bodyguard; Kamayta, a corps commander; and Aagem, commander of the mercenaries.

The battle had begun about 4 p.m. At about 7 o'clock, the lead elements of the Division of Ptah, with Ramses' vizier in the lead, emerged from the Forest of Robaui. The arrival of that third Egyptian division threatened the Hittite rear.

The Egyptian account says the Hittites retreated inside Kadesh, but it is improbable that so many men could have stayed inside the city. More likely, Muwutallis retired toward Aleppo.

The next morning, Ramses proclaimed that he had won a great victory. In a sense, it had been a triumph. After blundering into a devastating ambush, the young king had escaped death or capture and, displaying courageous leadership, had rallied his scattered troops. Even so, the Egyptians had suffered heavy casualties, Kadesh's defenses were unbroken, and Muwutallis' army, though badly bloodied, was still intact, with more than 1,000 chariots still at his disposal. Chastened, Ramses prudently gathered the remnants of his army and marched toward Damascus.

Muwutallis, too, had had enough, although once safely back at Hattusas, he, too, proclaimed a great victory. Later, he tried to foment another revolt against the Egyptians, but he died while Ramses was preparing to crush the uprising. Among other successes, Ramses took Dapur, south of Aleppo, in 1290 BC.

The Battle of Kadesh holds great interest to scholars of military strategy but, as pointed out by Egyptian press attaché and Egyptologist Ahmed Nouby Moussa, its epilogue was equally historic in the realm of international diplomacy. After a dynastic struggle, Khattusilis III succeeded Muwutallis and subsequently invited Egyptian plenipotentiaries to Hattusas for what would amount to the first summit conference between two equally matched powers. In 1280 BC, Ramses and Khattusilis signed history's oldest recorded international agreement, establishing a condominium between the two empires. After 13 years of peace, Ramses sealed the treaty by marrying one of Khattusilis' daughters. With his northeastern borders secure, the Egyptian king ruled until 1235 BC—a reign of 67 years, during which his name would be literally etched in stone as Ramses the Great.

Upset at Issus

*King Darius III had cut off the Macedonian upstart who
had dared invade his mighty empire—but then Alexander
moved to slash his way out of the trap.*

By Harry J. Maihafer

In 333 BC, as Macedonian forces bivouacked at Gordium in Asia Minor, they
were led by a confident, aggressive 23-year-old warrior-king who would
become known to history as Alexander the Great.

Three years earlier, upon the murder of his father, Philip II of Macedon, Alexander had inherited an army superior to any other the world
had yet seen. He had also inherited a mission—to cross the Hellespont
and liberate those Greeks who for generations had been living under Persian control.

It was not a new idea. Ten years before Alexander was even born, the
veteran Athenian pamphleteer Isocrates had published an "Address to
Philip," calling for a Panhellenic offensive against Persia under Philip's leadership. Even before that, the various Greek city-states had discussed such a
crusade, one that would avenge Xerxes' invasion of a century and a half earlier. The Greeks had forgotten neither the sacrileges committed against the
temples of their gods nor the humiliating settlement that had ceded the Hellenic cities of Asia Minor to Persia's "Great King."

Until the emergence of Philip, however, the idea of a Panhellenic "movement" had made little progress among competing Greek states. Athens, for
example, while a center of wisdom and culture, had never been able to sustain a dominant role politically or militarily. A great crusade needed a leader
like Philip to head it, even though sophisticated Athenians might view him
as little more than a crude barbarian.

Philip, however, unable to count on the cooperation, let alone the loyalty, of other Greek states and well aware of Persia's military superiority,
was forced to bide his time. In the next few years he put together a superior,
well-drilled army of foot soldiers and cavalry, one with the mighty Macedonian phalanx as a nucleus. Simultaneously, he was also seeing to the training of his son, giving him the brilliant Aristotle as tutor and assigning him a
significant military role while he was still in his teens.

Young Alexander more than fulfilled Philip's expectations. He was a
splendid student and a gifted athlete, and at the age of 18 at the Battle of
Chaeronia on September 1, 338 BC, he had fought heroically while command-

ing Macedonia's finest cavalry unit. It was an Alexander-led cavalry charge that broke the Theban line and exposed the Athenian flank and rear, leading to an overwhelming Macedonian victory and the conquest of the Greek city-state. Thus it was, upon Philip's death, that Alexander was able to become both army leader and king—he was seen as one who really deserved those titles, by ability as well as by birth. Two months later, the Hellenic League met at Corinth and there—with little choice and under a good bit of coercion—it named Alexander captain-general of the League's forces for the invasion of Persia. To spur things along, Alexander even introduced a delegate from Ephesus in Asia Minor who claimed to be speaking on behalf of "the Greeks of Asia" and who urged Alexander "to undertake a war of liberation" on their behalf.

Finally, in the early spring of 334, Alexander set out from Pella at the head of his expeditionary force and marched for the Hellespont. With him were some 43,000 infantry and 6,000 cavalry. Of these, 12,000 infantry and 1,800 cavalry were Macedonians; the remainder were mostly tribal levies or mercenaries. The Hellenic League begrudgingly provided a number of ships for the expedition, but little else. Of the 43,000 infantry, only 7,000 were contributed by the League; of the 6,000 cavalry, the League provided a mere 600 (calling the force "Panhellenic" was clearly bowing to a misnomer, but it made for good propaganda). Thanks to Alexander's inquiring scientific mind, the expedition also was accompanied by a whole host of botanists, zoologists and surveyors.

After crossing the Dardanelles, Alexander began taking over certain Greek towns. While he called his actions "liberation," in truth the people were merely exchanging one satrap for another. The shrewd Alexander said they no longer must pay tribute to Persia; however, since they were now members of the Hellenic League, they would be given the "opportunity" of contributing to the support of "their" army!

As his army encamped at Gordium in 333 BC, Alexander could look back on a year of solid triumph. Only once had he faced serious opposition, and that was at the Granicus River, where he had convincingly defeated an army led by Memnon, a Greek general fighting for Persia.

Nevertheless, Alexander had his problems, not the least of which was a shortage of funds with which to pay his mercenaries. And to his rear, a Persian fleet far superior to that of the League was threatening his line of communications. Meanwhile, Memnon, who now had a score to settle, had been named commander of all Persian forces in Asia Minor and was menacing not only the towns to Alexander's rear but even Greece itself. His army had already captured key Greek islands, and on the Greek mainland, Memnon's agents were handing out bribes and doing whatever they could to stir up trouble. Sparta, it was said, was more than willing to revolt as soon as Memnon gave the word.

The question for Alexander, of course, was whether to retreat to secure his home base or to go forward and take on the entire Persian Empire, a vast conglomerate stretching from the Red Sea to the Caspian, from the Hellspont to beyond the Hindu Kush. He needed an omen, if not for his own sake (he may have already made up his mind), then at least as a positive sign for his superstitious troops.

Fortunately, Gordium provided just such as opportunity. On the acropolis above the city sat the ancient Phrygian palace of King Midas. Nearby was an ox cart with a shaft secured to its yoke by a knot of tough cornel bark. The knot (of a type known to sailors as a "Turk's head") was closely woven and had no visible loose ends. According to legend, the man who could undo the knot would someday "rule all Asia."

Surely this was a challenge not to be missed. It was out of the question, in fact, to leave Gordium without accepting that challenge. Alexander climbed the hill and approached the cart as a crowd of curious Macedonians and Phrygians gathered around. They watched intently as Alexander struggled with the knot and became frustrated. The atmosphere grew tense—what would it portend if he should fail?

Alexander, stepping back, called out, "What does it matter how I loose it?" With that, he drew his sword, and in one powerful stroke severed the knot. That night, there came thunder and lightning, which the seers conveniently interpreted to mean the gods were pleased with the actions of this so-called Son of Zeus who had cut the Gordian knot (according to Greek legend, the knot came from Gordius, king of Phrygia).

Some historians said that Alexander merely drew out the dowel peg that ran through the shaft and yoke, thus releasing the thongs; others said that the incident never happened at all. The sword story persists, however, and surely seems true to character. In any case, his course was clear—he would go forward!

By mid-July, Alexander began receiving ominous reports about goings-on in Persia. Evidently his triumphs, and especially his victory at the Granicus River, had at last provoked the full attention of Persian King Darius III. The Great King had moved from Susa to Babylon and begun assembling a mighty horde. Alexander's army, having "lost" increments of garrison troops dropped off at various points along the way, was down to about 30,000. Darius, calling on the entire Persian Empire, was capable of assembling a force numbering in the hundreds of thousands.

Alexander's expedition continued south, crossing 75 miles of parched, volcanic upland in a forced march, then passed through a narrow mountain defile known as the Cilician Gates. At the same time, Persian reinforcements were streaming into Babylon. On September 3, Alexander reached Tarsus, where he fell ill with a violent fever. Physicians were summoned, but most were unwilling to treat him, fearing they would be accused either of negligence or murder were he to die. (This was understandable; it was well known that Darius had offered a reward to anyone who managed to slay Alexander.)

As the fever worsened, Philip of Arcanania, a physician Alexander had known since childhood, was brave enough to step forward and offer treatment. He suggested a certain purgative drug, cautioning that there would be an element of danger. As the dose was being made up, Alexander received a letter from his general Parmenio saying that Philip had been bribed by Darius—the medicine he provided to Alexander would in fact be a deadly poison!

Unhesitatingly, Alexander took the letter to Philip and told him to read it. While Philip was still reading, Alexander surprised him by picking up the medicine and gulping it down. The purge had a violent effect, but three days later the fever was broken and Alexander began to recover. The most relieved man in camp no doubt was Philip, the physician!

By that time, pontoon bridges had been constructed over the Euphrates. Darius, with an army reported to have numbered as many as 500,000 men—although, allowing for the Greeks' penchant for inflating Persian numbers, it was more likely a fraction of that size—began crossing the river and advancing toward the Greek invaders.

While he convalesced, Alexander sent ahead Parmenio, his senior and ablest general, to capture the little harbor town of Issus and to watch the only two passes (the Amanic Gates northeast of Issus and the Syrian Gates farther south) through which Darius could bring his army into Cilicia. Finally, Alexander himself passed through Issus, leaving there his sick and wounded (evidently feeling the town was safe from attack), and continued south, passing through a constricted place known as the Pillars of Jonah.

On his right, now, was the Mediterranean Sea; on his left, the rugged Amanus Mountains. As he advanced, scouts arrived with chilling reports— the Persian army, numbering in the hundreds of thousands, was gathering in the vast plain east of the mountains.

Alexander had always taken pride in his ability to anticipate an opponent's actions. At that point, perhaps acting on false information deliberately "leaked" by the Persians, he decided Darius would make his approach through the Syrian Gates, specifically via the Beilan Pass. He proceeded to pitch camp near the pass and waited. This time, however, he was wrong. Days passed, and the attack never materialized.

Alexander had underestimated his opponent. Darius III was a wily, ruthless monarch, who three years earlier had taken over a throne made vacant through an assassination arranged by Bagoas, his scheming grand vizier. Darius showed his gratitude and headed off any further intrigue by promptly forcing Bagoas to drink the poison he had often administered to others. Truly this was a man of many moves, one Alexander could ill afford to underrate.

But he did, and as a result—perhaps for the first time ever—Alexander was both outsmarted and outmaneuvered. Darius, taking part of his force, advanced rapidly to the north, swept through the Amanic Gates and positioned himself astride the Greeks' line of communication in the vicinity of Issus.

In Issus itself, Persians captured most of Alexander's hospital cases, lopped off their hands and sealed their wrists with pitch. Those unfortunates were then paraded through Darius' camp, and after being suitably impressed, were turned loose and told to report what they had seen. (More than a century earlier, a similar terror tactic had been employed by Xerxes.) Soon, cavalry scouts pounded into Alexander's camp to spread the grim message that he and his not-so-great host were cut off.

What had occurred was any commander's worst nightmare—an enemy in force astride one's lifeline. Alexander's Macedonians were far from home with no hope of help or reinforcement. A lesser man might have panicked, but Alexander, supremely confident in the ability of his troops and his own destiny, moved quickly to regain the initiative. He faced his army about, sent cavalry units northward to secure his route past the Pillars of Jonah, and then dispatched other horsemen to scout out Darius' position.

The Macedonians hurried north in an incredible forced march, covering 70 miles in two days. The bone-weary foot soldiers were made even more wretched by a torrential rain that washed out their tents and left the men sodden and miserable. Nevertheless, when the weather cleared and the charismatic, ever-optimistic Alexander addressed them, his enthusiasm was contagious. When he finished his speech with a reference to Xenophon and the Ten Thousand (Xenophon of Athens had led some 10,000 Greeks on a tortuous 4,000-mile retreat following the Battle of Cunaza in 401 BC), the troops were on their feet, banging swords against shields and cheering lustily.

Late in the afternoon, just beyond the Pillars of Jonah, the Macedonians and their allies made camp, ate a hot meal, and saw to their weapons. Alexander and his lieutenants made an inspection tour, walking among the hoplites, who included both the *pezetaeri*, or foot companions, with their long spears called *sarissas*, and the *hypaspists*, or shield-bearing guards, with their swords and one-handed pikes. Nearby were the *psiloi*, well-organized and substantially armed light infantry.

Farther off, and strung out more loosely, were irregular wild tribesmen from many lands, skilled archers, slingers and darters.

Next, after mounting his horse, the legendary Bucephalus, Alexander reviewed the cavalry, trotting past the lancers, the horse bowmen and scores of rough mercanaries. Finally, he came to his finest troops, squadrons of crack horsemen from Thessaly and Greece, including his favorite unit, the Cavalry Companions. The latter group, an elite unit of Macedonian bluebloods, was the one with which he would ride into battle.

22

Well after dark, while his troops secured a few hours' rest, Alexander climbed a nearby hill and by torchlight made sacrifice to the gods. Looking to the north toward Issus, he could make out thousands of twinkling campfires in the Persian camp. It was not a reassuring sight for the Macedonian leader. Next morning, scouts were dispatched to reconnoiter the Persian position. As reports came in, Alexander realized he was facing a man with no small military ability. Darius had deployed his army skillfully on the far side of the narrow Pinarus River. His line extended across the entire Issus valley, its right resting on the sea, its left anchored in the foothills to the east.

Alexander set his phalanxes in motion, telling his commanders to maintain an easy, steady pace that would not tire the men needlessly—they would soon be needing every last bit of strength and endurance.

Darius had positioned a large cavalry screen south of the Pinarus to mask his dispositions, so Alexander was still uncertain as to the center of his opponent's strength. He did note know that Darius' best troops, ironically, were the Persian's Greek mercenaries, seasoned veterans who would fight especially hard. Viewed as traitors to the Hellenic League, they could expect no quarter, and they would give none in return. The Persians' Asiatic levies were a different matter. Alexander felt sure these ill-trained irregulars could never stand up to the Macedonian phalanxes. Up ahead, Alexander saw a scrub plain, about 2½ miles wide. To his left was the sparkling blue Mediterranean. Across his front, now becoming more visible, was the shallow Pinarus, behind which was a dark mass of infantry fronted by a line of archers. To his right were foothills in which Persian cavalry seemed to be deploying. Was that where Darius planned his main effort?

The phalanxes had been advancing in column. Now, as the leading unit halted just out of archery range, the other phalanxes came abreast. Next, Alexander deployed his cavalry. Parmenio would take command of the squadrons on the left.

"Do not lose contact with the sea," he told Parmenio. "The enemy may try to turn our left flank. Do not let him!" Alexander himself then went to the right, which he felt would be the decisive point. With him were his best troops, the Thessalian cavalry and his own Macedonian Cavalry Companions.

Some horsemen and archers made a quick sally into the foothills on the right, and the Persian cavalry screen promptly withdrew. With that, the Persian disposition became a bit more visible. In the center of the line was the Royal Bodyguard, 2,000 hand-picked tropps whose spear butts were decorated with golden quinces. Behind them was their Great King in an imposing ornamental chariot. On either side, filling out the line, were the best of Darius' infantry—the Greek mercenaries plus the *cardaces*, the latter lightly-armed Persian youths who had just completed their military training. As part of their defense, the Persians had placed upright sharpened stakes along the riverbank, especially at those points where the river was danger-ously low.

Massed behind the front line were the thousands of Persian irregulars. With grim satisfaction, Alexander noted that while Darius had the advantage of numerical superiority, the comparative narrowness of the valley effec-tively kept him from making much use of that advantage.

Suddenly, he saw Darius' true battle plan as the Persian cavalry, includ-ing those who had begun the day acting as a screen, now moved swiftly behind the Persian front line and took up positions near the sea. It became obvious that their main attack, led by the able Nabarzanes, would be made against the Macedonian left!

Alexander dispatched the Thessalian cavalry to reinforce Parmenio, along with instructions to bend back, but always to maintain contact with the sea—in military terms, to "refuse the flank."

The moment had come. Raising his sword, Alexander gave the signal to launch the attack. A trumpet rang out and the phalanxes move forward, with successive elements echeloned to the left in the formation known as an "oblique order." On the far right, Alexander and his Cavalry Companions, shrieking like fiends, galloped across the river in an all-out charge, scatter-ing the archers and light infantry nearest the mountain. Within moments, the Persian flank had crumbled.

As the troops facing Alexander were fleeing in disorder, the first Mace-donian phalanx was becoming engaged, and for them the going was not so easy. With long spears bristling, they had moved forward and had been met by swarms of arrows—in the words of one ancient writer, "such a shower of missiles that they collided with one another in the air." After splashing across the river, the foot companions had been forced to climb a steep, bramble-covered bank, after which they had been slowed by the sharpened-stake palisades. Understandably, even the well-disciplined Macedonians were having difficulty maintaining cohesion, and to make matters worse, they were up against Darius' best Greek mercenaries.

The fighting became fierce and bloody. Swords cut into flesh, arrows found their targets, spears were driven home, and soon the screams of the wounded were mixed with the shouts of battle and the clang of sword upon shield. Men fell in jumbled confusion, body piling upon body as Alexander's veterans clashed with Persian veterans, equally tough and professional.

With the phalanx slowed and the Cavalry Companions still moving ahead, a break formed in the Macedonian line. Moving to exploit it, a wedge of Dar-ius' mercenaries drove into the gap, swinging their swords in vicious arcs and inflicting heavy casualties, among them some 120 Macedonian officers. At that point, Alexander wheeled his Cavalry Companions to the left and charged at full speed into the Persian flank. Amid a tremendous din, forcing their way through the bodies of dying horses and men, the Companions drove forward against the mercenaries, who then had to fight in two directions. It was too much—the mercenaries began to give way. With that, Alexander swung his whole right wing so as to roll up the Persian line.

A few hundred yards away, Alexander saw the ornamental chariot of Darius, which he now used as his personal aiming point. Darius was surrounded by his Royal Household Cavalry, loyal defenders of the Great King led by his brother Oxathres. They fought bravely but were no match for the Companions. Darius' chariot horses, wounded by arrows and terrified by the screams and the confusion, began to plunge and rear, at one point almost pulling the unwilling king straight into the Greek line.

As Darius fought to control his chariot, Alexander continued hacking his way forward, swinging his sword left and right, ignoring the personal danger, even when someone managed to slash his thigh with a dagger. Darius, seeing his bodyguards dying and fearing for his own safety, abandoned his ornate chariot for a lighter, more mobile one and raced to safety.

For the moment, Alexander was unable to pursue the fleeing Persian king. His help was needed in the center, where the phalanxes were heavily engaged, and on the far flank, where Parmenio and the Thessalian cavalry were engaged in a fierce struggle with Nabarzanes and his heavily armored Persian horsemen.

Alexander and the Cavalry Companions, joined by succeeding echelons of Macedonian phalanxes, continued to roll up the line. The embattled Persians, who had been struck from two directions at once and abandoned by their king, lost all semblance of cohesion. Before long, their entire formation was shattered; the only remaining resistance to the Macedonian forces came from small groups whose members, one by one, were throwing down their arms.

Nabarzanes, looking to his rear, saw the Persian line had disintegrated. Then, learning that his king had fled, he prudently decided to follow. Within the next few minutes the entire Persian army (including the Asiatic levies who had played no part in the battle) turned into a panicky, chaotic, fleeing mob. Some of the escaping infantry were even ridden down by their own cavalry.

Fleeing Persians continued to be cut down, both by pursuing horsemen and by clouds of arrows. (Ptolemy, one of Alexander's lieutenants, later wrote that he and his squadron had ridden across a patch of deep water bridged by the piled-up bodies of the dead.)

With the battle won, Alexander set off in pursuit of Darius. The daylight was fading by that time, however, and the chase was hampered by the fleeing mass of humanity blocking his path. Nevertheless, Alexander and the Companions, threading their way through the remnants of the Persian Imperial Army, kept going for some 25 miles—only after dark did they give up the chase and return to camp. (Darius had escaped for the moment, but his days were numbered. Three years later, after being decisively routed by Alexander in their ultimate confrontation at Gaugamela, and once again fleeing the battlefield, he was murdered by traitorous companions to keep him from falling into Alexander's hands.)

Back near Issus, meanwhile, Alexander's men had found Darius' base camp to be rich in plunder. Looting the Persian tents, they found jeweled swords, inlaid furniture, priceless tapestries, and countless vessels of gold and silver. Darius' own luxurious belongings were left untouched, since custom decreed they now belonged to Alexander himself.

Alexander returned to camp tired, hot and sweaty, and decided that he would refresh himself by soaking in the ornate bathtub found among the Great King's possessions. When he at first referred to it as Darius' tub, his followers happily pointed out that it, like everything else the Persian king had left behind him, was no longer Darius', but Alexander's.

Later that night, Alexander heard the sound of wailing. In a nearby tent, Darius' mother, wife and children were mourning the Great King, whom they had been told was dead. As for themselves, they fully expected to be used shamefully and then executed. However, at Alexander's direction, the women were told that Darius still lived. Moreover, they were told that they themselves not only would be safeguarded but also would be allowed to keep all the titles, honors and perquisites befitting their royal status. Some historians have said that Alexander's generous treatment of the captured women was nothing but a shrewd political gesture. Be that as it may, in the story of any battle, an act of chivalry and compassion stands out in shining contrast!

Classic Double Encirclement

As Hannibal Barca's polyglot Carthaginian
expeditionary force marched on Rome, he found himself
facing the strongest Roman army he had
yet encountered, at Cannae.

By Greg Yocherer

Dawn of that August morning in 216 BC found Hannibal, commander of Carthage's army in Italy, peering down at the plain separating his vantage point from the waters of the Adriatic Sea some three miles away. The Roman enemy was already advancing—an army of more than 85,000 men, aligned in the standard offensive formation of the widely feared legions. Hannibal's force, some 56,000 in number, faced long, very long odds.

The third century BC already had witnessed the growth of Rome and Carthage as the foremost powers of the central Mediterranean. Rome had developed slowly over the previous five centuries and now was the dominant military power on the Italian peninsula. There had been frequent reverses, but Rome was able to build and solidify its holdings through political means, such as extending full or partial Roman citizenship to conquered cities or deserving individuals. A large degree of autonomy was granted to the peoples Rome defeated in exchange for military help when Rome needed it. In that way, Rome was able to expand its territory and build its pool of available manpower without diluting its strength by creating armies of occupation.

Future rival Carthage was a city located near present-day Tunis, Tunisia, and was founded by colonists from Phoenician Tyre. Instead of gradually conquering and assimilating neighboring cities, Carthage grew through maritime commerce. Its empire was based on overseas trading stations in Spain, Sicily, Sardinia, Corsica, the Balearic Islands and along the North African coast. The hinterlands near those trading stations provided markets for Carthaginian commerce, manpower for Carthage's armies and sources of wealth such as silver and gold mines. The income from the mines paid for mercenary armies, and people living in the area immediately surrounding Carthage were not given the freedoms such as those granted by Rome. No strong bond of loyalty was forged between Carthage and the immediate satellite area because of Carthage's exploitation of the indigenous peoples and the Carthaginian tendency to respond to resistance with great cruelty. When military might was needed, the population of the city of Carthage

27

found it expedient to use its mercenary troops, drawn from its economic spheres of influence.

As the two states grew, they came into conflict in Sicily. The city of Messina, located at the northeastern tip of Sicily, appealed to Rome for protection from nearby Syracuse. Carthage regarded Roman intervention as an intrusion into its domain, and the First Punic (Latin for Phoenician) War resulted (264-241 BC). It was a costly conflict, to a large extent due to Roman lives lost while that city attempted to become a sea power. In 255 BC, the Romans lost 180 ships and 95,000 men in a single storm off the Sicilian coast, and in 253 BC, another storm cost Rome an additional 150 vessels and their crews. A third Roman fleet later was ground to pieces off the rocky coast of southern Sicily in yet another storm.

Characteristic Roman persistence in the face of adversity finally brought victory—and the expulsion of the Carthaginians from Sicily. By the end of the years-long war, Carthage's naval supremacy in the western and central Mediterranean had been broken. To be sure, Carthage's ability to build and man a fleet had not been seriously impaired, but Carthage did not aggressively challenge the Romans at sea in subsequent conflicts. The reasons for that seeming lethargy on the part of expert seafaring people will never be known, as no Carthaginian history of the Punic Wars has survived. Our information today comes from Roman sources.

Hamilcar Barca, Hannibal's father, had been one of Carthage's principal generals in the first war and had held out in Carthage's last stronghold in western Sicily for a considerable period. Though finally defeated, he did not suffer the fate sometimes meted out to unsuccessful Carthaginian generals—crucifixion.

At the conclusion of the First Punic War, Carthage's mercenaries rose in revolt, aided by disaffected elements from the lands surrounding the city. Rome took advantage of her rival's distraction and, in spite of the recent peace agreement, took control of Sardinia and Corsica and forced Carthage to pay a large indemnity. Carthage finally won the mercenary war, but the loss of Sicily, Sardinia and Corsica left her economic empire crippled and reduced the area from which she could hire troops.

Hamilcar took it upon himself to rebuild Carthaginian fortunes by occupying Spain. The city of Gades (Cadiz), located on the Atlantic Ocean outside the Pillars of Hercules, was older than Carthage and, like her North African ally, had started as a Phoenician colony. Carthage itself had traded in Spain and used Spanish mercenaries for many years. Hamilcar decided to build on those foundations and formally placed large sections of Spain under Carthaginian rule. That would provide a base for military operations against Rome (which Hamilcar felt were inevitable anyway), give access to the large silver and gold deposits of the country, and draw closer the region's excellent Iberian and Celt-Iberian mercenaries, both useful in combating the Romans.

Hamilcar Barca and Hasdrubal the Splendid, his son-in-law and successor, subdued a large portion of southern and eastern Spain and established the city of Cartegena (New Carthage) on the southeastern coast as the capital of Carthaginian Spain. The city-state's leadership in the new land remained in the hands of one family, the Barcids. To minimize the unreliability of mercenary troops and recognize the loyalty of Spanish tribesmen to a worthy leader, the Barcid clan built an empire based on close relationships with local tribal leaders, rather than with the distant city of Carthage. Hasdrubal the Splendid utilized diplomacy and marriage to an influential chief's daughter to cement relations with the indigenous tribes. Hamilcar's three sons, Hannibal, Hasdrubal and Mago, would continue the work of Hamilcar and the first Hasdrubal—and nearly bring Rome to its knees during the Second Punic War.

Few details of Hannibal's youth have survived. At age 5, he was with his father in Sicily at the end of the first war. At 9, he accompanied Hamilcar to Spain and spent his adolescent years there while the empire was created.

In 226 BC, Hasdrubal the Splendid had reached an agreement with Rome that recognized the Ebro River in northeastern Spain as the northern limit of Carthaginian interests in the area. Five years later, Hasdrubal was assassinated, and Hamilcar's son Hannibal became the leader. At about that time, Rome began involving itself in the affairs of Saguntum, a city on the Mediterranean coast of Spain well south of the Ebro and therefore presumably in Carthaginian territory. Hannibal viewed the Roman moves as a prelude to the type of intervention that had touched off the first war. Hannibal laid siege to the town, which fell after eight months.

Hannibal's strategic insight now became evident. From study of the First Punic War, Hannibal realized that Carthage could not prevail in a war far from Rome's heartland. The huge populations at Rome's disposal made a simple war of attrition a losing proposition for Carthage. Hannibal decided to fight in Italy itself, making Rome's people bear the burden of the war while at the same time weakening the loyalty of Rome's allies in Italy. Concurrently, military alliances could be negotiated with Rome's enemies, notably Macedonia and Syracuse. And since Carthage's fleet was no longer a match for Rome's, the invasion of Italy would be by land.

To that end, Hannibal did his best to negotiate with tribes in his line of march well in advance of the onset of hostilities; he also concluded alliances with various north Italian Celtic tribes that were traditional enemies of Rome.

Hannibal's was the first civilized army to cross the Alps. Exposure, desertion, accidents and fierce resistance by mountain tribes reduced his army from 40,000 to 26,000 during the trip, and most of the elephants accompanying the remarkable host also perished. Fortunately, once the Carthaginian force reached Italy, the Celtic alliances provided replacements that brought the army back to its original strength.

Shortly thereafter, Hannibal fought two battles that demonstrated his mettle as a field commander and his determination to destroy rather than merely defeat his enemy. At the Trebia River in December 218 BC, only 10,000 Romans escaped an ambush out of 40,000 engaged, and at Lake Trasimene in April 217 BC, virtually an entire Roman force of 25,000 was killed or captured. From then on, the Romans were reluctant to fight a large-scale engagement. Hannibal, for his part, was careful to treat prisoners from Rome's allied cities courteously, often freeing them without ransom to encourage disaffection with Rome's cause. Captured Roman citizens, on the other hand, were held for ransom used to pay Hannibal's men or, failing that, were often sold into slavery. The Carthaginian army lived off the land, causing as much damage to the economy as possible.

After the battle at Lake Trasimene, Hannibal moved his army to southern Italy in order to recruit additional help in that quarter. And there, Hannibal's depredations forced the Romans to become more aggressive. Two new consuls, Caius Terentius Varro and Aemilius Paulus, were given command of the combined legions of Rome with orders to make an end to the feared Carthaginian. Normally, the two consuls would have independent commands, but, by custom, when their forces were combined, command of the whole alternated daily. Hannibal's efficient intelligence system soon informed him that Varro was the more impetuous of his opponents, and so Hannibal decided to force an action on a day Varro was in overall command.

Hannibal seized a grain depot to lure the Romans to the site he had chosen for battle. The depot was located at the small village of Cannae, south of Rome and on the Adriatic side of the "boot" of Italy.

The Roman force available for battle was large by the standards of the day. Eight full legions of infantry, some 40,000 men, were augmented by 40,000 allied infantrymen. About 2,400 Roman cavalry and 4,000 allied horse completed the army, for a total strength of 86,400.

In battle, the Roman infantry usually advanced on a broad front, with cavalry screens on the flanks. The heavy infantry was preceded by skirmishers, who opened the engagement with flights of javelins and then retired to the rear of the formation. They were able to pass through the Roman formation because deliberate gaps were left in each line. The basic fighting unit of the heavy infantry was the maniple of about 160 men divided into two centuries. Rather than forming a continuous line, the two centuries were deployed one behind the other, leaving the gaps used by the retiring skirmishers. At the point of attack or when in a defensive posture, the rear centuries could be moved up to fill the gaps.

The *hastati* made up the first line of Roman heavy infantry. They were equipped with a heavy shield, a helmet, light and heavy *pila* (javelins) and a short, straight sword. The *princeps* were the second line of heavy infantry. They were armed like the *hastati*, but were somewhat older and more experienced soldiers. The *princeps'* centuries formed behind those of the *hastati*, but were offset to block the gaps in the *hastati* line. The third line, made up of the old veteran troops called *tritarii*, had its centuries form behind the gaps in the second line, giving an overall checkerboard effect to the formation. The *triarii* had a thrusting spear in place of the *pila* of the first two lines.

In the hands of a skilled commander, the flexibility possible with this formation was advantageous, particularly against older military formations such as the phalanx. Unfortunately, the Roman method of appointing new consuls each year and rotating command daily if the consuls were deployed together made it unlikely that top military talent would be allowed to pursue a coherent plan. Roman courage, discipline and patriotism were rarely lacking, but the coming battle of Cannae would highlight the need for changes in the selection and responsibilities of army commanders.

Aside from the top commanders, very few Carthaginians were present in Hannibal's army. His basic components at Cannae consisted of North African, Spanish and Celtic personnel. Perhaps the steadiest foot soldiers available to Hannibal were the Liby-Phoenician heavy infantry, a manisfestation of Carthage's origins as a Phoenician colony. The Phoenicians living in Africa (Libya) were subject to Carthaginian military service and acquitted themselves well. Originally armed like Greek Hoplites, they now began equipping with Roman arms captured at the Trebia River and Lake Trasimene.

In addition to 12,000 of those African infantrymen, Hannibal had 4,000 Numidian horsemen at Cannae. These unarmored light cavalrymen were extremely mobile and excellent for reconnaissance work or for pursuit of a defeated enemy. Armed only with javelins and light shields, they had little value as shock troops.

Some 8,000 Spanish infantry remained with Hannibal. About half of those were light troops, perhaps slingers from the Balearic Islands who were renowned for that speciality. The heavy infantry used javelins, as did the Romans, but the basic weapon was the sword, with which they were more than a match for the average legionary.

Indeed, not only was the Spaniard a more skilled swordsman, but his weapon was distinctly superior to that of his Roman adversary. Fine Spanish iron coupled with commendable workmanship resulted in a straight, double-edged blade that was later copied by the Romans for their own use as the *gladius hispanicus*. Celt-Iberians had a unique weapon of their own, a long, slightly curved sword, well-suited for cut-and-thrust combat called the *falcata*.

In addition to the infantry, 2,000 Spanish cavalry were available to Hannibal. They were heavily armed and were used as heavy cavalry, but the excellent quality of their horses allowed them to rival the speed of the Numidians.

About 25,000 Celtic infantry and 5,000 Celtic cavalry made up the remainder of Hannibal's force. Those wild tribesmen lived for war, but without the guidance of a commander like Hannibal, their lack of discipline made them unreliable. They were excellent swordsmen, but only the wealthiest wore armor. Often the Celt fought naked, equipped solely with sword, shield and helmet. At the time of Cannae, Hannibal was arming those men with captured Roman weapons. He liked to use the Celts as shock troops that would cause disruption in enemy ranks prior to committing his African infantry. Of course, heavy Celtic casualties resulted, but they accepted their losses as the natural result of occupying the position of honor.

At Cannae (present-day Barletta, Italy), the Romans were determined to crush Hannibal's center. They formed extremely deep battle lines in order to bring maximum pressure to bear against the middle of the Carthaginian line. On the Roman right, the legion cavalry, some 2,400 strong, faced Hannibal's Spaniards and Celts, totaling 7,000. That mismatch would prove a decisive element in the battle's surprising outcome. On the Roman left, the 4,000 allied cavalry faced an equal number of Numidians.

Hannibal aligned his infantry in an unusual manner. The center of his position was convex, facing outward toward the advancing Romans. The wings bent backward from the center. Alternating units of Spanish and Celtic swordsmen held this convex line, and they were greatly outnumbered by the oncoming Romans. Hannibal positioned himself at the left end of this line, and his youngest brother, Mago, held the right. Each end of the line was anchored by a dense square of African infantry, the location of which ensured that they would not be engaged until long after those at the center.

As the Romans advanced, a hot west wind blew dust in their faces and obscured their vision. At a range of about 35 yards, the Romans hurled their light javelins, causing casualties among the Spaniards and Celts. Those *pila* often caused problems even if they only penetrated a man's shield, because the shaft was difficult to remove and weighed the shield down, making the man vulnerable to an oncoming legionary.

At closer range, the Romans threw their heavier *pila*, and then the infantry lines crashed together, the agile Celts and Spaniards against the disciplined Roman masses. In time, the weight of the Roman assault began to take effect on Hannibal's troops, and the center of the Carthaginian line receded. As Hannibal's men were forced back, they found themselves slowly backing up a slope. The top of the slope formed a "V" if viewed from above, and the Spaniards and Celts now formed a concave line that conformed to that V, with the African squares still anchored to their original positions at the tips. Due to the nature of the terrain, the Romans fought uphill as they advanced and at the same time were restricted into a narrowing front as their mass of men entered the V.

Although the Roman infantrymen did not know it, their fate was all but sealed by that time. Hannibal had planned for his cavalry to strike the decisive blows while his infantry fought a large-scale delaying action. As the battle opened, Hannibal launched the Spanish and Celtic cavalry on his left against the outnumbered Roman horse. The consul Aemilius accompanied those cavalrymen, who could not withstand the weight of the Carthaginian assault. Aemilius was wounded and the bulk of the Roman horse was driven from the field, uncovering that flank of the Roman army. While this occurred on the Carthaginian left, the Numidians on the right had been inconclusively engaged with the horsemen of Rome's allies.

Hasdrubal, the Carthaginian cavalry commander on the left, reorganized his units and proceeded to ride behind the Roman infantry to the far side of the battlefield, where the stalemated cavalry fight continued between the Numidians and Rome's allies. The allied horsemen now were taken by surprise and were crushed between the two Carthaginian forces. The allied cavalry fled the field, taking the consul Varro with them. At that point, Aemilius was dead or dying, and Varro, the other commander, no longer was with the Roman army. The Roman and allied cavalrymen had been killed, captured or driven from the field. The Numidians were in pursuit of the allied horsemen, leaving the Celts and Spaniards as the only effective cavalry force in the area.

By that time, the Roman infantry had fought its way up the slope and into the closed end of the V, the point. As the men became more tightly packed into a confined space, fewer of them could use their weapons effectively. Romans in the rear ranks continued to push forward, but found they had little room to maneuver. The prevailing winds continued to blow dust into the faces of the advancing legionaries, making it difficult for them to appreciate their dangerous predicament.

At that moment, the African squares anchoring the Carthaginian flanks turned inward and advanced, further constricting the Roman infantry. Hasdrubal assaulted the Roman rear with his heavy cavalry, assisted by the Carthaginian light infantry. The encirclement was complete. Many Romans first discovered the danger when they felt the searing pain of being hamstrung by the knives and swords of the Balearic slingers. The courage of the Roman soldiers was amply demonstrated—the legions fought on even though all hope was gone.

Gradually, though, the pocket of resistance was reduced in size as thousands of Romans were killed. And when, finally, it was over, the Roman army had been truly annihilated. Of the original force of 86,400 about 50,000 were dead, with about 4,500 others taken prisoner. About 17,000 Romans took refuge in two fortified camps nearby, but after further resistance cost 2,000 more fatalities, the remaining 15,000 surrendered. In all, some 71,500 Romans were dead or captured—83 percent of the entire army. Carthaginian losses were less than 6,000, most of them suffered by the Celts.

It is a measure of the greatness of the Roman people that they did not give up after a disaster of such magnitude, especially after the previous defeats at the Trebia and Lake Trasimene. When the Roman Senate next convened, 177 vacancies had to be filled due to the casualties suffered at Cannae, but the Romans did not hesitate to continue the war.

Cannae represented the apex of Hannibal's career, although he has been criticized for not attempting to end the war by sacking Rome itself at that point. Hannibal remained in Italy for 13 more years, but the determination of the Romans to fight on, regardless of losses, eventually gave them the opportunity to defeat the great Carthaginian.

The failure of Carthage to build a fleet strong enough to challenge that of the Romans made Hannibal's task enormously difficult. He attempted to reduce Rome's naval advantage by occupying Italian coastal cities, home for the bulk of Rome's sailors. Could Hannibal have held them, the odds against the Carthaginian fleet would have improved, but his limited manpower made it difficult for him to detach sufficient garrisons to prevent Roman recapture of the port cities.

For 15 years in all, from 218 to 203 BC, Hannibal occupied large areas of Italy. He fought and defeated the Romans on numerous occasions but could not break their spirit. After Cannae, the Romans again became cautious about entering into full-scale battle against Hannibal, but their command of the sea and their decision to invade Spain, in spite of Hannibal's continued presence on Italian soil, made reinforcement of Hannibal's army a problem. Gradually, the troops who had crossed the Alps with Hannibal dwindled in number as age, disease and wounds claimed them. Hannibal was able to maintain his army in the field by replacing casualties with men from the Italian peninsula, first with Celts from the north and later, when this source was cut off, with Bruttians and Lucanians from the south.

But Carthage's lack of naval strength prevented Hannibal's alliances with Syracuse and Macedonia from bearing fruit. The Roman navy captured the text of the treaty between Hannibal and Philip V of Macedon, and by the time the latter received a duplicate copy and acted upon it, a Roman fleet prevented his troops from crossing the Adriatic to Italy. Hannibal could not go to the aid of Syracuse when it was besieged by Roman troops because the Roman fleet prevented him from crossing the narrow Straits of Messina, and Syracuse fell.

In spite of all the difficulties, Hannibal proved to be a gifted leader, able to get the very best from his men. His army was composed of mercenaries with no real ideological commitment to the Carthaginian cause, yet no record exists of any mutiny during its 15 years of campaigning in Italy. The army did not merely endure, it maintained a high level of morale and fighting spirit. After nearly a decade in Italy, the 500-man Numidian garrison of Salabria chose to fight to the death in the streets defending their post when they might have cut their way to safety. Such conduct was especially remarkable for mercenaries having no great patriotic motivation.

Spain was taken from Carthage and the Barcid family after Hannibal's brother Hasdrubal duplicated the crossing of the Alps with a relief force, a desperate move that gave the Romans in Spain a free hand. Hasdrubal was unable to effect a union with Hannibal before being confronted by a strong Roman army in 207 BC. In the ensuing battle, Hasdrubal was defeated and killed. The first news Hannibal had of his brother's arrival in Italy was when his head was catapulted into Hannibal's camp. The loss of Spain cost Carthage an excellent source of mercenaries, along with the absolutely vital gold and silver mines needed to finance the use of mercenaries from other countries.

In October of 203 BC, Publius Cornelius Scipio, the conqueror of Spain, invaded North Africa and forced Hannibal's recall to defend Carthage itself. Hannibal's defeat at Zama at the hands of Scipio in the following spring, caused largely by a deficiency of cavalry strength, ended the Second Punic War.

Hannibal rose to a position of prominence in Carthage after the war and took steps that helped Carthage recover economically from the conflict. Rome viewed Carthage's revival with suspicion, and Hannibal was forced to flee to the east, where he committed suicide in 183 BC rather than fall into Roman hands.

Spartacus,
Terror of Rome

*Rome's legions were sorely challenged by rebellious slaves
and gladiators led up and down the Italian boot
by a most determined Thracian.*

By Kenneth P. Czech

In 73 BC, the populace of Rome trembled at the grave rumors that their city was about to be attacked by a rabble army of gladiators and rebelling slaves. The vaunted Roman legions had been defeated, their noble standards captured. News of atrocities against slaveholding landowners dominated conversation in Rome's marketplaces and public buildings. The very name of the slave rebellion's leader, Spartacus, generated terror.

Slave insurrections were not really new to Rome. Extreme cruelty to slaves had sparked a revolt on the island of Sicily in 135 BC. More than 70,000 slaves had taken up arms and effectively battled local militia until a Roman army led by Publius Rupilius triumphed over the rebels two years later. A second servile war erupted on the island in 104 BC, when 40,000 slaves rampaged through its farmlands. After four years of bloody fighting, the last remnants of that rebel horde were captured by Roman consul Manius Aquillius and shipped to Rome to fight wild beasts in the arena.

But those revolts had been in far-off Sicily. The new insurrection threatened Rome itself, a city where a great percentage of the inhabitants were slaves. To make matters worse, several legions had already been demolished by the slave army.

Forming the nucleus of the threat were gladiators—prisoners of war, convicts and slaves specially trained to fight and kill one another as entertainment for crowds packing amphitheaters throughout Latin lands. Notoriously tough and highly skilled, the gladiators surging toward Rome had little to lose. Facing death in the arena on an almost daily basis, these warrior-slaves felt their only key to freedom lay in crushing Rome itself.

Combats between trained warriors had first surfaced to commemorate funerals during the First Punic War in 264 BC. In 174 BC, 74 gladiators fought each other during a three-day span as part of special funeral ceremonies for wealthy Romans. The first officially sponsored gladiatorial "games" were held nearly 70 years later, and they were an instant success with the public. As the Roman appetite for blood sports grew, thousands of prisoners captured in Rome's numerous wars of conquest were trundled off to specially constructed training centers, or "schools," to prepare them for the games.

The gladiators took their name from the Latin word *gladius*, the short sword favored by many of the combatants. Early gladiators were outfitted with an ornately wrought visored helmet, a shield and an armored sleeve worn on the right arm, after the fashion of Samnite warriors defeated by Rome in the late 3rd century BC.

Samnite-style gladiators relied on their swords. Other gladiator styles evolved from the national themes of the lands conquered by Rome. Thracian-style gladiators, for instance, carried a *sica*—a curved, short-bladed scimitar—and a round buckler. Gallic-style gladiators wielded long swords and rectangular or oval shields. Another gladiator type, more exotically accoutered and called a *retiarius*, fought with a trident, a dagger and a fishing net strung to the wrist by a thong that was designed to ensnare an opponent and draw him into harpooning range.

Pairing the warriors was done by drawing lots. Mercy was rarely offered in the arena, with crowds often controlling the immediate fortunes of a wounded gladiator by signaling or calling for life or death. While several noted Roman writers applauded the games as invigorating spectacles, the writer-philosopher Seneca abhorred them, commenting: "I come home more greedy, more cruel and inhuman, because I have been among human beings.... Man, a sacred thing to man, is killed for sport and merriment."

A number of gladiator-training schools sprang up throughout Italy, concentrated near the town of Capua, north of present-day Naples. At such schools, gladiators received training in a variety of weapons, though they usually specialized in one. Diets were carefully observed, and a strict exercise regimen was maintained. Discipline and punishment were harsh.

It may have been pure brutality that convinced 78 gladiators to rebel at the school of Lentulus Batiatus, near Capua, in 73 BC. The gladiators, who had been severely treated, sallied from their quarters and overpowered their guards with "cleavers and spits seized from some kitchen," reported Roman historian Plutarch. After scrambling over the school's walls, the slaves were fortunate to find a wagon transporting gladiators' weapons to another city. Armed with these familiar—if not military-issue—weapons, the little band had suddenly become a dangerous fighting force.

Masterminding the revolt, according to the sources, was Spartacus, a Thracian by birth who may even have once served as an auxiliary in the Roman army before being sold into slavery. Sharing command were two Gauls: Crixus and Oenamus. The triumvirate raided the countryside, terrorizing landowners in the lush Campania farming district. Field hands and house slaves, many armed with farm tools and kitchen utensils, declared their own freedom by joining the gladiators.

As word of the insurrection spread, Spartacus led his force up the slopes of the dormant volcano Vesuvius. Close on his heels was a hastily assembled army of 3,000 militia under the command of Clodius Glaber. Poorly trained and untested, the militia was usually sent to control riots or outbreaks of brigandage, while the solid legions of the regular army were used primarily in foreign conquests.

Glaber deployed his troops at the base of Vesuvius and blocked the sole road leading to its crest. In his mind, the gladiators were effectively cut off from the plains and could be starved into submission. Not about to be besieged, however, Spartacus ordered his men to hack the abundant vines growing near the crest and fashion them into crude ladders. After sunset, the slaves descended on their ladders and fell upon the few sentries Glaber had bothered to post. In minutes, the gladiators were slashing their way through the slumbering Roman camp, routing the militia and seizing valuable stocks of military arms and armor.

Two legions of militia under the command of the praetor Publius Varinius then were dispatched from Rome to track the insurgents and bring them to justice. Unknown to the Romans, the gladiators' army had swollen to nearly 40,000, including bands of shepherds who were familiar with the countryside and acted as scouts. Lacking knowledge of the terrain, Varinius was further hampered by disease brought on by damp autumn weather—and by an outbreak of insubordination among his own troops. Perhaps even worse was his own refusal to consider the slaves a serious fighting force.

Spartacus was determined to annihilate his pursuers. Near Vesuvius, he surprised an advance column of 2,000 men under Varinius' lieutenant Furius and destroyed it. Using his scouts to good advantage, the gladiator discovered another party of Romans under Cossinius at a camp and bath near Herculaneum. In a swirling battle, Spartacus nearly captured Cossinius, then pursued him as he fled. The Roman and the remnants of his column were brought to bay and slaughtered.

Slipping southward, Spartacus' army continued to grow. Varinius trailed him into Lucania, where he suddenly found the rebels deployed in battle formation. The insubordination that had plagued Varinius earlier now flared up once more. Some soldiers refused to advance, while others fled. The Roman praetor (a magistrate next below the rank of consul) continued his attack but was badly mauled. Varinius escaped, though his horse and his official standards and insignia were seized, adding to the Roman humiliation. Captured legionaries were forced to fight each other as gladiators or were crucified, just as some Romans crucified captured slaves.

Spartacus and his army marched north, reoccupying Campania and destroying a Roman corps under Gaius Thoranius that had been left there by Varinius to restore order. Spartacus undoubtedly realized that his ragtag force had been lucky so far. It had defeated several Roman forces, but the

38

rebels had not yet faced the rugged veterans of wars in Spain, Gaul and Germany. The Thracian advocated marching his horde to the Alps in hopes of eluding Rome's long reach. Unfortunately for the slaves, another faction, led by the Gaul Crixus, was full of confidence after helping to crush the Roman militia and argued that Rome itself should be attacked. Taking as many as 30,000 men, including a contingent of German and Gallic gladiators, Crixus broke with Spartacus to plunder neighboring villages and towns.

No longer considering the gladiator uprising as a mere outbreak of brigandage, the Roman Senate decided to send two more armies against the slaves in the spring of 72 BC. Commanded by the consuls Lucius Gellius and Gnaeus Lentulus, four Roman legions took to the field. It was relatively easy to follow the trail left by Crixus and his band as they levied tribute in the Apulia region at the heel of the Italian peninsula. Gellius sent two legions under his praetor Quintus Arrius to hem in the gladiators against the coast. Surprised by the Romans near Mount Garganus, Crixus found himself surrounded. Despite furious fighting, the Gaul and two-thirds of his army were cut down.

Spartacus, meantime, had made good use of his winter respite while camped in the Appenine Mountains. His men scoured the area, raiding estates and towns, particularly in search of horses. The slave leader hoped to build and train a cavalry unit to be his eyes as his rabble marched toward the Alps. Towns such as Consentia and Metapontum were stormed, their newly released slaves joining ranks with Spartacus and swelling the army to more than 70,000. Any freed slaves capable of bearing arms received rudimentary training.

In the spring of 72 BC, the gladiator army trekked northward, pursued by the consuls and their legions. In three separate engagements, Spartacus first defeated Lentulus, who had attempted to surround the slaves, and then both Gellius and the praetor Arrius, who had recently slain Crixus and most of his Gauls. At Mutina in the Cisalpine Gaul region of northern Italy, the governor, Caius Cassius, made a futile attempt to stem the slaves' trek with an army of 10,000 men. Spartacus' horde collapsed Cassius' center, slaying many of the legionaries, and Cassius barely escaped with his life. To appease the ghost of Crixus, 300 Romans were sacrificed or forced to fight each other as gladiators.

With Cassius' army demolished, the path to freedom over the Alps now lay clear. Surprisingly, however, Spartacus chose to lead his slaves back into Italy. Perhaps a contingent of his gladiators preferred looting the peninsula as Crixus had, and Spartacus may have feared that a further division of his force could be disastrous if Roman legions pursued them and forced them into battle. He may have even entertained the idea of raiding Rome, the source of enslavement of so many peoples. For whatever reasons, the Thracian led his mob southward.

Rome was beside itself with anxiety. The gladiator army was estimated at between 75,000 and 125,000. With the losses of the various legions, the city was short of available troops and able commanders. The most experienced generals, such as Quintus Metellus and Gnaeus Pompeius (Pompey), were stationed with their battle-hardened legions in rebellious Spain, while Lucius Lucullus kept an eye on troublesome Asia Minor. For the moment, only poorly trained local levies remained to defend Rome.

The Roman Senate finally gave supreme military command to the praetor Marcus Licinius Crassus, the only man who offered to take the post. A multimillionaire, Crassus had built his fortune through astute real estate deals. More important, he had gained valuable experience while serving under the command of the great Roman general Lucius Cornelius Sulla, who had died in 78 BC.

Crassus inherited the remnants of the legions of Publius Varinius that had fled the battlefield in their earlier disastrous engagement with the gladiators, in addition to several newly raised legions.

News then reached the Romans that Spartacus was marching through Picenum, along Italy's central Adriatic coast. Crassus ordered his lieutenant Mummius to lead two of the new legions in a circle behind the slave rabble, but, as Plutarch noted, "not to join battle nor even skirmish with them." Unfortunately for Crassus, Mummius unwisely attacked the gladiators from the rear, obviously thinking that he would have the advantage of surprise. In the ensuing melee, many of the legionaries were slain, and hundreds of others broke rank and fled.

Crassus was livid with anger. Assembling the shattered remains of Mummius' legions, he ordered 500 men accused of cowardice to be divided into 50 groups of 10 each. Lots were drawn in each group, with one unlucky soldier chosen for execution. The entire army was forced to witness the deaths of their comrades as warning to any others who considered disobedience.

With discipline re-established, the new general proceeded to retrain and rearm his troops. Each soldier became proficient in the use of the short-bladed *gladius*, ideal for either thrusting or slashing. In addition, the Roman levies were drilled in the use of the *pilum*, an iron-headed spear whose metal neck, extending to a wooden shaft, would snap downward after hitting an object to prevent its being thrown back by an enemy. The legions were also divided into regiments, called cohorts, of 480 men each and were instructed how to maneuver on the field of battle. A complete legion stood ready for action with roughly 5,000 men.

With eight new legions under his command, Crassus pursued Spartacus the length of Italy, getting the best of him in a running battle in the Lucania region in the south. Stung, the gladiator army limped through Bruttium on the toe of the Italian peninsula, finally reaching the coastal city of Rhegium across the Strait of Messina from Sicily. Spartacus managed to contact Sicilian pirates, paying them handsomely in gold and treasure looted from countless estates to ferry thousands of his men to Sicily, where he hoped to rekindle the slave rebellion that had erupted there barely a generation earlier. The pirates, however, deceived the rebels. They accepted the payment, but failed to take their fleet to the approved rendezvous. For the moment, the gladiator army was literally left high and dry on the Bruttium peninsula.

Crassus, in the meantime, realized he had the slaves trapped. Rather than face the cornered gladiators in a pitched battle, he ordered his legions to construct a wall completely across the peninsula to hem in the enemy and starve them into submission. The legionaries excavated a ditch 15 feet deep and wide across the 32-mile distance, then fashioned a wood and stone wall along one edge of the ditch.

Spartacus, for a time, ignored the Roman wall. He desperately searched for some other means to transport his army but could not devise one. With winter setting in and supplies running low, he determined his only recourse was to smash through the barricade across the peninsula. The Thracian "waited for a snowy night and a wintery storm," noted Plutarch, "when he filled up a small portion of the ditch with earth and timber and the boughs of trees," and battered his way through.

With the freed gladiators once more tramping toward Lucania, Rome panicked. The Senate authorized the return of Pompey from Spain and Lucullus from his recent wars with King Mithridates VI of Pontus, to bolster the legions of Crassus. Fearing that the glory of subduing the gladiators would be won by those political rivals, Crassus redoubled his efforts.

Fortunately for the Romans, the gladiators were once again weakened by internal squabbling. Two more Gauls, Ganicus and Cestus, broke away from the main army to plunder area villages and estates. Encamped at the Lucanian Lake, that splinter band was surprised by Crassus and his legions. With no retreat possible, the gladiators fought with the desperate fury of cornered men. More than 12,000 rebels fell in the battle before Spartacus arrived to rescue the survivors.

Pursued by the Romans, Spartacus led his army to the mountains of Petelia. Several legions under Crassus' lieutenants Scrophas and Quintus harassed the slaves by making several daring attacks on their rear. Then, Spartacus suddenly wheeled his force about and fell on the Romans. In the furious battle that followed, Scrophas was wounded, and his legionaries barely managed to drag him to safety. The defeat became a rout, as Romans streamed away by the score.

News reached the slaves that Pompey and Lucullus had been dispatched with their legions and were at that moment marching to put an end to the insurrection. Spartacus advised his followers to continue their retreat through the Petelian heights, but many of his officers advocated heading south to Apulia to reach the seaport of Brundisium on the heel of the Italian peninsula. There, it was hoped, they could capture merchant ships in a desperate escape attempt.

With the legions of his political rivals rapidly approaching, Crassus was determined to bring Spartacus to a decisive battle. His legions hounded the gladiators as they fled southward. Stragglers were rapidly picked off and executed. When word reached him that Lucullus had landed at Brundisium and was marching inland, Crassus knew he had the Thracian at his mercy.

Spartacus found himself trapped between the two armies, with the legions of Pompey still on their way. Drawing his force up to face Crassus, the weaker of the two opponents. Spartacus commanded that his horse should be brought to him. Drawing his sword, the slave leader stabbed the animal to show his men that there would be no further retreat—only victory or death.

Sweeping forward in a wave of humanity, the slaves sought to overwhelm the Romans by sheer numbers. Spying Crassus through the swirling melee, Spartacus fought to reach the Roman general. With weapons flying around him, the Thracian nearly reached his goal, slaying two centurions in individual combat before being surrounded by the enemy. Ancient Roman sources agree that although he was severely wounded, he continued to wield his spear and shield until the Romans swarmed over him and a small contingent of bodyguards.

The Roman victory was complete. Almost the entire gladiator army was annihilated, its remnants scattering to the nearby hills. Although Crassus was accorded the victory, his own decimated legions were unable to track down all the fugitives. That dubious honor was left to Pompey, who had recently arrived on the scene. Rebel slaves were hunted without mercy throughout southern Italy, many of them fighting until they were cut down by the legions. More than 6,000 captured slaves, according to Appian, were "crucified along the whole road from Capua to Rome."

The Third Servile War, as Spartacus' rebellion officially came to be known, was the last of the major slave insurrections that Rome would experience. The fear engendered by the revolt, however, would haunt the Roman psyche for centuries to come. During the reign of Nero (54-68 AD), panic erupted when gladiators at Praeneste attempted a breakout. "Their army guards overpowered them" before the revolt could spread, according to one historian, "but the Roman public, as always terrified or fascinated by revolution, were already talking of ancient calamities such as the rising of Spartacus."

Gladiatorial games, in spite of the dangers posed by strong-willed warriors such as Spartacus, continued to grow in popularity. The Roman public became so thirsty for the spectacle that politicians often sponsored elaborate games to win votes. During the rule of Emperor Marcus Ulpius Traianus

(Trajan), 4,941 pairs of gladiators saw combat through 117 days of festivities. By the time the games peaked in the 4th century AD, 175 days a year were devoted to the sport.

Societal changes and the influx of barbarian peoples into the Roman Empire ultimately ended the popularity of the gladiator contests. In 404 AD, the Emperor Honorius banned the games.

Besiegers Besieged

*At Alesia, Gaius Julius Caesar surrounded the Gallic defenders
with ring upon ring of his own defensive works.*

By Donald O'Reilly

Just 58 years before the birth of Christ, the territories controlled by Rome incorporated almost all the shores of the Mediterranean Sea and dozens of city-states, tribes, cultures and languages. Italians dominated, but the greatest danger to Rome was the murderous feuding of the political factions within Italy. The hereditary Senate and its great landowners were challenged by self-proclaimed leaders of the common people. Often aristocrats who were considered traitors to their class, men such as Gaius Julius Caesar and Marc Antony, opposed the establishment and made no pretense of favoring democracy. Their appeal was to fierce personal loyalties rather than abstract principles. After bloody civil war had repeatedly ravaged the Italian peninsula, the Senate felt considerable relief when Caesar, the most ambitious contender for power, accepted command of the army in northern Italy and Cisalpine and Transalpine Gaul, with orders to stop the incursions of Celtic barbarians into the province known today as the French Riviera.

Perhaps he would be battling beyond the Alps long enough to fade from the political scene, or, with luck, he might be killed by the Gauls, as had been his father-in-law. And if not, perhaps his conquests would satisfy his financial ambitions.

The Senate underestimated Caesar's greed. He had no sooner arrived in Massilia (Marseille) than he appropriated the province's treasury as his own. In the years to come, he would stay in the political limelight despite his absence from Italy by writing a stream of news dispatches of his adventures, a real-life suspense story tacked to marketplace walls and soon the popular gossip of the streets of Italy. Assembled as Caesar's war commentaries, they provide posterity with a brilliant description of his military exploits.

Caesar, of course, was the hero of his own account. And it was remarkably accurate for the most part, but it can be assumed that he omitted or glossed over matters that were less than edifying to his political supporters.

The army of Rome consisted of two elements, the legions of 6,000 citizens each when at full complement, and the smaller auxiliary units of 500 or 1,000 men who were not Roman citizens, plus various allied forces under Roman direction. Every Roman soldier was a volunteer and thoroughly professional.

The typical legionary carried more than 50 pounds of armor and weapons. Auxiliaries wore little armor and functioned as scouts, flankers and skirmishers, their formations more open, like those of the barbarian tribes from which they were usually recruited.

The legionary battle formation was a solid wall of hundreds of men standing shoulder to shoulder three ranks deep, each man first casting the javelin, then resorting to the spear and finally to the short sword. A wounded man was immediately replaced by the soldier behind him. After 15 to 20 minutes of hand-to-hand fighting—more exhausting than heavyweight boxing and without the rest between rounds—the second rank took the place of the first. The youngest men were in the first rank, the oldest in the rear. The centurions—who, in effect, ranged in rank from staff sergeant to colonel—usually kept close to the center of action. Their high casualty rate, acknowledged by Caesar, reflected that fact.

In comparison, the Gauls (as the Romans called them) or Celts (as they called themselves) were by no means professionals. They preferred the swift raid and swifter disappearance—guerrilla tactics—in contrast to Rome's foot-slogging and carefully planned system of war making. The Celts were farmers taking arms to defend their homes, most of them without body armor. A struggle between a well-armored infantryman and one without armor, as the writer Seneca would remark of a contest between armored and unarmored gladiators, "is no contest, it is murder." The leaders of the Celts had armor but fought on horseback; they favored foolhardy courage and acts of bravado that seldom prevailed against the coldly systematic Roman battle drill.

The Roman formations were vulnerable when taken by surprise by cavalry or by fast-running footmen assaulting their flanks or rear. Most Roman defeats in Gaul could be blamed upon such enemy tactics. The legions were slow to maneuver and to face a new direction. The broken terrain of valleys, high hills, forests and meadows so typical of France (Gaul) was especially dangerous for the Romans.

The Gauls were a civilized people, if stone-walled towns, skilled metalwork, pottery and weaving denote civilization. No nomads, they lived year-round in permanent villages, satellites of fortified hill towns called *oppida*. Because they were civilized, they could be forced to engage in the set-piece battles that gave Romans the advantage—the Gauls had to defend the *oppida*, which contained vital metal workshops, tradesmen and temples. Rome would prove to have much more limited success in campaigns against uncivilized peoples who wandered in pursuit of hunting, herding or new farmland. Beyond the Rhine and Danube there were tribal folk who had no towns to defend, only temporary villages.

The Romans were superbly skilled at rapidly digging trenches and raising fieldworks. Most Gauls disdained use of the ax, pick and shovel, preferring to fight in the open rather than set up defensive works. It would prove to be their undoing. In metalwork, too, the small workshops were no match in output for the Roman mass production of iron weapons of war. Moreover, Rome could import metal by sea from distant sources anywhere across the Mediterranean.

Even so, there were Celtic pressures upon Roman territory, a reaction to the movement of German tribes into Gaul. One such incursion pushed the Celts of Switzerland, the Helvetii, southwestward into the lands of the Aedui, a powerful tribe of Savoy allied to Rome—and source of many auxiliaries. A prominent Aedui chief, Dumnorix, son-in-law of the Helvetic king, had been asked to secretly arrange refuge for the Helvetii among the Sequani, the western neighbors of the Aedui. To get there, the Helvetii invaded the Roman province of Transalpine Gaul, governed by Caesar. That prompted Caesar to mobilize his forces and recruit more men. Moving on to Aedui territory, the Helvetii proceeded to ravage and plunder. Divitiacus, the older brother of Aedui Chief Dumnorix, thereupon appealed to the Roman Senate for aid. The Senate refused.

Caesar was left with little choice but to react against the Helvetii and ignore the Senate, which had long been hostile to him. In a campaign marked by many bold moves, he then conquered the 380,000-strong Helvetii. He next engaged the Germans who had crossed the Rhine. And having defeated them, he recruited their cavalry as allies. It was a hallmark of Roman policy, like that of many later empires, to pit one foe against another. To divide and conquer the Celts, though, was not necessary. They already were involved in constant intrigue and conflict, one tribe against another, though without the utter ruthlessness of Roman ambitions. War to them was largely raiding, rather than mass executions or the enslavement of entire populations.

The Aedui was the only tribe claiming loyalty to the Romans, whose supply lines from Italy into Gaul passed right through their territory. Moreover, Aedui grain was essential to maintain the Roman forces. But from the beginning of his campaigns in Gaul, Caesar would be vexed by the unreliability of the Aedui he was protecting. Dumnorix, as leader of their cavalry, had been the first to turn tail when he encountered the Helvetii, who had paid him for passage through his tribe's land. Evidence then emerged that he had been duped. The Sequani and Germans had secretly conspired to use the Helvetii against the Aedui. Dumnorix chose to shrug off the matter, preoccupying himself with jealousy at what he saw as the usurpation of his authority by his older brother Divitiacus, whom Caesar trusted and respected.

Instead of vital grain, more and more promises from Dumnorix were arriving in the Roman camps. Confronting Divitiacus with proofs of his brother's complicity, Caesar was restrained from punishing Dumnorix only by his elder brother's pleas—and the fact that if Dumnorix fell before Roman swords, his brother would be blamed by the tribe and would lose his pro-Roman influence.

Dumnorix was taken hostage, well-treated but nonetheless held as a prisoner in Caesar's entourage. Hostage-taking, a custom among the Celts, was effective because of the intensity of family and personal loyalties. It succeeded in forestalling open and bloody battle so long as the hostage was treated well.

Divitiacus was probably a Druid, a member of the educated priestly class or "philosophers among the Gauls," as Caesar called them. They were exempt from military service. Although literate, the Druids committed all their knowledge to memory, scorning writing as a "weakness of the mind." Their secret knowledge secured their power and influence.

Druidism was not a specific religion. There were many creeds and philosophies among the Gauls. Druids led ceremonies of public worship that were considered a patriotic duty by the Celtic tribesmen regardless of personal convictions, an attitude the Romans shared. Druidic and Christian worship would be virtually the only creeds banned by Rome, the former because it inspired Celtic nationalism, although the Roman explanation was that the Druids made human sacrifices. (Caesar stated that the victims were criminals.)

The Druids, in effect, were their society's lawyers and judges, doctors and teachers, and women ranked among them. Ruling manipulatively, they appealed to both superstition and intellect, depending upon the makeup of their audience. Many people were convinced that some Druids could predict the future, an ability no doubt aided by their many informants.

Usually wary of war, the Druids were in the habit of claiming all booty taken in a battle victory so that it could be tossed into a pond as sacrifice to the gods. The large hoard of Roman weapons, armor and silverware unearthed by archaeologists at Vimöse, in Denmark, attests to that practice.

While consistently maneuvering to secure Aedui interests, the Druid Divitiacus repeatedly intervened to soften Roman policy toward defeated tribes, offering the Aedui as guarantors of their good behavior. He had the wisdom to see Rome's power and held that discretion was the better part of valor for his people, a point that seemingly eluded his charismatic but vainglorious brother.

In six years, Caesar campaigned from the Alps and the Rhine to the Bay of Biscay and the English Channel, twice invading Britain, that "mysterious island," as he called it. With the help of the slave dealers accompanying him, he became the equivalent of a billionaire. In the process, whatever illusions anyone had about him vanished.

In Belgium, fighting what he described as the "bravest of all the Gauls," he reduced 60,000 warriors of the Nervii tribe to 500. Let his own words tell of the assault on the fortified *oppidum* of the Atuatuci, allies of the Nervii: "They were a brave lot, and in this last desperate bid, courage was all they could rely upon. We had the advantage of position, being able to direct our fire from earthworks and siege-towers. About 4,000 of them were killed and the survivors forced back into town. Next day, the gates, being undefended, were driven in and our troops made their entry. I had the entire population sold at auction in one lot, and the purchasers' returns showed a total of 53,000 souls."

Upon the invasion of Britain in 54 BC, the hostage Dumnorix was ordered to go with the Roman forces. Accustomed to intrigue, he took this as pretext that outside Gallic territory he would meet with a fatal "accident." He fled on horseback, pursued by Roman horsemen warned against killing him—if it was avoidable. Intercepted, he resisted violently, shouting, "I'm the free citizen of a free state!" The Romans killed him.

After his brother's death, Divitiacus disappears from Caesar's memoirs. His brother's death probably did cost Divitiacus his effective leadership over his people, who were increasingly restive under Roman domination. At the same time, the free tribes throughout Gaul had come to the realization that their piecemeal resistance efforts were doomed. The only way to defeat the Romans was to achieve complete unity under one leader for all Gaul.

In 52 BC, while Caesar was enrolling new troops in northern Italy, the leaders of many tribes gathered near Chartres, the center of Druidic organization in Gaul. They plotted a unified onslaught against the Romans greater than anything previously attempted. The supreme leader was Vercingetorix, a young aristocrat of the Arvernii tribe from the rugged, unconquered heartland of Gaul, the area today known as the Auvergne. His father had died trying to acquire the chieftainship of all Gaul, and Vercingetorix now demanded that his forces swear solemn oaths to the gods to destroy the Roman invaders. Hostages were taken from all the tribes joining him. Chieftains refusing to provide hostages were publicly killed, tortured or mutilated as examples to the rest.

With the advantage of surprise and swiftness, the rebels swept southward upon what is now Orleans on the Loire River and killed its entire Roman population, including the civilian in charge of the Roman grain supply in Gaul. In 12 hours, news of the massacre traveled 150 miles by word of mouth.

Caesar's forces, scattered throughout Gaul, faced starvation within months. He never really said so in writing, but what else can explain his subsequent actions? He ordered his more distant troops sent toward him and Roman territory, while he sent soldiers' slaves and wounded men who had been on light duty into the fields to gather grain. Some of the slaves, captured and brought to Vercingetorix, were made to declare to the assembled Celtic war host that the Romans were reduced to near starvation. It was a premature announcement.

The Celts, for their part, boasted an impressive town at Avaricum (modern Bourges) near the Loire River. Its inhabitants chose to hold it against Caesar's advance despite Vercingetorix's desire to raze it to the ground as part of a scorched-earth strategy. It contained a large store of grain. In weeks of hard labor, the Romans erected siege works against the counterefforts of the town's ingenious defenders, many of whom were miners skilled at feats of engineering. In the end, of 40,000 people of the tribe holding the town, only 800 were not killed by the Romans, who erupted into a frenzy of vengeance for the deaths at Orleans.

The Roman fury may have been motivated as much by the pangs of hunger as revenge. The grain stores were taken intact, but there was probably little to share with any great number of prisoners. Caesar admitted, but passed over lightly, the "fatigue and undernourishment" of his troops at Avaricum.

News arrived that the Aedui, who had been assisting his operations in Gaul, had split into feuding parties. Two rival chiefs claimed to have been elected to the one-year term of the tribal presidency. Fearing that one might ally with Vercingetorix, Caesar summoned their tribal council and bluntly ordered that the supposedly pro-Roman claimant be accepted. For Caesar, it was a political blunder he could have avoided had he still had the benefit of Divitiacus' usual informed advice. Convictolitavis, endorsed by the Druids and generously bribed by Caesar, had repressed his resentment of the Romans as long as he could bear. He used part of the bribe to buy the support of the Aedui in a plot to double-cross the Romans. For once, Caesar was naive.

As a result, Litaviccus, the Aedui commander of 10,000 warriors en route to join the Romans as allies, stopped his men on the march and asked them to reconsider their loyalties. He related deeds of Roman treachery and murder. Believing him, his barbaric troops changed their line of march and headed to the town of Gergovia, near the headwaters of the Loire, to reinforce Vercingetorix. Meanwhile, messengers were sent by Litaviccus to stir up all the Aedui against Rome.

In his camp about midnight, Caesar was abruptly alerted by a loyal chief who begged him not to blame the entire tribe for the actions of a few deceiving the many. Caesar immediately ordered his troops to be awakened and set out with the major part of them on a forced march that met the Aedui force 23 miles away. Cavalry headed the column of four legions traveling without their usual heavy gear. Careful not to attack, Caesar sent among the Aedui some of the very chiefs said to have been murdered by the Romans. Litaviccus fled. His army yielded without a fight.

Meanwhile, the Aedui in villages and towns were murdering Romans without even questioning the assertions of Litaviccus' agents. Such was the heedless impetuosity of the Gallic character, according to Caesar. That soon ceased. Once again, however, six years after the problem had first arisen, there was the ominous threat that Aedui grain would not be sent to the Roman camps. But this time other Roman armies, their grain supply destroyed, were retreating toward Caesar in hope of supply.

It was no time to display weakness. Boldly, too boldly, Caesar advanced to attack the citadel of Gergovia held by Vercingetorix. Attacking the stronghold, near modern Autun, the Romans suffered an unexpected setback, losing nearly 700 men and 46 centurions, plus many wounded. Caesar said the reason was that the legionaries, in their enthusiasm, had charged uphill against the stone walls of the citadel before receiving orders. Adding to the dismay of the Romans, a large Aedui force sent to protect their flank was mistaken for a hostile tribal force, a misapprehension causing near panic in the Roman ranks. Caesar ordered a withdrawal, but only the elite *Legio* (Legion) X did so in good order.

Caesar described a centurion of *Legio* VII, Marcus Petronius, cut off by his enemies as he attacked a gateway of the town. Petronius shouted to his men: "I can't go with you, but it's my fault you are in this fix. Too eager to make a show, that's me. I'll do what I can for you." He than rushed among the enemy, killing two of them and driving the rest back from the gate. His comrades tried to save him, but again he cried: "It's no use. I've lost too much blood. I'm finished. Run for it while you can. Get back to the legion!"

A moment later, Petronius fell fighting. But he had saved his men.

Abandoning the attack on Gergovia, Caesar marched northward to join the troops of Titus Labienus, who had just taken, and burned, Lutetia on the site of what would become Paris. After the linkup, the combined Roman force was comprised of 12 legions and many auxiliaries, including the German cavalry recalled from beyond the Rhine. The force of 80,000 men marched south along the Armancon, apparently intending to reach the Rhône and the riverboats there that would carry them to Roman-occupied Narbonensis in southern Gaul. Almost all the Roman forces in Gaul were with Caesar, in retreat after six years of conquest.

Meanwhile, Vercingetorix had moved from Bibrace, near Gergovia, to block the retreat, rallying the tribes at the *oppidum* of Alesia (pronounced Ah-lay-zeeah). To delay the approaching Romans, his cavalry attacked at Ampilly-le-Sec, on a headwater of the Seine. Alerted by *pioneri*, their scouts, the Romans were ready. Allied German cavalry defeated the Celtic horsemen and drove them into a waiting formation of Roman infantry. The Celtic horsemen were demoralized by the loss of 3,000 of their warrior aristocracy and retreated with Caesar's army in pursuit. The battle nevertheless had given Vercingetorix time to bring herds of cattle onto the mesalike summit of Alesia. He also confiscated wheat from the local tribesmen, the Mandubii, allies of the Aedui and not enemies of Rome. Villagers objecting to the loss of their entire food supply were summarily butchered as examples to the rest.

Alesia (today Alise Ste. Reine, between Dijon and Auxerre) was strategically situated between the headwaters of the Loire and the Rhône, the two greatest rivers of Gaul. Situated on a mesa (modern Mont Auxois), it was a natural fortress, its steep slopes isolated on every side by valleys cut in eons past by streams surviving as the Oze and Ozerain. Rising more than 400 feet from the valleys, its cliff sides were reinforced by stone walls. It was impossible to bring siege trenches and towers directly to its walls, but its isolation would also make it difficult for its defenders to escape.

Vercingetorix's army numbered about 80,000. Many of his men were anxious at the thought of the impending battle, which they realized would be the most terrible of many that had bled Gaul. In one night, as much to prevent desertion as to impede the Romans, Vercingetorix had a 6-foot-deep trench dug from the Oze to the Ozerain, and the earth removed piled on top on one side in Roman military fashion, forming a *vallum*. This entrenchment guarded the eastern foot of Alesia's heights.

The first clash of the rival armies within sight of Alesia began with the Celtic cavalry attacking the Romans on the plain west of the town. Moving in two columns, one emerging from the north and the other from the south of Alesia's heights, the Celts never reached the Roman infantry. Caesar's German cavalry met them in the field, charge after charge continuing intensely throughout the day. Compared to the Gallic horses, those of the Germans were mere ponies, small and ugly in Caesar's opinion but of remarkable stamina. Each German horse carried into battle a rider and a soldier armed with bow and arrow, the latter ready to fight on foot. Riders and footmen took turns protecting each other.

The Celtic cavalry was ultimately routed, galloping to Vercingetorix's entrenched camp. The riders were hotly pursued and suffered more losses when forced to dismount because of the narrowness of the gates to the camp.

As was typical of him, Vercingetorix acted decisively. That night he ordered all the surviving cavalry to return to their distant homes in order to raise a relief column from tribes throughout Gaul. Meanwhile, he would hold Alesia. He had food supplies for one month.

Both sides now had placed everything on the next throw of fate's dice. Both Romans and Gauls were trapped. For the Romans to withdraw meant the likely destruction of their rear guard. The Celts dared not retreat until the relief army had arrived.

Having abandoned the valley bottoms to the Romans rather than be subject to Roman attack from the surrounding hillsides, the Gauls waited. The Romans occupied the plains. Routinely, at the end of every day's march, Roman troops dug a *vallum* in rectangular outline within an hour. On this occasion they outdid themselves. Caesar commanded that Alesia be completely encircled by a broad band of defenses 10 miles in circumference. The main redoubt consisted of a 12-foot-high rampart surmounted by a palisade, with towers erected at 130-yard intervals. A *vallum* 20 feet wide was dug linking the streams at the western foot of Alesia. The Roman camps kept the streams and *vallum* between themselves and the Celts on the heights. The Romans crossed the streams to construct elaborate works to retard a surprise attack by the defenders. Trenches 5 feet deep and lined with sharpened branches were dug in front of the main Roman fortifications. In front of those "boundary posts," thousands of pits were dug and fitted at the bottom with sharpened stakes, called "lilies" by the Romans. "Goads"—foot-long wooden blocks embedded with steel hooks—were planted in the soil to mangle feet and legs. These would slow a charge in daylight, and at night, invisible, they would be particularly effective. The works completed, the Romans withdrew across the streams, flooded the largest *vallum*, dug a second one, and erected as many as 600 three-story siege towers. As a precaution against attack by an outside relief force, Caesar also had a second ring of fortifications built, facing outward on the flattest ground available and covering a circumference of 14 miles.

With his food supply dwindling, Vercingetorix ordered all noncombatants in Alesia out of its fortifications. Thousands of women, children, the sick, wounded and elderly were to starve to death in the next few weeks between the lines of the opposing armies. When only a few days' food remained, the Gallic relief army arrived—240,000 infantry and 8,000 cavalry. Their commander, an Atrebian named Commius, had served with Caesar in Britain. His chief lieutenants were Vercassivellaunus, cousin of Vercingetorix, and two Aeduans, Viridomarus and Eporedorix. The Gauls camped on the heights, a few miles to the southwest of Alesia. And without bothering to fortify their position, they immediately sent their cavalry to attack the Romans.

Caesar's German horsemen intercepted them. This time the Gauls mingled infantry and riders, imitating the tactic that had previously mauled them. The battle lasted from midday until sunset, resolving little. Neither set of horsemen could be expected to assault fortifications.

For several days the Gauls busily assembled ladders, planking, bundles of hay, bags of earth, ropes, hooks and the myriad other items needed to take the Roman fortifications. Under cover of night the relief force approached the Roman lines. Abruptly shouting their war cry, they alerted their countrymen in Alesia, who soon raced pell-mell down the hillside to assault the Roman lines, which were now sandwiched between two onslaughts. All night long a confused battle raged. But the Roman defensive works served them well. As dawn neared, both Gallic forces fell back, unable to break the Roman lines. They knew that they could manage only one more attack before the food supplies within Alesia would vanish.

Scouting the Roman lines encircling the hill town, the leaders of the Gallic relief force located a weak point in the outer fortifications. Throughout the next night, Vercassivellaunus led 60,000 on a clockwise march behind the hills in order to be ready to attack from the valley north of Alesia between the heights that today are called Mont Rhea and Montagne de Bussy. Concealed behind Mont Rhea, they rested until midday. Then the remaining Gallic cavalry moved against the southern lines of the Romans to distract them from the infantry assault about to be launched. The Romans to the north of Alesia, unable to see this surge of cavalry, were surprised by the cries of thousands of voices, the source of which they could not locate. In well-organized waves, the relief army charged them, each wave relieved by another when it was exhausted. Men advanced in tightly formed shield walls, which protected bodies and heads, while those behind them piled hay and earth in the pits and trenches of the Romans. By sheer weight of numbers, the Gauls forced the Romans back. Caesar, atop Mont Flavigny, south of Alesia, the highest observation point available to him, realized that the critical moment had arrived. He sent six cohorts (3,000 troops) under Titus Labienus to bolster the badly pressed northern line.

Vercingetorix, meanwhile, launched his forces from Alesia against the southern Roman lines. The lines below Caesar's lookout post began to crumble, the siege towers abandoned in smoke and flames. Caesar ordered Marcus Brutus with fresh troops to save the situation. They arrived, but struggled without success.

Labienus, hard pressed on the northwest near Mont Rhea, formed up 12,000 men and informed Caesar that he urgently needed reinforcements. Gathering all the troops he had available and deliberately making himself conspicuous by wearing a red cloak on horseback as he led the reinforcements, Caesar hastened to support Labienus. He played his trump card. The German cavalry left the Roman lines to attack the tribesmen who were pushing Labienus' forces to the point of desperation. The Gauls had almost achieved victory when the charging German cavalry saved the brass eagles of Roman ensigns from capture. Attacked from the rear by the horsemen, the Gauls fell back, disorganized. The result was carnage, relieved only when the pursuing Romans became fatigued. Sedullus, chief of the Lemovices, was killed. Vercassivellaunus was captured. Vercingetorix, too, broke off his attack and returned to the heights of Alesia.

Within days, faced with famine, Vercingetorix addressed the assembly of chiefs and advised them to deal with him however they thought most satisfactory to the Romans—either kill him or hand him over to the enemy. They surrendered Vercingetorix and all their forces. After six years as a prisoner in the city of Rome, in the same sunless dungeon that would later hold Saint Peter, Vercingetorix was executed. Much earlier, every Roman soldier at Alesia received one of its defenders as a slave. Officers obtained dozens and even hundreds as their personal property. Thereafter, the Roman military actions in Gaul were largely mop-up operations.

Today, only a handful of words in French are of Celtic origin. One of those is *garçon*—boy or servant. That one word quite concisely tells of the relationship of the Gauls to the Romans after Alesia. Estimates vary, but Romans probably killed 5 million persons in Gaul and enslaved as many. Ironically, it was the Gauls in the Roman army and the German auxiliaries— only a few years earlier they had been Rome's enemies—who now tipped the balance numerically for Caesar. Despite the Aedui's vacillating aid to Vercingetorix, Caesar allowed them and the Arvernii to escape enslavement. They had been allies reluctantly turned against him and would be useful as middlemen.

In the years that followed, Labienus would die fighting against Caesar, whose politics he came to despise. Brutus, whom Caesar regarded as virtually an adopted son, would be a part of the plot to assassinate Caesar in the Senate in 44 BC. Defeated by Marc Antony, Brutus committed suicide, as would Antony, subsequent to his defeat by Caesar's nephew and a rival contender to power, Octavian, who then went on to become Augustus, the first Roman emperor. The army had become the political essence of Rome, its internal feuds, as merciless as gang wars, massively multiplied.

Cao Cao: Ancient China's Military Master

A genius at warfare, Chinese warlord Cao Cao faced a seemingly overwhelming challenge by his longtime rival Yuan Shao in the region of the Yellow River.

By Karl W. Eikenberry

More than 17 centuries after his death, the ancient general Cao Cao still "lives" among the Chinese people as their favorite villain in Beijing opera, and as the cunning and complex genius who dominates the widely read classic novel, *Romance of the Three Kingdoms.*

Beyond the caricature, however, lies one of the most remarkable figures of world military history. In a determined effort to reunify China, Cao fought continuously for more than 30 years in expeditions that included large cavalry engagements along the western reaches of the Yellow River, pitched battles against barbarian armies in the Manchurian foothills, and riverine and amphibious combat along the Chang Jiang (Yangtze River). Of his many military operations, however, it was the Guandu campaign that brought out all the characteristics that distinguished Cao's way of war—his emphasis on logistics, clarity of strategic goals, tactical flexibility and forceful yet open style of command.

Cao Cao was born in 155 AD in what is now Anhui province in east-central China. His name, incidentally, comprises two distinct Chinese characters with separate tonal pronunciations, but, under the Pinyin Romanization system they are both written in English as "Cao" and pronounced approximately as "Tsiao." Cao's family was of modest background, his father the adopted son of a court eunuch. He was raised during a time of growing economic and political turmoil, as the ruling Han Dynasty (206 BC to 220 AD), Asia's analogue to the Roman Empire, found itself with diminishing sources of revenue—both a cause and an effect of increasing peasant rebellions and attacks by feudal separatist forces.

Named as a minor government official in 174, Cao was appointed chief commandant of cavalry of Pei province (his native land) 10 years later. His future attention to strategic and tactical mobility seems to have been influenced by the experience he gained as a mounted soldier. Cao soon earned recognition for his sweeping victories over the "Yellow Turban" rebels, whose widespread uprising was shaking the foundations of the empire. It was recorded that his forces killed the enemy by the "tens of thousands." As Cao's fame grew, one commentator at the time said of Cao that he was "a good servant in time of peace, and a dangerous chieftain in time of trouble."

In 188, Cao was elevated to the post of "Colonel of the Western Garden," but so was his future rival, Yuan Shao. When the Han Dynasty ruler died one year later, the warlord Dong Zhuo seized power by occupying the capital at Luoyang, taking control of the government and forcing the new emperor to accept "puppet" status.

Cao refused to be co-opted; instead, he fled, sold his family property and raised an army of opposition, comprised of some 5,000 soldiers. In 190, Cao's forces suffered a defeat in battle against Dong's army, during which he was unable to persuade his more timid allies to attack. He thereupon decided to retire with his army to strengthen a base of operations around Yan province (contemporary Henan province in northeast-central China). Launching a series of campaigns against bandit forces ravaging the lands of Yan, Cao gradually brought stability to the region.

He demonstrated a singular ability to identify and strike at the enemy's most vulnerable point. For instance, when the rebel leader known as "Poison Yu" surrounded the important town of Wuyang, Cao elected to go after Yu's lightly defended base camp rather than lift the siege directly. As expected, Yu broke off his attack and hastened back to protect his supplies, enabling Cao to fight him on more favorable terms.

Cao's reputation as a dynamic and charismatic leader continued to spread. When one of his commanders, Bao Xin, was killed in battle and his unit was unable to recover the body, Cao ordered a carving made of wood in the likeness of Bao and mourned it. It was recorded by the ancient Chinese historians that, although Cao's army lacked numbers, "he encouraged them, made open rewards and clear punishments, and took advantage of enemy weaknesses to spring his own surprises."

Cao's power base increased substantially after his victory over a major Yellow Turban force in 192. He selected the best of the surrendering units and incorporated them into his own army. Then, while looking for an opening to bring the emperor under his own "protection" and earn the political legitimacy that such a move offered, he continued to consolidate his domains. Promoting aggressive, capable subordinates and encouraging candor, Cao developed a superb group of commanders and staff officers.

He also listened to their advice. When, in 195, Cao contemplated a major offensive to the east, his key adviser, Xun Yu, argued against it. Xun said that the harvest had already been gathered in Cao's intended area of operations and that the enemy would be waiting with "strong walls and empty fields." Nothing could be captured or plundered, and in 10 days Cao's army of 100,000 would be in danger before even fighting its first battle. "It is always better to judge the situation of the time and make no move to endanger your base of operations," Xun added. "Yet your present plans have no connection to [this principle]." Cao abandoned the idea. His prudence in tailoring his ambition to fit logistical realities would prove critical in the future.

Cao Cao continued to gather momentum—in 196, after the assassination of Dong Zhuo and the consequent resumption of disorder in the capital, he brought the emperor and the imperial court under his direct control, moving them to his recently conquered Xu province (bordering Yan to the east-southeast). He also initiated the *tun tian* military-style agricultural colony system to increase grain production and lessen the tax burden on the peasants. His order noted that only with abundant food could the state be stabilized and the army made strong. Again, his concentration on the material basis of war set him apart from his foes. The great historian Sima Guang wrote, "Cao could make campaigns in every direction and have no trouble with his supplies, and so he could conquer all of his rivals."

Cao's officials and generals continued to find their initiative rewarded. When his brave subordinate Yu Jin came across Cao's favored Jingzhou Troops looting in the midst of a chaotic withdrawal by the army, Yu attacked them and succeeded in re-establishing order. Yu's colleagues urged him to go immediately to Cao and explain his actions, since the officers of the Jingzhou Troops had already lodged a complaint. But Yu Jin replied that the enemy was nearing and it was more important to dig trenches and prepare fortifications. Only after the preparations had been completed did he travel to Cao's headquarters, where Cao told him: "In the misfortune at the Yu River [which had precipitated the withdrawal], I was helpless and confused. But you kept control in the confusion, you have punished cruelty, and you have strengthened our defenses. You never fail to maintain good conduct, and how could the most famous generals of the past have done any better?" He thereupon promoted Yu to the rank of marquis.

On another occasion, a prefect named Man Chong, upon learning of serious crimes being committed by three associates of one of Cao's close relatives, had them swiftly beheaded to pre-empt a pardon. When Cao learned of Man's decisiveness, he said, "That's the way a responsible man behaves." As a result, Cao Cao continued to attract men of talent.

Over the next three years, Cao moved steadily to eliminate his rivals at court by political maneuvering and force of arms. Even so, the predominant power in China was his old rival Yuan Shao, who commanded a large army and ruled over several important provinces to the north and northwest of Cao's state. The Yuan clan had served the Han court in key positions for generations, and its family name and influence among the landed gentry class made Yuan Shao a formidable opponent. When Cao Cao received a letter written in arrogant terms from Yuan, his trusted subordinates Xun Yu and Guo Jia counseled him to persevere.

They pointed out 10 advantages he had over Yuan: (1) showing consideration to his subordinates and acting naturally; (2) serving and obeying the emperor while Yuan was cast in the role of a rebel; (3) maintaining firm control of his people and making his rules clear, while Yuan was weak-willed and too gentle; (4) remaining outwardly easy and simple while inwardly being shrewd and clever, using men well and trusting them, and judging personal relationships with subordinates by their ability; (5) making plans and taking action quickly while coping with changing situations, whereas Yuan made many plans but reached few decisions; (6) attracting people who wished to serve, while Yuan drew those who only loved words and ornamental show; (7) disregarding small things and remaining committed to the great affairs that affect all of the empire; (8) treating subordinates fairly and disregarding slander; (9) promoting those who are right and using law to correct those who do wrong; (10) commanding soldiers with "spiritlike" qualities—resulting in the army's trusting Cao and the enemy's fearing him—whereas Yuan did not grasp the essentials of war.

As might be expected, then, Cao and his generals were confident that Yuan Shao would simply not measure up to the demands of a long war, and they prepared accordingly.

In anticipation of an offensive by Yuan Shao, in the autumn of 199 Cao moved to fortify an important site called Guandu, located south of the Yellow River. In January 200, Yuan ordered his army of some 100,000, including 10,000 cavalry, to move south from its staging area north of the Yellow River, intent on advancing across a broad front to take advantage of his numerical superiority. But General Yu Jin held up Yuan's advance guard at the town of Liyang on the north side of the river, allowing Cao to rapidly concentrate his army of some 20,000 around Guandu. Yuan, in turn, was compelled to bring up his main body to seize Liyang and gain mastery over the north bank of the Yellow River.

Yuan then immediately dispatched his commander Yan Liang to the south side of the river to lay siege to the town of Baima. Cao, with the goal of freeing his units at Baima and regaining the initiative, accepted the recommendation of his strategist Xun Yu, who said they should "make noise in the east, then attack in the west" (the Chinese expression for using a feint in support of the actual main effort).

In response, Cao sent a force from Guandu that closed up toward the Yellow River, threatening to cross at the Yan Ford, roll up Yuan's right flank and lay waste to his rear area. Yuan countered by dispatching a large formation to guard the north side of the crossing site. Unknown to Yuan, however, Cao's outstanding cavalry commanders, Guan Yu and Zhang Liao, leading an advance guard, had sped farther east along the south side of the Yellow River and were positioned to attack the units encircling Baima. Yan Liang was caught off guard, his elements were routed by Guan and Zhang, and the siege was lifted.

Yuan's lieutenants urged caution, but he instead conducted a major crossing at Yan Ford and sent his lieutenants Liu Bei and Wen Chou forward with a detachment of some 5,000 cavalry. Cao learned of the detachment's approach and arrayed his supply trains on the sides of the road, pretending to abandon them. With a force of 600 mounted soldiers lying in ambush, Cao waited until the enemy cavalry broke ranks to begin plundering and then launched a furious attack. Wen Chou was killed, Liu Bei fled, and Cao once again had managed to disrupt Yuan's offensive and cut into his advantage in numbers.

Yuan's army still possessed overall superiority and remained on the strategic offensive. Liu Bei was sent with a raiding party to attack Cao's supply points south of Guandu, but Cao Ren (Cao's cousin and an extremely capable general in his own right) drove him off. By July 200, Yuan had massed his forces around a base at Wuyang, about 20 kilometers north of Cao's Guandu strongpoint. The next month, he ordered his main body to advance and close up to Cao's fortifications. Yuan's army then dug extensive fieldworks, probably stretching over 10 kilometers from east to west.

A foray launched by Cao was unsuccessful, and his army was forced onto the defensive. The two armies parried for the next month. When Yuan's engineers constructed wooden towers from which archers fired down into their adversary's encampment, Cao's engineers countered by knocking them out of action with stones hurled by "thunder cars" (ancient Chinese ballistae). Yuan then attempted to sap Cao's lines, but was stymied by his foe's aggressive countermining.

Although his key advisers recommended bypassing Guandu and attacking Cao's weakly defended capital at Xuchang to the south, Yuan remained set on forcing the withdrawal of his opponent by frontal assaults, which he hoped would lead to an opportunity to annihilate Cao in decisive battle.

With supplies running low, his forces exhausted and his people beginning to turn to Yuan Shao, Cao considered retreating. But again soliciting advice, Cao listened to Xun Yu, who dispatched a message, saying, "Your command is only a tenth of [Yuan's], yet you have marked the ground and hold it. You have him by the throat and he cannot advance. You have managed this now for six months. It's clear his strength is exhausted and changes must result. This is the time to use an extraordinary strategy. Don't miss the opportunity."

Regaining his confidence, Cao rallied his soldiers and told them they would defeat Yuan within 15 days.

Cao now focused on the vulnerability of Yuan's extended supply lines. A raiding party intercepted several thousand of Yuan's supply wagons moving toward Guandu and put them to the torch. Then, in October, Yuan's commander, Chunyu Qiong, escorted a huge convoy of grain with some

10,000 soldiers, aiming to deliver the food to supply bases in the rear area. Yuan's generals proposed sending out cavalry to counter Cao's raiders but their advice was ignored. Xu You, one of Yuan's senior officers, reached the limit of his endurance upon learning that one of his relatives had been arrested by a Yuan official for wrongdoing. He departed for Cao's camp.

Cao, upon hearing that Xu You had defected and arrived in his camp, immediately ran out of his tent barefoot, clapped his hands and said, "You have come from far away, and now I will surely be successful!" Warming to his newly acquired status, Xu learned from Cao that he had only one month's food supply remaining and no reinforcements available. Xu then informed Cao that Chunyu Qiong was guarding a great many supply wagons at Wucao, about 35 kilometers northeast of Guandu. He reported that security was lax and said if Cao were to raid it with light forces, he could burn all the accumulated supplies there. Deprived of its logistic train, Yuan's army would collapse within three days.

Cao seized the moment. Placing Cao Ren in charge of the defenses at Guandu, he led some 5,000 cavalry and light infantrymen over side trails toward Wucao. Moving at night with their horses' mouths gagged, the raiding force carried Yuan army banners, ready to pretend to be a friendly relief column to any enemy they encountered. Before dawn on the day of their attack, Cao's soldiers surrounded the Wucao supply base and lit the firewood they had carried with them from Guandu. Chunyu's defenders were thrown into a panic, and Cao struck. But with the breaking of daylight, Chunyu could see Cao's forces were not overwhelming in numbers, and he advanced from his fortifications to do battle.

When Yuan Shao was notified of Cao's surprise attack, he immediately sent a mounted force to reinforce Chunyu Qiong. His son, Yuan Tan, told his father they should move against the Guandu fortifications in Cao's absence and eliminate his base of operations. Yuan Shao agreed and ordered his generals Gao Lan and Zhang He to attack. Zhang pleaded with Yuan to instead send a large element to relieve Chunyu, arguing that if Wucao fell their army would collapse. Yuan, predictably, did not listen, and his army's assault on Cao's base camp was repulsed. In the meantime, one of Cao's lieutenants reported the approach of Yuan's counterattack forces toward Wucao. Cao, probably realizing the time of decision of the entire campaign was at hand, replied, "Don't tell me about them again until they are right behind us!" Inspiring his troops, he finally overwhelmed Chunyu's security elements, chased off Yuan's reinforcements and burned all the stores at Wucao.

Fear gripped the soldiers in Yuan's camp as word of the Wucao disaster spread and recriminations were exchanged among their leaders. Gao Lan and Zhang He destroyed Yuan's siege engines and entered Cao's lines to surrender. As Xu You had predicted, Yuan's army pulled back in total disorder. Cao followed up with an aggressive pursuit. More than 70,000 of Yuan's soldiers were killed or captured south of the Yellow River, and Yuan and his son managed to escape with only some 800 cavalrymen. An incident that took place after the rout of Yuan's forces helps to illuminate Cao's style of leadership. When Yuan's papers were collected from his abandoned headquarters, secret correspondence between Yuan and officers in Cao's army was discovered. But Cao had all the papers burned, saying simply, "When Yuan Shao was strong, even I was not sure of myself. How much more the case for my army?"

By gaining mastery over the provinces Yuan had ruled, Cao now became the most powerful warlord in China. Still maintaining the appearance of serving the Han emperor, he brought central and northern China firmly under his control, culminating his efforts in 207 at the Battle of White Wolf Mountain in Manchuria with a brilliant victory over a combined Chinese and northern barbarian army. In the following year, however, he suffered the only real disaster of his military career when the allied army of Liu Bei (assisted by one of the most gifted strategists in Chinese history, Zhuge Liang) and Sun Quan destroyed Cao's forces in the famous Battle of Red Cliffs.

The struggle for the "Mandate of Heaven" from that point on was waged, for the most part, between the states of Wei in the north (Cao Cao), Shu Han in the southwest (Liu Bei), and Wu in the southeast (Sun Quan). Cao recovered from his setback and waged war continuously, both to consolidate and to expand his power. After his death in 220, his son, Cao Pi, went on to proclaim himself emperor, giving his late father the title of Emperor Wu. Sima Yi (who had served as a young officer under Cao Cao), in turn, overthrew the Caos and set up his family in their stead. China then fell into even greater anarchy until its reunification under the Sui Dynasty in 581, followed by the Tang Dynasty in the 7th century.

Cao Cao's battlefield success can be attributed in large measure to his attention to logistics, his ability to identify and exploit enemy weaknesses, and his brilliant command techniques. Cao provided what are perhaps the first known commentaries on that classic military treatise, *The Art of War*, by Sun Zi (also known to us today as Sun Tzu). Ancient Chinese historians also recorded that Cao himself wrote a book on military tactics and strategy more than 100,000 characters long, but to date it has not been recovered. In his annotations to *The Art of War*, he made several references to the influence of logistics on warfare. He noted that even a small fortress, if solid and amply supplied with food, was difficult to take. He wrote that, in armed conflict, it was important for an army to attack and take food supplies from the enemy.

Cao's genius lay in his persistence in building up and protecting his own sources of supply, as evidenced by his introduction of military agricultural colonies, his construction of the Guandu fortress almost a year prior to the commencement of operations against Yuan Shao, and the contrasting speed with which he moved to eliminate the threat that Liu Bei's raids posed to his rear areas.

Cao also displayed a real talent for analyzing his opponent's major strategic vulnerabilities (similar to Prussian military theorist Karl von Clausewitz's "centers of gravity"), and then concentrating his resources to attack them. What makes Cao truly stand out is the ease with which he could modify his tactics to accommodate changing conditions while remaining committed to his long-term goals. For example, Cao had told his subordinates at the outset of the Guandu campaign that the contradictions within Yuan's command would inevitably lead to his downfall. Given the lack of unity and cohesiveness among Yuan's generals, it seems that Cao intuitively knew he would eventually triumph by keeping Yuan tactically off-balance, protracting their contest of arms and waiting for opportunity to knock.

Displaying remarkable patience, he refused to make frontal attacks while Yuan maintained numerical superiority. Cao later wrote, "Use the most solid to attack the most empty." He avoided set-piece battles and instead tried to destroy the enemy through pursuit: "Attack what is important [to the enemy]; cut off his resupply route and guard his line of retreat...."

As can be seen by his relief of Baima, his ambush of Yuan's advance guard south of the Yan Ford, his linear warfare at Guandu and the lightning raid against Wucao, Cao Cao was always alert to new tactical possibilities and could change directions quickly.

Probably influenced by his humble origins, Cao seemed to be a more accessible and open commander than his rivals. His success in recruiting men of talent was often mentioned by Chinese historians of antiquity. Although he was a strict disciplinarian, Cao was effective in retaining the loyalty of his officers and soldiers. Throughout his career, Cao publicly praised and rewarded those generals who best seemed to understand his intent and could act independently. His assignment of tasks usually reflected a shrewd understanding of his leaders' strengths and limitations.

Cao was famous, as well, for looking after the welfare of his veterans. Numerous edicts that he issued ordered government officials to use land grants, food distribution and loans to attend to the financial needs of the families of soldiers killed in battle. It is evident, too, that Cao Cao added to his effectiveness through his display of courage and force of presence on the battlefield. Cao, by adhering to the timeless doctrine that a commander should always accompany his "main effort," ensured victories at Baima and Wucao through his own inspiring leadership at moments of crisis.

The biography of Cao Cao written in *The Chronicle of the Three Kingdoms*, an imperially sanctioned history of the times, noted: "In accordance with different situations, he took extraordinary strategems; by deceiving the enemy, he won victory; he varied his tactics in demonic fashion. In the face of the enemy on the battlefield, he remained unperturbed, as if he had no intention whatever of fighting; but seizing the opportunity, he would strike for victory in the highest spirits....He knew his men well and was adept in judging them; it was difficult to dazzle him by false display. It was thus that he laid the foundations of his great work."

Cao Cao's way of war was as ingenious and distinctive as that of Alexander the Great, Hannibal Barca, Gaius Julius Caesar and the other great captains of Western ancient military history, any of whom could have applauded Cao's Guandu campaign as worthy of his own best efforts in military endeavor.

Confrontation at the Lech

*That King Otto of Saxony had gathered so many
contentious German duchies together under his command
was an accomplishment in itself, but would it be
enough to stop the rampaging Magyar hordes?*

By Jon Guttman

On August 9, 955, Augsburg was a city fighting for its life. Magyar invaders had denuded the countryside around the old city, then pitched their tents and dug earthworks for a determined siege. Initially, the city's garrison, under the inspired leadership of Bishop Ulrich, resisted stoutly, even conducting at least one offensive sortie beyond the city's walls with the fearless warrior-bishop accompanying them in his holy vestments instead of armor. Soon, however, the nomadic raiders had completely surrounded Augsburg and demonstrated a disturbing sophistication in the art of siegecraft as the siege-engines they had built approached the doomed city, pushed forward by Slavic captives whipped from behind by their Magyar masters. While Bishop Ulrich chanted the familiar psalm, "Yea, though I walk through the valley of the shadow of death," Augsburg's defenders tensely waited at the ramparts with little hope of fending off these murderous invaders from the east—and also well aware that they could expect no mercy from them.

The Magyar tribes that first entered the Carpathian basin in 896 are generally believed to have originated along the River Ob, west of the central Ural Mountains, the general position of the most easterly (Ugrian) branch of the Finno-Ugric linguistic group. Originally hunters and fishermen, they settled down to farming and raising livestock in the valleys of the southeastern Urals from about 2,000 BC, but changes in climate in the millennium that followed, combined with their taming of horses, caused them to revert to the life of equestrian nomads. After intermittent movements north and south, during which they were culturally and linguistically subjected to Iranian influence, the peoples who would come to be identified as Magyars broke away from other Ugrians sometime around 500 BC to lead their semi-nomadic existence in what is now Bashkiria, north of the Caspian Sea between the middle Volga region and the southern Urals. Borrowing from neighboring peoples, such as the Alans, Persians and Turkic Bulgars, they synthesized a culture and social structure of their own.

The religion of the Magyars was animist in nature, with the horse a sacred animal and the *turul*—a predatory eagle—their totemic emblem.

64

Shamans provided a bridge between the material and the spiritual world, with a mythical black shaman, representing winter, darkness and evil, in perpetual, seasonal strife with a white shaman of spring, light and goodness (a folk theme that was later readily transferred by Hungarian Christians into the equally popular metaphor of St. George and the Dragon).

By 500 AD, the Magyars were dominated by a warrior class of horsemen whose effectiveness was enhanced by the use of light, curved sabers and stirrups, as well as a Magyar-designed saddle that was lightweight and comfortable for the horse as well as its rider. War booty and foreign slaves (especially Slavs, who commanded a high price in the Byzantine markets) became staples of their livelihood, although the cultivation of land during seasonal periods of temporary settlement was never abandoned.

The principle Magyar weapon was a composite bow of straighter design than those used by other nomads of the steppes. For closer combat, the well-equipped Magyar carried a light spear, a curved saber and sometimes a mace. Shields were seldom used. Chieftains wore felt or leather lamellar protection in the style of the Scandanavians and eastern Slavs, and the aristocratic warrior elite possessed finely-crafted metal armor.

From about 500 on, the Magyars were part of a tribal confederation called the Ten Arrows, or *Onogur*—whence the later term "Hungary" originated—which was in turn subordinate to the Khazar *kaganate* (kingdom). The Khazars were a Turkic people whose aristocracy maintained a precariously balanced neutrality between the neighboring Muslim and Byzantine empires, avoiding religious commitment to either power by converting to Judaism. Numerous individuals within the Magyar tribes also converted to Judaism under the Khazar influence. A somewhat smaller number also embraced Islam. Both "religions of the Book" were tolerated and their adherents accepted as equals by the predominating Magyar pagans.

After 800, the Khazar *kaganate* began to decline and the Magyars, under pressure from another fierce Turkic people, the Pechenegs, moved to a place they called Etelköz (land between the rivers), which lay between the lower Danube and Dniestr Rivers.

Besides their religious influence on many within the tribe, the Khazars left their mark on the Magyar political structure. Such central power as existed among the tribal chiefs at that time came to be shared by three men: the *kende*, commander of the warriors; the *gyula*, chief military commander; and the *harka*, who saw to civilian administration and judicial affairs. In 895, the Magyars' *harka* was Tétény, Kurszán was the *kende* and Arpád the *gyula*.

In that year, while Arpád and his son Levente were on campaign against the Bulgars with most of the Magyar army, the Pechenegs—possibly at the invitation of the Bulgars—stormed across the River Don to attack the inadequately protected Magyar settlements and slaughtered great numbers of Magyar women and children. The survivors migrated west, taking refuge in the Transylvanian mountains.

Seeking a stronger alliance among the Magyar tribes, Arpád called upon the seven greatest chieftains to cut their wrists, gather their blood in a helmet, and drink from it. He then led his people further west in search of a more secure homeland.

Astounding though it would later seem in retrospect, the Magyar invasion of Europe came by invitation. Not long after the death of Charlemagne in 814, the united empire he had built in western Europe broke up. The most fragmentation occurred among the duchies of Germany. The political scene was dominated by counts and margraves and their vassals and *milites*—contentious noblemen whose relationship to anyone claiming to represent central authority was marked more by mistrust than loyalty.

The appearance of the Magyars only served to encourage that state of affairs. In 892, Arnulf, king of the western Carolingian territories, broke down great defensive earthworks to enlist the Magyars' aid against Duke Sviat–opluk of Moravia. He got more than he bargained for.

Arpád led his powerful force into the Carpathian basin, in a horse-borne blitzkrieg that the Magyars came to call "The Conquest." Between 896 and 906, they drove the Bulgars out of the Great Plain and Transylvania, drove the Franks from Transdanubia and destroyed the Kingdom of Moravia. When Arnulf died, his own people found themselves fair game for Magyar raids as well.

Not since the sweeps by Attila's Huns in 451 AD had Europe faced invaders comparable to the Magyars. In fact, the speed and range of their raids even surpassed those of the Hunnic invaders. Besides being superb horsemen, the Magyars displayed remarkable endurance, matched by that of their horses, whose stamina was conserved by the Magyars' practice of riding with spare mounts.

In 899, 5,000 Magyars swept into the Po valley, driving as far west as Pavia. Berengar I, the Lombard emperor of Northern Italy, raised an army of 15,000 men to confront the barbarians, who retreated before his larger force. After mauling Berengar's vanguard when it caught up with them at Verona, the Magyars resumed their flight across the River Brenta, and camped on its far bank as the main Lombard force overtook them.

The Magyars offered to give up their booty, their arms and their horses if Berengar would grant them safe conduct to leave Italy, but he contemptuously rejected the offer. Left with nothing to lose but their lives, the Magyars reaffirmed their warriors' creed—"To fall fighting like men is not to die, but to live"—and suddenly took the offensive. The overconfident Lombards were caught while resting and eating when the Magyars charged across the river, and were decimated. After easily running down and slaughtering those who tried to flee, the Magyars left Italy and returned to their newly claimed homeland in triumph.

In 904, Kurszán was invited to a peace feast by the Bavarians, who then murdered him and his retinue. Declaring Kurszán's death a form of divine punishment in accordance with Magyar pagan traditions, Arpád assumed the power of *kende* as well as *gyula*. At the same time, he made preparations for war with the Bavarians.

In 907, a Magyar raiding force was intercepted near Augsburg by Ludwig II, the 14-year-old son of Arnulf who regarded himself not only as king of Bavaria, but as emperor of Charlemagne's kingdom (although that claim was not acknowledged by other German rulers, who referred to him as Ludwig the Child). Around daybreak, the Magyars swept into the Bavarian camp from all sides. Some German warriors never awoke from their beds, pinned to them by arrows. Many who survived the barrage struggled into their mail as they stumbled from their tents, only to have their heads split by Magyar sabers. For about seven hours, Ludwig's surviving warriors fought the Magyars to a stalemate. Then, when the Magyar cavalry broke into disorderly retreat, Ludwig bravely—but, as it turned out, unwisely—led them after the retreating enemy, only to fall into a waiting ambush.

Ludwig narrowly escaped the slaughter, but afterward he wasted no time mobilizing an even larger host, estimated at between 30,000 to 40,000 men. In that summer of 907, Ludwig, hoping to emulate Charlemagne's victory over the Avars, advanced into Magyar territory with his cavalry and infantry divided on either side of the Danube River and supported by a riverine fleet on the Danube itself. Arpád responded to the threat by personally leading an equally sizable Magyar force to confront Ludwig at Ennsburg, near the present-day Slovakian capital city of Bratislava. The battle commenced on July 3, with Arpád concentrating his forces against Ludwig's southern army. After routing that force, the Magyar warriors swam across the Danube overnight and surprised the northern unit the following day. In addition to destroying the Bavarians on land, select members of Arpád's army who had an extraordinary talent for holding their breath swam underneath Ludwig's riverboats, drilled or punched holes in their hulls and sank them—a technique that would later be used by the Hungarians against an Ottoman river fleet during the Siege of Belgrade in July 1456.

The remnants of Ludwig's army took refuge in the fortress at Ennsburg, but after a desultory attempt to storm the castle on July 7, the Magyars retired in apparent disorder. Again, Ludwig and his troops sallied forth to pursue the barbarians—only to dash once more into a trap as Arpád's horsemen regrouped and turned on their pursuers. Ludwig was again fortunate to escape with his life, while the victorious Magyars expanded their territorial domain into the upper Enns region. Arpád, however, paid a heavy personal price for the greatest single victory of his brilliant military career. Three of his grandsons had died in the battle, and he himself had sustained wounds from which he would die a few days later. Nevertheless, in a little over a decade he had invaded and occupied the lands from Transylvania to the old Roman province of Pannonia. From that geographic base, the depredations of the Magyars in Europe really began in earnest. Before the year was out, they would cross the Rhine River, then move south into Provence in an orgy of looting and destruction.

The Magyar terror was not without purpose. The women they carried off in their raids were not casual rape victims but intended brides, meant to replace those slaughtered by the Pechenegs and restore population-sustaining family units to the semi-nomadic settlement that the Hungarians sought to establish in the conquered territories. The area around their base of operations was to be laid waste in order to establish a protective no man's land around it. The Magyars had no territorial ambitions beyond the buffer zone, but they mounted periodic raids to keep the Germans too weak and off-balance to threaten their newly won homeland.

Villages and monasteries burned while clerics wondered what their lords were doing about the new scourge from the east. The majority of the feuding nobles were in fact paying tribute to the Magyars, vying to have their realms spared and to persuade the Magyars to ravage the lands of their rivals. To pay for that extortion money, the nobles increased the taxes on their subjects, keeping a percentage for themselves. In 910, King Ludwig himself agreed to pay a heavy tribute to the Magyars. After his death the next year at the age of 18, his successor, Conrad I, was forced to do the same.

After the death of King Conrad in 918, Henry of Saxony was elected to succeed him. He was hawking for birds when he was informed of his election, and was known thereafter as Henry the Fowler.

The Magyars subjected Henry to careful scrutiny, for the election of a new king tended to void the tribute-paying agreement of his predecessor. During an encounter in 924, Henry managed to capture a Magyar chieftain, but magnanimously released his captive in return for immunity from further Magyar raids in Saxony for nine years. Henry agreed to continue paying tribute over those nine years, but made use of the time he had thus literally bought to strengthen his hand for the future, by rebuilding border fortifications in Saxony and Thuringia, and levying all male subjects above the age of 13 into a strong army or *exercitus*.

A noteworthy feature of Henry's new Saxon army was greater reliance on cavalry than before. Horse-breeding was encouraged in order to enlarge the mounted element, whose equestrian skills were perfected through mock combat games—an idea revived from the days of Charlemagne, and the forerunner of the medieval tournament. Through such means, the Saxons developed a new elite, the heavily mailed cavalryman or *miles armatus*, from whom would evolve the medieval knight.

In 933, Henry's rearmament program could no longer be ignored. The Magyars decided that a show of force was in order to keep Henry in his place; they advanced into Saxony, slaughtering men and enslaving women and children as they came. Although ill at the time, Henry mobilized his *miles armati*, reinforced with cavalry from Bavaria and Franconia, to confront the invaders on March 15 at Riade on the Saale River, a few miles south of Merseburg.

Before the forces clashed, the Saxons loudly sang the *Kyrie eleison* (Lord have mercy upon us), to which the Magyars countered with an awesome battle chant of their own. Henry then led his infantry and peasant light cavalry forward in an orderly advance, taking care that none of his men charged ahead, to be swallowed up in the Magyar horde. When the Magyars charged, they found themselves suddenly under attack by Henry's main force of armored cavalry, which had been held in concealment up to that moment. The Magyars loosed a shower of arrows at the oncoming horsemen, but this time the knights, anticipating the volley, raised their shields in unison to deflect it, then galloped full tilt into the enemy before they could fire another. Awed by these new, more disciplined tactics, the Magyars broke and retreated—their first real setback since the Conquest.

In 936, Henry the Fowler died, but he had already arranged for the election of Otto, his eldest son by his second wife, to succeed him. Henry's faith in his red-haired son's ability to carry on where he had left off would prove to be thoroughly justified.

From the moment of his coronation at Aix-la-Chapelle, Otto was forced to prove that his qualifications to rule the German duchies were more than hereditary. In 936, 939 and 941, he had to put down rebellions, the latter two involving his brother, Henry. Otto emerged victorious from all those challenges, strengthening his power by replacing the defeated rebel dukes with loyal members of his own family. Of the latter, the most able was his younger brother, Bruno of Sankt Gallen, who served as archchaplain, later chancellor, and, after 953, as Archbishop of Cologne as well as Duke of Lorraine.

Otto's ambitions in the east gave the Magyars ample cause for concern. In 937, he founded a new monastery at the more eastern location of Magdeburg and later established bishoprics at Havelburg and Brandenburg. He lent military support to the enterprises of fellow Germans against the Slavs, and at the same time promoted the expansion of German settlers into their lands—the first serious precedent for the *Drang nach Osten* (compulsion toward the East) that would effect German-Slavic relations for a millennium to come. Otto also began encroaching into northern territories at the expense of the Bohemians, compelling their ruler, Duke Boleslav I, to accept his suzerainty in 950.

In 951, Otto followed the path of the Magyars into Italy, with results as different as the intentions. His invasion was in response to an appeal from the Burgundian princess Adelaide, widow of King Lothair II of Lombardy, who had been imprisoned by the ambitious King Berengar II of Ivrea. Otto defeated Berengar, freed Adelaide and, since his own queen, Edgitha, had died early in his reign, he proposed marriage to the newly liberated princess. From Adelaide's standpoint, the handsome and energetic young Saxon king had literally been a savior in shining armor, so her acceptance of his troth was a foregone conclusion.

No sooner were the two wed, however, than Otto faced another rebellion among his German vassals. Foremost among the rebels was Duke Conrad the Red of Franconia, who would not submit to the Saxon king until 954.

While Otto struggled to increase his power, disunity was developing among the Magyars. A rivalry was growing between Bulczú, the administrative *harka*, and Lél, the military *gyula*. Moreover, some of the *hadnagyok* were declining to join in the large Magyar forays, or going off to conduct raids on their own. In spite of their growing differences, however, Bulczú and Lél were in agreement over the need to reverse the setback suffered against Henry the Fowler at Riade, and to put paid to the growing threat posed by his successor.

Around 925, the Magyars had forged an alliance with Hugh of Provence, King of Italy, and in 942 Hugh called upon them to assist him against his Italian rivals and against the Muslim caliphate of Cordoba, which was threatening Provence's western borders. The most ambitious Magyar raid in years occurred in 947, striking into Italy as far south as Apulia. In 948, Bulczú went to Byzantium and was baptized a Christian. By so doing, he established friendly enough relations with the Byzantine Empire to secure the southern Hungarian borders from incursions that might divert the Magyars' attention from their coming western campaigns.

In 954, Conrad of Franconia made a treaty with the Magyars, granting them safe passage across the Rhine River at Worms and through the duchy of Lorraine in exchange for their military support against Otto. Lél did provide Conrad with some warriors, but led the bulk of his army on the largest and most devastating raid in Magyar history. Crossing the Meuse, his warriors ravaged northeastern France and Burgundy, sacked the cities of Reims and Châlons, then moved southwest into Aquitaine. Aided and abetted by a safe passage provided by Hugh through Provence, the Magyars rode through the Great St. Bernard Pass into Lombardy, then moved on through the Carnic Alps to pillage the Drava and Danube valleys.

The Great Magyar Raid, as Lél's epic sweep came to be called, was a masterpiece of mobile brigandage, but he failed both in bringing victory to Duke Conrad or in squelching Otto's ambitions. As the Magyars rode through Germany, they again found themselves in demand by the feuding German factions, but this time Lél seemed to be indiscriminate in punishing them all. In so doing, he only strengthened the hand of Otto, who marched into Bavaria at the head of what now appeared to be a liberating army. Otto and Lél's main forces missed each other, and the Magyars returned home to prepare a return engagement. Otto, meanwhile, contented himself with subduing Conrad's rebellion and compelling the duke to forfeit his duchy as retribution.

Otto then turned his attention to the Magyars. He recognized how their raids had both exacerbated and exploited the rivalries among the German duchies. Given the depredations of Lél's last raid, however, Otto was now in an ideal position to persuade the various German kings and dukes to set aside their differences and unite under him against the common foreign threat. Among those who Otto skillfully managed to win over to his side was the recently vanquished Duke Conrad. As one of the king's chief lieutenants in the campaign to come, Conrad's loyalty and valor would prove decisive.

In the summer of 955, the Magyars returned in the greatest numbers seen in Central Europe in many years, seemingly determined to settle once and for all their right to roam unrestricted throughout Europe. On August 8, they invested Augsburg, this time intending to make a fearful example of the city itself. Up until that time, the Magyars had not been known to assault fortified places. Sometimes they would impose a blockade, but more often they would limit their raiding to targets that could be overrun and sacked quickly. At Augsburg, however, they came prepared, equipped and determined to scale or breach the walls.

Then, the next day, the siege operations suddenly stopped. Word had arrived that Otto's army was fast approaching. Popular lore states that a rebel Bavarian lord, Berthold of Reisenburg, gave the Magyars that information, but that is highly unlikely, given the fact that Berthold was not punished by Otto later, and by the fact that the Magyars, with their network of scouts, hardly needed a traitor to keep them informed of an enemy army's movements. Calling together their raiding parties by means of smoke signals, the Magyars eagerly prepared for the battle that would remove the Saxon thorn from their side. Not only Lél, the military commander, but Bulczú, the civil administrator rode at the head of their men, both rival leaders keen for a place in the folk sagas for their part in this important victory.

Otto's host encamped near the River Lech, a tributary of the Danube that formed a natural boundary between the duchies of Swabia on its western bank and Bavaria to the east. Otto's army represented a triumph of diplomacy—in addition to Bavarians, Swabians and Franconians, he had a unit of 1,000 Bohemians (Czechs), personally commanded by their Duke Boleslav. King Otto's own unit, the *legio regia*, was a royal guard of Saxon and Franconian warriors, the bulk of his Saxon vassals having remained behind to pursue operations against Slavic pagans and to be ready to defend Saxony if the Magyars evaded Otto's force and tried to raid his homeland. Also absent was Bruno of Sankt Gallen—Otto apparently decided that his brother could not have mobilized his vassals in Lorraine in time to join him north of Augsburg, and therefore chose to have him stay in his own wealthy duchy, again to defend it against possible Magyar raids. With the addition of

Slavic auxiliaries and warriors who had slipped out of Augsburg, Otto's over-all forces probably totaled 8,000 men. The Magyars' numbers are generally believed to have been greater than Otto's force, but may in fact have been somewhat smaller.

The location of the Battle of Lechfeld has been the subject of some dispute, since the name "field of the Lech" could apply to either side of the river. The most familiar account places it on the western side, with Otto's army arriving from west-northwest. Eyewitness accounts of the battle, however, provide some convincing evidence that it may have been fought on the east side. If the latter were true, then it would do much to explain why the Magyars—who were arrogant but not stupid—would seek a head-on confrontation with armored knights after having been defeated by them at Riade 22 years earlier. If Otto did indeed arrive from the northeast and came down the east side of the Lech, he would have been in position to place his force between the Magyars at Augsburg and their home base. In so doing, he would have compelled them to attempt a breakout from the potential trap—and, in so doing, engage Otto on his terms. That Otto may have taken that route instead of coming directly to Augsburg's aid suggests that, in addition to being a strong and cunning leader, he may also have had a cannier grasp of strategy than history has given him credit for.

That night, a fast was ordered among the Christians to prepare them spiritually for the battle to come; many of them were probably too tense to eat in any case.

On the next morning, August 10, all the German lords swore mutual allegiance. They then said mass and advanced with lances and standards held high, in a loose column of eight groups, or "legions," by nationality. Three Bavarian legions made up the vanguard—which in itself is evidence that Otto was on the eastern, Bavarian side of the Lech, rather than the Swabian side—followed by a war band of Franconians. Behind them, Otto's Saxons rode in formation beneath the banner of St. Michael, vanquisher of the Devil, while their king himself brandished the fabled "Spear of Destiny," whose antique point was alleged to have tipped the spear with which the Roman soldier Gaius Cassius Longinus pierced the side of Jesus Christ during the crucifixion. Two legions of Swabians followed Otto's *legio regia*, and Duke Boleslav's Bohemian legion constituted the rearguard. Otto carefully chose broken terrain over which to move his force forward, in order to frustrate any mass charges by the Magyars before he could deploy his legions into line for a cavalry rush of his own.

As they advanced, however, the Germans failed to notice a contingent of Magyars moving rapidly along their flank on the other side of the river, whose banks were overgrown with foliage. Those raiders crossed the river, and even as Otto began to engage the main Hungarian force, they fell upon his rearguard and his army's baggage train.

Under a hail of arrows and a fearsome onslaught of howling Magyars, the Bohemian and Swabian rearguard faltered, then broke. Their panicky flight caused the Franconians also to begin to disintegrate. With a third of his force routed, Otto's position became critical. At that time, however, a failure to coordinate their effort cost the Hungarians their chance to encircle and annihilate the Germans. Instead of following up their success, the Magyars of the flanking group contented themselves with looting the German baggage train.

Otto, on the other hand, continued to demonstrate his mastery of the diverse kingdoms and duchies under his command. In an effort to protect his threatened rear, he dispatched Duke Conrad to deal with the crisis. Conrad succeeded in rallying the remaining Franconians and led a counterattack that caught the Magyars in the act of retiring with their booty and hastened them on their way, freeing many prisoners in the process. The crisis averted, the battle now shifted completely to the front, where Otto redeployed his column into a battle line and charged in good order

Lél ordered his cavalry to stage a feigned flight, but Otto, like his father at Riade, was not about to let that old ruse break up his formations. Urging his men forward, Otto relentlessly kept up the pressure. As at Riade, the Magyars disengaged and withdrew to their main camp south of Augsburg to recover their pack horses, baggage train and booty. One of Augsburg's defenders later stated that they gave little indication of being a defeated force until they passed close by the city walls.

As the Magyars retired to the Lech, however, the battle entered its decisive phase. Otto's army either caught up with them on the west side of the river or positioned itself on the east side to cut off their withdrawal. In any case, fighting resumed in earnest, as the howling Magyar horsemen hurled themselves at their pursuers.

Brandishing aloft his "Spear of Destiny," Otto is said to have shouted above the din of the fighting, "They surpass us, I know, in numbers, but neither in weapons nor in courage. We know also that they are quite without the help of God, which is of the greatest comfort to us." Whether or not anyone heard those encouraging words, the Germans slowly began to gain the advantage in spirit and morale as the bravest warriors battled on in the summer heat. Amid that desperate fight for survival, Duke Conrad, in a state of near-exhaustion, momentarily loosened the mail around his helmet and an instant later fell choking to the ground, his throat pierced by a Magyar arrow.

By then, however, even the mightiest Magyar warriors were falling back. The Germans had won the day, but only after taking heavy losses during 10 hours of some of the most intense fighting that Central Europe had witnessed in centuries. Realizing that his victory and the unity that had made it possible represented an opportunity that might never come again, King Otto resolved to follow it through for all it was worth. Most of those Magyars who gamely fought on were the bravest and best-armed of the *hadnagyok*; as they were cut down, the Hungarian retreat—now real, not feigned—degenerated into a general rout.

Some Magyars leaped into the River Lech, only to drown on the opposite bank when the foliage that lined it collapsed under their weight. At more fordable parts of the river, they were intercepted by Otto's men and either cut down or drowned. Others tried to hide in outlying villages, but were burned out or cremated inside by the Germans. The stunned survivors who managed to get to the eastern bank of the Lech reorganized only enough to make their way through what is now Austria, across the Leitha River. Otto did not pursue them, correctly judging that another, even larger Magyar army had remained behind (remembering what had happened when Arpád had left his home settlement unguarded against the Pechenegs, the great chieftain's heirs usually did not participate in raiding abroad, keeping a substantial contingent of warriors defensively close to home). Instead, Otto turned his attention to those invaders still trapped on the west side of the Lech. In particular, he ordered Duke Henry of Bavaria to station his men along the east bank of the Lech to ensure that no more of them escaped alive.

Over the next two days, the Germans hunted down and slaughtered as many Magyars as they could, in a ruthless follow-up that was more decisive than the battle itself. Lél and a sizable group of *hadnagyok* tried to break through, only to run afoul of Duke Boleslav's Bohemian legion, which annihilated the Magyars and took Lél prisoner. A Hungarian legend claims that Lél, when brought before Otto, struck him down with the golden clarion that he still held, and killed the Saxon king before he himself was executed; another claims that he did so to Duke Conrad. Whatever gesture of defiance was shown by Lél, however, Otto certainly lived to have the satisfaction of seeing him hang, along with Bulczú and hundreds of Magyar *hadnagyok* who had been captured by the Bavarians.

Many of the Augsburgers also fell victim to the German army's orgy of destruction, which was comparable to any they had known from the Magyars. Still, in one dramatic battle, the barbarian menace from the east had been eliminated. Lechfeld's consequences, however, were to be even more far-reaching for both sides.

Otto was congratulated for his great victory by the Byzantine emperor, who bestowed upon him the title of "Emperor." As with his other claims, Otto made that more than a hollow title. In 961, he was again summoned to Italy, this time by Pope John XII. On February 962, he arrived in Rome and was crowned emperor for his support, at which point he issued a decree of his own, the *Privilegeum Ottonianum*, which linked papacy and empire and reconfirmed the temporal power of the popes that had first been confirmed by Charlemagne. In this case, however, the popes would be feudal vassals to the emperor.

The next year, John XII found out how seriously the decree was to be taken when he showed disloyalty to Otto and was promptly deposed and replaced by Otto's own candidate, Leo VIII. After Leo's death in 965, Otto had to march into Italy a third time, overpowering Roman opposition to install another pope, John XIII, in 966.

On May 7, 973, Otto I died and was buried at the cathedral in his beloved city of Magdeburg. As the first Holy Roman emperor, he had linked the German monarchy with Italy in a fateful rivalry for power that would continue for centuries. He had also laid the foundations of the German state, a precedent that would inspire generations of ambitious German kings and statesmen to follow.

More astonishing than the ascendancy of Otto the Great from his victory at Lechfeld was the recovery of the Magyars from their defeat. Forced to choose between adjusting to the ways of their western neighbors or following the succession of barbarians who had invaded Europe and wandered back into the east, the Hungarians uniquely chose the former course. The most serious effort to reconcile Hungary with its European neighbors was pursued by Vajk, who after taking the reins of government in 997, renamed himself Stephen (István in Hungarian), restructured the Hungarian political system along German lines, made Western Christianity the state religion of Hungary, stripped Eastern Christian, Jewish and Muslim *hadnagyok* of their noble status, and outlawed paganism entirely. Such profound changes were not accomplished without bitter resistance, but Stephen, partly with German help—and largely thanks to the fact that the majority of Magyar warriors left after the Battle of Lechfeld belonged to the defending army left at home and were directly loyal to him—eventually succeeded in establishing a permanent state modeled along similar lines to Otto's empire. On December 25, 1000, Stephen's stern measures bore fruit as he was crowned king by Pope Sylvester II and Hungary declared an apostolic state. Ironically, later German attempts to invade or dominate Hungary would be soundly defeated by the strong kingdom in whose creation they had assisted.

Although not very innovative militarily, King Otto I's victory at Lechfeld stands as a classic example of the importance of a strong leader with a sound sense of strategy and tactics, combined with the ability to maintain control of the units under his command. The battle's political consequences were more profound than its protagonists could ever have imagined. Most far-reaching were the national traditions established in the battle's aftermath—the unification of the German state, and the phoenix-like ability of the Hungarian people to recover from the first of a long succession of crises, conquests and disasters.

Brian Boru's Costly Last Victory

*The Irish High King wanted to unite his people,
but his enemies—including the Viking Brodir of Man—
stopped him at Clontarf in 1014.*

By Terry L. Gore

As the dreaded Norse longboats cut sleekly toward the shore dimly outlined in the evening dusk, the lights of the Irish army's distant campfires could be seen a mile or so inland. The ruse had worked for Brodir of Man. The Vikings had fooled the Irish High King (*Ard Ri*), Brian Boru into thinking they had deserted their allies at the fortress of Dublin.

In reality, the Norsemen had simply sailed out of sight, to return in the darkness in hopes of catching the Irish unprepared for the enemy's reappearance the next morning. The Vikings also knew that the pious Brian would be loath to do battle on such a holy day as April 23, 1014, Good Friday.

More important to Brodir than such sacrosanct niceties were the treasures he would possess after he had destroyed the Irish armies. Not only the wealth of the kingdom, but also the high kingship itself might be his. Of course, others coveted the same things—including his ally Sigtrygg, the king of Dublin, and Sigurd, the earl of the Orkney Isles. But they could be dealt with after the Irish—including Brian Boru—had been destroyed. First things first.

Ireland, to this day not noted for unity, consisted of 100 to 200 different tribal kingdoms in the early 11th century, as well as various Norse and Danish settlements scattered among the provinces of Ulster, Leinster, Connaught, Munster and Meath. Sparsely populated and with few large villages, Ireland had become popular with the colonizing Scandinavians in the 9th century. It was not long before the invaders began to arrange marriage alliances with Irish noble families and assimilate into the culture of the island. Many Irish boys were adopted by Norse settlers and became vicious fighters known as *Gall-Gael* ("Foreign Irish") to the native Irish, who also referred to them as "Sons of Death."

Living in close proximity, the Irish warriors and Scandinavians fought constantly, with tribal factions joining one side or the other as circumstances dictated. From such violent relations, blood feuds developed over the generations.

Although no standing army as such existed in Ireland, clan chieftains (*Ri Tuatha*) owed military service to their tribe and had an obligation to defend tribal lands when they appeared threatened. Each tribal chief provided a number of warriors from his own personal war band, as well as the warriors of his subchiefs, to his immediate superior—the number of warriors varying from a handful to hundreds, depending on the clan or tribal unit. The kings, troubled by the fickleness of their subjects, employed bands of mercenaries as bodyguards, although they had a habit of deserting to a higher bidder at inopportune times. By the mid-9th century, most such mercenaries were Scotsmen or Norsemen.

The Irish warriors, educated by older, experienced soldiers, were brought up in a climate of almost continuous warfare. It was the custom, say the ancient histories, for the young men of Ulaid to prove their mettle by going to Connaught and killing a man. Though the Irish appear to have been ferocious warriors, their actual military service obligations lasted a grand total of three fortnights every three years. Undoubtedly, local leaders spent much of their wealth hiring mercenaries or paying for nonaggression treaties with their Scandinavian neighbors.

Most of the old chronicles depict the weaponry of the Irish as identical to that of the Norsemen. The chiefs wore chain mail and helmets and wielded heavy two-handed axes. The vast majority of warriors, however, fought unarmored with spear, ax, shield and sword.

The Irish chiefs also employed large numbers of kerns, lightly armed skirmishers who used javelins—apparently longer-ranged missile weapons were considered a less-than-honorable method of inflicting casualties, even though weapons such as bows and slings had been used from the earliest times.

A common Irish battle custom was to cut off the heads of slain enemies; another was to place a sword or spearpoint between an enemy's teeth while accepting the unfortunate warrior's surrender. Such ceremonies undoubtedly encouraged the antagonists to summon up their utmost skill and bravery to avoid being publicly humiliated.

In this violent, war-torn land, the Norsemen behaved just as viciously toward the Irish. The Viking raiders, commanded by their earls and kings, numbered up to 1,000 men per leader; the leader paid and supplied the adventurers. The Viking *huscarl* (housecarl) became synonymous with this hardy warrior race, well-armored and loyal to the death to his earl.

Not all Vikings, however, were well-armed and armored. Though the bulk of the raiders became well-off as pirates, those new to the profession or conscripted out of need were more akin to the comparatively primitive Irish in dress and weaponry.

The standard Viking tactic was to form their divisions into shield walls, five or more men deep and close enough together to lock shields, allowing 1½ feet per man; that prevented missiles from doing much harm. Vikings used the old-style German "boar's head," or swine array, attack formation, with their most heavily armored and best-armed men in the front ranks and those more lightly armored filling in behind. This formation concentrated plenty of impact on a small frontage—a necessary tactic if the enemy's shield wall was to be broken. While their methods may sound simplistic today, the combination of honor-bound loyalty to the leader, superior armament and the incentives of loot and glory made the 11th-century Viking warriors formidable opponents on land or at sea.

The Irish, loyal to their individual tribes, were poorly equipped in comparison to their Scandinavian adversaries. Still, fighting not for pillage but to protect their homes and families in most cases, the Irish managed to give a good account of themselves when battling the invaders. The Irish prepared fortified encampments at night and entertained themselves with jugglers, poets and musicians to keep their spirits up during the grueling campaigns. When in battle, the Irish would often make an impromptu mad dash at the enemy lines, hoping to smash into the enemy formation with enough momentum to cause their foe to break ranks and lose cohesiveness.

Unlike the Vikings, who felt that any form of deceit, subterfuge or underhandedness simply proved the wisdom of a leader, the Irish frowned on the use of stealth and guile, though ambushes were considered a normal form of warfare. Irish history is replete with its share of treachery, but when matters came down to a pitched battle, the Irish were often known to extend courtesies to their enemies, a practice that perplexed the Scandinavians. In the year 1002, for instance, Brian Boru marched to Tara (the Irish capital) to demand that the High King Malachi either submit or do battle. Malachi asked for a month's delay—time to muster his army—and Brian, upholding the Irish tradition of honorable fairness in war, granted his request. The Irish sense of honor brought the grantor of such graces even greater glory in the end—provided that he was the victor!

Even though the Irish and Scandinavian warriors were culturally similar, they retained their ethnic pride and prejudices. During the centuries before the Battle of Clontarf, historical momentum was building toward a final cataclysmic battle that would decide whether Ireland would remain Celtic or become another Scandinavian colony. To finally bring the issue to a bloody climax, it only required an Irish leader who was sufficiently charismatic and physically powerful to unite the clans.

Brian mac Cenneidigh was born in Thomond, a northern region in the province of Munster now known as County Clare, around 941 AD. He was the youngest of 12 brothers, all but two of whom would be killed in battle. Members of the Dal Caissan tribe, the brothers fought continuous wars against the Danes and rival Leinstermen until Brian's brother, Mahon, broke the Viking armies at the Battle of Sulchoid in 968.

Mahon assumed the mantle of provincial king in 968, but he was assassinated eight years afterward. Brian succeeded him. He caught and killed the assassins who had murdered Mahon and then proceeded to bring the southern half of Ireland under his rule. According to the ancient chronicle known as the *Cogadh*, "He was not a stone in place of an egg, nor a wisp of hay in place of a club; but he was a hero in place of a hero."

Civil war, an endemic element of Irish history, did not abate during the latter part of the 10th century. Malachi claimed the high kingship of Ireland in 980, after defeating the Danes at the Battle of Tara the year before. Brian and Malachi then proceeded to fight a 20-year war before being forced to join forces just before the turn of the century to defeat an invading Danish army at Glenmama. They killed 7,000 of the enemy, sacked Dublin and ravaged Leinster in the process. Malachi, acknowledging Brian's military prowess and growing popularity, offered him the kingship of more than half the land, but Brian would be satisfied with nothing less than the title of high king. By 1002, Brian's military strength proved overwhelming, and Malachi abdicated the throne. Brian wasted no time in occupying it. His added honorary sobriquet of *Boru* might roughly be translated as "of the tributes."

Though contemporaries described Brian Boru as an idealized, fearless king who fostered Irish nationalism, the reality was that Brian, intelligent enough to know the value of "good press," generated political support with lavish patronage of the church, and used plenty of Scandinavian-style cunning in his political dealings. One of the legends he spread regarding his tenure as high king was that "a richly dressed lady could walk from one end of Ireland to the other without anyone taking her jewelry or anything else." In effect, he appeared to contemporaries as the mystical type of leader that King Arthur represented for the Britons.

Around the turn of the century, Brian broke a peace treaty with the king of Meath, attacking and defeating him. By 1005, he had used Norse-Irish renegades to mount raiding expeditions against the western shores of Britain, at the same time guaranteeing Danish settlers in Ireland their territories in return for their military support. Still, the ethnic hatred smoldered. The *Cogadh* text notes that around 1013 Norsemen had been billeted in many Irish homes for some time. The moment came when Brian instructed his countrymen in each household to kill their "guests" on a given night as they slept and light a torch to signal that the deed was done. Such was the reality of warfare in the age of heroes.

By the time he was 60, Brian had defeated Vikings and Irish contenders alike, setting the stage for a strong dynasty to rule over the fragmented island.

But then, the king of Leinster, Mael Morda, rose in revolt in 1012, refusing to acknowledge Brian's rule. Casting about for allies, he joined up with the always troublesome Dublin Norse in open defiance of the high king. Brian tried diplomatically to dissolve this alliance by giving his daughter to Sigtrygg Silkbeard, the king of Dublin, while he himself married the legendary Gormlaith, mother of Sigtrygg, sister to King Mael Morda of Leinster and former spouse of none other than Malachi! It was a political alliance that had too many powerful personages involved to be a success.

While transporting his "tree tribute" (a tax in the form of masts for ships), King Mael Morda broke a button off a tunic given to him by Brian. He asked his sister Gormlaith to mend it, but she started to scold and shame him for accepting anything from her husband Brian and being subject to his rule. Stung by his sister's insults to his honor and manhood, Mael Morda murdered one of Brian's heralds and rode off to his old allies, the Dublin Norse. Sigtrygg, ever anxious for a fight, wasted no time in welcoming his uncle, and immediately attacked an Irish ally of Brian's, raising the banner of insurrection. Various disaffected and rebellious Irish clans quickly threw in their lot with the Dublin Norse.

Brian, incensed by Gormlaith's meddling and intrigues, had her imprisoned while he marched for three months through the rebellious lands, raising havoc of his own before dispatching his son Murchad to raid the lands around Dublin.

Gormlaith, though imprisoned, did not sit idly by and accept her fate. At 50 years of age, she had retained her beauty; she had little trouble persuading Sigurd, the earl of the Orkney Isles (who was half Irish), to come to her rescue. Sigurd not only desired Gormlaith, but he also wanted to sit in Brian's seat as high king, like his countrymen Svein and Cnut had done in England. Sigtrygg also had sent an appeal for help to Sigurd, promising Gormlaith's hand in marriage and support for Sigurd's aspirations to the throne. It seemed that the ever-so-reasonable Sigtrygg only wanted Sigurd to guarantee his continued rule over Dublin. But Sigtrygg had other plans. Attempting to garner as much military help as possible, the wily Dubliner promised Gormlaith to another renowned warrior of the age—to Brodir of Man (the Isle of Man).

Brodir, described by the Irish as a Christian "magician" with hair so long he had to tuck it in his belt, and with mailed armor that reportedly could not be pierced by steel, made the same "deal" with Sigtrygg that Sigurd had made—Brodir was promised the Irish throne as well as a bride in return for military assistance. Sigtrygg went so far as to tempt his own brother, but his brother, disgusted with the treacherous double-dealings of his sibling, joined the army of Brian Boru instead. Still, the Norsemen of Sigurd and Brodir, more than 2,000 of them, were a force to be feared.

As the forces formed during the winter of 1013-1014, Brian, informed of the mustering of Vikings and rebellious Irish clans in Dublin, called in his own allies—his old enemy Malachi and the clans of Meath, the clans of Connacht, Munster and his own Dal Caissans, as well as a thousand foreign mercenaries. Once the muster had been completed, Brian sent his second oldest son, Donnchad, on a raiding expedition into the rebellious Irish territories, while Brian himself took the main army and marched through Leinster toward Dublin. Brian's strategy was sound. By attacking and continuing to harass the rebel bases, he saw to it that many of the rebellious clans would refuse to leave their threatened homes and march to Dublin. The rebel army never reached the size it potentially could have because Brian cleverly managed to neutralize a sizable portion of it.

As Sigurd and other adventurers who had joined him sailed into the tributaries outside Dublin, they were met by Sigtrygg, Mael Morda's Leinstermen, the Dublin Vikings and the Irish rebels from various clans. Shortly thereafter, Brodir of Man and his warriors arrived. The allied army resisting Brian Boru reportedly also contained English, *Gall-Gael*, Welsh, Flemish and French warriors, as well as a handful of Normans. This amalgamation of troops allegedly fought for promised land and pillage, as well as for glory and honor. Yet, to read of their determined hand-to-hand combat, revenge for age-old wrongs seems as much a determinant as anything else.

As he approached Dublin, Brian Boru's Irish army suffered a serious blow. Perhaps because of old quarrels, the men of Meath, commanded by ex-high king Malachi, drew off from the rest of the army and refused to take part in the battle plans. Although upset by the reluctance of his ally, Brian then was heartened by "news" that the Viking forces had boarded their longships and headed out to sea, apparently deserting Sigtrygg. Unknown to the Irish leaders, of course, Sigtrygg, Brodir and Earl Sigurd had planned that ruse to lull the Irish into a sense of false security. The Norsemen sailed out of sight and immediately turned around, arriving back on the darkened beaches near Clontarf after sunset and thus ensuring that a battle would be fought on Good Friday.

Brian's army, depleted by Malachi's refusal to fight, still managed to muster 7,000 or so warriors. Not only were Brian's Irish troops present, but there were also warriors from Scotland and Norway, and a contingent of newly Christianized Manx Vikings—all of whom prepared to fight the more heavily armored allied force.

The night before the battle, the Norsemen were informed that Sigurd had brought a sacred raven banner, woven by his mother, which had the magical properties of ensuring victory for the army if carried before it—but also promising death to its bearers. He tried to downplay that part of the prophecy; even so, he would have a difficult time finding volunteers to bear his mother's banner the next morning.

As dawn broke, the Norsemen assembled on the shores near Clontarf before their beached boats, a mile and a half from the walls of Dublin. If Brian Boru and his followers were totally aghast at such a surprise, it was not immediately apparent. Indeed, adversarial warriors in the fortress were graciously allowed by the Irish to leave their walled fortress unmolested and join the Vikings forming up near the shore.

Brian, though reluctant to take an active part in a battle on Good Friday, did ride before his assembling forces, carrying a crucifix in one hand and a sword in the other. He gave a short but inspiring speech to his warriors assembled to do battle and then retired to the rear, accompanied by a number of personal escorting guards, who formed a shield wall around him. The Irish, incensed by years of bloody skirmishes, of loved ones being killed or captured and homes destroyed, prepared to take bloody revenge on the hated Norse and their renegade allies.

The Viking-allied army formed up into five battle divisions on the field; a sixth remained in Dublin, where Sigtrygg also stayed with 1,000 of his Dublin Vikings manning the walls, effectively guaranteeing himself a ringside seat without fear of personal harm. His son commanded the extreme left division of the allied army as leader of all those Dublin warriors who desired to fight in the open that day, perhaps another 1,000 men. Next in line stood a strong, 3,000-man force of Leinstermen in two divisions, commanded by Brian's rebellious brother-in-law, Mael Morda. Armed and armored the same as the Irish clans opposite them, these fighters were the weakest link in the allied line. Sigurd's Orkney Vikings manned the center—1,000 well-armored, ax-wielding veterans of many wars. And finally, on the right were stationed Brodir's Vikings, 1,000 or more of them, eager to come to grips with the supposedly inferior foe. Brodir's men anchored their flank on the banks of Dublin Bay, where the longboats lay beached.

Opposite the Viking allies, Brian's forces also formed into regional divisions. On the Irish right, 1,000 foreign mercenaries and Manx Vikings assembled opposite the Dublin Vikings. Next to them, 1,500 clansmen of Connacht were gathered under their kings, while more than 2,000 Munster warriors under Brian's son Murchad continued the front, flanked by 1,400 Dal Caissans on the extreme left—they were led by Murchad's 15-year-old son, Tordhelbach, and Brian's brother, Cuduiligh. Off to the right of the army and several hundred yards to the rear stood the 1,500 warriors of Meath, under the reluctant Malachi, watching and waiting—perhaps to see which side prevailed before becoming involved.

As the forces formed up into their respective battle arrays, a Danish chief roared a challenge across the field to an Irish leader, "Where's Domhnall?" Came the reply, "Here, thou reptile," and reportedly each man soon fell with the other's sword in his breast and holding the adversary's hair. Such was the grim, no-quarter combat that would be the norm this day.

Several other names were called out as more individuals advanced to the middle ground between the armies to settle grudges and family feuds. The massed onlookers cheered on the various combatants who strode into the no-man's land between the two forces to offer or accept a challenge. As the individual contests were fought between old enemies, the two armies slowly began to move toward each other in the early morning light.

Inevitably, the forces closed with crushing impact, their brutal edged weapons crashing down on helmet and shield. Swinging his deadly ax with frightful effect, Brodir fought his way through the first ranks of his enemies, pushing back the Irishmen before him until a renowned warrior, Wolf the Quarrelsome, sought him out and hit him twice with such force that the Viking fell back, only managing to escape Wolf's ax by ignominiously fleeing into the woods to his right.

In the center, the Leinstermen of Mael Morda dealt harshly with the Munster clans opposing them. They pushed their fellow Irishmen back, and Sigurd's Orkney Vikings added to the Irish despair by smashing into the already engaged and lightly armed Munstermen.

Sigurd fought hard, following his "magical" raven banner and watching the prophecies of the seers come to pass. An Irish leader led a mad, impetuous attack directed at the raven standard and viciously killed the Vikings near it. He slew the standard-bearer, who was immediately replaced by another, but he, too, fell to the Irish blades.

According to the old histories, Earl Sigurd ordered the chieftain Thorstein to pick up the fallen standard, but Asmund the White warned that he would die if he took it. Thorstein walked away. Sigurd then turned to another chieftain, who told him to carry it himself. Sigurd, unwilling to show cowardice or fear, did pick up the banner, but placed it under his cloak, hoping to avoid the Irish blades. His ruse was to no avail—Brian's son Murchad sought him out and felled the Orkney leader with a spear thrust.

Brodir's men, still a threat even with their leader hiding in the woods, were attacked by the omnipresent Murchad, who led his personal bodyguard of 140 "king's sons" along the line of battle, bolstering morale and valor by his presence in the Irish ranks. As in most battles of this period, a leader's example could not honorably be ignored, and men would fight to the death to gain his notice, respect and encouragement.

Murchad's assault broke the Manx Vikings, who, with their leader gone, began to flee to their ships. That left the Leinstermen isolated, although they continued to press the Munster clans hard after hours of bloody push and shove. Curiously, the ebb and flow of battle was often interrupted while men from both sides drew back from each other to gain a few moments of mutually needed rest.

Although victorious so far, Mael Morda's Leinster clansmen were tired, disordered and severely weakened by the heavy losses sustained in hours of battle. Rallying, the Munstermen mounted a desperate counterattack against Mael Morda's troops, and in a wild, frenzied, tooth-and-nail fight, Mael Morda and the Munster chieftain killed each other.

On the Viking left, meanwhile, the Dublin warriors fought toe to toe against the foreign mercenaries Brian had hired. Here, the axes and spears of the professional warriors cut through Danish mail with deadly effect.

Slowly, the Dubliners were forced to fight a delaying action they could not maintain. They lost touch with the supporting Leinstermen on their right. And as the Leinster clans became even further isolated, several groups of them joined the Orkney Vikings on their immediate flank, the two forces momentarily holding in the face of increasing Irish pressure.

Somewhere at this point in the battle, either the Norwegian Prince Anwud or Eric of Denmark fought his way through to the exhausted Murchad, who still managed to throw the attacking Viking to the ground, and wrenched off his mail shirt. In the course of the struggle, the Viking stabbed Murchad in the stomach with his knife, but moments later Murchad recovered the sword that the Norseman had dropped and beheaded him with it. Finally, Murchad collapsed, to die of his wound the following day. His final combat was yet another example of the propensity for leaders of note to seek each other out and fight their own individual battles throughout the daylong contest.

The deadly axes of the foreign auxiliaries finally broke the Dubliners, who began to run for their fortress. The Orkney Vikings, finding their allies evaporating around them and seeing that Earl Sigurd and the "magical" raven banner had fallen, also began to break ranks and retreat to their ships.

The diffident Malachi had held his men in place all day, watching their fellow countrymen bleed and die on the fields before them. Now that the enemy appeared to be in retreat, however, he ordered his Meath warriors to join the battle. Any possibility of the Vikings rallying died in that final attack. As the Dublin Vikings streamed toward the single bridge into Dublin, they were caught by Malachi's fresh Irish warriors, and in the ensuing panic only a handful of survivors managed to return to Sigtrygg's garrison.

On the other flank, the Orkney and Manx Vikings had nowhere to run. During the course of the long battle, the tide had come in, cutting the Norsemen off from the safety of their ships. Faced with the choice of being cut down by Irish blades or a hazardous swim, most elected to run into the sea. As the Vikings fled into the water, Brian's 15-year-old grandson Tordhelbach, caught up in the fury of battle, chased two Danes into the ocean and dragged them under, drowning himself in the process.

Not all the defeated Vikings would be killed, however. Thorstein, the Viking who had wisely refused to carry Sigurd's raven banner, was exhausted and resigned to his fate. He had paused to tie his shoelace when the Munstermen caught him and asked why he had not continued to run. Thorstein replied, "Because I can't get home tonight, since I am at home out in Iceland." The Irish, generous in their victory, allowed the Icelander to live.

Not so with another leading participant. It seems Brodir and some of his Vikings, hiding in the woods, saw Brian just outside, lightly guarded while most of his men were off in furious pursuit of the fugitives. The Vikings fell upon the few Irish retainers, decapitating Brian with one blow. Then they retreated, Brodir yelling, "Now let man tell man that Brodir felled Brian." Soon afterward, however, they were subdued and taken prisoner by the enraged Irish. According to the Viking sagas, Wolf the Quarrelsome ordered that Brodir's men be killed and that Brodir himself should die a lingering coward's death.

Losses to both sides were incredibly high. Out of a total of between 7,000 and 8,000 combatants, the estimated allied loss was more than 6,000, including almost all the leaders. Irish losses were at least 1,600, and perhaps as high as 4,000, including their king, Brian Boru.

The next day, Donnchad arrived and tried to tempt Sigtrygg out of Dublin, but to no avail. So, on Easter Sunday, the dead Irish leaders were gathered up along with the wounded, and the Irish warriors marched home, leaving behind the stripped bodies of several thousand corpses. Brian Boru and his son Murchad were ceremonially buried at Armagh.

With his troops still fresh and at full strength, latecomer Malachi claimed the Irish throne once again—and there were few left to oppose him. Sigtrygg held out in Dublin until his death in 1042, while the surviving Danes and Norsemen were assimilated into the Irish populace and culture. Donnchad succeeded Malachi as high king in 1022, but was deposed by a rebellious faction in the 1050s, when wars fought over the throne became even more brutal, ending only with an Anglo-Norman invasion in the next century.

The stories, songs and poems of glory and battlefield prowess at Clontarf that appeared over the next few hundred years took on a unique importance. In the late Middle Ages, if Irish families could not claim an ancestor killed at the battle, they were not considered truly noble.

Battering a Wall of Shields

*Occupying the ridge top was Harold, his shield wall
surely invincible. Attacking up the slope was William.
The outcome would be truly historic....*

By Don Hollway

In the city of York the celebration had gone on for days. Revelers thronged the streets, and the sound of rejoicing went on late into the autumn nights — and nowhere with more gladness than in the great hall where sat the king.

For Harold Godwinson, it was the supreme moment. Only the previous week the city had been conquered by Norwegian invaders whose king, Harald Sigurdsson—also known as Hardraada, or "Hard Ruler"—and Harold's own brother, Tostig, contested his right to rule. But on September 25, 1066, in the greatest battle England had ever seen, Harold's Anglo-Saxon army then had surprised and slaughtered the Norsemen, including Harald Hardraada and Tostig, at Stamford Bridge. Only Duke William of Normandy now remained to challenge Harold. And with no Norman invasion apparently threatening, Harold seemed at last the undisputed king.

But then came the rude shock the evening of October 1 — a weary rider brought news that Duke William had invaded after all! His army was already laying waste the countryside around Hastings, to the south. Worse, Harold's already once-mauled troops were three times farther than William's from London. The king sent messengers ahead to gather reinforcements and at dawn led his exhausted men south to defend his crown for a second time in just days.

The stage for this particular confrontation, however, had been set long before. The drama of disputed succession went back to when the line of Anglo-Saxon kings descending from Alfred the Great had culminated in Edward, called the Confessor. But Edward, half-Norman and raised in Normandy, was not well liked by the native Saxon aristocracy led by his father-in-law, Godwin Earl of Wessex. In 1051 the earl and his sons staged an unsuccessful revolt, and Edward exiled them. During that high point of Norman influence at the Anglo-Saxon court, young Duke William paid a visit to London.

The man granted an audience with King Edward had come a long way from an illegitimate birth in perennially embattled Normandy, where the warlords habitually feuded with each other and with every duke who tried to unite them. The title had passed to William at the age of 7 or 8, even though he was Robert I's illegitimate son by the daughter of a local tanner.

Sensitive about his birth, William reacted in his siege of Alençon, when its people sought to protect their walls from Norman fire with vinegar-soaked animal skins. William took the skins as a personal insult because his maternal grandfather had been a humble tanner. After he overcame the town by night assault, he had the citizens' hands and feet cut off. Aside from such cruelty, William was, at 23, a natural leader. Distantly related to Edward, he was Norman, and he felt secure enough at home to aspire to rule England. To the childless Edward, he could have seemed a natural heir to the English crown, and though no official agreement was made, William went home with the impression it would be his.

But the Anglo-Saxon earls soon returned to power and forced Edward to banish the Normans. Godwin died soon after, and his son Harold Godwinson inherited his position as Earl of Wessex, the power behind Edward's throne. Good-natured and likable, Harold proved an able diplomat and commander, fighting so skillfully in Wales that the Welsh delivered their king's head as a peace offering. As virtual ruler of England he came to be known as *Dux Anglorum*, Duke of the English, and *Dei Gratia Dux*, Duke by the Grace of God, and even *Subregulus*, Underking.

By 1064, Duke William was well aware of the threat the earl posed to his ambition. When Harold came to France on a diplomatic mission and was taken prisoner by a neighboring count, William secured his release. The two men seemed to take an instant liking to each other. Harold joined William on a raid into Brittany; the duke knighted him in the Norman fashion. That in itself implied the earl owed William allegiance—it seems, furthermore, that Harold swore an oath of fealty on the bones of a saint. If he ever had any royal aspirations, the contention long has been, he relinquished them that summer in Normandy.

On the other side of the Channel, meanwhile, Edward suffered an apparent stroke on Christmas Eve 1065, reviving only long enough to designate Harold Godwinson his heir. Whether he really reneged on an oath of fealty to William will probably never be clear. Events moved fast—the assembled English nobles confirmed Edward's decision. Edward was buried, and Harold was crowned the very next day.

Duke William, as leader of an always-warring realm, could hardly ignore such an affront to his honor. And so, locked by circumstances into conflicting paths, both he and Harold laid plans for the invasion that must surely follow.

Many of the Norman nobles were unconvinced an invasion could be mounted, but William used promises of land and loot to rally his reluctant barons and to recruit mercenaries from all over Europe. He also secured the blessing of the pope, which gave his cause credibility among European powers.

Harold at first had little trouble organizing the defense of England. It seemed God was on his side. "At that time," said the *Anglo-Saxon Chronicle*, "throughout all England, a portent such as men had never seen before was seen in the heavens." A comet, which was later named Halley's, appeared in the sky in mid-April of 1066. With such a "long-haired star" as a sign of change and misfortune, few men could doubt Harold's warnings.

The call to arms drew men from all over southern England. Each earl brought along his personal retinue of bodyguards, or *housecarls*. These professional soldiers, well equipped with knee-length chain-mail armor and yard-long, kite-shaped shields, were expert with all weapons, especially the great, two-handed Viking battle-ax and the short, single-edged blade called the seax (or "sax"). They had fought with Harold in Wales and formed the hard core of his army.

The rank and file came from the peasant levy called the *fyrd*, vast in number but inexperienced and poorly armed. Worst of all, their tour of duty was limited to about two months, cut short by the need to return to their farms in time for the harvest.

So Harold found his army, perhaps the most powerful in Europe at that time, dwindling in strength as the summer came and went with no sign of the expected Norman invasion. In fact the Normans, who were no sailors, were awaiting a favorable wind to carry them to England. The Norwegians attacked first, drawing the English north and leaving the southern coastline undefended. As a result, the Normans landed unopposed at Pevensey on September 28.

Harold brought his battered force back from Stamford Bridge on October 6. While his men regrouped in London, the king visited the shrine of the Holy Cross at Waltham, where a miraculous stone crucifix of unknown origin supposedly stood.

Historians and strategists have since faulted Harold for not waiting longer in London to rebuild his forces. Possibly the enemy army was simply larger than he expected, or the victory in York made him overconfident, but more likely Harold simply wanted to pin the Normans down. Hastings, at the foot of the north road to London, stood on a peninsula between the tidal River Brede and the harbor of Bulverhythe. If Harold's army could block any Norman advance overland, and his fleet stop any retreat or resupply, winter would win the war for Harold.

The site on which he chose to do battle could not have been better suited for his purposes. The only road out of the peninsula was straddled by a cross-ridge, flanked by ravines impassable by cavalry. Behind the ridge rose the forest of Andredsweald; at its foot lay a marshy valley that the Anglo-Saxons in their Germanic tongue called *Santlache*, "sand lake." The French later corrupted that name, as they did most of the Anglo-Saxon language, to *Sanguelac*, "lake of blood." Today, the site is known as Senlac.

On the evening of Friday, October 13, after a hasty 60-mile march from London, Harold's army took command of the ridge. His men, it is alleged, spent the night drinking and singing bawdy songs. More likely they were exhausted. And in their camp some miles away, the Normans used the time—if their own chroniclers are to be believed—in prayer. For his part, William, unprepared for a long campaign in enemy country, could be thankful Harold had offered battle so soon.

Early on the sunny Saturday morning following, the two armies, each more than 7,000 strong, faced one another across the valley of Senlac. Along the crest of the ridge stood the Anglo-Saxons, arrayed behind a wall of overlapping shields 600 yards across and bristling with spears. The *housecarls*, prepared for the most severe punishment, manned the front line, with *fyrd-men* six deep behind them. Harold's brothers, the Earls Gyrth and Leofwine, probably commanded the flanks. Harold himself stood in the midst of his host, beneath the dragon standard of Anglo-Saxon kings and his personal banner, gem-encrusted and emblazoned with a fighting man.

William and his host had risen early and marched six miles to confront their foe. Now, seeing the flags, Duke William swore that if he were victorious he would build an abbey where they stood.

The Normans were deployed in three divisions, each with archers, infantry and cavalry—and all in the valley. On the left, the mercenaries of Brittany, Maine and Anjou followed the Breton Count Alan Fergant. On the right, Count Eustace of Boulogne commanded the French and Flemish. William's Normans formed the center, led by his own half brother, Bishop Odo, who later commissioned the famous Bayeux Tapestry depicting the battle. The duke set up his command post across the valley, beneath the papal banner.

William at first donned his mail *hauberk* backward, seemingly an evil omen. But the duke just laughed as he turned it around. "My dukedom shall be turned into a kingdom," he said.

Before the battle commenced, a Norman minstrel by the name of Taillefer begged William's permission to strike the first blow. As the two armies watched, he then cantered his horse up the hill to the shield wall, singing and tossing his weapons in the air. So dumbfounded were the Anglo-Saxons by this display that he managed to kill at least two of them before being himself overwhelmed.

It was about 9 a.m. "The terrible sound of trumpets on both sides," wrote Duke William's chaplain, William of Poitiers, "signalled the beginning of the battle."

The duke's strategy, if unimaginative, was classic: soften up the enemy with artillery, send in the infantry to break the line, then turn the cavalry loose on the scattered survivors.

Line abreast, the Norman archers trudged up the slope. The Bayeux Tapestry shows them, some well equipped, even armored, but carrying short, short-range bows. At 50 paces they formed up, drew and let fly, shooting up the incline. The arrows clattered harmlessly on the wall of overlapping shields. But they went unanswered by the Anglo-Saxons, few of whom knew how to handle a bow. In England, hunting was a privilege of the rich. The *housecarls* could only stand and take it while the Normans feathered their shields with volley after volley.

Though the English line remained largely untouched, William sent forward his infantry. The mailed foot soldiers advanced past the archers, but before they could come to grips with the English, it was their turn to be showered—with lances and javelins, throwing axes and even, from the poorer ranks, stones tied to sticks. Then, with each side calling on God's help and shouting insults in a language the other did not understand, the two lines smashed together. Blood spattered the knee-high grass, and the crash of weapons echoed across the valley, soon to be drowned out by the cries of wounded men.

In this contest of infantry the *housecarls* proved superior. Before his footmen gave way, however, William ordered his cavalry to their aid. In a wave the knights charged up the slope, pitched their javelins ahead of them, and rushed at the shield wall.

Chivalric tradition had not yet taken root in England. The men of the *fyrd* preferred to fight in the old-fashioned Viking way—on foot, man to man. But if the Anglo-Saxons were unused to fighting cavalry, the Norman knights were unprepared for the Viking ax, with which an experienced man could behead a horse or split a mounted knight to the saddle.

Now, the shield wall's hedge of spears held off the Normans' trained chargers while the *housecarls* stepped clear for room to swing their murderous axes. The screams of dismembered war horses added to the din.

With the full strength of both sides engaged, the slaughter went on until afternoon. The battle at that point began to go against the Normans. The Breton division fell back first, the horsemen turning their animals about and galloping back down the hill, through their own infantry and archers, who then joined the flight, too.

Whether that retreat was real or not remains debatable. Normans had used the technique of feigned retreat before, in France and Sicily, and may in fact have picked it up from the Bretons. However, it is generally thought that this first flight at Hastings was genuine, in no small part because the Bretons fled straight down into the Senlac marsh.

The men of the English right wing saw the knights below struggling with their mired horses, and to the left they viewed the exposed flank of the Norman army. The raw recruits in the *fyrd* could not resist the opportunity. Dropping their spears, drawing their seaxes, they plunged down the hill to the attack.

Outflanked, the Normans in the center panicked and fell back, and then the French. In the confusion, a rumor went through the army that Duke William had been killed.

Duke William, in fact, was still at his command post on Telham Hill. Seeing his attack collapse, he mounted his horse and spurred down into the melee. On the Bayeux Tapestry he is seen waving a wooden club called a *baculus*—capable of breaking bones through armor, an authority symbol left over from pagan days—and raising his one-piece, conical helmet to show his face and say: "Look at me well! I am still alive, and by the grace of God I will yet prove victor!"

Under his curses and threats, the Norman right and center steadied, for unlike the left wing, they had not been pursued. Most of the Anglo-Saxons still held the ridge; only those on the left had disobeyed their king's orders and deserted the defensive position. Perhaps that was a fatal mistake by inexperienced troops. Or perhaps the mistake was that the rest of the English army did not support them. Certainly the Normans had been thrown into confusion—at that moment a concerted charge downhill might have upended horses and spilled knights to the ground, where the knife-wielding *fyrdmen* could finish them off.

But no order came to attack. Either Harold did not realize his opportunity, or perhaps, as he fought on foot in the middle of a huge army, his order was lost.

Instead of the Norman left, it now was the English right that was exposed. William saw his chance and sent his horsemen charging up across the slope and into the gap. The attacking *fyrdmen* found not their own men but enemy knights behind them. Surrounded, some managed to make a stand on a little hillock—which still rises from the valley—but the swirling hordes of knights cut them down.

Both sides now paused to regroup. Each man checked himself for wounds gone unnoticed in the heat of battle, counted friends lost and those still alive, wiped the gore from notched weapons, or perhaps washed down a bit of food while he had the chance. For no one reckoned the battle over yet; despite the carnage, nothing had changed. Duke William had nothing to lose by a second assault.

It began about midafternoon, but the battle now was between *housecarls* and cavalry. Again the crest of the ridge became a swirling meat grinder of slashing blades. This time it was the Norman right that "broke," a retreat that almost certainly was faked. The English left wing dutifully pursued. Duke William, once again favored with good luck, immediately sent his knights around again to cut off and annihilate the unwary Anglo-Saxons.

Now dead Normans littered the top of the ridge, and dead English covered the slope. Probably 1,000 Anglo-Saxons had been killed in each of the two or possibly three abortive counterattacks, including both of Harold's brothers. Before Gyrth died, he managed to put a spear into William's horse, one of several killed under the duke that day. The duke, apparently thinking Gyrth was Harold, shouted, "Take the crown you have earned from us!" and

91

struck him down.

But the Norman infantry had been cut to pieces and the cavalry deci-mated, all for nothing. The English still held the ridge, those in the rear ranks moving forward to fill the gaps in the line. The battle would become one of attrition.

In the valley, Duke William faced the prospect of defeat. It seemed he could throw his knights against the *housecarls* all day, but unless he carried the fight to the ill-prepared *fyrdmen* sheltering behind the mounted English, the day would be lost. In the end he went back to his original plan, ordering his archers to attack again. But this time he commanded them to fire their arrows not into the shield wall but over it, in a high arc and down onto the heads of the Anglo-Saxons.

For the first time the mass of men behind the shield wall felt the full fury of the arrow barrage. There was no cover; the men were packed so tightly that even the dead could not fall. Only a minority wore armor or carried shields; no helmets protected their heads from the descending clouds of shafts. Even the *housecarls* had to raise their shields for protection, an action that then exposed them to direct frontal fire. Their line shortened, and as it did, the two ends pulled away from the ravines protecting the flanks. For the first time, the Normans found it possible to go around the shield wall.

And now William ordered forward one last assault. Up the hill went the Norman knights, many of them by now fighting on foot. They waded forward through grass that was blood-soaked and tangled with severed limbs, com-ing to grips with the *housecarls* while still-mounted Normans swept around and behind the Anglo-Saxons.

For some time, though, the issue remained in doubt. The English line bent back on itself, around the banners of royalty and the king. Duke Wil-liam, fighting his way around the English right, spotted Harold as the king stood chopping down Norman knights. The duke began to work toward him.

With his defenses crumbling around him. Harold Godwinson awaited the inevitable. At about 4 o'clock, perhaps sensing that his moment—and England's—had come, he turned his face heavenward, only to receive an arrow in the eye.

Harold, his face covered in blood, managed to pull out the shaft and hurl it aside, but could not continue the fight. And at that moment four Norman knights—some sources say William was one of them—finally burst through the defenders and set upon the wounded king. The first drove a spear into his chest; a sword blow from the second nearly decapitated him and drove him to the ground.

With the king slain, the Anglo-Saxon resistance collapsed, though many of the *housecarls,* as was their way, probably fought to the death around the body of their commander. The survivors fled into the woods behind the ridge—even so, they still managed to trap and slaughter some of the pursuing knights in a ravine later named by the French the Malfosse, or "Evil Ditch."

Harold's body, stripped of its armor and thrown on a heap with the other Anglo-Saxon dead, was so mutilated as to be barely recognizable. Rejecting offers of ransom for the corpse, Duke William had it wrapped in purple and taken for burial to the shore at Hastings.

William, crowned king of England that Christmas at Westminster, was not to have an easy time defending his new empire. Most historians regard the Norman rule in England as beneficial in the long term, but in those early years, few Anglo-Saxons would have agreed. William ruthlessly crushed all opposition, replacing the native nobility with his own, dividing up the country among them and studding it with Norman castles. Still, rebellions continued for half a decade. Viking raids, encroachments by the French, and revolts led by his own son also kept William's armies busy. In 1087 he died after a riding accident while at war in France.

At its greatest extent, the empire he founded reached from Scotland to the Pyrenees. More important to history, though, England, previously considered part of Scandinavia, had been brought into the European fold. Within a few hundred years, Normandy itself again fell under French sway, but by that time the Normans had themselves become Anglicized. The dynasty of William, born the Bastard but called by history the Conqueror, lasted for more than three centuries, but his legacy remains to the present day.

Odds Against the Black Prince

As Edward of Woodstock, Prince of Wales, engaged
'John the Good' at medieval Poitiers, the French would regret
the decision to dismount their knights in armor and fight
on foot. Still, they inflicted heavy casualties in the initial
slugfest of sword, mace, club, knife and dagger.

By John Schlight

Traveling in hostile territory, deep in the enemy's homeland, the "Black Prince" Edward looked upon a battlefield prospect as bleak as any that ever faced a general at the head of a small army. No more, it seemed, would there be the raiding and booty-taking he and his men had enjoyed for months, unimpeded.

For now, within shouting distance of his own ancestral home of Poitiers in west-central France, Edward of Woodstock, Prince of Wales, was stopped short by a clearly superior force with a king, the king of France, at its head.

It was no enviable position for an Englishman so far from home with no possibility of reinforcement—nor even any supply line. His soldiers, fatigued by forced-march in an effort to elude the pursuing enemy, were tired and probably unable to bear the shock of a cavalry charge. It would be frontal, too, because the French force thought to be chasing from behind somehow had found a shortcut, had swung around in front of the English to cut off their retreat through the countryside of Aquitaine.

His supplies already dangerously low, Edward was further hampered by a considerable baggage train, many of its wagons groaning with booty he hated to give up after all the easy months of plunder and pillage in French cities and villages. To make matters worse, his scouts reported that the French army encamped just four miles ahead was being reinforced by added men-at-arms and infantry from nearby Poitiers. The French force, led by King John II, "John the Good," had swelled to about 16,000 men, more than double the size of Edward's marauding contingent.

Even so, it wasn't so much battle the celebrated Black Prince feared—it was blockade, by which the French conceivably could force him to surrender.

In fact, that was the very course being urged upon John the Good in his sea of white tents outside the walls of medieval Poitiers. There, among the colored pavilions of his nobles, among swirling banners of all variety, the king met with his staff to decide just what to do. As knights in armor, their horses, crossbowmen and foot soldiers milled about nearby, one of John's two marshals, Clermont, argued against going into battle with the English.

The French could defeat Prince Edward simply by surrounding him, cutting off his food supply and awaiting his certain surrender, noted Clermont quite sensibly. But hotter heads were to prevail, and his advice, running contrary to the battle-minded spirit of chivalry, would be vetoed.

The French, of course, did have a superior force mustered at the gates of Poitiers. They did...but now Scotsman William Douglas offered King John a fresh piece of advice: Dismount your troops.

That was singular, perhaps even rash, strategy indeed. Yet perhaps not: only a decade earlier, English foot soldiers had inflicted disastrous defeat upon mounted French knights at Crécy. Douglas, an ally who had brought 200 Scots men-at-arms to the French, in effect was suggesting that John the Good adopt the supposedly proven English tactics for the battle ahead. And John, reported the early chronicler Geoffrey le Baker, "foolishly agreed to the counsel of this busybody."

Leaving only a small force of 300 men on horseback, the French king ordered all others to stand ready on foot, without their horses. The 300 would remain mounted as an initial shock force; the others...well, by the mid-14th century, the knights of Europe no longer favored the fairly light and flexible coats of chain mail they once embraced. Many now were wedded to heavy, cumbersome plate armor.

The 60 pounds of plate was a bearable weight for a man on horseback, but when he was on foot in his armor, when he had to walk or run some distance to close with the enemy, the same 60 pounds of deadweight could be an insufferable burden. King John's decision to dismount his men therefore could be considered a rather blind imitation of another's tactics in earlier battle—in this case, Crécy, where the French had lost when their horses, painfully pierced by showering arrows, reared and turned on their own oncoming soldiers, with disastrous confusion resulting. The decision now, at Poitiers, to leave the horses behind probably was an attempt to avoid a recurrence of that earlier disaster.

Probably, for there has been only fair agreement among observers and writers on the general outlines of the pending battle; they varied and sometimes are contradictory on detail. The past century of labor by historians, textual exegetes, psychologists, ballistics experts, military history buffs and visitors to the battlefield has resolved most of the ambiguities, however. With some inference, the historian today can develop an account which, while appearing occasionally fanciful, does reconcile the apparent contradictions and does bring us as close as we may ever be to what actually happened.

Like all such events, the battle of Poitiers was preceded by a chain of events that led to the inevitable confrontation between Edward, Prince of Wales, and King John the Good in 1356.

For one thing, those were the days of savage English raids upon the

French known as *chevauchées,* their objective vengeful destruction, plunder of fineries from the more advanced French society, or the seizing of captives for ransom. Then, too, the French in 1337 had tried to regain control of Gascony, the last continental remnant of England's 12th-century empire encompassing more than half of present-day France. King Edward III of England struck back in return for such treatment of his fief of Gascony. He carried his banner across the English Channel and into France with a rather dubious claim to the French throne. But territorial conquest soon became secondary to the profits of plundering as the Hundred Years War continued. Thus, the *chevauchées.*

The decisive English victory at Crécy on August 26, 1346, and the cession of Calais to England in the following year—that and the Black Death, a combination of bubonic plague and pneumonia that wiped out a full third of the European population in 1348 and 1349—quieted the feudal principals for several years. By 1355, though, Edward was ready to resume his harassment of the Continent, undeterred by the fact that King John II of France was his own cousin, a Valois who also was Edward's overlord for his continental lands.

Providing opportunity for Edward was John the Good's capacity for weakness and vacillation, even panic at critical moments, together with the discontent of his bourgeoisie and challenges by several of his most powerful lords.

Among them was his cousin, Charles de Navarre, who by allying himself with the English king, managed to strike terror into the heart of the French monarch. All in all, Edward judged the moment propitious for further adventures against his cousin John.

In the fall of 1355, Edward launched an assault against the French that would be three-pronged...eventually. The king himself would take a force to the recently acquired Calais, while Henry Plantagenet of Grosmont, Earl of Derby and Duke of Lancaster would sail with a second army to Normandy to join forces with Charles the Bad, King of Navarre and Count of Evreux. Finally, the king's oldest and favorite son, Edward, Prince of Wales, would lead a contingent to friendly Gascony in the south. Then, with those pro-English enclaves as jumping off points, the three armies were to unite for an attack on the French king.

Young Edward, known as the Black Prince for the color of his armor, sailed from Plymouth in September with more than 40 ships loaded, an early chronicler reports, with "jewels, hauberks, helmets, lances, shields, bows, arrows, and more besides [horses, for one]." The 25-year-old prince soon landed at Bordeaux with 1,000 knights, 2,000 archers and 2,000 foot soldiers. He than set out on a one-month, 500-mile *chevauchée* of devastation across southern France that reached to within a few miles of the Mediterranean before he returned to Bordeaux. As Maj. Gen. William T. Sherman did in Georgia five centuries later, Prince Edward cut a destructive swath difficult to forget—it elicited comment even from the hardened chroniclers of the day, gentlemen normally quite inured to tales of violence.

The expedition began peacefully enough as the prince passed through the friendly territory of western Gascony, but turned bloody when he entered the county of Armagnac to the south. Cities in his path that resisted—and some that did not—he burned to the ground, slaying their inhabitants, destroying churches, mills and homes, seizing food and wine, and carting away silver plate, gold, carpets and other valuables in his wagons.

Inexplicably, the prince's progress went unopposed by either the French marshal Clermont, who had forces in the area, or by the count of Armagnac, whose territory was being raped. The English army's greatest obstacle was the heat and dust of Languedoc and the scarcity of water. At the end of one particular day's march, noted a contemporary chronicler, "the army camped in the open fields where, for lack of water, they gave the horses wine to drink." The next day "they were drunk and could not keep a steady footing, with the result that many horses were lost." On another occasion, we are told, Edward's soldiers had to bathe in wine.

Returning to Bordeaux with his prizes, the prince passed the winter and spring there. In July 1356, Henry, Duke of Lancaster, arrived in Normandy with another English army. The following month, Black Prince Edward set out northward through Limousin and Berry on a march designed to draw the French king southward away from Henry and from the prince's father, King Edward, who was expected on the continent with yet another English force. The absence of reliable communications kept from the prince the news that Lancaster's men already had been routed by the French and that King Edward's invasion had been aborted by his need to remain in England to face a Scottish revolt in the north. The Black Prince in fact was on his own.

Leaving a large part of his army behind in Gascony as security against reprisals for his earlier raids in Armagnac, the prince set out from Bergerac on the Dordogne River on August 4, with a force of 3,500 mounted men-at-arms, mostly Gascon, 2,500 mounted English archers, and 1,000 foot soldiers. This small, mobile force was well suited for raiding the countryside and tempting the Valois monarch, but not for doing battle with the French. If King John took the bait, Edward would race back to Bordeaux and leave northern France exposed, he thought, to Henry's raids.

Since it mattered little how far north he marched before John learned of his presence and took out after him, the prince proceeded at a leisurely pace, averaging 10 miles a day, gathering provisions and plunder, resting his men and horses as he went. Sacking towns en route, he met little resistance until he arrived at Vierzon, some 40 miles south of the Loire on August 28. There, a small, irregular French scouting party tried without success to ambush his army and, after being scattered, retreated to the castle at Romorantin, 20 miles away. The prince followed and for six days besieged the fortification, which fell to him on September 3. By now, though, the French king had learned that the prince was in the neighborhood; John the Good's army was flooding across the Loire at Tour and Blois to confront the invader.

Uncertain of John's whereabouts, the Black Prince marched his men along the Loire to Tours, of half a mind to cross the river and link up with Lancaster, for such was the *ad hoc* nature of many medieval strategic decisions. Unable to find a crossing, and learning belatedly that the French were approaching, he thought better of his intention of joining Lancaster, broke camp and began a flight southward along the main trunk road that ran from Paris to Bordeaux. John, whose forces were increasing but still only equal in size to those of the English, followed. Once again, poor intelligence worked to the Black Prince's disadvantage. Upon reaching Chattelerault on the road to Bordeaux, and believing that he had shaken his pursuer, he idled for two critical days at the town while John, forcing a march, closed to within one day of him.

A score of miles ahead along the road lay Poitiers, and there an irony hardly could have escaped the notice of the Black Prince. Poitiers was the ancestral home and hub from which his forebears, Eleanor of Aquitaine and Richard the Lion Hearted, had controlled, in England's name, the very land through which he now was fleeing as a fugitive. The former queen's palace stood out starkly in the city's landscape, mute testimony to the lost empire that the Black Prince was trying to restore. A century and a half earlier, he would have been welcomed into Poitiers with celebrations and music for which the region was famous. Now the city was strongly fortified, its citizens loyal to the French king—Edward had to find a way to circumvent the town.

Leaving the main road north of the city, his army proceeded south along the path of an old Roman road that skirted Poitiers to the east. When the army was three miles abeam the city, however, his scouts stumbled on the rear guard of the French king's forces. In a brilliant maneuver, John had departed the main road farther north than had the prince, passed unnoticed by the English force on its left and now was heading due west from Chauvigny into Poitiers. He had swung around in front of the English to cut off their retreat.

The reconnaissance unit dispersed the French, who fled to join their main army, already encamped outside the walls of Poitiers. The Black Prince and his men, now in grave danger, already had covered 16 grueling miles that day, slowed by their infantry and large baggage train. They now were forced to press on for two more miles before finding a suitable place to camp, while their scouts reported the French army, four miles away, was being reinforced from the city.

The Black Prince's goal remained to avoid battle and escape to Bordeaux with his booty intact. His soldiers were tired, and unprepared to withstand the frightening cavalry charge of the French. While his greatest fear was that John would blockade him, forcing him to surrender, Edward had to consider the possibility that a showdown might occur. The key was to choose a position that would allow him to go either way—retreat if he could, or fight if he must.

On the following morning, a Sunday, Edward arranged his troops in just such a position on the crest of a small hill facing Poitiers, five miles to the northwest. The left of his 2,000-yard-long front line was guarded by a small river, the Moisson, and his rear by the Houaille wood, into which he could retreat if need be. The Moisson snaked around from his left and flowed beyond the wood at his back, where it was spanned by a ford to the prince's left and by a stone bridge several miles away to his right rear in the village of Nouaille. Across his front spread a hedge-enclosed vineyard whose four-foot-high vines provided a serious obstacle to a cavalry charge and excellent cover for his dismounted archers. A narrow lane marked the only direct passage through the maze of undergrowth.

The Black Prince positioned his forces in the day's customary three battalions, or "battles," one behind the other. Since escape was uppermost in his mind, he made the first battalion stronger than the others, to act as a defensive shield while the rest of his troops prepared to depart. That battalion, under the command of the Earls of Salisbury and Suffolk, had at its front, just behind the hedge, most of Edward's 1,000 archers, backed up by a sizable force of men-at-arms, all on foot. Behind that front line was the second battalion, a much smaller group of men-at-arms led by the Earls of Warwick and Oxford. Since that battalion was supposed to escort the wagons during the retreat, it was mounted to provide needed mobility. Finally, at the rear, the prince was in charge of a large group of Gascon men-at-arms, many of them on horseback. A large convoy of wagons was placed at the vulnerable right side of the front line to discourage any flank attack from that quarter. The wagons containing the marauding army's most valued possessions were in the rear and to the left of the entire formation, in a flight declivity that led down to the ford in the river.

Meanwhile, hard by Poitiers, the French had been undecided about their best course at first, King John's counsel having been somewhat divided. As seen earlier, though, the decision was to do battle rather than blockade, was to dismount most of the French king's men.

For the march to the battlefield, then, John arranged his forces into a vanguard and three columns. In the vanguard, led by the marshals Clermont and Audenham, he first placed his 300 still-mounted, fully-armored men-at-arms, followed in order by a contingent of German mercenaries, 2,000 spearmen on foot and 2,000 unarmored Genoese crossbowmen. His son, Charles, the Dauphin and Duke of Normandy, commanded the first battalion, which consisted of dismounted men-at-arms. The king's 20-year-old brother, Philip, Duke of Orléans, led the second battalion, also dismounted. At the rear, with

5,000 to 6,000 dismounted knights was the king. Except for the 300 men up front, the entire army was on foot. In an attempt to confuse the English and avoid capture, meanwhile, John had 19 of his own men don the royal colors and place his decorations on their shields.

And so, both sides now were drawn up in battle order.

Just as the battle was about to begin, however, a large retinue of clerics and lawyers appeared on the field, led by the papal envoy, Cardinal de Périgord. He spoke first to the prince and then to the king, with appeal for each to arrange a truce. Both commanders did agree to postpone the battle and discuss the suggestion, and all of Sunday passed in negotiation. When it became apparent that they could not avoid a clash, someone proposed that 100 men from each side fight it out and that the army of the defeated leave the field. The prospect of missing out on glory, booty and ransom was enough to defeat that suggestion. Although Clermont advised John to accept a truce, the other marshal, Audenham, William Douglas and others persuaded the king that the English force was weak, outnumbered, tired, and should not be allowed to escape.

John would agree to a truce only on terms unacceptable to the Black Prince—return of all captured prisoners and castles, and abandonment of all claims to the French throne. Edward, as his father's agent, was not empowered to make such concessions, and the day ended with resumed preparation for battle. While the parties had been conferring, meanwhile, the French took advantage of the pause to bring up 1,000 more knights and a large group of townspeople to add to their ranks. While the diplomats talked, both sides sent out scouting parties to reconnoiter the opposing forces.

The next morning, the armies formed their battle lines about two miles apart. Occupying the lower ground, the French could not see how the English were arranged. The Black Prince, still uncertain of John's intentions, had completed his plan for retreat. Leaving his strong first battalion up front behind the hedge as a cover, he ordered Warwick's second battalion and part of his own third line to begin escorting the wagons with their valuables back across the ford in the Moisson. If the French failed to attack while he was moving his prizes to safety, he apparently thought that he would continue his escape by gradually withdrawing elements from the front line to act as a rear guard for the retreating force. If, on the other hand, the French attacked, the front line would hold them until Warwick and the prince returned from the ford.

The French now did march forward in columns and, when they were about 600 yards from the crest of the hill, they saw the prince's banner disappear over its shoulder. Interpreting the sight as a full-blown retreat and afraid lest the English escape, they quickly formed into lines; their marshals ordered an attack.

The 300 mounted knights in the vanguard led the charge up the hill, followed in turn by the dismounted German auxiliaries, the French spearmen and the Genoese crossbowmen. Unable to ride through the vineyard, the horsemen were channeled into the single lane that passed through the bushes. There, they were met by a withering storm of arrows on their flanks and front, an onslaught that virtually annihilated them. Audenham was captured and Clermont, struck down from his horse and unable to promise ransom convincingly, was butchered on the spot.

Unlike the situation at Crécy, however, the destruction of the mounted unit did not prevent the footmen behind from advancing up the slope to the top of the hill. Infiltrating through the vineyard, stepping over the dead and dying bodies in the lane, the Germans closed in hand-to-hand combat with the English, while the following wave of unarmored spearmen raced up the incline and the crossbowmen fired their deadly bolts into Salisbury's battalion. The English situation was desperate, its line at the breaking point.

Hearing the commotion, Warwick and Prince Edward wheeled their two battalions around and returned from the wagons. Instead of resuming his former position behind Salisbury, however, Warwick brought his troops into line to the left and slightly forward of the first battalion, from which point his archers fired into the right flank of the advancing enemy infantry. Completely surprised by this unexpected assault on their right, the unprotected French foot soldiers broke off and retreated down the hill. In so doing, they ran into their own first battalion, the Dauphin's, which was rushing up to support them. The resulting confusion gave the English a brief breathing spell, during which the prince brought up his contingent to support Salisbury.

The Dauphin's unit managed to struggle through its own retreating vanguard and close with the reinforced English line. The heavy armor of the dismounted Frenchmen protected them from Warwick's arrows on their right, but the strain of having run half a mile in full armor weakened them for the ensuing struggle, as men of both infantry units, casting aside spears and longbows, slugged it out with swords, maces, clubs, knives and daggers. For the moment, the English outnumbered the enemy, but John had two fresh battalions ready for action, whereas the Black Prince was already using his reserves. The Dauphin's force was soon cut to shreds and began to withdraw down the hill, but it had inflicted heavy casualties. Many of the Black Prince's men were wounded and retired from the field. The rest were fatigued from having repelled two strong assaults. Their supply of weapons and ammunition depleted, the English soldiers now took advantage of the lull to take lances and daggers from the fallen to replace their own broken weapons. Archers "pulled arrows out of wretches who were still half alive," reported contemporary chronicler le Baker.

An immediate attack by the second French battalion probably would have won the day for King John. The Duke of Orléans' battalion, however,

101

had failed to appear. For reasons that forever will remain a mystery, Philip's entire battalion of knights mounted their horses, which were nearby, and rode off to the north. Once again, the medieval lack of discipline and centralized command proved disastrous for the French. The sudden disappearance of so many thousands of men tilted the scales strongly in favor of the English—so strongly, in fact, that King John, with but 5,000 or 6,000 men remaining, should have left the field. But his impetuosity and devotion to the spirit of chivalry mandated otherwise—foolishly, he ordered his knights, still on foot, to march the mile to the English line.

Edward, meanwhile, told the leader of his Gascons, Jean de Grailly, *Captal de Buch*, to mount up 200 knights and archers, and secretly lead them around the French left, to come up behind. Placing his own 6,000 men on horses, the Black Prince now led them against the oncoming French. John's footmen withstood the initial shock of the charge, and a furious battle ensued. For about half an hour, the two groups hacked away at each other, crushing skulls with axes, thrusting spears between the joints of plate armor, stabbing and mangling. When the struggle was at its height, de Buch appeared with his contingent at the French rear. Small though his force was, its appearance threw panic into the French, who now appeared surrounded.

The Black Prince was in the center of the fight, "hewing at the French with his sharp sword, cutting lances, parrying thrusts, bringing the enemy's efforts to nothing, raising the fallen and teaching the enemy what the true fury of war meant" (le Baker). John proved no less valiant, showing "the zeal of a young knight, doing great deeds, training some, killing others, cutting or bruising faces, gutting or beheading others" (le Baker again). But the outcome of the battle already had been determined by earlier decisions. The French were driven back to Poitiers, with the English chasing them and picking up numerous prisoners along the way. Among those captured were King John himself and his young son Philip, along with 60 counts and 1,000 other noblemen. The victorious Black Prince retired to his tent, where he received the captured king with all the honor due a sovereign.

After several days of tending the wounded and burying the dead, Edward returned to Bordeaux with his wagon train, to which now was added an even more lucrative prize—a French king and a large portion of the French nobility.

The battle near Poitiers had far-reaching effects on both kingdoms. Politically, the Duke of Orléans' flight weakened further in the eyes of the French peasantry and townsmen the already faltering credibility of the nobility. Conversely, England's political benefits were enormous. By an agreement four years later, King Edward's sovereignty over Gascony and all of Aquitaine—one third of France—was recognized.

The economic results were equally disastrous for the French and beneficial for the English. Although the French people excused John, who had acquitted himself well in the battle, the financial implications of his capture, along with so many nobles, were to plague the French economy for years. The king's ransom was set at three million gold crowns (about $750,000), then a vast sum which only added to an already crushing tax burden on the French peasant. In addition, the French countryside was scourged for years after the battle by "Free Companies" of English and Gascon brigands who found themselves unemployed and knew only the art of war.

The military scene that emerged after the battle at Poitiers reflected developments in the larger European society. An oft-repeated interpretation of the battle as a victory of infantry over cavalry, marking the demise of the age of the horseman, is not in all respects valid. After all, the English victors were mounted and the vanquished fought on foot. Yet, taken in conjunction with the other major military engagements of the Hundred Years War, the battle does mark a period of decline for the cavalry in the face of brilliant use of missile weapons by the English Plantagenets. The longbow marked the first step, to be followed shortly by firearms, in the ascendancy of missile weapons over the mounted charge.

The English won by employing more forward-looking techniques and weapons than their foe—by training and discipline that allowed them to combine their arms more effectively than did the French, by using to the fullest the inherent advantages of defense and imaginative employment of the longbow. The French, on the other hand, lost (but not by much) through conservative adherence to feudal rules, tactics and weapons—lack of control over units, insistence on chivalric charges (even though on foot), and retention of the crossbow. The battle, like the age, was half feudal and half modern. The modern half won, but by a hair.

Battle with Bitter Legacy

*At Kosovo in 1389, a lightning stroke by Turkish Prince Bayazid
sealed the fate of Serbia for the next 500 years...spawning
a legacy that haunts the Balkans even today.*

By David M. Castlewitz

A tomb sits on the Plain of the Blackbirds, near where the rivulet known
as the Lab flows into the Sitnica River. The Serbs call this region Kosovo
Polye. It was the heart of the Serbian Empire for most of the Middle Ages, a
valley of 4,200 square miles surrounded by hills, with Mount Kopaonik to the
north and snowcapped Mount Shar to the south. Today, it lies within the
borders of a truncated and strife-torn Yugoslavia, where Albania, Herzegov-
ina and Macedonia meet.

The quiet tomb on this empty plain is a monument made of brick. Thick
portals of chocolate-colored wood guard the entry, and the building sports
a domed roof, above which is a crescent, symbol of the Muslim Turks who
surged out of Anatolia and westward toward Europe in the 14th century. In
this mausoleum lie the partial remains of Murad I, the Ottoman Sultan who,
in 1389, defeated a Serbian-led Slavic Union intent on defending its homes
and way of life against the invaders from the east. Murad died at Kosovo in
1389, but not before destroying Serbian independence for the next 500 years.

In the early morning hours of St. Vitus Day—June 15, 1389, according to
the old calendar in use at that time, June 28 in the current one—the Serbian
army prepared for battle. The Serbs were camped along the right bank of the
Lab, terrain well suited to heavy cavalry and large infantry formations. The
Serbian left wing was led by *Vojvoda* (Duke) Vlatko Vuković, who had been
sent by King Tvrtko I of Bosnia. The right was commanded by Dimitrije
Vojonović, a Serbian noble. Prince Lazar Hrebeljanović, *knez* (king) of the
Serbs, was in command of the center. His reserve force of infantry was led
by Vuk Branković, the husband of his eldest daughter, Mara.

Assembled in the area of Niš and Kumanovo were the forces of Murad I.
The Ottomans were flushed with pride and fresh from a succession of small
victories in neighboring Bulgaria, where they had crushed Prince Sisman
and extended their rapidly expanding empire as far as the banks of the
Danube River. Sisman, who had sought to save his throne and perhaps regain
the ancient glory of his country, was now Murad's vassal. The Turks seemed
to be unstoppable.

Led by skilled veterans and imbued with a sense of righteousness, these descendants of a tiny band of nomadic tribesmen were poised to knife into the Balkans and inflict a bleeding wound that would fester for centuries. Their leader Murad, 70 years old, had led his warring nation for 30 years, tackling enemies in Asia Minor, penetrating Europe and establishing Adrianople as his capital. A recent defeat at the hands of the Bosnians had not given him pause in his quest for territory, slaves and new citizens to tax. It had only served to whet his appetite for vengeance and conquest.

Serbian Prince Lazar did not want to fight. His army's morale was low. Although Hungary was an ally, he had not had time to garner that powerful kingdom's support against the Turkish invasion. And of his Slavic vassals, many were engaged in local rivalries or withstanding revolts that were tying down reinforcements from the north. There was disharmony even among his generals and nobles. His son-in-law Branković had become embroiled in a feud with Miloš Obilić, the husband of Lazar's younger daughter, Vukosava. The sisters had grown from squabbling children into adult enemies, and now, at the worst of times for Serbia, their husbands had been brought into the fray.

In addition to strife in his own camp, Lazar had to face the fact that potential friends had become his foes. Several Bulgarian and Serbian princes were ready to fight for the Turks. Men like Marko and Andrias, rulers of western Macedonia, became servants to Murad when the Ottoman army swept into Macedonia, Thrace and Bulgaria. Even Prince Sisman, who only the year before had fought Murad, released troops to the invaders, while Byzantine Emperor John Palaeologus supplied the sultan with men from his faltering empire. According to the feudal conventions that ruled the era, such leaders now were pledged to their conquerors. Feudal princes served their lords, not their people.

Lazar tried to take comfort in the knowledge that his union of Slavs was defending Christianity against the onslaught of Islamic conquest. While the Church did not declare his enterprise a holy crusade and attempt to garner more support for Serbia from the rest of Europe, there were many who realized that the Balkans stood as a bulwark against Islamic expansion into Europe proper. Christian Albanian chieftains, closely allied with the Serbs, marched to his banner under the leadership of John Castriota, who had mobilized a volunteer force of combined Serbian and Albanian infantrymen. Some Croatian units, caught up in the crusading fervor, also joined him.

Deep in the memories of some, as well as the songs of the bards, were tales of the Turks' atrocities. When the Ottomans took Thrace in the 1360s, they massacred the defenders of the fortress at Chorlu and decapitated its commander. The act had been calculated to weave fear through the hearts of the Balkan defenders, but it had only served to strengthen their resolve.

On the night before battle, Lazar prepared himself and his followers by offering prayers and toasts of wine served in a golden goblet. He beseeched his fellow countrymen—and the assortment of Albanian tribesmen and Balkan volunteers who had flocked to his army—to be brave and true to their faith, saying to them, "The earthly kingdom is short-lived, but the Heavenly One is forever." Lazar regarded this war with the Turks as Christianity's last chance to defend Eastern Europe against Islam.

Such tragic forboding had not always marked the reign of Prince Lazar. Popular, respected by the Church as well as the Serbian nobility, he had been proclaimed *knez* after King Vukashin died fighting Murad's forces at the Second Battle of Maritza in 1371. In addition to being a skilled soldier and a cultured man, Lazar enjoyed legitimacy as the Serbian ruler due to his marriage to Militza, the great-granddaughter of Stefan Nemanja, founder of the Nemanjić dynasty and the man who had challenged the Byzantine Empire in the late 12th century and won recognition for the independence of his kingdom.

Backed by such support, Lazar fought the Turks wherever they appeared along the Serbian frontier. In 1381, and again in 1386, he thwarted Murad's westward expansion. Tvrtko I, his Bosnian ally, gave further aid to the cause by defeating the Turks when they crossed the Vardar River and entered his territory in 1388. Murad's army was outnumbered, and fully four-fifths of it was destroyed. For the Slavs, that was reason to rejoice. The Turks seemed less than invincible after all.

But the Ottoman forces the Balkan princes had stopped in Bosnia represented more of a reconnaissance-in-force than an army. A man of intelligence and resolution, both a statesman and a strategist, Sultan Murad slowly crafted an efficient war machine. He consolidated his position in Bulgaria's interior and prepared for a much wider war with Serbia. Once he had secured the Bulgarian passes through the Balkan Mountains, he turned again to face Prince Lazar's Slavic Union.

In 1326, during the reign of Sultan Urkhon, the Ottomans gained a foothold in Europe when 80 men crossed the Hellespont on three rafts and attacked the castle of Tzympe, on the peninsula of Gallipoli. The raid was led by Murad's older brother, Sulayman, who was designated to succeed their father, Urkhon, as sultan. In a short time, with the help of an earthquake that the Ottomans interpreted as God's approval of their actions, the Turks secured this strategic site on the Sea of Marmora and held it as their gateway to a greater prize: Eastern Europe.

Three years after the raid on Gallipoli, Sulayman was killed when he fell from his horse. Urkhon received the news with dismay and soon died from grief at the age of 72. Murad, the son of a Greek girl forcibly taken by Urkhon, was anointed supreme lord of the Ottomans.

By the time Murad inherited the Ottoman sultanate, its nearest rival, the once-powerful Byzantine Empire, had been reduced to a crumbling shell of its former self. The Byzantine capital, Constantinople, was rife with civil war.

Thus, the great eastern heir of Imperial Rome was left only in bystander status as the Ottoman Turks marched westward.

According to legend, the Ottomans were descended from a roving warrior band of 400 horsemen led by a tribal chieftain named Ertoghrul, who chose to side with a Seljuk sultan in a skirmish with Mongol marauders sometime in the latter part of the 13th century. Rewarded with land and the gratitude of the Seljuks, Ertoghrul's people settled in Anatolia. After he died in 1288, his son, Osman, took the mantle of leadership and extended his people's rule to the Black Sea and the Bosphorus. The Seljuk presence in Anatolia was crumbling; the Osmanlis, followers of Osman, expertly filled the vacuum.

Enamored with Islam, the Ottomans adopted that religion as their own, blending its martial call with their innate warrior nature. When Murad I, Osman's grandson, ascended to the throne in 1359, the old Byzantine Empire sat closed off in the city of Constantinople, and the entire Anatolian Plain belonged to the Turks. Thessally, Macedonia, and western Thrace would soon be added as a new empire, poised to burst east and west. Fortune, land, slaves and taxes were the Ottomans' prime concerns, with the spread of Islam in the conquered lands almost an afterthought. The Ottomans professed respect for the religions of their conquered peoples. The vanquished, however, sometimes employed conversion to Islam as their best means to evade slavery and punitive taxation.

In 1389, with Bulgaria subdued, Sultan Murad penetrated deeper into the Balkans. He assaulted the Serbian fortress at Niś, where, for 25 days, the Serbs held out with all the heroics of a cornered and desperate people. When Niś fell, Murad received word that Lazar had assembled his army at Kosovo. Immediately seizing this opportunity to crush Serbian resistance in one decisive stroke, Murad marched to meet his enemy. Confident of victory, he ordered that the castles, churches, cities and villages that his armies captured should be left intact, not destroyed. Serbia was a rich and fertile country, and Murad wanted it to be useful for both his vassals and Muslim colonists imported from Asia Minor. Conquering scorched earth would add little to his empire's coffers.

Awaiting the coming battle near the Lab, Murad took counsel from his veteran advisers. He had surrounded himself with skilled strategists who had served him well in previous campaigns. Following advice given by Evrenos Bey, a Greek who commanded the Ottoman army, Murad planned his attack for the dawn hours. Lazar and his nobles, meanwhile, prayed in the Samodrezha Church.

That night, a vile wind whipped the rocky plain. While Lazar admonished his followers to put aside personal quarrels, extinguish their distrust of one another, solidify this union of Slavic peoples and fight for victory, Sultan Murad prayed to God that the evil wind would abate. When morning broke, the air was calm and the Ottoman generals and captains marshaled their soldiers.

Murad commanded the center of the line with his personal guard of cavalry and Jannissaries, the latter being the elite corps of archers and infantry that had begun as the sultan's Imperial Guard and graduated to being one of the most fearsome fighting units in history. All of them were slaves, some born Christians, all the sons of the vanquished who had been taken as children, converted to Islam, and rigorously trained to fight for their sultan.

On the right flank stood Murad's first born son Bayezid, commanding an assortment of Eastern European troops. Murad's other son, Yakub, commanded the Asians who comprised the Ottoman left flank. Two thousand Turkish archers initiated the battle by launching a brutal frontal attack, and the irregular infantry, the *azabs*, were let loose to harass and tire the enemy. Cannons, a European invention, were employed by the Turks for the first time. The cumbersome fieldpieces were made of brass, which became the Ottomans' favorite metal, since they had huge copper deposits in Anatolia and very little iron.

Enduring the punishment hurled at them by the archers and artillery, the Serbs began moving into attack formation. They massed on Murad's left, then struck in one long, undulating wave, as though confident that they could break the onslaught by sheer will. Breaking through Yakub's contingent, they routed the East Europeans, whom they probably considered traitors to the cause of Balkan independence, and then poured into the archers' ranks. A Turkish regiment, boxed in and outmaneuvered, disintegrated.

The Turkish left wing began to crumble, and it looked as if the Serbian assault would indeed carry the day for the Slavic Union. When Bayezid received the news of the disaster on the Turkish left flank, however, he wheeled from the right in a daring counterattack. Known as *Yilderim*— "Lightning"—among the Ottomans, Bayezid dashed into the battle swinging an iron mace while his men struck like a massive hammer at the Serbian flank.

Thwarted by Bayezid's quick-thinking action, the Serbian attack lost its impetus. Battered, the Serbs fell back in disarray, and now victory slipped quickly from their grasp. Seeing that, Lazar's son-in-law Branković either lost his nerve or acted on a plan that had been prearranged with Murad. Taking his 12,000-man reserve with him—including the Croatian contingent, which up to that point had played only a minor role in the battle—he fled the battlefield, leaving Lazar and his loyalists in the proverbial lurch.

The day's battle had ebbed and flowed from Balkan victory to Balkan defeat, but still the Serbs rallied to renew their attack. Prince Lazar personally whipped up enthusiasm and led his demoralized forces on a new foray into the Ottomans' ranks. But his army, disheartened as a body and obviously still facing defeat, dwindled as soldiers died, fell wounded or deserted the cause.

Regardless of his flagging fortunes, Lazar fought on. The night before, sensing that he was surrounded by men who might betray him, he had added a plea for unity to his toasts for victory. Turning to Miloš Obilić, one of his sons-in-law, he had sought assurances of support. Lifting his golden goblet, Lazar had said, "Do not be faithless and take this golden cup from me as a souvenir." Miloš was indignant at the suggestion that he would betray his czar. Now, watching his soldiers desert and knowing that Branković had betrayed him by leaving the field, Lazar learned that Miloš had been seen crossing over to the Ottoman lines.

Serbian morale plummeted. Lazar, wounded, was forced to throw down his sword and surrender, while what remained of his decimated army rapidly withdrew and dispersed across the plain. The war was over. Serbia had lost. Lazar was Murad's prisoner.

According to the chroniclers, the erstwhile czar encountered a dying Miloš when he was taken into the Ottoman camp. Perhaps from his son-in-law, or from a guard, he learned what had happened after Miloš crossed the lines.

Bent on proving his father-in-law wrong as to his loyalty, Miloš had presented himself to Sultan Murad as a traitor and claimed to have information that might help the Ottomans. Because of his high rank, he was ushered into Murad's tent. There, Miloš knelt in submission to kiss the sultan's feet—and then suddenly he whipped out a concealed dagger and stabbed Murad twice in the chest. Ali Pasha, one of Murad's advisers, tried to intervene and was struck dead with the same weapon. Unable to escape, Miloš lunged at his angry captors and was quickly cut down. The outraged Turks then left him to die from his wounds.

As a result of Miloš' double deception, Murad's abdomen was cut open from roughly his groin to his chest. Yet still the 70-year-old campaigner grimly clung to life, while his physicians put his intestines back in his stomach and bound the terrible wound in a sheepskin. Murad knew he would not recover, but he was determined to stay alive long enough to have the satisfaction of seeing his enemies die before he did.

Prince Lazar, on learning of Miloš' heroics, gave the man his blessing before being led to the dying sultan, whose final act in this short war was to condemn Lazar and the other captured Serbian nobles to death. The czar would be the first to die, although Lazar's nobles begged to be beheaded first, thus assuring their sovereign a few more minutes of life. The request was denied and Murad's son Bayezid prepared to carry out his father's orders.

One of Lazar's followers, Krajimir of Toplicta, asked to be allowed to hold his robe open under Lazar so the czar's head would not touch the ground as it fell. Bayezid responded to that expression of loyalty with his permission. Assembled outside Murad's tent, the Serbs awaited execution, and Lazar turned to his nobles to offer a final farewell. As he began to speak, the Turks roughly pushed him to his knees, but before the sword struck his neck, Lazar managed to utter, "My God, receive my soul."

Soon after all the captured nobles had been beheaded, Murad succumbed at last to his own wounds. Bayezid, as the eldest son, was proclaimed sultan of the Ottomans. To counter possible civil strife or rivalry, he took his brother Yakub prisoner and had him strangled with a bowstring, thereby assuring that no rival descendant could counter his claim to their father's throne. That act of fratricide—perhaps impetuous, perhaps born from the knowledge that his brother was a popular commander who enjoyed the personal loyalty of his troops—began an Ottoman tradition that doomed a sultan's younger sons for generations thereafter.

Secure now in his position as the victor of Kosovo and sultan of the Turks, Bayezid felt that he could afford to be gracious. He allowed the Serbs to retrieve Lazar's head—that and the body were conducted to Prishtina and laid to rest at the Church of Vaznesenje Hristovo. Lazar's son Stephen, one of the few nobles to have escaped the Turks, sought and was granted terms of surrender from Bayezid. Serbia was not incorporated into the Ottoman Empire as a nameless Turkish province, or *sandjak*; instead, it became a vassal state, with all the privileges and responsibilities that vassalage imposed. Stephen paid the Ottomans taxes, provided soldiers for the sultan's army and became the Turks' first line of defense against a possibly resurgent Christian Eastern Europe. He also surrendered his sister Olivera, and Bayezid took her as a personal prize, adding the princess to his harem.

Where Murad was killed, the Turks eventually built a tomb and enshrined the fallen sultan by depositing his intestines in a coffin. The body was conducted back to Turkey, to the town of Broussa. Two Serbian nobles were forced to join the escort. When the body was laid to rest, they were executed by decapitation.

Bayezid soon after returned with his army to Asia Minor and fought a series of campaigns designed to enlarge the empire. In 1396, he destroyed a Western crusading army, jointly led by Burgundian Count Jean de Nevers and Hungarian Emperor Sigismund, at Nicopolis. A decisive factor in Bayezid's victory was the cavalry provided by his newly acquired vassal, Serbia. Bayezid also succeeded in dominating nearly all of Anatolia but was unsuccessful in his siege of Constantinople, the last Christian outpost in his domain. That setback was followed by a deeper tragedy, an incursion by Timur-i-Lenk (better known in the West as Tamerlane), whose Islamic Tatar empire bordered the Ottomans' on the east. To keep Bayezid from encroaching on his holdings, Tamerlane invaded Anatolia, and on July 20, 1402, he outmaneuvered and routed the Turkish army at Ankara. Sultan Bayezid was captured, imprisoned in a wagon with iron bars, and forced to accompany the victorious army and endure the humiliation of seeing his harem (including Olivera) in Tamerlane's hands. Finally, according to some accounts, Bayezid took poison and died.

Lazar's wife, Militza, meanwhile, had sought refuge in religion. She became a nun, renouncing the material world for a life of solitude and prayer. She was joined by a companion, Princess Euphemia, whose husband had been killed by the Turks in an earlier battle. An embroideress of great talent, Euphemia spent her time in the convent fashioning a pall to drape upon Lazar's body where the severed head rested against the neck.

To the Dechani Monastery, the largest of Serbia's medieval churches, Militza gave a unique gift. It was a giant candle that she said should be lit only when the defeat at Kosovo had been avenged. More than 500 years had to pass before Serbian King Peter Karadjordjević I fulfilled her wish, in 1913, although Serbia had finally been established as an independent kingdom 35 years before that, by the Treaty of Berlin in 1878.

Eventually the Serbian Church declared Czar Lazar a saint and a martyr, and his remains were moved to the Ravanicsa Monastery. Meanwhile, Muslims swarmed into Serbia and Bosnia and established colonies. When the Turks moved into northern Serbia, Lazar was disinterred and removed to Srem, which was in Hungary. Then, in 1941, in response to the pilfering and desecration of Serbian national shrines by the Nazi-supported independent state of Croatia, Czar Lazar was taken to rest at the altar of an Orthodox cathedral in Belgrade. The long-dead prince currently lies in a robe of faded red and gold brocade. A cloth, the one embroidered by Euphemia, hides the gap where his head is separated from his neck. His hands, black and mummified, are crossed over his loins. His feet have shrunken. They are encased in modern stockings and fitted into medieval boots of blue silk, woven with gold thread.

Less than 40 years after gaining its independence, Serbia would again be overrun by invaders. The assassination of Austrian Archduke Franz Ferdinand Sarajevo in 1914 led to a world war many times more devastating and treacherous than the great war that Lazar Hrebeljanović had fought.

More recently, the legacy of Kosovo continues to haunt the Balkans in the form of recurring ethnic hatred between the Serbs and those southern Slavs who still practice the Muslim faith of the Turkish invaders—a bitter blood feud that has outlived the Ottoman occupation to the present day. Kosovo itself would be the scene of later battles and civil disturbances throughout those bitter centuries.

Empire's Sun Eclipsed

Spain's peerless tercios, *or infantry,*
kept their fierce reputation intact at Rocroi —
but died in so doing when they were outmaneuvered
by Louis II Bourbon, duc *d'Enghien*

By Timothy Baker Shutt

The dawning weather was clear and mild in the fields and woods south of Rocroi, three miles from the border of the Spanish Netherlands and northern France. The sun shone low and golden through the new leaves, and the fresh grass was heavy with dew.

But the French commander, Louis II de Bourbon, *duc* d'Enghien, was apprehensive anyway. Five days before, his sovereign, Louis XIII of France, had died after a reign of 33 years. To make matters worse, in the previous December, Cardinal Richelieu, the diplomatic bulwark of the Bourbon throne, had passed to whatever heavenly reward awaited a religious adviser so unscrupulously secular—and so canny. Louis XIV, the new king, would eventually lead France to glory, but in 1643, Louis XIV was only 5 years old. The government, such as it was, lay in the hands of Richelieu's handpicked successor, Giulio Raimondo Mazzarino—a k a Cardinal Mazarin—and the hands of Anne of Austria, Louis XIV's redoubtable Spanish mother. It remained to be seen, however, whether their power would find acceptance.

Enghien, for one, felt nervous enough about their prospects that, with a battle imminent, he did not tell his troops of their king's death. He had with him on that bright morning of May 19, 1643, 7,000 horse and 15,000 foot— ordinarily a sturdy enough contingent, and all the more so since under the impetus of the late Richelieu's recent reforms, the French army had improved rapidly. But before them lay 26,000 troops under the command of Francisco de Melo, among them 8,000 Spanish *tercios*, the pride of the Hapsburgs, and for more than a century the most feared and effective infantrymen in the world—victors in Italy, in the Netherlands, victors at Lepanto and in the Philippines, conquerors of Mexico and of Peru.

De Melo had begun the year's campaigning by crossing over from Spanish Flanders to invest the fortified town of Rocroi. Enghien's task was simple—to lift the siege—and the previous day he had already successfully weathered two potential crises. To approach his chosen field of battle, he had led his troops through a series of narrow woodland paths, courting ambush and disaster in the hope of luring de Melo from his position for a quick double-outflanking movement on the town of Rocroi itself. De Melo had not fallen for the bait, but neither had he surprised Enghien on unfavorable terrain. Enghien, accordingly, was able, on the afternoon of May 18, to deploy his troops on his chosen ground, skillfully screening his infantry with his cavalrymen.

Once the French arrangements were complete, however, Enghien again found himself in extreme peril. As the shadows lengthened and Enghien prepared his attack, the *Comte* de Senneterre, commanding the French left, decided on his own initiative to bypass the Spaniards altogether and swept off into a flanking swamp in an effort to angle toward Rocroi itself. De Melo was gleefully preparing to strike when the irate Enghien recalled Senneterre and, as the dusk deepened, covered his retreat.

Despite the season, it was a long night as the armies waited in position—waited for the dawn and the certain clash that would follow. Impetuous and strong-willed as he was, Enghien would have been more than human had he not suffered from some misgivings. He had, after all, never before served as a commander—no matter how high Richelieu's opinion of him had been, no matter how eminent his family, and no matter how favorable the omens (shortly before his death, Louis XIII had awakened from a fitful sleep to tell the young duke's father that he had dreamed that Enghien had won "a great victory"). More to the point, perhaps, the *Duc* d'Enghien was only 21 years old.

Even people who pride themselves upon their knowledge of European history tend to get a little hazy when the Thirty Years' War is mentioned. The name itself reveals that the affair was difficult and prolonged. And—thanks perhaps to the efforts of German playwright Berthold Brecht and Mother Courage and Her Children—many readers know that it was bloody. So indeed it was—and like the most savage kinds of modern warfare, as rough on civilians as on soldiers. In the 1600s, commissariat arrangements were crude, and armies generally fed themselves on plunder and pillage. A campaign or two was quite enough to depopulate a district, and over the course of the Thirty Years' War many parts of what is now Germany, where most of the fighting took place, lost more than half their people. But who was fighting whom, and what was everybody fighting about? That is what is confusing.

It must have confused people at the time, too, because between 1618, when hostilities started, and 1648, when the Treaty of Westphalia finally put an end to the fighting, both the parties involved and the issues at stake had changed almost entirely—had changed, in fact, several times.

It all started out relatively simply as a quarrel about who should be King of Bohemia, the western portion of modern Czechoslovakia—a Roman Catholic or a Protestant. Ferdinand II, the Hapsburg Holy Roman Emperor and an ardent Catholic, had a splendid candidate in mind—himself—and duly ascended the throne. But a Bohemian revolt installed the Protestant Frederick

V, Elector of the Palatine, in his place. Frederick V was well-connected—his wife was the daughter of James I of England—and many Protestants hoped he could make a go of things, but, in November 1620, his troops were thrashed by the forces of the Catholic League under the able (and admirable) General Johann Tserclaes, Count Tilly, at the Battle of White Mountain. Frederick and his wife hurriedly left Prague. All clear enough thus far.

Then, for a while, the conflict expanded into what amounted to a Europe-wide Catholic-Protestant holy war, intermixed all the while with Imperial politics. The Danes, under King Christian IV, intervened and won for a time. The Swedes intervened, under the leadership of King Gustavus II Adolphus, and won even more consistently and decisively. At Breitenfeld in 1631, the Swedish rapid volley and field artillery so convincingly bested the Imperial forces that for the moment the war seemed won for the Protestant side.

But the next year at Lützen, the great Gustavus was killed, and though his forces fought on to victory, inspired by their leader's fall, their offensive impetus was spent. Over the long haul, under the leadership of the amoral but chillingly capable General Albrecht von Wallenstein, the Catholic side had gained ground, despite the successes of the Swedes and Danes. More to the point, perhaps, the Catholic House of Hapsburg had gained ground.

By a combination of judicious marriage, successful exploration and simple fighting, the Hapsburgs entered the 17th century easily the most powerful dynasty in Europe. One branch of the family ruled the Spanish Empire, which included, besides the Americas and the Philippines (and more silver than anyone had thought existed), much of the Netherlands as well. The other ruled Austria and controlled the Holy Roman Empire.

Catholic or not, the success of the Hapsburgs began to make Bourbon France uneasy. The Netherlands lay to the north, the Holy Roman Empire to the east, and Spain to the south—Hapsburg dominions all. The Bourbons felt surrounded and threatened. And so, in 1635, in the 17th year of the conflict, Catholic France came into the war on the Protestant side—not to preserve Protestantism (which would soon, in fact, be illegal in France), but rather to contain the power of Spain and Austria.

Meanwhile, the Empire, the Swedes and various German states on both sides continued a war that more or less resembled the original conflict. But from 1635, the Bourbon-Hapsburg conflict was decisive. And that, of course, was what had drawn both de Melo and Enghien to the French frontier citadel of Rocroi.

Seventeenth-century warfare was more a matter of sieges than of maneuver—the development of the so-called *trace italienne* in the late Renaissance had rendered strong points almost impregnable to direct assault—and far too powerful to ignore. As a result, military campaigns hinged on the result of lengthy investments, and pitched battles occurred most often between besiegers and would-be relief columns. So at Rocroi, de Melo and his troops were prepared to fight Enghien, but their main business was taking the defenses behind them. Before they could continue the siege, however, they had to dispose of Enghien. It would not prove an easy task.

As dawn gave way to day on May 19, Enghien made the first move. The Hapsburg troops were deployed a mile or so southwest of Rocroi itself, blocking Enghien's advance, the line of battle extending from the northwest to the southeast. There was a swamp on the Spanish right and a small spur of woodland on the left separating the Spanish and the French. De Melo had placed cavalry detachments on both these flanks, taking personal control of the right wing and leaving the left to the leadership of the Duke of Albuquerque. In the Hapsburg center, the Flemish general the *Comte* de Fontaine commanded three lines of infantry—Walloons, Italians and Germans in the rear, and in front the celebrated *tercios*, the pride of Spain and the terror of infidels and heretics everywhere. It was a formidable formation.

Enghien's deployment matched that of his opponents. The cavalry on the French left opposite de Melo; the French infantry stood in the center opposite the *tercios* and Fontaine; and Enghien's cavalry, on the right, opposed the Duke of Albuquerque, hidden for the moment behind a fringe of trees.

The day before, Albuquerque had deployed a skirmish line of musketeers in the woods to give him advance warning of Enghien's intentions, and now, shortly after dawn, Enghien brushed them aside and mounted a two-pronged attack on Albuquerque's position, Enghien himself charging head-on, and his subordinate the *Comte* de Gassion taking the Spaniards on the flank. For a time the Spanish troopers held the surging Frenchmen at bay, but soon the Hapsburg line began to buckle.

It was the decisive moment of the battle. De Melo, meanwhile, was more than holding his own against the French left flank. There, Enghien's Lieutenant François l'Hopital had mounted a charge at the same time as Enghien, but had met with far less success. De Melo's cavalry had held, and as Enghien looked across the melee, he saw the Spaniards driving their disordered French counterparts back. Reserves were on the way—perhaps the left might advance after all—but l'Hopital and Senneterre were clearly in trouble.

And in the center, the French infantry, despite Richelieu's reforms, was proving no match for Flemish General Fontaine's Spanish veterans. Slowly, foot by foot, the Frenchmen were beginning to fall back, barely even holding their own. They could not withstand the Spanish much longer.

Enghien's corner of the battle was effectively won, but the rest of the army was hard-pressed. He was in danger of losing the field despite his personal triumph. What was the young commander to do? He paused for a moment as the smoke of battle swirled around him, and at once the answer was clear. Discharging Gassion to pursue Albuquerque's routed cavalry, he began to cut his way through the Hapsburg infantry, to make his way to l'Hopital's side. The *tercios*' hands were already full, fighting the French before them. They could not stop him. They did not try to. And Enghien sliced quickly between the less-experienced Walloon and Italian lines behind the *tercios*.

De Melo's cavalrymen, now in hot pursuit of Senneterre and l'Hopital, were suddenly overtaken from behind. Nonplussed and confronted by enemies both in the front and to the rear, the Spanish held briefly, then fled into the swampland to the northwest.

Thus it was that the *tercios*—all 8,000, less the relatively few casualties already inflicted, and still undefeated thus far—suddenly found themselves alone on the field, with nothing but their tradition and mettle to support them, and nothing to do but hold on in the ever-diminishing hope of reinforcements. They did the best they could.

The French infantry mounted an attack. Spanish volleys crushed it. Enghien ordered his cavalry to join in. The *tercios* drove the French back again. Enghien redeployed and drove forward. Again the Spaniards held. And again. And yet once again.

By now it was late afternoon; the Hapsburg army had been dismembered for hours, both wings long since reduced to scattered fragments. But still its Spanish heart beat on. Tired, bloodied, outnumbered and hopeless, abandoned by all of their comrades, the *tercios* held their ground.

At length, however, Enghien's commanders Gassion and Senneterre returned from pursuit of the broken Hapsburg cavalry. The remaining Spanish infantrymen now found themselves entirely surrounded. Their commander Fontaine was already dead, and their losses had been severe. As Enghien prepared for a final attack, the few remaining Spanish officers decided that honor had been satisfied and signaled for a truce.

Enghien was more than willing to grant one. The field was already his, and the *tercios* had fought gloriously—no point in killing more of them or in sacrificing his own troops. As he rode forward to parley, however, a few of the Spanish, unaware of the truce, suddenly opened fire in the belief that the final assault had begun. And so, in fact, it had—if only because of their own volley. The irate Frenchmen swarmed over their position, aflame with anger at what they saw as Spanish treachery. Enghien tried to stem the tide, but it was no use. The exhausted Spaniards called in vain for quarter, but had to fight on. Enghien was able to save only the few who were able to work their way through the melee and surrender to him in person.

As the shadows lengthened, however, the guns at last fell silent, swords were sheathed and the shouting stopped. There was no one left on the field to kill—and Spain was a military giant no more. At dawn, 18,000 Hapsburg infantrymen had manned the lines. By nightfall, 8,000 were dead, most of the *tercios* among them, and 7,000 had been captured.

Rocroi did not end the Thirty Years' War. The fighting dragged on for five more years. And it did not end what historian Geoffrey Parker called the "other thirty years war" between Spain and France, which continued intermittently until the Battle of the Dunes and the Treaty of the Pyrenees in 1659. But it did mark the end of Spain as a first-class world power.

The Spanish Empire was the first upon which the sun never set, and from shortly after 1492, when Ferdinand and Isabella took Granada and Columbus discovered the New World, until Rocroi in 1643, Spain had been the most powerful nation on earth. There had been problems, of course: the very wealth of the New World had flooded Spain with so much silver and driven prices in Spain so high that Spanish agriculture and industry (such as it was) began to wither. Spain could, by the end, produce nothing that could not be made more cheaply elsewhere. The Spanish taxation system was a disaster, and Spain defaulted on her loans so frequently that borrowing became a very costly alternative. The Spanish monarchy was consistently forced to pay exorbitant interest rates. Catalonia was chronically rebellious, and in 1640 Spain lost Portugal (and more important, Portugal's colonies). But despite such difficulties, until 1643, Spanish arms had proven capable of taking up the slack.

That is what made Rocroi such a disaster for Spain. The Spanish infantry had represented the backbone of Spanish greatness, and the final bloodbath at Rocroi left no remnant from which to rebuild. The *tercios* were gone. There was no one left even to train their replacements. As C.V. Wedgwood observed, they had not lost their reputation—they remained formidable troops to the end—"but they had died to keep it." And, old, powerful Spain had died with them.

The mantle of supremacy passed to the French. And they, when their 5-year-old monarch achieved his majority, would begin their own "splendid century" under the leadership of the "Sun King," Louis XIV.

The *Duc* d'Enghien, who upon the death of his father inherited the title of Prince de Condé in December 1646, would contribute many more victories to France's rise, earning the sobriquet of "The Great Condé."

Soon after the conclusion of the Thirty Years' War, the issue of how to pay for it set political forces in motion in France that led to a rebellion of the nobility known to history as the *Fronde*. Condé participated, and in 1652 Mazarin, the de facto regent, ordered his arrest. Ironically enough, Condé deserted to Spain, and until the late 1650s proffered his services to the Spanish crown, fighting French armies under the command of his erstwhile partner in arms, the equally gifted Henri de la Tour d'Auvergne, *vicomte* de Turenne. After several engagements between these two great captains, the question of who was the better tactician was decided on June 14, 1658, when Turenne defeated Condé in the Battle of the Dunes near Dunkirk.

At the conclusion of the French-Spanish conflict, however, in 1659, Louis XIV married the Spanish *infanta* Maria Theresa, and Condé was pardoned.

Once again, he took to the field—in the War of Revolution and the Dutch War—and ably served his forgiving sovereign as late as 1675. But never better than he had on that May morning 32 years before, when in an instant he decided to cut his way across the Hapsburg center, and in so doing put to rest what Richelieu had termed "the unbridled ambition of Spain," and accordingly laid the military foundation of the golden age of France.

Charge Signaled by Thunderclap

*At Marston Moor in 1644, the decisive victory
by Oliver Cromwell's Roundheads
doomed the Royalist cause.*

By John Woolford

A great change had come to the English Civil War in 1644. For a start, with the Scots and the Irish now brought into the fray, it ceased to be exclusively English. Many familiar faces, amateurs at war, were gone. But German-born Prince Rupert of Brunswick, the king's nephew, was still there for King Charles I, recruiting and training forces on the Welsh border, and Robert Devereux, 3rd Earl of Essex, still guarded London with an army that denied Rupert's aspirations of conquest while itself being unable to conquer.

In December 1643, Sir Ralph Hopton, the most successful Royalist general next to Rupert, had been turned back from Arundel in Sussex and from Alresford in Hampshire. By now Hopton's magnificent Cornish infantry, which had stormed the heights of Lansdowne Hill and had held the defenseless town of Devizes in that hopeful summer of 1643, had returned home. The campaigns of both sides had stalled in the south.

Control of the House of Commons was in the hands of younger, harder men, such as Oliver St. John and Sir Henry Vane the Younger. Vane had negotiated Scotland's entry into the war, and 20,000 men were about to march into England to preserve Scotland from English prelates and to impose Presbyterianism on England—or so they thought.

Oliver Cromwell, that superbly efficient amateur soldier of the Eastern Counties who in a few months had made himself into a thorough professional, had the spiritual force to make himself master of his regiments of cavalry, and then to make his regiments the masters of the armies of Parliament. In a few years he would rule England, and under him Britain would become the master of America's eastern seaboard as well as an equal and sometimes feared voice in the councils of Europe.

"Few indeed loved his government," wrote the historian Thomas Macaulay nearly two centuries later, "but those who hated it most hated it less than they feared it. Had it been a worse government, it might perhaps have been overthrown in spite of all its strength. Had it been a weaker government, it would certainly have been overthrown in spite of all its merits.

119

But it had moderation enough to abstain from those oppressions which drive men mad; and it had a force and energy which none but men driven mad by oppression would venture to encounter."

Yet Cromwell, who became a military dictator with the power of a king, though he spurned the title of king, came from the class of small gentry that was often on the side of Charles in the Civil War. An uncle of Cromwell's had entertained James VI of Scotland in 1603 when that Stuart monarch was on the way to London to accept the English crown as King James I. In the 1620s, Cromwell became a not very prominent member of the House of Commons. In the 1630s, he supported his cousin, John Hampden, in his resistance to the Ship Money Tax, which was imposed by King Charles without Parliamentary approval. A poor speaker who tended to ramble, the unprepossessing Cromwell was nevertheless picked out by Hampden as likely to become "the greatest man in England" if war should come. Cromwell's utter conviction that he had sought and found the will of God impressed his listeners far more than his speaking ability or appearance.

Cromwell had been at the Battle of Edgehill on October 23, 1642, and became convinced that Parliament should recruit for its cavalry God-fearing men with a spiritual certainty that would enable them to prevail against the "men of honour" to be found fighting for the Royalists. Mere "serving men and tapsters," he told Hampden, would never do.

He showed great energy in the recruiting of cavalry to fight under Earl Edward Montagu of Manchester in the Eastern Counties Association, and he was largely responsible for turning back the southward movement of Marquis William Cavendish of Newcastle's forces at Winceby in Lincolnshire on October 10, 1643.

Colonel Cromwell's regiment of horse soon swelled to 1,400 strong. He trained his men to charge at a "good round trot," although they also must have belted in at full gallop as contact was made. His troopers wore leather jackets that were often covered by armor. They were drilled to pull up on command after a charge so that Cromwell could regroup them and charge again if need be. Rupert's men, following the more traditional battle tactic of the day, would tear through the enemy like dogs jumping through a hoop and then return to the battlefield so exhausted they could hardly charge again. At Naseby in 1645, they drove the rebel horse clean off the field, kept going, then returned to find the rest of the battle was lost. At Marston Moor, by contrast, Cromwell's men were able to make two separate charges on different parts of the field. It was a new degree of battlefield discipline that Rupert never mastered.

Cromwell's inspired leadership in 1643 was a portent of the increasingly powerful role he would come to play in succeeding events, his drive fueled by the religious conversion some years before that had led him to believe in a personal God who spoke to his servant, Oliver Cromwell. Cromwell was a true Puritan Independent, believing that each person should find his own way to God, just as he had. The Independents were to become the rulers of England after the war—to the disgust of the Presbyterians—and Cromwell's soldiers were to be known for their preaching officers, who soon had an immense influence over their fiercely Protestant men. Puritans, who were strong in trade and commerce, and who were thus literate enough to read the Bible, provided an ever-present recruiting ground for Cromwell's forces. The Royalists rightly feared the Puritans, but they did not fully understand the group's potential influence.

In contrast to Cromwell, the man of certainty, King Charles gave his generals no proper directive for 1644. Instead, he thrashed about in all directions, calling a Parliament to assemble in Oxford; negotiating with the Scots through the Duke of Hamilton and with the Scottish Royalists through James Graham, the Marquis of Montrose; urging his lord deputy in Ireland, the Earl of Ormonde, to conclude a treaty with the Catholic Confederacy, thus releasing Protestant troops to serve in England; negotiating behind Ormonde's back for a Catholic army; and negotiating (using his wife, Henrietta Maria, as intermediary) with any European country that might help him.

The assembling of 200 members of the Parliament at Oxford created a serious rival government to the House of Commons in London, which had trouble raising more than 200 members itself once war had begun. The Oxford Parliament was joined by the bulk of the House of Lords, leaving rebellious London's upper house with a mere 25 or so members.

Charles' other bright ideas came to very little. No European aid reached the king. The Irish negotiations remained a hopeless muddle, and the thousands of Irish soldiers that Charles wanted would remain quite remote and useless. Hamilton's pleadings with the Scots were in vain, and even though Montrose had scored a series of remarkable victories for the Royalists in 1644-46 (at Tippermuir, Inverlochy, etc.), he was unable to shift the political weight of the stubborn northern kingdom.

In the spring of 1644, the Scots under Earl Alexander Leslie of Leven were besieging Newcastle and had sent patrols as far south as Durham. Blocked in Lincolnshire by Cromwell and the Earl of Manchester, the northern Royalists under the Marquis of Newcastle retreated to the walled city of York. Much of the cavalry was sent out to ride for Newark, where it reinforced a Royalist garrison that never surrendered until ordered to by Charles in 1646. Some 5,000 men were retained to defend York. Around York there eventually gathered three Roundhead (Parliamentary) armies: that of Lord Fairfax, which had been driven to take refuge in Hull during the Royalist successes of 1643; the Scots, except the portion besieging Newcastle; and Manchester's troops of the Eastern Counties Association.

While the Royalist situation worsened in the north, in March Rupert suddenly curved across the middle of England to Newark, where he forced the surrender of 6,000 Parliamentary troops besieging the place under Sir John Meldrum. The whole of Lincolnshire again fell to the Royalists.

The news from Newark brought new urgency to the deliberations of the Parliamentary Committee of the Two Kingdoms, which was trying to direct the war from Westminster. Cromwell called up all the men he could muster and then firmly held East Anglia. Rupert returned to Oxford and next, in May, headed for Lancashire, where he intended to pick off Parliamentary garrisons before marching to the relief of York.

On May 6, the Earl of Manchester stormed Lincoln before leaving with Cromwell to join the siege of York. On the other side of the Pennines, Rupert took Stockport on May 25, and Bolton three days later. At Bolton, 1,600 Roundheads were killed and the town was savagely sacked in reprisal (typical in the 17th century) for refusing to surrender. Early in June, Rupert was in Liverpool, now joined by Lord George Goring and the Newark cavalry. Rupert measured the strength he would need to help relieve York, but he intended to take the town of Manchester first. Other events now impinged upon the campaign.

Rupert had worked out a plan to defend Oxford with outlying garrisons, backed by a reserve of cavalry held in Oxford that could go to the help of any garrison that was in danger. At the urging of the notoriously unstable Sir John Digby, Charles abandoned Reading and Abingdon, which were promptly occupied by the Earl of Essex and Sir William Waller. Charles bolted out of Oxford with 3,000 cavalry on June 2 and headed for Evesham. Digby admitted later that "had Essex and Waller either pursued us or attacked Oxford, we had been lost."

Fortunately for Charles, Essex marched for the southwest in an attempt to occupy Cornwall, a departure that allowed Charles to turn on Waller at Cropedy Bridge and win a substantial victory on June 29. However, Charles was disconcerted enough to have written a letter to Rupert on June 14 from Bewdley that caused Rupert to break off his Lancashire campaign and march for York.

"If York be lost," said Charles, "I shall esteem my crown little less, unless supported by your sudden march to me, and a miraculous conquest in the South before the effects of the Northern power can be found here."

Charles meant, in effect, that if York were lost, there would still be hope for him if Rupert could join him and write off the Roundhead forces in the south before the "Northern power"—the Scots and others—could come to their aid.

The letter went on: "But if York be relieved, and you beat the rebel armies of both Kingdoms which were before it—then, but otherwise not, I may possibly make a shift upon the defensive to spin out time until you come to assist me; wherefore I command and conjure you…that, all new enterprises laid aside, you immediately march according to your first intention, with all your force, to the relief of York."

By this convoluted sentence (which gives us a glimpse of his muddle-headedness) Charles implied that he could hold on in the south until Rupert had relieved York and won a great battle. He befuddled the issue with the three words "but otherwise not," which suggested that if Rupert could not relieve York and "beat the rebel armies," then Charles could not "spin out time" in the south. That did not square with the earlier suggestion that all might be well if Rupert could march south "before the effects of the Northern power can be found here."

Rupert probably knew that Charles had no idea how to frame clear instructions, so he did the only thing possible—he marched out of Preston on June 23 to cross the Pennines on the way to York.

Cromwell and his lieutenants knew Rupert was at Knaresborough on June 30. On July 1, they faced west along the York-Knaresborough road, pulling some of their forces back over the bridge of boats at Poppleton. They soon realized that they had not adequately anticipated the enemy's movements.

Rupert shot across the map like a line on a graph, crossing the Ure at Boroughbridge and the Swale at Thornton Bridge before dropping to the south, with the Ouse River protecting his right flank. That night, he seized the bridge of boats at Poppleton and sent his messengers into York over the very trenches the Roundheads had so speedily abandoned. His infantry had marched more than 20 miles that day; the cavalry had ridden even farther. It was a remarkable piece of strategy, but the advantage gained was to be negated within a few hours.

The Roundheads drew off toward Tadcaster to guard the route to Newark and the south. Horse and foot were strung out like stretched elastic as Rupert's men began to appear behind them on Marston Moor at dawn on July 2.

Rupert had snatched a few hours of sleep in the Forest of Galtres. He then sent a peremptory message to the Marquis of Newcastle demanding he be present with his forces on the moor at 4 a.m. Newcastle replied by saying he was "made of nothing but thankfulness and obedience to your Highness's commands," but not until 9 a.m. did he arrive with a small party. "My Lord, I wish you had come sooner with your forces," said Rupert dolefully, "but I hope we shall yet have a glorious day."

Newcastle was a patrician who had been born in 1592; he was a learned man—John Dryden and Ben Jonson were among his friends in the course of his 84 years—but he made no claim to being a great general. "He loved monarchy," wrote Sir Edward Hyde, "as it was the foundation and support of his own greatness; and the Church, as it was well constituted for the splendour and security of the Crown; and religion, as it cherished and maintained that order and obedience that was necessary to both." (In contrast, the 60-year-old Earl of Leven, the Scots commander, was said to be almost illiterate, although he held a Swedish knighthood.)

Newcastle's military adviser was James King, Lord Eythin, who had been with Rupert in 1638 at Lemgo in Germany when Rupert was taken prisoner. Eythin had not covered himself with glory then, and now Newcastle was faced with the fact that the 25-year-old nephew of King Charles was his Royalist commander.

At Gloucester and again at Newbury in 1643, Rupert had been balked and overruled. At Newark, he had been his own boss. Now once again his plans were thwarted by powerful older men. Newcastle was not going to meet Rupert—an upstart half his age—on a moor at 4 a.m., forsooth! Nine o'clock was a much more civilized hour, and even that was earlier than he was used to.

Lord Eythin made no attempt to get his men moving that morning of July 2. When he did turn up that afternoon, he grumbled to Rupert that a plan of battle was all very well, "but there is no such thing in the field."

Somewhere around midday, the Roundheads realized the Royalists were gathering on Marston Moor, and they frantically began giving ground. Rupert contemplated sending his cavalry to swirl among the disordered enemy, but presumably felt he was not strong enough to withstand a counterattack without the support of Newcastle's men. He hesitated and settled for watching while Cromwell, Manchester, Leven and the Fairfaxes moved their forces into battle order. His hesitation was to lose the war.

Many similarities come to mind between Marston Moor and the battle that decided another civil war two centuries later: Gettysburg. The Confederate commander, Robert E. Lee, had lost his great deputy, Lt. Gen. T. J. "Stonewall" Jackson, at Chancellorsville, despite winning the battle. At Lansdown, the Royalists had won the battle, but had lost the incomparable Sir Bevil Grenvile, who, if he had lived, might have become to Rupert what Jackson could have been to Lee. At Gettysburg, the Confederates would fail to seize the commanding heights as they arrived on the field and then would delay the great assault that might have shattered the Union. The man filling Jackson's role, Lt. Gen. James Longstreet, is often blamed for the South's defeat. At Marston Moor, Eythin prevented the prompt assembly of the Royalists when they could have destroyed the scattered Roundheads with ease. At 4 p.m. the Royalists were finally ready for battle—but by then so were the Parliamentarians.

"Is Cromwell there?" Rupert asked a Parliamentary straggler who had been taken prisoner earlier that day. Cromwell was indeed present, with 2,500 cavalry, backed by a reserve of 800 Scots on Parliament's left.

Rupert had about 17,000 men. On his right were some 2,600 cavalry under Maj. Gen. Sir John Urry (or Hurry), a many-time deserter from both sides. It is strange that on this vital day he was Rupert's main cavalry commander, but he did his work professionally, interspersing blocks of 50 musketeers with the squadrons of horse. This was a popular Swedish idea, intended to break up an enemy charge before it came within sword-slashing range. Lord John Byron commanded the first line, and Lord Moly-neaux the second. There was no reserve, apart from Rupert's personal guard of "Bluecoats."

In the Royalist center were Newcastle's "Whitecoats," so-called because of their coats of undyed wool. These were the men who had borne the brunt of the fighting for York, and this day they would die by the thousand for a lost cause. On the left was Lord George Goring's cavalry of some 2,000 to 3,000 men. Goring was a heavy drinker who did not get along with the other Royalist leaders, but at Marston Moor he nearly won the battle.

In the Parliamentary center were six infantry brigades in the first line, two each under Manchester and Lord Fairfax, and another two of Scots under Lt. Gen. William Baillie. In the second line, all the infantry were Scots except for another of Manchester's brigades. On the right were 2,000 or 3,000 cavalry under Sir Thomas Fairfax, son of Ferdinando, 2nd Baron Fairfax.

The Roundheads had about 23,000 men, according to recent research, not the 27,000 once reported. They certainly outnumbered the Royalists, but not so much that Rupert, after being reinforced by the York garrison, was afraid to meet the enemy.

The two armies were only 400 yards apart, separated by a ditch and the track running from the village of Long Marston to Tockwith. Along the Parliamentary front were 25 cannons, which were irritating rather than murderous. The most efficient artillery of the time was the large siege cannon, which was too cumbersome for battlefield use.

After the Roundheads had chanted their evening psalms, it was thought there would be no fighting that day. The Parliamentary infantry stood in a field of wet rye. Just after 7 p.m. there was a shower of rain, and Rupert went off to have his dinner. "We'll charge them in the morning," he said to Newcastle, who retired to his coach to smoke a pipe. At 7:30 p.m. a thunderclap smote their ears, and, as if on signal, Cromwell charged.

We do not know what Cromwell had said at a hurried conclave on Marston Hill a little earlier, but now the entire Roundhead army moved forward, "like unto so many thick clouds," as Manchester's chaplain Simeon Ash put it. A Roundhead participant in the charge described the onrush of the left wing: "In a moment we were past the ditch into the moor, upon equal grounds with the enemy, our men going in a running march."

From these descriptions it appears Cromwell's horse hit the enemy in well-ordered squadrons. There was no sudden tearing through the enemy, as Rupert so loved to do. By unified weight they heaved back the Royalist right. Lord Byron did not help by advancing to meet the charge head-on and getting in the way of the musketeers.

As soon as he heard the sound of battle, Rupert leapt into the saddle and charged into the fray at the head of his reserve of Bluecoats. They fought furiously and punched back the crust of Cromwell's cavalry. At about that time, Cromwell was slightly wounded in the neck and withdrew for some minutes to have the cut patched.

Someone ordered up the Scottish reserve, and Cromwell soon returned to urge them on in person. Suddenly, the Parliamentary weight prevailed, and Rupert's horse was flying back along the road to York.

Elsewhere, the Royalists appeared to have won the battle. Newcastle's Whitecoats had made a colossal attack on the Parliamentary infantry, and the Scots in the second line could hardly hold them. The first line was in complete disorder, and it seemed that the driving pikes of the Whitecoats might lift the Roundheads clean off the field. On the Royalist left, Lord Goring had launched his cavalry in the sort of tearaway charge Rupert might have produced had he not been so hesitant. The Parliamentary right had been torn away as a man's shoulder might be torn away by a cannon ball, and the Earl of Leven and one or two other worthies went with it. Back down the roads leading to the south went news of the trampling of Parliament's main armies, and in Newark a peal of bells was rung in honor of a Royalist triumph.

The time now was getting toward 8:30 p.m., and there was at most an hour of daylight left. Cromwell had pulled his cavalry round behind the Royalists and had halted either in or near Wilstrop Wood. Most of Rupert's cavalry had fled beyond it, and Cromwell let them go while he and his men coolly evaluated what else needed to be done on that hectic field.

Lord Ferdinando Fairfax, father of Sir Thomas, had joined the rout of the infantry, but to his right with some of the cavalry was still the redoubtable Sir Thomas. In the midst of the confusion he threw away the white scarf by which many of the Parliamentarians distinguished themselves (those were the days before regular uniforms), and he rode amid the turmoil right through the rampaging Royalist cavalry. It is not certain who first found Cromwell at Wilstrop Wood with news of the chaos on the Parliamentary right, but it might have been Fairfax. At any rate, Fairfax would have been sufficiently coolheaded to put Cromwell in the picture. And Cromwell knew what to do.

At 8:30 Goring's cavalry was slicing away the right flank of the wavering Roundhead infantry, and some of his men had even reached Marston Hill. Suddenly from behind them, from where they might have thought Rupert's Bluecoats were waiting, came a sweeping, violent charge of 2,500 horsemen led by Cromwell in person. And these men were fresh—remember, they had paused after the rout of Rupert's cavalry, and had not just returned from a chase.

Lord Maitland's regiment of Scots was still holding its ground with pike and musket, and the grand sweep of Cromwell's cavalry did the rest. From being the victors, Goring's horse became the fugitives, the mere backwash of a river trying to contend with an incoming tide. By 9 o'clock the battle was over as a contest, and Cromwell was the master of the field (with which his nominal superiors, Manchester, Leven and Lord Fairfax, had lost touch).

There was a bloody postscript. The gallant Whitecoats refused to surrender to an army that included many Scots. They were penned in White Sike Close, and they fought on far into the night under a full moon while Cromwell's cavalry had the hideous work of cutting away their outer ranks, layer by layer. The Whitecoats who were wounded spent their last strength thrusting upwards from the ground with pikes and scythes to maim the horses of their attackers. Late that night some 30 or so men surrendered; the rest were dead or so badly wounded they could no longer bear arms.

The Royalist dead numbered between 3,000 and 7,000, probably nearer the latter figure when it is recollected that 3,000 Whitecoats alone must have died. Roundhead losses are reckoned to have been less than 1,000 dead and wounded, but it was a narrow squeak. For without Cromwell, those figures could easily have been reversed. Rupert still managed to find 6,000 horsemen with which he escaped back over the hills into Lancashire.

A few days later, Yorkshire troops under Sir Thomas Fairfax entered York under an agreement that no "foreign" troops would garrison the city. Sir Thomas, one of the most civilized men in that war, saw to it that the stained-glass windows of York Minster (containing more than 2 million separate pieces) were not damaged by the iconoclasts among the Roundheads.

The results of the battle were cataclysmic. Apart from Newark, the whole of the north and the English midlands had fallen to Parliament in two hours. The biggest battle fought on British soil was a Parliamentary landslide. Cromwell was free to turn his attention to the south.

The Scots now returned to the siege of Newcastle. Fairfax the Younger mopped up Royalist garrisons just as Rupert, only a few weeks before, had mopped up Parliamentary garrisons. "Truly England and the Church of God hath had a great favour from the Lord in this great victory given unto us," wrote Cromwell to his brother-in-law. "God made them as stubble to our swords," he went on. "We charged their regiments of foot with our horse and routed all we charged."

The Marquis of Newcastle declined to help Rupert pick up the pieces; instead, he left the country. He returned at the time of the Restoration in 1660 and lived to the ripe old age of 84. The Earl of Manchester, nominal commander of the Parliamentarians at Marston Moor, returned to East Anglia for a time, where he contemplated the future with increasing doubt.

In the south, Charles had followed Essex into Cornwall, and at Lostwithiel on September 2 some 8,000 Parliamentarians surrendered—the greatest surrender of the war. Charles marched back to Wiltshire, entered Salisbury in high spirits, and at the end of October fought another drawn battle at Newbury against twice his numbers. He thought the war had been dragged back onto an even keel, but it had not. Nothing could undo the effect of those shattering charges of Cromwell's men, half-humorously and half-fearfully dubbed "Ironsides" by Rupert himself. From now on, Parliament would be able to concentrate its forces in the south and the midlands, where the war would be decided.

Cromwell and Manchester came to a parting of the ways at Newbury. Manchester pointed out that no matter how often Charles was beaten, he was king still, and that one defeat would ruin Parliament. Cromwell would have no truck with that defeatism, and he and his friends in the House of Commons dictated the course the war was to take from then on. A new army, the New Model (which included some New Englanders in its ranks) was to take the field in 1645, and under Sir Thomas Fairfax it was to win the Battle of Naseby. It was not an army to be bound to any one district, like the Eastern Counties Association or the Cornish Infantry, but would march and fight anywhere. It was England's first real standing army, and it introduced among its men (New Englanders and all) the red coats that were to be British uniform until the facts of 19th- and 20th-century war (and the climate in India and South Africa) led to the introduction of khaki.

The powerful Oliver Cromwell, lieutenant general of horse in the New Model army, grew even more powerful after Marston Moor. After the execution of King Charles I on January 30, 1649, Cromwell's sweep to military dictatorship could not be stopped.

Yet, that was not to be the end—the reaction, when it came, was against the military republic and not against the monarchy. In 1660, when Charles II was restored, both the Earl of Manchester and the Marquis of Newcastle were on his staff—an example of the constant changing of partners in the waltz of history. And it can be argued that the two hours at Marston Moor ensured the triumph of the constitutional monarchy just as much as it spelled the end of the ambitions of Charles I.

Stressed to the Breaking Point

In order to reach Blenheim, the Duke of Marlborough
adopted a bold course that shocked his adversaries.
His strategy in the field was equally unorthodox,
a puzzle to the confident French.

By Eric Niderost

It was the start of a friendship that would alter the course of European history. On the afternoon of June 10, 1704, John Churchill, Duke of Marlborough and supreme commander of the English Army, met his ally Prince Eugene of Savoy in Mannheim, a sleepy little village in southern Germany. It was the second year of the War of the Spanish Succession, a conflict that pitted the France of King Louis XIV against England, the Netherlands and the Hapsburg emperor in Vienna. Marlborough and Eugene were the principal generals in the anti-French coalition, and what they decided here at Mannheim would determine the course of the campaign.

The rendezvous was conducted with a kind of Baroque splendor that typified the age. Bewigged and beribboned officers bowed low and doffed their hats, and the air was filled with courtly compliments. All eyes were drawn to Marlborough and Eugene as the main actors in the unfolding drama—and the contrasts between the two men could not have been more startling.

Prince Eugene of Savoy was 41, a swarthy little man of mixed Italian-French extraction. His long hawk face and prominent nose were framed by a luxuriant wig, yet his shabby brown coat gave him an almost monkish appearance—ironic, since Louis XIV had once called him *"le petite abbé."* As he talked, Eugene would plunge his hands deep into the lining of his coat pocket to extract the finely ground Spanish snuff he carried there. As a general in the service of the Hapsburgs, however, the unimpressive-looking Eugene had carved out a formidable military reputation.

The Duke of Marlborough was 54, a relatively old man by the life expectancy of the day. By all accounts, he was still a handsome man, youthful in looks, courtly in manner, and graceful in carriage. He had a pink complexion and the slight hint of jowls, counterbalanced by a commanding gaze. Due in part to the suspicion of the late King of England, William III, he had seen little active campaigning in the last 10 years. To that degree he was an unknown quantity, yet there was something about the man that inspired confidence.

Marlborough played his role as host to perfection, and Eugene began to warm to this ruddy-faced Englishman. The Duke escorted his new friend to a lavish banquet—the diners supped on the finest silver plate and drank the choicest vintages. Amid the flickering banquet candles, a partnership was forged that would have far-reaching consequences.

The war had begun when the dying King of Spain, Charles II, bequeathed his throne and overseas empire to Philip, Duke of Anjou, the 17-year-old grandson of France's Louis XIV. Louis and his ministers promptly declared young Philip king of Spain and the Indies. In Vienna, however, Holy Roman Emperor Leopold I fretted that the Spanish throne, so long a Hapsburg possession, was about to be lost to his family forever. Without a moment's hesitation, the haughty Hapsburg began preparations for war.

At first England and the Netherlands stood aloof, but then events took an ominous turn when French troops invaded the Spanish Netherlands— present-day Belgium—and seized important border fortresses. For 40 years Louis XIV, the "Sun King," was the richest and most powerful monarch in Europe, and his brilliant reign illumined the entire continent. Thanks to his powerful patronage, French language and culture spread throughout Europe. But if he were admired, he was also greatly feared. Louis' seizure of the fortresses seemed a blatant act of aggression, a first step toward complete domination of Europe.

To counter French moves, a Grand Alliance of England, the Netherlands, and the Holy Roman Empire (Austria and some smaller German states) was formed in 1701. War with France followed in May 1702. The chief architect of the Alliance, King William III of England, died soon after the outbreak of hostilities, but the new monarch, Queen Anne, supported his bellicose aims. Anne retained John Churchill as captain-general of English forces and minister extraordinary to the Netherlands—and, as further mark of royal favor, created him Duke of Marlborough a few months later. The queen thus made Marlborough supreme in both military and diplomatic spheres, a crucial distinction. As events would show, he needed every bit of his authority to overcome internal opposition and lead his forces to victory.

By early 1704 the war had been raging for almost two years—a time of ever-mounting frustration for Marlborough. His Dutch allies were a volatile lot, united only in their hatred of Louis. Time and again, the Duke's brilliant campaign plans were dashed on the rocks of Dutch intransigence. On four separate occasions, masterful maneuvers—maneuvers designed to seize important objectives and bring the French army to bay—came to grief due to backstage Dutch opposition.

While fighting flared in Spain and Italy, there were really only two decisive fronts—Flanders and Southern Germany. In Flanders, Marlborough guarded Holland from a French army of 46,000 under Marshal François *duc* de Villeroi. In southern Germany, Elector Maximilian Emmanuel of Bavaria had lately joined France, lured by Louis' promise of making him emperor in place of Leopold. A Franco-Bavarian army of about 45,000 men hovered around Ulm, jointly commanded by the Elector and Marshal Ferdinand *comte* de Marsin. In order to protect the French lines of communication, some 30,000 French troops were stationed at Strasbourg with Marshal Camille *comte* de Tallard. In April, Tallard led 10,000 reinforcements to the elector and Marsin, boosting their numbers to at least 55,000 troops.

Poring over his maps, Marlborough could see that Vienna was threatened by the French and Bavarians. And Austria was the linchpin of the Grand Alliance—if Vienna fell, the coalition would collapse like a house of cards. With Franco-Bavarian forces poised on the very edge of Austria, the troops under Prince Eugene and Prince Ludwig, Margrave of Baden, might be overwhelmed. Only the Elector Emmanuel's short-sighted greed had saved Vienna thus far—over French objections, he delayed attacking the city and tried to annex the Tyrol instead—but such a respite, Marlborough knew, was only temporary.

The crisis was a tonic to Marlborough, sharpening his genius as nothing else could. In answer to the French menace, and against all expectations, he would leave the Netherlands and march 300 miles south to relieve Vienna. The proposed march was one of the boldest military designs ever conceived: a long, potentially arduous trek that exposed the flank of his army nearly the entire length of the journey.

Given the transportation and supply systems of the time, the march might well be a logistical nightmare—but if he could destroy the Franco-Bavarian army, the whole strategic picture would change. Vienna would be saved, and with it the Grand Alliance. With luck, Bavaria might even be persuaded to switch sides and cast its lot with the British-led allies.

Once Marlborough decided on this course of action, planning proceeded under a heavy cloak of secrecy. To mask his intentions from the Dutch, who feared the French would overrun them in the duke's absence, Marlborough proposed a limited German campaign on the Moselle River. After some foot-dragging, the Dutch reluctantly agreed. For his part, Marlborough had no fears for the safety of Holland—he surmised the French would rather follow him than invade the Netherlands.

The town of Bedburg, about 20 miles northeast of Cologne, was selected as the starting point for Marlborough's grand design. The duke began the march with 31 squadrons and 66 battalions—approximately 21,000 men, of whom about 16,000 were English. Like rivulets combining to form a mighty river, Marlborough's force would be augmented by allied troops en route, including contingents from Austria, Prussia and Denmark. By the time he reached the Danube, his numbers would swell to at least 40,000—and that figure did not include an Imperial Austrian army under Prince Eugene.

At first light on May 20, 1704, the English army departed Bedburg for the Rhineland town of Coblenz, the first major lap of the journey. The cavalry led the way, and next came the long snakes of red-coated infantry, muskets swaying on their shoulders, gaitered legs kicking up dust swirls as they went. A series of wagon convoys followed the troops, a rattling procession that eventually stretched for miles. First, there were the supply carts whose axles groaned under the weight of nails, ropes, saddlery, medical supplies and bricks to make bread ovens. Hundreds of ammunition wagons also moved along the rutted track. Finally, officers' baggage carts brought up the rear, filled to the brim with furniture, silver plate and candlesticks—in short, all the things a gentleman needed while engaged on active campaign.

As they trudged along, the men were cheered by the thought of leaving Holland, with its flat terrain and all-too-familiar campaigning grounds. A spirit of adventure pervaded the ranks, and before long the rough-hewn soldiers swapped jokes and stories and peppered the air with the most profane oaths. Marlborough, however, was haunted by fears of arriving too late. The spectre of Prince Eugene being overwhelmed and Vienna taken dominated his thoughts—so much so that he decided to take the cavalry and press on ahead.

The English army soon approached Coblenz, a multi-spired town at the confluence of the Rhine and the Moselle rivers. The cavalry crossed a bobbing bridge of boats over the Moselle and continued southward, followed two days later by the bulk of the army. Once past Coblenz, the route of march paralleled the great Rhine River itself for a time, revealing magnificent vistas at every turn.

It was a paradise to men used to more northerly climes. As the soldiers went through small German villages, their footfalls reverberating off the narrow, cobblestoned streets, sturdy German burghers would emerge from their half-timbered houses to gape at the martial spectacle.

Marlborough's meticulous planning was beginning to produce results. Provisions were funneled in at selected points all along the march, and local German sutlers were well paid for their services, a startling contrast to the French habit of foraging (often pillaging) for supplies. Given the primitive transportation systems of the time, the duke and his staff had worked wonders. Apart from his men's needs, Marlborough had 14,000 cavalry horses, 5,000 artillery horses, and 4,000 draught animals to provide for. The horses alone needed 100 tons of oats a day to remain in good health.

Nothing escaped Marlborough's methodical eye: when the army arrived in Heidelburg, the infantry found fresh footwear waiting for them. Weeks before, the duke's funds had set German cobblers to work, and here was the result. A full 14 battalions were newly shod, thanks to the duke's thoughtful gesture.

To avoid fatigue, Marlborough established a daily routine that was unprecedented among European armies. The march would begin about 3 a.m., when the cool of the night protected the men from the sweltering heat of the day, and the cover of darkness hid troop movements from the French. As soon as a halt was called, about 9 a.m., the men pitched their tents, broke out cooking kettles, and spent the balance of the day at their leisure.

The march continued at a steady pace, though during its latter stages the columns were pelted by cold rains that transformed the roads into quagmires. On June 27, Marlborough's army reached the vicinity of Ulm. The march had been brought to a successful conclusion: in 35 days, the Duke had traversed nearly 300 miles, and the men were as fresh as when they began the journey. Marlborough now had a force to be reckoned with, amounting to nearly 50,000 men. The captain-general was also in contact with Ludwig of Baden's allied army.

While the English columns trudged south, confusion had reigned in the French camp. True to Marlborough's prediction, Marshal Villeroi left the Netherlands and followed the duke, though on a parallel course and at a very respectful distance. Villeroi linked up with Tallard, and together they awaited further developments at Landau in Lorraine. The French were thrown into a panic when they discovered Marlborough was on the Danube; in effect he was between the Villeroi-Tallard army at Landau and the elector's forces in Bavaria. After some deliberation, King Louis decreed that Marshal Tallard would take some of the finest French regiments available—a force of some 35,000 men—and rush to the aid of the elector. Tallard complied, but his haste was his undoing: German peasants, enraged by French looting, killed many stragglers, and hundreds of the entirely essential French cavalry horses were felled by a disease called glanders.

Now that Marlborough was on the Danube, the next question revolved around his future intentions. An invasion of Bavaria was contemplated, but first the key fortress of Schellenburg would have to be taken. Time was growing short—if the Franco-Bavarian army were not brought to battle soon, Vienna could still be lost. Marlborough ordered that the fortress be taken by storm. Though the Franco-Bavarian garrison resisted fiercely, Dutch and British infantry managed to overrun the fortress.

For the next few weeks there was a lull in the campaign. Hoping to "persuade" the elector to abandon the French alliance, Marlborough sent out parties that burned and ravaged Bavarian villages. While destructive, the effort was half-hearted and produced none of the desired results.

On August 6, Tallard's 35,000 men effected a junction with the elector and Marsin, boosting the Franco-Bavarian army to 60,000. With the French and Bavarians concentrated at last, Marlborough decided it was time to strike. After dispatching Margrave Ludwig with 15,000 men to besiege Ingolstadt (some say it was to get rid of an obstinate fool), Marlborough and Eugene proceeded to the vicinity of Hochstadt with an army of 53,000. Of those troops, only 9,000 were British, but Marlborough enjoyed the full cooperation of all the allied units.

With Eugene at his side, Marlborough rode out to the village of Tapfheim for a look at the enemy dispositions. The church tower of the hamlet afforded an excellent view of the Franco-Bavarian camps, a sea of tents that filled the horizon.

Tallard had a reputation for being a dilettante at war, but nevertheless he had chosen a very strong topographical position. On the far right, the mighty Danube flowed, its banks fringed by reeds and its surface broken by small islands and shoals. On the extreme left, undulating ground formed a series of small hills, many of them clothed with verdant stands of pine. A small, sluggish stream, the Nebel, fronted much of the French line, its brackish waters following a meandering course until emptying into the Danube.

The French right rested on the village of Blenheim (locally "Blindheim"), a cluster of red-roofed stone cottages that nestled where the Nebel flowed into the Danube. In many ways, Blenheim was the key to the French position—if the village could be taken, Tallard's line could be rolled up in short order.

From Blenheim to the next village, Oberglau, there stretched a plain of about four miles. Its rich, alluvial soil, dark brown and fertile, was covered by vast expanses of wheat fields, now cut to stubble by local harvesters. The stubble fields, yellow-golden in the August sun, were ideal places to deploy troops—if the marshy Nebel could be crossed first. From Oberglau to the next hamlet, Lutzingen, the terrain was an attacker's nightmare, seamed as it was by ditches, broken by low hills, and carpeted by woods, thickets and brambles.

In the chill, pre-dawn hours of August 13, 1704, the allied army roused itself for the coming battle. Amid the flurry of activity, Marlborough made his way to Eugene's tent and together they refined the allied battle plan.

The duke would attack where he was least expected, right across the Nebel and directly in front of the French center. Before the main assault was launched, Lord John Cutts of Gowan (nicknamed "Salamander" because of his relish for the hottest fire), would be given the task of attacking the French right at Blenheim, in concert with Prince Eugene's assaults on the French left. With the enemy flanks tied down, Marlborough's hands would be free to deliver the deciding blow in the center.

As an added bonus, strong allied attacks on the French flanks might panic the enemy into weakening his center. Once French troops were siphoned off, Marlborough would bridge the Nebel, deploy in the stubble fields beyond, then punch through the French defenses before Tallard knew what was happening. It was an admirable plan, but it entailed enormous risks: if Marlborough were caught in mid-crossing, his forces could be divided and utterly destroyed.

Meanwhile, behind the marshy moat of the Nebel, the Franco-Bavarian camps slept peacefully, untroubled by dreams of impending doom. All was tranquil, save for outlying districts where French foragers scoured the countryside for food. French pickets noticed the bustle in the allied camp, but when it was reported, Tallard convinced himself the activity signaled an allied retreat.

General Jean *comte* de Mérode-Westerloo, a Flemish officer in French service, was asleep in a barn when he was rudely awakened by his servant. The man was in a high fever of excitement and babbled something about the enemy being upon them. When Mérode-Westerloo laughingly expressed disbelief, the servant threw open the barn door to let the count see for himself. In the far distance, beyond the Nebel, the allied army could be seen advancing at a measured pace. Serried ranks of infantry in blue and scarlet, bayonets fixed and at the ready, moved forward with parade-ground precision.

As the alarm spread, the Franco-Bavarian camps seethed with activity. Aides-de-camp rode to and fro, cavalrymen scrambled into the saddle, and French officers kicked their sleeping men into ranks. Two French cannon were fired to recall the foragers, and Marshal Tallard held a hasty conference with Elector Max Emmanuel and Marshal Marsin.

Fortunately for the French, Marlborough was forced to call a halt at the approaches of the Nebel while he waited for news of Eugene—until the prince was in position on the allied right, the battle proper could not begin. Relieved to be given this precious respite, the French commanders outlined their course of action. Since time did not permit complicated maneuvers, it was decided the Franco-Bavarian troops would fight right where they had camped the day before. Opinion was divided over how to deal with Marlborough's threat over the Nebel. Tallard decided he would allow Marlborough to cross in strength, then launch a heavy frontal attack in concert with French flank attacks from Blenheim and Oberglau. Since he had a healthy respect for the disciplined firepower of the English, the elector remained skeptical. He urged that the Nebel line be defended, a proposal that fell on deaf ears.

In the meantime, Marlborough was growing concerned as to Eugene's whereabouts. As an indication of his worry, he dispatched his most trusted aide, William Cadogan, to find out what had befallen the prince. While they waited, the allied troops were ordered to stand down, and since this was a Sunday, chaplains began to conduct their worship services.

Suddenly an iron cannonball crashed into the infantry ranks, tearing a bloody gap as it bounded forward. The shot had come from a French battery near Blenheim and signaled the start of a general bombardment of Marlborough's whole line. Unruffled by that turn of events, chaplains continued the services, offering prayers to the Prince of Peace amid the carnage of war. Hymns mingled with the screams of the wounded and the booming reports of the cannon. Allied cannon flamed in counterbattery, but since Marlborough had less artillery, his men received the worst of the encounter.

Toward midday, the allied troops sat down to eat, though an iron hail fell upon their ranks. Finally, a courier galloped up with the heartening news: in spite of the rough terrain, Eugene's men were in position. Marlborough mounted his horse, turned to the circle of bewigged officers around him, and said simply, "Gentlemen, to your posts." The Battle of Blenheim was about to begin.

If all went well, Marlborough's brother Charles Churchill would lead allied infantry over the Nebel while Eugene contained the French left and Lord Cutts attacked the French right at Blenheim.

Of all the participants, Cutts had perhaps the most difficult assignment. Blenheim was an immensely strong position, and the peculiar architecture of its 300-odd stone houses made it even more so. Since each dwelling was a self-contained unit, housing living quarters and stables under one roof, the cottages could be transformed into small fortresses with relative ease. To bolster an already strong defense, the French threw up barricades of over-turned carts and wagons, barn doors and furniture in the village streets. To garrison Blenheim, Tallard allotted nine battalions and a further 18 battalions in reserve—a total of nearly 13,000 men.

It was past noon when Cutts finally received the order to advance on Blenheim. For two hours and more, his men had stoically endured a galling fire from a French battery near the village. Since the guns, commanded by a Swiss officer named Zurlauben, were particularly well served, even the depression of the Nebel stream bank afforded no protection to the allied troops.

Cutts had four brigades—two British, one Hessian and one Hanoverian—at his disposal, and it was a crack British brigade, composed of five battalions of well-trained troops, that had the honor of leading the assault. The redcoats set out at once, a swath of scarlet under the intense glare of the August sun.

The scarlet columns drew closer and closer to Blenheim, yet the French held their fire. Then, when the leading ranks were a scant 30 paces from their objective, the French unleashed a devastating volley into their midst. The storm of musketry shredded the approaching columns, but the redcoats merely stepped over the bodies of their fallen comrades and pressed forward. Against all odds, the survivors gained the French fortifications, while the French fusillade continued to cut through British ranks with grim impartiality. The redcoats stabbed through the cracks of the barricades with their bayonets, fired over the parapets with their muskets, and even tried to tear openings with their bare hands in their grim determination to succeed.

But no body of troops, however disciplined, could long withstand that holocaust, and the battered English battalions began to fall back. Seeing that movement, several squadrons of elite French mounted *gendarmes* advanced upon the retreating English, their upraised sabers poised to strike. Still reeling from their bloody repulse, the British were unable to mount an effective defense against this new threat. The fleeing soldiers fell like wheat before a scythe as the *gendarmes* sabered the terrified fugitives almost at will.

In the ensuing melee, a Scots battalion—the 21st—lost its colors. But the *gendarmes* ran headlong into the leveled muskets of a Hessian infantry brigade. A withering volley brought men and horses down in a tumbled heap, and in the resulting carnage the lost colors were retrieved.

The situation momentarily stabilized, Cutts ordered a fresh attack on Blenheim. Once again, the scarlet tide crashed against the village barricades, and though Blenheim remained in French hands, the heavily besieged garrison was hard pressed. The French commander at Blenheim, Philippe *marquis* de Clérambault, was becoming rapidly unnerved by the persistence of the English attacks. Thousands of English voices—deep, resonant and terrifying—kept up a steady cheering amidst the rattle of musketry and the screams of the wounded. Panicked by the din, the frightened marquis ordered 11 reserve battalions into Blenheim, exactly as Marlborough hoped the French would do.

While the battle swirled and eddied around Blenheim, Marlborough was crossing the Nebel in front of the French center. Earlier, during the morning's cannonade, the duke's engineers had been at work bridging the marshy stream. Loads of brushwood carpeted its approaches, then pontoon bridges were thrown across it.

To help facilitate the crossing, Marlborough adopted an unorthodox formation. Cavalry and infantry were arranged in a layered fashion—6,000 foot soldiers led the way, followed by the massed squadrons of 8,000 cavalry troopers. An additional 6,000 infantry brought up the rear, completing the formation.

The French were puzzled by Marlborough's deployment, but would discover its effectiveness before the day was out. A superb tactician, the duke placed great confidence in the platoon volleys of his infantry. Once over the Nebel, the infantry would form a barrier of bristling muskets, a wall the rest of the formation could shelter behind as it completed the passage of the Nebel.

While the engineers hurried to complete their task, the French cannonade continued unabated. Whistling cannonballs chopped bloody holes in the waiting infantry, but after each hit, the men merely closed ranks and sent the wounded to the rear. To steady his men, Marlborough exposed himself to the hottest fire, a conspicuous target in his gold and scarlet coat, cascading wig and tricorne hat. Mounted on a magnificent charger, the star of the Order of the Garter sparkling on his breast, the duke calmly rode through the assembled regiments as if reviewing the troops at Hyde Park. Without warning, a cannonball gouged the earth beneath his mount's feet, kicking up a cloud of dust that temporarily obscured both horse and rider. For one heart-pounding moment, it seemed that the commander in chief was surely hit. But no—to everyone's immense relief, Marlborough emerged unscathed, his peacock brilliance merely dulled by a coat of dust.

Near Blenheim, a cavalry action occurred that was the psychological turning point of the entire battle. It began when five squadrons of English dragoons splashed through the waters of the Nebel and arrayed themselves at the foot of a rise near the village. Eight squadrons of French *gendarmes*— the same elite cavalry that had been bloodied earlier—spied the movement and rushed forward to expel the invaders. With pounding hooves and flowing manes, the French horses broke into a full gallop, the downward slope of the hill giving them added momentum.

Instead of waiting for the anticipated shock, the English dragoons unsheathed their swords, divided up into three groups, then enveloped the onrushing Frenchmen in front and flank. After a flurry of swordplay, the *gendarmes* were utterly routed and fled the field with the dragoons in hot pursuit. Marshal Tallard witnessed the defeat of his proud regiment with utter disbelief. As he later attested, from that moment he lost faith in ultimate victory.

Still, a French triumph was yet a possibility, even at that late hour. About 3 p.m., the Prince of Holstein-Beck led his men against the French at Oberglau's cluster of farm buildings around a church. When only two of Holstein-Beck's 10 battalions were across the Nebel, the French attacked with all the troops they could muster, including the fire-eating "Wild Geese," Irish emigrés in French service. In short order, Holstein-Beck was mortally wounded and his troops were cut to pieces. As the remnants were thrown back into the Nebel, it seemed the French were on the verge of driving a wedge between Marlborough and Eugene on the allied right.

The crisis of the battle was now at hand. Marlborough, grasping the urgency of the situation, dispatched a courier to Eugene with a plea for aid. Prince Eugene was having troubles of his own—at his wing, the rocky ravines and brush-choked ditches were hard to cross and hotly contested by the stubborn Franco-Bavarians. The Prince was a pygmy in stature but a giant in courage—he personally led attacks, was nearly captured by the enemy, and when he saw two deserters fleeing the field, he shot them down with his own hand. His Prussian and Danish infantry gained ground, but when Marlborough's appeal reached him he was still hard pressed. Nevertheless, he ordered his Imperial cuirassiers to attack the French breakthrough at Oberglau without a moment's hesitation. Thanks to Eugene's generous and timely aid, the French were driven back and the allied line saved. The friendship born weeks before at Mannheim had now come to fruition.

With the situation eased, Marlborough could devote his attention to the French center. His massive crossing of the Nebel had been brought off without a hitch; no less than 28 battalions of infantry (about 14,000 men) and 71 squadrons of cavalry (about 5,000 horsemen) were poised to deliver the decisive blow.

Against that formidable array, the French could muster perhaps 60 squadrons of cavalry but only nine battalions of infantry. And the available infantry, for that matter, were raw conscripts—Tallard's best soldiers were at Blenheim, packed in the smoky, sweltering streets and so crowded together most could not even raise their muskets to fire.

It was now past five o'clock, and sensing perhaps that he was at the pinnacle of his career, Marlborough placed himself at the head of his men and personally led them forward. The allied formations, great oblong blocks of blue and scarlet that stretched a full mile across, began their general advance with trumpets blowing and drums beating, Though a slight rise fronted the French center, and clouds of smoke from cannon fire and burning buildings obscured parts of the field, the advancing troops managed to make good progress.

Louis François d'Aumont, *duc* d'Humières, resplendent in a golden cuirass, launched squadron after squadron against Marlborough's infantry, but the harried horsemen could make little impression on the solid walls of bayonets. The French infantry, brave but unseasoned, were also swept away by the steady volleys of the allied soldiers.

Marlborough now massed his cavalry in two parallel lines that ran nearly three miles across and ordered them forward to administer the *coup-de-grâce*. The ground reverberated with the pounding of thousands of hooves as the allied troopers galloped inexorably toward the weakening French center. Awaiting them were the French *Maison du Roy*, or King's Household Troops, formidable warriors noted for their pride and panache. The *Maison du Roy* seemed about to accept the allied challenge when they suddenly drew rein, fired a ragged pistol volley, then turned and fled the field. With their precipitous flight, what was left of Tallard's center evaporated like a morning mist. The Battle of Blenheim was won.

When the news of the center's debacle reached the Elector and Marshal Marsin, they broke off the engagement with Prince Eugene and retreated in good order, bloodied but unbowed. Others were not so lucky. Allied troops completely invested Blenheim, sealing the fate of the thousands of French soldiers who still swarmed in its houses and gardens. In a fit of despair or an addled attempt to escape, the *Marquis* de Clérambault, the man who had done so much to ensure French defeat by his panic, plunged into the Danube and drowned.

The trapped Blenheim garrison included some of the proudest regiments in the French Army—Provence, Artois, Navarre, La Reine—names that echoed through the years as a roll call of *La Gloire*. After an attempt to break out failed, the marooned regiments accepted their fate and surrendered en masse to the allies. With tears coursing down their cheeks, the men of one regiment, Navarre, burned their colors rather than deliver them as trophies to their enemies.

Even before the surrender, an exhausted Marlborough—he had spent 17 hours in the saddle—hastily scribbled a note to his beloved wife Sarah telling her of the "Glorious Victory." And glorious victory it was. Estimates vary, but it appears the French lost 23,000 killed, wounded, and drowned, and a further 15,000 as prisoners, for a total of 38,000 out of 60,000 engaged. The allies suffered much lighter casualties, 4,500 killed and 7,500 wounded. An immense booty fell into allied hands, including 100 cannon, 3,600 tents, 34 coaches, and 8 casks of silver. The effects of Blenheim were dramatic and far-reaching. Vienna was saved, and with it the Grand Alliance. But most of all, the myth of French battlefield invincibility was shattered. Apart from a brief renaissance under Marshal Maurice *comte* de Saxe, the French Army never really recovered from Blenheim, a decline that lasted until the French Revolution—and Napoleon.

As one of Marlborough's generals, George Hamilton, Earl of Orkney, put it, the monumental Battle of Blenheim was the "greatest fought in 50 years."

Storming Prague's Heights

Sick to his stomach, Frederick the Great
allowed his field marshals to run the battle—
until he had to step in after all.

By Christopher I. Gomola

The first weeks of the year 1757 were not exactly pleasant ones for Prussian King Friedrick Wilhelm II, better known today as Frederick the Great. In total contrast, the previous year had witnessed his successful pre-emptive strike into Saxony, starting the destructive Seven Years' War, and his subsequent victory over an Austrian army in the Battle of Lobositz on October 1, 1756.

But Frederick now was painfully aware that the new year would pose challenges much more trying than the drubbing of a third-rate power like Saxony.

In 1756, Frederick had expected simply a final showdown with his archenemy, the Hapsburg empress Maria Theresa, over the disputed province of Silesia, which Prussia had wrested away from Austria during the War of the Austrian Succession. Far from a localized dynastic struggle over a small piece of territory, however, the events unfolding in early 1757 were turning into a war drawing in all the major powers of Europe. King Frederick was quick to realize that the protection of Silesia from Austrian designs was no longer the primary goal of this new war. Rather, the object was the very survival of the kingdom of Prussia in an increasingly anti-Prussian world.

The greatest danger facing him was the gradual movement of two bitter rivals, Bourbon France and Hapsburg Austria, into an anti-Prussian coalition. Frederick could thank Maria Theresa's Chancellor Wenzel von Kaunitz, who, in the years preceding the war, had engineered the "diplomatic revolution" by gathering the various major powers on the Continent into a loose alliance to isolate Prussia and thus curb her growing ambitions.

In May 1756, weeks before Frederick's attack on Saxony, France and Austria had concluded the Treaty of Versailles, a defensive alliance between the two nations. About the same time, the Austrian ambassador in St. Petersburg was informed by Russian officials that Empress Elizabeth Petrovna was prepared to come to Austria's aid should Prussia provoke a war.

Frederick's open aggression against Saxony in August only pushed Russia and France closer to Austria. By early 1757, not only France and Russia but Sweden, as well as a host of minor German states, were openly siding with Austria. Collectively, those nations could put 400,000 troops in the field against Prussia. In contrast, Frederick had only one significant Continental ally, Hanover. Great Britain, whose reigning monarch was the Hanoverian King George II, was also pro-Prussian, although a better description of its stand might be anti-French. Although the British would aid Frederick financially with huge subsidies, militarily their eyes were focused on North America and India.

With such a grave situation facing King Frederick in the early part of 1757, convention would have dictated that for the upcoming campaign he should remain on the defensive, hoping to fend off the Austrians along the southern borders of Saxony and Silesia while at the same time preparing for eventual Russian and French onslaughts from the east and west.

One reason Frederick was such a dangerous and successful commander was that he never felt bound by convention.

In this case, Frederick realized it would take considerable time for the coalition opposing him to fully muster its forces. France first must contend with the Hanoverian army, and to the east, the Russian forces, though potentially immense in numbers, would surely move at their usual sluggish pace and probably would not pose a threat to East Prussia until late summer. Therefore, Frederick felt, his best move would be a rapid strike into Austrian territory in early spring. If he could decisively defeat the Austrians on their own territory, there was a chance that Maria Theresa would sue for peace. If Austria, the cornerstone of the coalition, could be knocked out of the war, France and Russia would certainly have to reconsider pursuing conflict against Prussia any longer. Even if Austria were not forced out of the war, it would be preferable to conduct a campaign on the enemy's land than on his own.

By early April, Frederick could present to his top field commanders his plans for the upcoming campaign. Four widely separated columns, collectively numbering some 116,000 men, would cross the Erzgebirge and Sudeten mountains and converge on the town of Leitmeritz, 80 miles to the north of the capital of Bohemia—Prague. Three of the columns, including Frederick's own, would be starting in Saxony and would have a relatively short march to Leitmeritz. The fourth, however, consisting of some 35,000 troops under Field Marshal Kurt von Schwerin, would have to make a 100-mile trek into Bohemia.

Once he was concentrated in the heart of Bohemia and, presumably, in possession of enough enemy magazines to keep his army supplied, Frederick intended to seek out and defeat any Austrian army he could reach. The Prussian king planned that his offensive should commence in the middle of April.

Frederick could not have hoped for a more unsuspecting opponent than Field Marshal Maximilian Ulysses Graf von Browne, who commanded the Austrian troops stationed in northern Bohemia. The first months of 1757 found Browne leisurely preparing for his own offensive into Saxony during the upcoming spring. The Austrian field marshal had divided his 110,000-man army into four forces of roughly equal size, stretching some 80 miles from Prague east to Koniggratz. A number of large magazines were constructed to supply his eventual thrust north, an offensive many in the Austrian court were certain would put the Prussian ogre in his place. By early April, the last thing on the minds of the Austrian high command—or Browne's mind, for that matter—was having to face a Prussian invasion. So painstakingly did King Frederick conceal his intentions that he even went to the trouble of having his troops erect fortifications in Saxony to further the charade of remaining on the defensive.

On April 18, the Prussian invasion commenced with Field Marshal Schwerin's force crossing into Bohemia from Silesia virtually unopposed. Even that move could not shake Browne from his conviction that the Prussians would not attempt any large-scale invasion. He dismissed Schwerin's move south as simply a foray designed to throw his own offensive off balance.

Browne was in for a rude awakening on the 20th and 22nd, though, as the remaining three Prussian columns, totaling some 81,000 men, came pouring over the Saxon-Bohemian border. Taken completely by surprise, the Austrian forces were thrown into a state of disarray. In the east, troops under General Christian Konigsegg tried to make a stand at Reichenberg on April 21, but after a brisk skirmish, they were driven off the field by Prussians commanded by Frederick's deputy, August Wilhelm Duke of Brunswick-Bevern. Schwerin's force continued to march west unopposed, linking up with Bevern's column around the town of Sobotka. Both commanders had come across a considerable amount of supplies left behind by the fleeing Austrians, and on April 28 they entered the town of Jung-Bunzlau to discover even more abandoned provisions. While all of that was going on, General Johan Serbelloni remained in Koniggratz with his 30,000 troops and did nothing to hinder the advance of Schwerin or Bevern.

Frederick's advance in the west was also going smoothly. On April 25 he finally caught up with Browne, who had assembled a sizable Austrian force at Budin on the south side of the Eger River. To Frederick it appeared that his much-sought-after major battle was in the offing, but Browne considered the situation much too dangerous and retreated toward Prague while the Prussians were still in the process of crossing the Eger. To the king's consolation, the Austrians had withdrawn in such haste and disorder that they left in Budin another sizable amount of stores, which now fell intact into Prussian hands.

It was under those circumstances that a new commander arrived on the scene for the Austrians. This was the inept and debauched Prince Charles Alexander of Lorraine, brother-in-law of Empress Maria Theresa, sent when even an astute commander could not have been encouraged by the state in which Prince Charles found the Austrian army at Prague. Morale among the troops was near rock bottom, and the army's top commanders seemed unable to formulate any type of defensive strategy short of retreat. After some contemplation, Prince Charles and Browne (who got along with each other in a less-than-amiable fashion) were able to decide that their best move would be to abandon the west bank of the Moldau River and assemble all available forces on the Zizkaberg Heights, a good defensive position just east of Prague. Also, to bolster their numbers, the two ordered Serbelloni to leave a small garrison at Koniggratz and immediately rush to Prague with the balance of his force.

Upon learning that the Austrians had crossed to the east bank of the Moldau, King Frederick, anxious to bring the enemy to battle, took the bulk of his army across the river as well, crossing just north of Prague. In order to keep the Austrians pinned to the east bank and to block any possible escape route, Frederick detached his Field Marshal James Keith and 30,000 troops to take up a position to the west of the city. After gaining a rough idea as to the Austrian positioning on Zizkaberg Heights, the Prussian king rested his army about two miles north of the enemy and decided to wait there until the rest of the Prussian forces arrived from the east. Half a century later, Napoleon would have lunged at the chance to attack and defeat two separate enemy armies attempting to unite. That, after all, was the basis of Bonaparte's celebrated "central position" strategy. But Prince Charles and Browne did nothing of the sort. Although the Austrians outnumbered Frederick's Prussians nearly 3 to 1, the Austrian commanders, satisfied with their apparently strong position, decided to stay put and let the Prussians come to them.

And so, during the early hours of May 6, Frederick's forces merged with those of Bevern and Schwerin, giving the Prussian king an army totaling 65,000 troops (not counting Keith's detachment). The result was a slight numerical advantage over Charles and Browne, who had 62,000 men under their command. In the meantime, though, Field Marshal Leopold von Daun, who had replaced the overcautious Serbelloni, was marching hard with the troops from Koniggratz. By the evening of May 5, he was within 15 miles of Prague.

Frederick was aware of Daun's movement and realized that his superiority in numbers would be lost if Daun reinforced Charles at Prague. Although the Prussian troops, especially those of Schwerin and Bevern, had covered a great deal of ground in the last few days and were probably in need of some rest, Frederick knew that time had run out. When he settled down late that evening to snatch a few hours of sleep, he knew that an all-decisive battle to deal Austria a knockout blow would have to come on the morrow, or not at all.

144

May 6 dawned a clear day, and the first glimpses of sunlight found Frederick and a small reconnaissance party riding just to the north of Zizkaberg Heights to observe the Austrian deployment. Physically, the Prussian king was not well. Stricken with some sort of stomach virus, he was experiencing a good deal of discomfort—he vomited several times during the early morning. Nevertheless, his mental capacity was not diminished. He quickly dismissed as suicidal any notion of assaulting the Austrian position from the north. The Austrian right flank on the east end of the heights, though, seemed to offer some possibilities.

Not feeling well enough to continue his personal reconnaissance, he entrusted Schwerin and General Hans Karl von Winterfeldt with the mission of scouting the Austrian right. When the two returned, they were able to report that the east slope of Zizkaberg Heights did indeed offer an excellent avenue to attack the Austrian rear, especially since it was nearly devoid of any troops. What the two Prussian commanders failed to notice, however, was the extensive marshland in this area, an oversight that was destined to haunt the Prussian planning.

Frederick's army began to move from its original position at 7 a.m. Initially, both Prince Charles and Browne were slow to react, but the sight of thousands of Prussians marching toward the towns of Hostawitz and Sterbohol eventually was enough to awaken the Austrian commanders to the fact that their right flank was Frederick's main target and that this wing was in need of rapid reinforcement.

Charles gave Browne permission to shift a good portion of the army to the east, with the result that the Prussian infantry assembling near the town of Hostawitz was faced by an ever-growing number of Austrian troops on the eastern edge of the heights. Browne also dispatched some 12,000 cavalry just to the southwest of Sterbohol to protect his new right flank. Upon seeing this new and unexpected development, Schwerin (who had been chosen by Frederick to command the flanking maneuver) was convinced that his only chance to gain the heights would be a rapid strike against the Austrians before Browne could form a cohesive line.

Schwerin began his attack about 10 a.m. with whatever troops were at hand, namely some 10,000 infantry and 6,000 cavalry. Frederick had his misgivings about how hastily his field marshal was throwing together the attack, but Schwerin insisted that it must be started immediately.

In order to secure his southern flank and tie down the Austrian horsemen in the area, Schwerin launched his own cavalry in a headlong attack against the enemy just to the south of Sterbohol. The result was a hotly contested cavalry skirmish, one in which neither side could gain the upper hand. After a considerable struggle, the matter was finally decided by the "Hussar King," General Johann (Hans) von Ziethen. He was well aware that his Prussian cavalry's flanks were protected on one side by a lake and on the other by a stream, while the Austrian cavalry's south flank lay wide open. Ziethen rounded up the Prussian cavalry reserve, which consisted of four regiments of hussars and a single dragoon regiment, and went crashing into the exposed southern flank of the Austrians. Their resistance soon crumbled, and in no time the surrounding fields were full of horsemen fleeing in complete disorder. According to one report, however, the Prussian hussars took more interest in looting captured enemy wagons than in pursuing the enemy. Whatever the case, the Austrian cavalry played no further role in the battle.

It was while the cavalry battle was still raging that, about one mile to the north, Schwerin began his main assault against the Austrians on the heights, with 10,000 troops sent forward from the area around Hostawitz. And here, bad planning on the Prussians' part came into play.

In all his haste to get the attack underway, Schwerin did not allow enough time for the Prussian artillery to reach supporting positions. In addition, the infantrymen moving forward soon began to flounder in the marshes and ponds south of Hostawitz, the key physical feature ignored earlier. The Prussian infantry, packed in formation shoulder to shoulder and greatly hampered by the inhospitable terrain, proved to be excellent targets for the Austrians, especially the well-situated battery on Homoly Hill. The expertly aimed cannon fire took a heavy toll of the hapless Prussians, many of whom found themselves waist-deep in marshes. Still the Prussians continued to press home their attack, leaving the fields behind them strewn with dead and wounded comrades.

As Frederick's infantry closed the range, the Austrians were able to let loose several devastating volleys of canister and musket fire, and soon the Prussian attack began to waiver. Winterfeldt, who was with the lead units, received a wound in his neck and fell to the ground unconscious. Upon seeing that, Schwerin rode directly into the fray and, after making sure that Winterfeldt would receive some medical attention, attempted to rally his shaken troops. He seized the regimental colors from one of his men and cried, "Onwards, my children!" as he bolted ahead. Barely a half-minute elapsed before he was hit by a canister blast—the old field marshal dropped the colors and fell to the ground, dead.

That was enough for his already discouraged troops. They fled en masse from the battlefield, leaving some 4,000 casualties behind. The initial Prussian assault-turned-rout had lasted barely more than 30 minutes.

Field Marshal Browne was elated by what he now saw before him—a very exposed Prussian center. He quickly assembled his forces for the counterattack, and at 11 a.m., he led his troops off the heights in pursuit of the fleeing Prussians. Not long after that, however, Browne was put out of action by a cannonball wound to a leg. (He died of the wound several weeks after the battle.) Nevertheless, the Austrians, minus their commander, plodded forward.

Until that point in the battle, King Frederick had played a relatively minor role. Earlier in the morning he had deferred to Schwerin's and Winterfeldt's judgment as to where to launch the initial attack, and later he had given Schwerin a more or less free hand in organizing and executing the ill-fated assault. Much of the king's lethargy could be explained by his illness, which hounded him throughout the day. But now, having had part of his army swept from the field, the urgency of the moment forced him to take control of the situation.

Frederick quickly positioned a fresh line of troops in place of those who had fled. The new line, consisting of more than 10,000 infantry, managed to halt the Austrian counterattack and stabilize the front. Indeed, the deployment, although born of desperation, would become the turning point in the battle, for at that very moment Frederick took note of a fatal flaw in the enemy's positioning. In all of their haste to advance from the heights, the Austrians had failed to bring forward enough troops to cover the flanks of the advancing units. Consequently, a sizable gap in the Austrian line opened up just to the west of Hostawitz. Into that opening Frederick poured 11 infantry regiments—roughly 15,000 men.

Four of his regiments moved to the south, while the remaining seven advanced due west to hit the remainder of the Austrian army (still facing north) in its right flank. Those moves effectively cut off the Austrian right wing, and by noon, the wing had disintegrated. The Austrians now were forced to remove their troublesome battery from Homoly Hill.

Although Frederick had turned the tide of the battle and completely uprooted the enemy position, the engagement was not quite over. There still remained the 40,000 Austrians of the left wing on the north end of the heights who had yet to fire a shot during the battle.

The early afternoon hours would see some brief but costly fighting as Frederick attempted to exploit the turned Austrian right and roll up the enemy line. It was around that time that the Austrians lost another commander, as Prince Charles, an epileptic, collapsed. He was removed to Prague.

While all the fighting had been going on near Hostawitz, the Prussian forces to the north of the battle area (the Prussian right wing), commanded by Prince Henry and General Christoph von Manstein, had sat idle. Taking it upon himself to become involved, General Manstein led his troops into action against the Austrians positioned south of the town of Hlaupetin. Manstein was able to clear the Austrians from that area, but was stopped when he reached the approaches to Tabor Hill, where the Austrians had situated an artillery battery. Reinforced by a reluctant Prince Henry (who felt Manstein should not have attacked without Frederick's consent), the Prussians managed to push the Austrians back to the vicinity of Hrdlorzez and Maleschitz. It was along a ravine running between these two towns that the Austrians managed to form an east-facing line. And it was in that configuration in the early afternoon that the Austrian army came under the final Prussian attacks of the day. A Prussian frontal assault against the position proved futile as well as bloody. Prince Henry finally saved the situation for the Prussians as he led an infantry regiment in an attack against the exposed Austrian left (or northern) flank in the vicinity of Hrdlorzez. This, coupled with fact that Frederick was fast approaching from the southeast with the Prussian left wing (troops from the initial late-morning breakthrough), forced the Austrians to begin to retire to the west. Although a few brisk skirmishes took place during the withdrawal, by 3 p.m. the Austrian army was safe behind the walls of Prague. That left the Prussians standing on the outside, having won the field but in no condition to finish off the bottled-up enemy.

The battle of Prague was Frederick's costliest battle to date, for by day's end he could count 14,300 casualties. Among the dead was his favorite field marshal, Schwerin, who, he once had said, was worth 10,000 men on a battlefield. Austrian losses amounted to 8,900 killed or wounded, while another 4,500 ended up as prisoners.

From the Prussian standpoint the outcome of the campaign hardly did justice to the vast amount of bloodshed. Although tactically it was indeed a great victory for the king of Prussia, strategically the battle of Prague meant very little. For propaganda purposes, Frederick was able to tout the fact that he again had succeeded in sweeping an enemy army from the battlefield, and it is true that Vienna and Empress Maria Theresa were greatly shaken by the battle's outcome. But she did not sue for peace as Frederick had hoped. Forty-six thousand Austrian troops now sat smugly in Prague, and knowing that he could advance no farther into Bohemia with such a potentially dangerous enemy force in his rear, Frederick had little choice but to try starving out the Austrians. That would require a great amount of time, and time was not on the king's side. The Prussians resorted to bombarding the city in late May and early June, but even that could not force Prince Charles and his garrison to surrender.

In the meantime, Frederick kept receiving disturbing reports that Field Marshal Daun was assembling a huge relief force to the east of Prague. By the second week of June, Daun was posing such a threat to Frederick that the Prussian king felt obliged to take part of his army away from the siege to keep Daun in check. What resulted on June 18 was the battle of Kolin, fought some 25 miles east of Prague. Frederick's outnumbered Prussians were mauled, losing more than 13,000 men in the process. The king's battered army fled northward, raised the siege of Prague, and retreated back into Saxony. The withdrawal effectively brought to an end Frederick the Great's costly foray through Bohemia, even if he did go on to many more successful campaigns against his European enemies.

For King, Clive and Company

*Barely lodged in India, their small numbers
dwarfed by those of the enemy, the British under
Robert Clive faced a battle that could
make or break an empire.*

By John H. Waller

At the dawn of the 17th century, a few intrepid English merchants, incorporated as the Honorable East India Company, set forth with sword and ledger to challenge the Portuguese, and then the Dutch, for domination of the lucrative spice trade in the East Indies. By the early 18th century, England's principal commercial rival in India was France, no less eager to tap the riches of that vast subcontinent.

But that was before, just before, the East India Company would best all rivals and metamorphose into the most powerful empire the world has known, ruling one-fifth of the world's population, commanding the most powerful army in Asia, and earning revenues greater than those of any country in Europe save France.

This extraordinary achievement was the work of giants, empire builders like Robert Clive, who may be said to have launched this same empire in 1757 at the Battle of Plassey—perhaps not a great battle as epic battles go, but one with consequences that would be enormous.

Despite the end of the War of Austrian Succession in Europe in 1748, Joseph Francois Dupleix, governor of the French in India, was bent upon winning the subcontinent, and he continued to press his contest with the English. By 1750, Dupleix, displaying a military genius sometimes compared to Napoleon Bonaparte's, had gained the upper hand. The English trading enclaves of Fort St. George in Madras and its subsidiary, Fort St. David, both perilously close to the French bastion at Pondicherry, found themselves threatened by Dupleix's overwhelming power. That was when Robert Clive, a fledgling in the East India Company, suddenly emerged from obscurity to propose a daring plan of action—march on Arcot, a few miles inland from Madras, and defeat the Indian *nawab*, or princely ruler, of that Carnatic region in southern India on whom French power depended.

A youthful Clive, in a fit of depression, had once tried to commit suicide. Twice he had pulled the trigger of his pistol; twice it failed to fire. Now convinced that providence had saved him for some important role in life, he gave up his effort to kill himself. And indeed, he had been saved for something momentous: the creation of a British empire in Asia. The beginning came at Arcot in 1751 when, with only a handful of Company soldiers, Clive seized the *nawab*'s fort and successfully resisted a siege mounted by the French who came to its rescue.

By that campaign, and an attack farther south at Trichinopoli, the power of the French and their Indian allies was broken. Clive had bested the great Dupleix. Now a hero, Clive spent two years in England basking in the adulation of his countrymen before returning to India with a new commission as a lieutenant colonel in the king's army—not simply the Company army—and an appointment as governor of Fort St. David.

In 1756, trouble erupted in north India when a French-encouraged Mogul uprising against the English in Bengal threatened the important trading factory at Calcutta. The Bengal problem began when the Mogul viceroy in Bengal, Suraj-ud-Daula, a young, vindictive despot who had brooded about the special position held by the English in Calcutta, decided to attack the Company settlement at Fort William. The English infidels, he feared, would one day wrest all Bengal from him—a prescient thought. Moreover, visions of Company treasure secreted in Fort William had fired the *nawab*'s lust for riches and further encouraged him in his action. For Suraj-ud-Daula the Europeans held no terror. In his ignorance he imagined that no more than 10,000 people inhabited the "petty" kingdoms of Europe.

In an inglorious chapter of English imperial history, Governor Roger Drake and most of the civilian administrators in Calcutta had fled with their dependents to English ships anchored in the roads. Fewer than 200 Englishmen were left behind to bear the brunt of Suraj-ud-Daula's attack. Most perished, suffocated in a small cell where they had been confined. The now famous Black Hole of Calcutta incident was emotionally described by one of the survivors, J.Z. Holwell, who had been left in charge when Drake so cowardly fled. The horror of some 146 prisoners herded into a cell 18 by 14 feet and ventilated by only one small, barred window during one of the hottest days of the year, has been etched in the minds of English schoolboys ever since.

The loss of the lucrative trading stations in Bengal, dramatized by the Black Hole atrocity, provoked the East India Company's Madras Council to seek retribution and restoration of the Company's fortunes in Bengal. Clive was the logical choice to lead an expeditionary force to retake Calcutta. The Madras commander in chief, Stringer Lawrence, was ill, while his next in command lacked experience and was little respected by the Madras Council. The reputation Clive had earned at Arcot, moreover, would be valuable in convincing both the Madras Council, under which he served, and the refugee Calcutta Council, still holed up precariously in Falta, downstream on the Hooghly River from Calcutta, that he should be given a free hand to conduct the campaign as he saw fit. Had it not been for that, rivalry between the two Company jurisdictions would have hopelessly hamstrung him.

Clive's force—consisting of 900 European soldiers of the Madras army; 250 men of the 39th Regiment, British troops on loan to Madras from the English army; and 1,500 native sepoys—finally sailed on October 16, 1756, aboard six Company transports escorted by five Royal Navy ships of the line under the command of Admiral Charles Watson. The excessive delay did cause problems—the monsoon season broke, and high winds drove the fleet off course to Ceylon before the British could beat their way back to the mouth of the Hooghly River leading to Calcutta. Two of the ships, carrying much needed supplies and a valuable contingent of troops, were so hopelessly separated from the fleet by the storms that they did not arrive in time to join the campaign. After that added delay, Clive and his expeditionary force reached Falta on December 15 to find the pathetic English survivors of the Calcutta debacle in dire straits. Half of 200 or so troops, hurriedly sent there by the Madras Council to protect them from further Mogul harassment, had died, while most of the others were incapacitated by disease.

If Governor Drake was grateful for the relief army, he did not show it. Instead he was angry that the force had not been put under his command. Clive withstood Drake's protests, promising only to keep him informed, and launched his own diplomatic initiative in an effort to reach a negotiated settlement with Suraj-ud-Daula. But Clive's messages to the *nawab* were never delivered; Manikchand, Mogul governor of Calcutta, refused to forward them to the *nawab* on grounds that they were not couched in adequately submissive terms. Now there seemingly remained only the military solution of taking Calcutta by storm—except that Suraj-ud-Daula was assembling an army in his capital of Murshidabad, some 100 miles upriver from Calcutta.

After a slight setback when Clive's exhausted forces were ambushed as they slept, the English seized the outlying fort of Budge-Budge. More accurately, the fort was "seized" by a drunken English sailor named Strahan who, without waiting for the signal to advance, staggered into the fort alone, only to find it abandoned. He joyously waved on his comrades to join him. When reprimanded for his rash act, Strahan promised never to capture another fort "single-handedly" as long as he lived.

On January 2, 1757, Clive's force took Calcutta with ease. Governor Manikchand, with all but a skeleton force, had retreated to a new defensive position at Hugli, on the river a few miles north of Calcutta. Almost immediately the English fell to bickering over command of Fort William. Admiral Watson, it seemed, had assumed command of Fort William and placed it in the charge of Captain Eyre Coote and his small detachment of the 39th King's Regiment, with instructions that Company sepoys should not enter. Clive stormed and fumed, before finally, by sheer force of will, convincing Watson that as commander of the campaign he needed command over its base. Clive got along well with Watson thereafter. Coote, however, never forgave Clive. This incident was symptomatic of the chronic friction between the Company's Indian army and the royal units from England on temporary duty in India, an issue that plagued many Company campaigns.

Clive, a Company officer at heart despite his king's commission, wrote a snippy letter to the Madras Council about the whole affair. It was just as well to withhold royal troops, he said, since Company sepoys made better troops anyway. In fact, Clive would soon raise an all-native army in Bengal made up of north Indian martial tribesmen to reinforce the Madras army in Bengal. The *Lal Patan*, or "Red Battalion," gloriously decked out in scarlet uniforms, ultimately became the basis of the vaunted Bengal army, backbone of the British raj.

For now, though, *Nawab* Suraj-ud-Daula moved with a massive army against Calcutta in an effort to regain Fort William. The *nawab* had 18,000 horse, 15,000 foot, 10,000 armed followers and 40 guns commanded by French gunners to pit against Clive's 2,000 men. Against those odds the Company cause seemed doomed—Clive's military skill and, more important, his daring would have to make the difference in the coming contest.

At first, Clive advanced in a thick morning fog. But when the fog cleared, the English, having gone too far, were appalled to find themselves surrounded by the *nawab*'s army. Nonetheless, Clive continued to push on. His bluff worked—the sudden appearance of the English looming out of the mist frightened the *nawab*, causing him to fall back, sustaining 1,300 casualties in the process. Already, Clive had outgeneraled and outwitted the *nawab*, and now the English could dictate the terms of peace. On February 9, both leaders signed a treaty restoring to the Company its former holdings and privileges in Bengal. With only 200 casualties, Clive had won back Calcutta, which he now proceeded to fortify.

Having accomplished his objective, Clive was supposed to return to Madras with his army. That he was frequently reminded of by the Madras Council, whose factories were ill-defended against possible new French aggression stimulated by a war (to become known as the Seven Years' War) that had broken out in Europe in May 1756. But Clive had his problems, too—the French in Bengal loomed as an even more menacing threat. Would they join forces with Suraj-ud-Daula, who was smoldering with dreams of revenge? Nursing his grudge against Clive, the *nawab* was, in fact, intriguing against the Company with the French commander at Chandernagore, Jean Law. His not-so-secret offer to join forces with the French against the English provoked Admiral Watson to threaten in a bombastic response, "I will kindle a flame in your country that all the water in the Ganges will not be able to extinguish."

Clive concluded that Bengal would never be safe from the capricious *nawab* as long as the French remained. For that matter, the French commander in chief, General Charles de Bussy, at Hyderabad far to the south, might well march on Bengal with the full force of the French army now that a state of war existed between England and France—or so reasoned Clive. (The French, in fact, had proposed that they and the English remain at peace in India.) It thus appeared that the French fort at Chandernagore, just north of Calcutta on the Hooghly River, must be taken. And this was no time for Clive to abandon Bengal and return to Madras.

After extracting Suraj-ud-Daula's grudging permission by threats, Clive marched against the French. The *nawab* knew Clive would attack anyway; he also felt vulnerable to both a possible Maratha attack from the west and an Afghan attack from Delhi, which the aggressive Afghan leader Ahmad Shah Abdali had occupied on a recent marauding expedition. On March 23, Clive defeated the French and forced the surrender of the Chandernagore garrison with its 300 European soldiers.

Clive still could not feel secure with the unpredictable Suraj-ud-Daula sitting on his throne in Murshidabad, supported by an army of some 50,000—larger than either the army of King Louis XV of France or that of Empress Maria Theresa of Austria. It could, if obviously so ordained, inundate the small English garrison at Fort William.

And now there appears another Clive: the master intriguer. Realizing that several of the *nawab*'s generals, alarmed at their ruler's "fickleness of temper," were disaffected, Clive began to weave an intricate web of conspiracy. Through the medium of a notorious opportunist, a wealthy Calcutta merchant named Amirchand, Clive reached a deal with the *nawab*'s chief of staff, Mir Jaffar: In exchange for the Bengal viceregal throne, Mir Jaffar and the troops under his command (and those of his confederates) would defect and join Clive at the crucial moment of battle in the forthcoming showdown with Suraj-ud-Daula. Clive also managed to win over the influential Hindu bankers in Murshidabad upon whom the *nawab* relied to finance his army.

The curtain went up and the charade began. On June 13, when a letter of Company grievances was rebuffed by the *nawab*—as Clive knew it would be—the English marched northward toward Murshidabad with a meager force of less than 1,000 Europeans and 2,000 native sepoys, all augmented by his newly raised Red Battalion and 100 English gunners with eight light 6-pounders and two small howitzers. Clive relied on deception in an effort to catch the *nawab* off guard—his attack was launched even as he made protestations of peace. But his attack was a dangerous gamble. If Mir Jaffar did not keep his end of the bargain, the badly outnumbered and outgunned English force would be doomed.

There was, in fact, growing evidence that Mir Jaffar was playing a double game and would not finally commit himself until he saw which side would win. So serious were Clive's apprehensions that he polled his officers as to the wisdom of proceeding, at a council of war held June 21. At first he sided with the majority, who were against attacking—much to the disgust of the hostile Captain Coote—but upon receiving a secret letter from Mir Jaffar with new assurances, Clive reversed himself. His decision to move forward would prove pivotal to the future of the empire.

By taking Katwa, 12 miles from the village of Plassey, on June 17, Clive's force gained valuable stores of grain, but more important, it gained shelter from the ferocious monsoon rains that struck the countryside the next day. The English then marched forward from Katwa on June 22.

Ignoring tactical advice proffered by Mir Jaffar in secret correspondence, Clive followed his own instincts and moved his force straight forward toward the village of Mankarah near Murshidabad, where the *nawab*'s army was bivouacked. That was risky, since it provided the *nawab*'s army opportunity to cut Clive's line of communications.

After an exhausting eight-hour march, Clive pitched camp in a mango grove a few miles north of Plassey. The strains of martial music, with horns tooting and cymbals banging, alerted the English that the *nawab*'s forces, which had also moved forward, were no more than a mile to the front— indeed, with 53 French fieldpieces in the vanguard trained on the English.

The eve of battle passed tensely in both camps. Suraj-ud-Daula was despondent as the moment of danger approached. He was having trouble with his troops, who resented not having been paid recently, and some of his officers seemed restless as well. Brooding alone that night, he was surprised by an intruder who had somehow managed to enter his tent. The *nawab* shouted for his guards to eject the thief, exclaiming wearily, "Already, they see me dead."

As dawn broke on June 23, the French gunners loosed a furious barrage, while drawn up and poised behind the artillery were 5,000 horses and 7,000 infantry under the *nawab*'s best and most reliable commander, Mir Mudin Khan. Most of the foot soldiers were armed with matchlocks, although some bore only pikes and swords. The cavalry was well-mounted and consisted of good fighters from north India. The artillery boasted 24- and 32-pounders drawn by oxen and followed by magnificently caparisoned war elephants used to maneuver the heavy pieces in combat.

The remaining 45,000 troops—under Mir Jaffar and his fellow conspirators Rajah Dulab Ram and Yar Lutf Khan—were deployed in an arc, anchored by the reliable Mudin Khan and his main force, curving around Clive's right flank toward the village of Plassey and nearly surrounding the English.

From his command post in a hunting box perched in the trees, Clive could see the precariousness of his position and realized that if Mir Jaffar double-crossed him and did not at least withhold his flanking troops from battle, the English would be in grave trouble.

The fateful confrontation at last took place at 8 o'clock in the morning. Clive's force had found shelter behind a mound in the mango grove and avoided the massive pounding from the French artillery while the English artillery could take a toll of their more exposed enemy. The gunners' duel lasted until midday with no decisive results. The English had resigned themselves to not being able to attack until nightfall, in view of the withering artillery fire, when suddenly the heavens opened and the monsoon rain fell in sheets. The French powder was drenched; their cannonading came to a sudden halt. Mir Mudin Khan, reasoning that the British ammunition must also be unusable, suddenly launched his attack. Having providently covered their powder with tarpaulins, the English could meet the onslaught with telling fire. The *nawab*'s attacking troops were driven back, and Mir Mudin Khan was mortally wounded in the fray.

The loss of Mir Mudin Khan was a crushing blow for Suraj-ud-Daula. He was now at the mercy of Mir Jaffar, who already had come under suspicion by hanging back and not closing the pincer in support of Mir Mudin Khan's attack. Suspecting treachery, the *nawab* called in Mir Jaffar and flung his turban at his feet in a gesture of appeal, pleading with him to respect his oath of loyalty, so recently sworn on the Koran. At that crucial moment, Mir Jaffar's co-conspirator, Rajah Dulab Ram, to whom an unsuspecting Suraj-ud-Daula now turned for advice, urged the distraught *nawab* to retreat. In a panic, Suraj-ud-Daula issued the fatal order to withdraw and was the first to flee. He sped by camel to Murshidabad with a bodyguard of 2,000 horsemen, leaving his army essentially leaderless.

Catching a quick nap in his hunting box-command post, the exhausted Clive was unaware of the drama unfolding in the *nawab*'s camp and had not witnessed the sudden withdrawal of Mir Mudin's main force. A subordinate, however, had seized the opportunity to engage the French artillerymen who had not joined in the retreat and two of the three flanking Indian divisions, whose troops continued to fight despite the orders to retire. Mir Jaffar had held back his own division, even if he did not actually join the English as he had promised.

Now aroused to action, Clive adroitly maneuvered his forces to meet the residual attacks and finally dislodged the artillery, a step making further resistance by the *nawab*'s stubborn remaining forces impossible. By 5 o'clock in the afternoon, victory had gone to the English. With only 23 killed in action, Clive had won a most decisive battle, but he had won it more by guile and intrigue than by force of arms.

The defeated Suraj-ud-Daula did not remain long in Murshidabad. Ignoring advice to give himself up to the English, he disguised himself as best he could and hurriedly embarked on a river barge, intent on reaching safety upriver at Patna and accompanied only by a casket of his choicest jewels, his favorite concubine and a trusted eunuch—bare necessities for survival. Before reaching his goal, however, he was spotted and betrayed by a disgruntled former servant who bore the *nawab* a grudge for having once sliced off his ears. The young ruler was brought back to Murshidabad, where he was summarily executed, his corpse then paraded through the streets on the back of an elephant.

To the end, Mir Jaffar's role had been ambivalent, but if he had not joined Clive in battle, he had at least held himself aloof from it, thereby saving the day for the English. Feeling guilty for his less-than-wholehearted commitment, Mir Jaffar was happily surprised when Clive embraced him and still offered him the viceregal throne of Bengal. Clive, now kingmaker, was a realist; he had no great respect for Mir Jaffar, but the new *nawab* would be indebted to the English and dependent upon them. Ultimately Mir Jaffar would try to betray the Company—and pay a price for his perfidy— but for the time being he made a useful puppet.

Mir Jaffar showed his gratitude toward Clive by giving him a monetary reward of 160,000 pounds sterling—a vast sum for its day. Clive's senior officers also received prize money, making them rich for life. This questionable practice, known as "shaking the pagoda tree," had become common among those Company officers fortunate enough to be accredited to native potentates. Returning Company officers laden with the treasures garnered by their positions and their patronage of wealthy puppet leaders were derisively (or perhaps enviously?) called "nabobs," a corruption of the Indian title *nawab*. Clive, who became the richest of them all, was later criticized in England, and ultimately an outraged Parliament put a stop to the practice. But if Clive had benefited personally, the Company had gained astonishing power and advantage from his exertions. It was fully reinstated to its position in Bengal and indemnified for all its losses endured under Suraj-ud-Daula. The Company, moreover, was given the rights of *remindar*, or landlord, for much of the rich land surrounding Calcutta. French competition had been eliminated, with the French property confiscated by the English. Clive's victory set in motion events of far-reaching consequences—politically, until India gained its independence after World War II in this century. And who can define or find end to the more social impact on India or the world at large?

Washington's Christmas Surprise

For the Americans stumbling through sleet and snow, pushing aside the river's ice floes, the battle ahead could make or break the Revolutionary cause. If General George Washington's calculated gamble failed, the 'Spirit of '76' might not survive into '77.

By William Press Miller

The soldiers marched silently, eight abreast, in the bitter pre-dawn cold of December 26, 1776. Snow was falling again, and George Washington exhorted his ragged men to press on down the icy road to Trenton, now just two miles away. "Soldiers, keep by your officers," he shouted. "For God's sake, keep by your officers!"

Suddenly, he heard shouts at the head of the column. Washington spurred his chestnut horse forward to investigate. Generals Nathanael Greene and Adam Stephen followed closely behind. Just visible through the swirling snow were 30 American soldiers in a narrow lane off Pennington Road. What were they doing? Where had they been? Had their actions alerted the enemy garrison in Trenton?

Washington demanded an explanation from the young officer in command. Richard Clough Anderson identified himself as a captain in the 5th Virginia Regiment. He said General Stephen had ordered him to cross the Delaware on Christmas Day, reconnoiter the Trenton vicinity and ascertain the location of the enemy outposts. About 7:30 the previous evening his men had come upon an enemy outpost in a blinding snowstorm. They had attacked the pickets, wounding several, and withdrawn into the woods.

Washington could not contain his fury. He turned to General Stephen and shouted, "You, sir, may have ruined all my plans by having put them on their guard!"

Washington knew that his army could not survive another defeat. Disaster after disaster had befallen it since August: Long Island, Kip's Bay, White Plains, Fort Washington, Fort Lee, the loss of New York City and most of New Jersey. Thousands of soldiers had been captured, wounded or killed. Tons of supplies and ammunition had been lost to the enemy. The Continental Congress had abandoned Philadelphia out of fear the British army would soon capture the American capital. The spirit of '76 was ebbing away, and

Washington realized that only some "bold stroke" could keep the Revolution alive. Yet he faced a desperate time limit—the enlistments of most of his soldiers would expire at year's end. He wrote financier Robert Morris that the British waited for only two events in order to begin their operations against Philadelphia. Those were the freezing of the Delaware River to allow a crossing by the troops and the dissolution of what Washington called "the poor remains of our debilitated Army."

Alertly, Washington had seized all his boats when his army retreated across the Delaware in early December. That stymied British plans, provided the river did not freeze. But what kind of an army would he have in 1777? He estimated he would have just 1,200 effectives to face 20,000 Royal troops in New Jersey. A defensive posture, therefore, was out of the question. He must attack before year's end, while he still had some strength.

After carefully evaluating the reports of his patrols and spies, Washington decided to strike the enemy garrison in the strategic town of Trenton, at the falls of the Delaware. Trenton was a forward position of the Royal forces occupying New Jersey. The British held a chain of posts stretching from Newark through the length of the state to Trenton and Bordentown on the Delaware. These posts secured the army's communications and provided protection for the Tory population. Trenton, a town of about 100 houses, commanded the upper reaches of the Delaware and was an important road junction.

Three crack Hessian regiments occupied the town, now nearly deserted. The Knyphausen Regiment, the Alt von Lossbert Fusilier Regiment and the Rall Grenadier Regiment had distinguished themselves at the battle for Fort Washington in November. Accounts of their ferocious assault and their ruthless use of the bayonet made the Hessians the most feared troops in the king's army. The inhabitants of New Jersey soon learned to flee at the approach of the blue-coated mercenaries with their miterlike headgear, blackened mustaches and long, powdered pigtails. The Hessians plundered Patriot and Tory alike with equal zeal, much to the dismay of the more far-sighted British officers.

Colonel Johann Gottlieb Rall, 50 years old and a 35-year veteran, proudly commanded the Hessian regiments in Trenton. His fighting prowess had earned him the nickname "the Lion." Combat with the American rebels on Long Island and at Fort Washington had convinced him that they were inferior fighting men, surely no match for his brave Hessians. He curtly refused to build redoubts guarding the approaches to Trenton, declaring: "Let them come! We want no trenches! We'll go at them with the bayonet!"

Washington did not underestimate his opponent's fighting mettle. He knew his men could not yet fight professional troops on the latter's terms. If the Hessians were allowed to form their battle lines, their discipline and élan probably would prevail. Thus, Washington's plan called for a three-pronged pre-dawn attack. He ordered the Continental regiments of Maj. Gens. John Sullivan and Nathanael Greene, a total of about 2,400 men, to cross the Delaware at McKonkey's Ferry, nine miles upstream from Trenton. Sullivan, a 36-year old New Hampshireman and future governor, had command of the right wing, designated to march down the River Road. Greene, a slightly lame Rhode Islander just 34 years of age, commanded the left wing, which would advance on parallel roads to Trenton. He still smarted from criticism of his judgment in the loss of Fort Washington the previous month. But General Washington had seen his military potential—something Greene would amply demonstrate in his brilliant Carolinas campaign in 1780 and 1781.

Washington sent orders for Brig. Gen. James Ewing's Pennsylvania and New Jersey militia, about 700 strong, to cross the Delaware just below Trenton prior to dawn. Their objective was the stone bridge spanning Assunpink Creek—its capture would block any retreat toward Bordentown and the other Hessian outposts south of Trenton.

Finally, the general instructed Colonel John Cadwalader, who commanded an estimated 1,800 Pennsylvania militia, Continentals and "Philadelphia Associators," to assemble his troops at Bristol, Pennsylvania, 11 miles downriver from Trenton. Washington ordered him to cross the river with the help of the Pennsylvania Navy and move against the Hessian garrisons at Bordentown and Mount Holly. If possible, Cadwalader was then to join the main army at Trenton.

At noon on Christmas Day 1776, the first regiments began marching to their assembly point at McKonkey's Ferry. They trudged over snow-covered roads that were tinged red here and there by bleeding feet. An officer wrote: "It is fearfully cold and raw and a snowstorm settling in. The wind is northeast and beats in the faces of the men. It will be a terrible night for the soldiers who have no shoes. Some of them have tied old rags around their feet; others are barefoot but I have not heard a man complain."

The army's morale, in fact, was exceptional, considering the disastrous events of recent months. Perhaps some men were inspired by Thomas Paine's recent patriotic call that began with these now famous words: "These are the times that try mens souls: the summer soldier and the sunshine patriot will in this crisis shrink from the service of his country; but he that stands it now deserves the love and thanks of man and woman. Tyranny, like Hell, is not easily conquered. Yet we have this consolation with us, that the harder the conflict, the more glorious the triumph."

Paine had published *The Crisis* just days earlier in Philadelphia, and Washington had ordered it read to each regiment on December 23. As the soldiers marched off to the ferry landing, they were also given Washington's dramatic password for the march: "Victory or Death." Many officers remarked on the high spirits of their men. Nineteen-year-old Alexander Hamilton, a captain in the New York State Company of Artillery, observed that his men were "ready, every devil of them...to storm hell's battlements in the night."

The sun set at 4:35 p.m., and the first boat to set out across the ice-strewn river carried a special detachment of 40 Virginians. Leading the men were two young officers, Captain William Washington, a distant relative of the general, and 18-year-old Lieutenant James Monroe, a future president of the United States. Their mission was to secure the roads leading to Trenton and to detain anyone they found.

Shortly after the Virginians landed, elements of General Stephen's brigade came across to establish a perimeter and to guide successive regiments to their assembly points. At about this time, word came from Cadwalader that his force downriver was having great difficulties. Washington scribbled a note saying: "I am determined, as the night is favorable, to cross the river and make the attack upon Trenton in the morning. If you can do nothing real, at least create as great a diversion as possible."

Despite detailed logistical planning, the frigid weather and the river ice hindered the crossings, causing Washington to fall behind schedule. Major James Wilkinson wrote: "The force of the current, the sharpness of the front, the darkness of the night, the ice which [was] made during the operation and a high wind rendered the passage of the river extremely difficult. And but for the stentorian lungs and extraordinary exertions of Colonel Knox, it could not have been effected." Portly Henry Knox, Washington's 26-year-old chief of artillery, ably marshaled the loading of the regiments onto 40-foot Durham boats. Those shallow-draft barges carried iron ore in peacetime, and their sturdiness and maneuverability proved critical to the success of the crossing.

More important was the effort of Colonel John Glover's 14th Massachusetts Continental Regiment, one of the few integrated units to serve during the Revolution. Most of its men were fishermen from Marblehead, Massachusetts "The Marbleheaders," as they were called, strained from sunset to 3 a.m. shuttling each regiment across the 800-foot-wide river. After the men and horses had been ferried across, the arduous task of loading Knox's 18 cannons began. An officer wrote: "The troops are all over, and the boats have gone back for the artillery. We are three hours behind the set time. Glover's men have had a hard time to force the boats through the floating ice with the snow drifting in their faces. I never have seen Washington so determined as he is now. He stands on the bank of the river, wrapped in his cloak, superintending the landing of the troops. He is calm and collected, but very determined. The storm is changing to sleet, and cuts like a knife."

It was past 3 a.m., after the last of the cannons had made it to the Jersey shore, when Washington carefully assessed the task still ahead—nine miles of snow-crusted roads to Trenton and less than four hours to daylight. He later reported to Congress: "This made me despair of surprising the town, as I well knew we could not reach it before the day was fairly broke. But as I was certain there was no making a retreat without being discovered and harassed on repassing the river, I determined to push on at all events." He had no way of knowing that ice in the river was foiling the crossings of both Ewing and Cadwalader—neither one would fight on New Jersey soil that morning.

Around 4 a.m., Washington ordered the army to march. General Stephen, 57, with his three depleted Virginia regiments totaling about 500 men, led the vanguard of Greene's division. The four artillery pieces of Captain Thomas Forrest's 2nd Company of Pennsylvania State Artillery accompanied them. Stephen's brigade was followed by those of Brig. Gens. Hugh Mercer, Alexis de Roche Fermoy and William Alexander Stirling, better known as "Lord Stirling."

Mercer was a 51-year-old Scotsman who had once served as personal physician to Prince Charles Edward Stuart during "Bonnie Prince Charlie's" ill-fated attempt to seize the British crown in 1745. After leaving Scotland, he established a practice in Fredericksburg, Virginia. He would be the great-grandfather of a future famous soldier, George S. Patton. Fermoy was one of those foreign adventurers of great ambition and inflated reputation who plagued Washington throughout the war. The Frenchman was reportedly quite fond of drink. Lord Stirling's claim to an earldom had been upheld by a British jury in 1759 but denied by the House of Lords. Now the wealthy New Jersey resident was fighting the king and Parliament, just like his staunch Jacobite father before him.

Sullivan's division was led by Colonel John Stark's veteran 1st New Hampshire Regiment. Stark, 58, had fought valiantly at Bunker Hill on June 17, 1775, earning a reputation as an aggressive leader. His regiment of tough frontiersmen was probably the best in the Continental Army. Brigadier General Arthur St. Clair, a Scotsman like Mercer, followed with his regiments. Last in the line of march were Colonel Paul Dudley Sargeant's New England regiments. Sargeant, 31, also had fought at Bunker Hill, where he was wounded.

Colonel Knox had allocated the artillery for both divisions identically: four pieces in the van, three in the center and two in the rear. The total of 18 cannons was two to three times the norm for a force of 2,400 men.

Washington's men marched first to Bear Tavern, 1½ miles inland from the river. The army suffered the full blast of the storm's sleet and snow, but at the tavern the silent columns turned southeastward down the River Road. For the rest of the march the wind was to their backs.

A few torches lit the way through the storm, and the officers, distinguishable by white pieces of paper stuck in their hats as field marks, endured the biting cold as stoically as their men. The men saw no lights nor any sign of life as they trudged on. The snow muffled their footsteps, and the howling wind drowned out the creaking and clattering of the artillery.

After 4½ miles, Washington called a halt at the hamlet of Birmingham. The weary men breakfasted on cold rations from their haversacks while Washington met with his division commanders. By torchlight, the officers synchronized their pocket watches. Washington later recalled: "I formed my detachments into two divisions, one to march by the lower or river road, the other by the upper or Pennington road. As the divisions had nearly the same distance to march, I ordered each of them, immediately upon forcing the out-guards, to push directly into the town, that they might charge the enemy before they had time to form." The remainder of the march was to be in strict silence, and all torches were ordered extinguished.

Washington, accompanied by the Philadelphia Troop of Light Horse, rode with Greene's vanguard. The last few miles were the most trying— sleet mixed with the snow, laying down an icy glaze everywhere. The soldiers stumbled and slid on the dark, unfamiliar roads.

In Trenton, meanwhile, the Hessian officer-of-the-day, Major Friedrich von Dechow, took one look at the storm outside and in a holiday spirit canceled the usual pre-dawn patrols. Dechow had served under Prussian King Frederick the Great and should have known better. But George Washington could not have asked for a better Christmas gift.

As his shivering men trudged on, Washington rode up and down the columns, encouraging the men in a low, solemn voice. Washington's horse slipped on an icy patch, and only the general's renowned horsemanship saved him from a dangerous fall. It was shortly thereafter that Washington confronted young Captain Anderson on the Pennington Road—and pressed on after the brief outburst at General Stephen.

With each step of the troops, the eastern sky glowed brighter. Dawn came at 7:23 a.m. A few minutes later, Washington's guides told him the column was nearing the first enemy outpost. The road exited the woods and ran through open fields the rest of the way to Trenton. Washington deployed his troops and then resumed the march. Colonel Charles Scott, 5th Virginia Regiment, told his men: "Take care now and fire low. Bring down your pieces. Fire at their legs. One man wounded in the leg is better than a dead one, for it takes two more to carry him off and there is three gone. Leg them, damn 'em. I say, leg them!"

The storm was still howling and visibility was poor. Just as the vanguard caught sight of Howell's cooper shop, the suspected enemy outpost, a Hessian officer suddenly stepped out of the front door. He wore the distinctive blue Hessian coat, and his black facings and straw-colored breeches marked him as a member of the Knyphausen Regiment. Lieutenant Andreas Wiederhold saw the approaching Continentals and immediately raised the alarm: *"Der Feind! Der Feind! Heraus! Heraus!"* (The enemy! The enemy! Turn out! Turn out!).

Seventeen men in tall brass headgear rushed out and formed a line. As they squinted into the storm, more and more dark forms emerged from the swirling snow, not just from the road but far off to both left and right. Wiederhold quickly realized this was not a raiding party like Anderson's of the night before.

The Americans volleyed thrice at overlong range to no effect. The Hessians held their fire until the attackers were much closer. At Wiederhold's command they fired, but the volley went wild in the storm. Wiederhold later reported: "I therefore retreated under constant fire until I reached Captain [Ernst Eber von] Altenbockum's company. While we had been engaging the enemy this company had formed a line in the street in front of the captain's quarters. I took a position at their right wing and together we fired at the enemy. But soon we were forced to retire in the same manner as before so that we would not be cut off from the garrison."

Washington was impressed by their discipline, and none too pleased to see that "for their numbers they behaved very well, keeping up a constant retreating fire from behind houses." But the Hessians were too few to stop the determined Americans.

Stephen's Virginians, "at a long trot," pushed down the road toward the high ground where King and Queen streets met the Pennington and Princeton roads. While the Virginians deployed at the upper end of town, Mercer's brigade set off across the fields to seize the houses fronting King Street.

Just three minutes after the Americans of Greene's division drove in Wiederhold's pickets, the crackle of musketry echoed from the direction of the river. Sullivan's division was attacking! Despite the daunting hardships, Washington's two columns had coordinated their attacks with almost Prussian precision. More important, they had achieved complete surprise.

The Hessian outpost on the River Road was in a country house called The Hermitage. There, Lieutenant Friederich von Grothhausen commanded about 50 Jägers, elite light infantry armed with short German rifles. They wore green coats with bright red facings, and unlike the Hessian grenadiers with their tall brass headgear, the Jägers wore dark tricorn hats.

Colonel Stark's New Hampshiremen quickly scattered the outlying pickets and advanced on The Hermitage. The Hessians there attempted to form, but when they saw hundreds of men charging at them through the snow, they broke and ran like raw militia. Most did not stop until safely beyond the Assunpink bridge. Along with them fled the only British in Trenton, 20 troopers from the 16th Light Dragoons, all of whom spurred their horses for Princeton without firing a shot.

Sullivan's other brigades were close on the heels of Stark's men as everyone now rushed toward Trenton. At the southwestern edge of town they encountered elements of Rall's Grenadier Regiment, quartered in an old barracks built during the French and Indian War. "The enemy made a momentary show of resistance by a wild and undirected fire from the windows of their quarters, which they abandoned as we advanced," recalled Major James Wilkinson.

Sullivan's men surged into the streets and alleys of lower Trenton and seized the Assunpink bridge. They found no sign of Ewing's militiamen, who were supposed to have blocked the southern escape route. Despite that lapse, only a few hundred Hessians escaped before the trap closed.

At about the same time that Sullivan's men were fighting their way into the lower end of Trenton, Washington galloped to the high ground at the north end of King and Queen streets. From there he had a commanding view.

Colonel Knox ordered Forrest to deploy his four cannons at the road junction. As the artillerymen pushed their pieces into position, Stephen's and Fermoy's brigades were ordered a few hundred yards eastward to seal off the road to Princeton. Within a few minutes the well-drilled Pennsylvanian gunners opened fire, sending cannonballs and grapeshot whistling down the main streets. They were soon joined by Alexander Hamilton's two 6-pounders.

At the Hessian headquarters on King Street, Colonel Rall's aide woke him with difficulty—Rall had spent all Christmas night drinking and gaming. He was groggy as he dressed; after several long minutes, he stepped out to the street and called for his horse. The sound of musketry echoed through the town; here and there a Hessian fell. Lieutenant Wiederhold later reported: "I took up a position in front of one of the first houses of the town and fired at the enemy who were forming in battle order on the upper side of town. It was only at this point that the Brigadier [Colonel Rall] finally appeared and he seemed to be quite dazed. I considered it my duty to report what had happened outside the town...I said that the enemy was strong in numbers, that they were not only above the town but also on both sides of the town." Wiederhold then hurried off to rejoin his regiment.

The Knyphausen Regiment, quartered at St. Michael's Church between King and Queen streets, was forming up under the direction of *Major* von Dechow, who was not only officer-of-the-day but also Rall's second-in-command. The von Lossberg Regiment was trying to form on King Street, along with elements of Rall's own regiment. But the American artillery was doing what Washington had planned. As Henry Knox recalled: "The hurry, fright, and confusion of the enemy was not unlike that which will be when the last trump[et] shall sound. They endeavored to form in the streets, the heads of which we had previously the possession of [with] cannon and howitzers. These in the twinkling of an eye, cleared the streets. The backs of the houses were resorted to for shelter. These proved ineffectual: the musketry soon dislodged them."

Hessian artillerymen did manage to wheel two cannons into action in front of Rall's headquarters. Hub-to-hub, they created a barricade across

King Street. Washington realized that the Hessian battery must be silenced. Orders went to the 3rd Virginia Regiment to seize the enemy cannons. The company of Captain William Washington led the regiment's charge down King Street. At young Washington's side was Lieutenant James Monroe. With a great shout, the Virginians rushed down the snow-covered street, keeping close to the houses and shops.

Hessian musketry and shot swept the street, but, incredibly, not a single attacker was hit. A Hessian soldier recorded: "The rebels attacked us ferociously. Near *Oberst* [Colonel] Rall's quarters there was a barricade of boards and in front of that stood our two company cannon. As the Americans were attempting to reach the cannon, we of Rall's Grenadier Regiment encountered them directly in front of Rall's headquarters. The fight was furious. The rebels dismantled the barricade and now we lost the greater part of our artillery and the rebels were about to use them. Then *Oberst* Rall led a counterattack on the rebels and the situation was thrown into utter confusion."

But then, according to Monroe, "Captain Washington rushed forward, attacked and put the troops around the cannon to flight and took possession of them." King and Queen streets were now swarming with ragged American troops. They fired at the Hessians from windows and from behind fences and trees, which confused and demoralized the Hessian troops. Colonel Francis Scheffer of the Alt von Lossberg Regiment had his horse shot out from under him. Several of his officers were already wounded. Unable to withstand the intense American fire, Colonel Rall ordered his men to withdraw to the fields east of town, between an apple orchard and the Friends' meeting house on Quaker Lane. There, some officers of the von Lossberg and Knyphausen regiments were attempting to rally their soldiers.

Captain Washington pressed his men forward. The Hessians volleyed and, in Monroe's words, Washington "received a severe wound and was taken from the field." Monroe assumed command and was advancing in the lead of his men when he, too, was shot down by a musket ball that passed through his breast into his shoulder. (Monroe carried that ball in his shoulder the rest of his life.)

Rall now ordered the regimental musicians to strike up a march. To the sound of fife and drums, the Hessian troops formed their lines and awaited the commands of their officers. To General Washington it appeared the Hessians were preparing to force their way northeastward to the Princeton Road. Anticipating Rall, he shifted Colonel Edward Hand's 1st Pennsylvania Regiment and Colonel Nicholas Hausseger's "German Battalion" to the extreme left of the American position.

A double line of American troops, supported by cannons, now stretched from the high ground all the way to Assunpink Creek. With snow and sleet pelting their faces, the Hessian officers could only guess at the actual number of enemy soldiers. Rall ordered his troops to advance, and mounted officers led the long blue lines forward. But Washington ordered his regiments to the attack. Unable to close within bayonet range, the shaken Hessians fell back toward the apple orchard.

Colonel Rall, at the urging of some of his officers, then decided he must retake the town and his cannons. The Hessians turned around, and Rall led them back toward Queen Street with the words, "All who are my grenadiers, forward!" A Hessian officer later wrote bitterly: "What madness this was! An open town which was useless to us and which he had only ten or fifteen minutes earlier left of his own free will and which was now filled with three or four thousand of the enemy and then to attempt to retake it with six to seven hundred men."

In the confusion of battle, the orders to the Knyphausen Regiment were garbled, and instead of joining the other regiments in the counterattack, *Major* von Dechow led his men southward toward the Assunpink. Even without the Knyphausen, the Rall and von Lossberg regiments stoically forced their way back to Queen Street. Officers and men fell, yet the ranks closed and the blue lines marched on. But against an enemy safely firing from windows and doorways, the Hessian counterattack could not be sustained. The blue lines began to waver. Colonel Rall valiantly tried to rally his men. Suddenly, two musket balls struck him in the side and he toppled from his horse, mortally wounded. The Hessian attack collapsed when the dispirited grenadiers saw their commander carried from the field.

In some disorder, the Hessians once again retreated to the open ground east of town. The Americans closed in. Knox ordered his artillerymen to push their cannons nearer to the Hessian regiments. Captain Forrest redeployed his battery between Queen Street and Quaker Lane, just a few hundred paces from the milling bluecoats. Captain Joseph Moulder's three pieces also were wheeled into place, and now seven cannons faced the Hessians at point-blank range. Other American cannons were being pushed closer as well. Meanwhile, Greene's regiments astride the Princeton Road advanced.

Some Americans began calling for the Hessians to surrender. The Hessians' position really was hopeless. Fifty-four-year-old Colonel Francis Scheffer, commander of the Alt von Lossberg Fusiliers, called out to an American officer for quarter. George Baylor, a young aide of Washington's, rode up, parleyed briefly with Scheffer, then spurred his horse on to General Washington and reported excitedly that the Hessians had surrendered. Washington could see the regimental flags being lowered and the enemy officers holding their hats up on the points of their swords in token of surrender. As the Hessian soldiers, too, threw down their muskets, a great cheer rose from the American lines.

But the crack of musketry still sounded from the fields near the Assunpink. Washington galloped down King Street toward the Assunpink bridge and the high ground beyond.

The Knyphausen Regiment that mistakenly had marched away from Trenton was headed toward the creek with its two cannons in tow. About the time Rall fell, *Major* von Dechow received a mortal thigh wound that saved him the indignity of a court-martial. He relinquished command to Captain Bernhard von Biesenrodt and advised him to surrender. Von Biesenrodt, however, was determined to save his regiment.

Thinking there must be a way out of this trap, he ordered Captain Jacob Baum to find a ford across the icy waters of the Assunpink. Baum and some privates found a spot and managed to get to the other side, but by then it was too late. St. Clair's cannons controlled the high ground south of the creek, the Hand and Hausseger regiments had closed in from the north, and Glover's Marbleheaders blocked the upper fords of the Assunpink.

An American officer on horseback shouted for the Hessians to lay down their arms. Von Biesenrodt sent Lieutenant Wiederhold, who had been fighting longer than any of the other Knyphausen officers, to seek terms. He spoke briefly with Major Wilkinson and returned to his captain. Von Biesenrodt had the audacity to reject the terms—his officers must be allowed to keep their swords. When Wiederhold reported that to Wilkinson, General St. Clair, who was now nearby, exploded, "Tell your commanding officer that if you do not surrender immediately I will blow you to bits!"

The American cannons supported his threat. That did it. Von Biesenrodt dejectedly ordered his men to ground their arms. (Captain Baum and a few of his men slipped away in the snowstorm, eventually delivering news of the shocking defeat to the British in Princeton.)

St. Clair dispatched Wilkinson to General Washington. Wilkinson found the general on King Street just as the dying Colonel Rall, supported by a file of sergeants, was presenting his sword in surrender. The young major told Washington that the last enemy regiment had struck its colors. Washington grasped the courier's hand and said with emotion, "Major Wilkinson, this is a glorious day for our country."

Indeed it was. Washington's army had achieved one of the most one-sided victories in the history of warfare. It had defeated some of the finest troops of Europe without the death of a single man (except for two privates who had died of exhaustion before even reaching Trenton). Just two officers and two privates had been wounded in the battle. In contrast, the Hessians lost their commanding officer, a major, two captains and a lieutenant, all dead; 101 men killed or wounded; and a stunning 868 officers and men captured. In addition, they lost all six of their field cannons, more than 1,000 muskets, their regimental flags, and all their baggage and loot. The Americans, in an hour, had totally destroyed three proud regiments and made the enemy's other Delaware River outposts untenable.

News of Washington's victory swept the country, reviving the Patriot cause. In retrospect, Trenton could be called the decisive battle of the

American Revolution. Without it, Washington's army would have dissolved and Washington himself probably would have lost command of any remnants. As George Otto Trevelyan, the great English historian, once wrote, "It may be doubted whether so small a number of men ever employed so short a space of time with greater and more lasting results upon the history of the world."

Shame with No Name

The unnamed battle known only as
Arthur St. Claire's Defeat was the greatest rout
of U.S. Army troops by American Indians,
but Miami Chief Little Turtle's victory
is largely forgotten today.

By John Hoyt Williams

Major General Arthur St. Clair, ranking officer of the United States Army, had left Fort Washington as the head of that infant organization's infantry and some 1,400 militia and volunteer levies, and with grim purpose in mind. From the future site of Cincinnati, Ohio, he was marching northeast to chastise hostile Miami, Shawnee and Delaware Indians who were camped some 100 miles away.

Old for active duty in the field at 57, and suffering from severe gout, St. Clair was acting on orders from two of his closest personal friends: President George Washington and Secretary of War Henry Knox.

Arthur St. Clair was neither a fool nor unqualified for the command thrust upon him. Born in Scotland, he had distinguished himself as a British officer in the French and Indian War. He resigned his commission in 1762 to marry a Bostonian and become a large landholder in Western Pennsylvania. An ardent patriot in his adopted land, he served with conspicuous success through the American Revolution, rising to become his state's only major general and a confidant of both Washington and the Marquis de Lafayette, who was impressed by the erudition of the Edinburgh University graduate. In 1787, St. Clair became president of the Continental Congress, and it was he who handed over power to Washington upon the latter's 1789 inauguration. St. Clair was soon named the first (and only) governor of the immense Northwest Territory (including what would become Ohio, Indiana, Illinois, Michigan, Iowa, Wisconsin and much of Minnesota).

That post was a high-stress one, because while St. Clair was expected to maintain peaceful relations with a score of Indian tribes and nations, increasing numbers of Anglo-American settlers were flooding west, making tension and friction inevitable. Valiantly he strove to calm the Indians—who could together field some 15,000 warriors without undue strain—signing treaties of peace, trade and boundary-setting with most of the Iroquois nation, the Sac, Ottawa, Wyandot, Chippewa and other major tribes in 1789 and 1790.

Remaining implacably hostile, however, were the Mohawk, Miami, Delaware, Shawnee and many tribes of the upper Wabash River, jointly capable of putting perhaps 5,000–6,000 warriors on any given warpath. These were spurred on by the British in Canada, who desired a permanent Indian buffer state to halt American westward expansion, and they were aided by bitter ex-Tories and renegades of all description, including the fiendish frontier psychopath, Simon Girty. Those Indians and their unsavory friends sought to halt the settlers at the Ohio River, a line they swore to hold.

Leader of the resistance was Michikiniqua of the Miami—better known to the whites as Little Turtle—whose braves were in a perpetual state of motion, raiding settlements, forts and river barges both within and without of the Northwest Territory. Little Turtle's attempts to band all the region's tribes together indicated a sound grasp of Indian geopolitics, but an ignorance of his enemy's and of the white man's numbers, strength and determination.

After an extended tour of much of his territory during the winter of 1789-1790, a dispirited Governor St. Clair suggested to Secretary Knox that a show of force against the disaffected Indians (whom he underestimated and termed "banditti") might be useful. It is worth noting that the entire authorized strength of the United States Army in 1790 was 718 officers and men, most of whom were scattered among a chain of forts in and along St. Clair's Territory: Forts Washington, Vincennes, Falls of the Ohio, Knox and Steuben. Those small garrisons were notoriously beset by problems of desertion and drunkenness.

Knox, who was always willing to spend money to "peacefully attach" the Indians to the United States, was loath to use force against them, for, he explained, this might "stain the character of the Nation." Congress was likewise hesitant. Aside from reluctance to increase the size (and expense) of the regular army, some members expressed other qualms: Representative Fitzsimmons of Virginia, with little prescience, exclaimed that "We already possess land sufficient—more, in fact, than we will be able to cultivate for a century to come."

Still, after the massacre of a government river convoy in May 1790, Knox and Congress authorized military action in August, in a plan drawn up by St. Clair. It stipulated that Major John Hamtramck would strike north along the Wabash from Vincennes with a force of 300 regulars and militia, while General Joseph Harmar would lead 300 regulars and 1,150 militia from Fort Washington into Miami country. The British were advised that neither expedition was meant to threaten Canadian interests.

In late September, the two forces moved out, the Vincennes expedition having to content itself with burning a few villages, for the Wabash tribes refused to either negotiate or fight and instead melted away into the forests. Harmar, whose militia "included many boys and infirm men who had been sent as substitutes," also confronted only shadows as he moved north and west. In October, however, when he unwisely split his forces, the shadows assumed a grim substance.

One wing of Harmar's force, about 300 strong and led by Colonel John Hardin, was ambushed and severely mauled by Little Turtle's Miami and Shawnee warriors under Wehyehpihehrsehnwah—known to the whites as Bluejacket—just south of today's Fort Wayne. A few days later, Harmar's men gleefully destroyed a number of Miami villages, and immediately began the march back to Fort Washington. As if in afterthought, the general sent Major John P. Wyllys back to the embers of the razed villages with 200 regulars and 200 militia to surprise the Miami when they returned.

Instead, it was Wyllys who was surprised—he found himself surrounded by Little Turtle's painted braves, Indians whose musketry was appallingly accurate. Toe to toe with Wyllys' men, the Indians accepted open battle with their firearms. The militia soon panicked and ran, and the major, with 182 of his men, fell dead among the whooping Miami.

With not a second lost, Harmar and his shrinking command retreated to the dubious protection of Fort Washington. Little Turtle, with his fame and exploits being sung around the campfires, soon formed a formidable confederacy with Bluejacket's Shawnee and the Delaware under Buckongehelas. Into their camps drifted cutthroats Girty, Alex McKee, Matt Elliot and a number of French-Canadian traders, purveying cheap whiskey and expensive firearms, while buying fresh scalps for the insatiable London trade.

A new, wide-ranging cycle of depredations spread out from their campfires, and hundreds more settlers were killed or taken captive. A member of an earlier expedition into the area characterized the Miami: "Like beasts of prey, they are patient, deceitful, and rendered by habit almost insensible to the common feelings of humanity." War and torture, it seemed, were their sports.

It was clear to St. Clair, Knox, Washington and Congress that the problem was no longer one of wandering Indian "banditti," but that of a powerful confederation standing in the path of westward migration. If not chastised, Little Turtle's alliance might well attract other disaffected tribes. Hence, in January 1791, the parsimonious Congress authorized expansion of the U.S. Army to 3,000 officers and men (a figure it never reached in this era) and set aside a fund of $300,000 for pacification of the territory. St. Clair was to command a new expedition and was empowered to call up militia units as well as three-month levies from Pennsylvania and Virginia. Last-minute peace missions were sent into Miami country, but to no avail.

St. Clair's instructions were to negotiate, if and when possible, rather than fight. If he did have to fight, he was to crush the Miami and their allies and force them to cede what is now Ohio and a large portion of Indiana, as well. A permanent fort was to be established in the heart of Miami country to guarantee the peace.

Slowly, the expedition began to take shape around Fort Washington. Two small regular army regiments, the veteran 1st and the newly-created 2nd, were collected there, along with a regular artillery company and two genuinely motley regiments of levies, whose common soldiers were paid a miserly $3 per month. One observer noted that the undisciplined levies were filled with "weak, diseased and unfit men from the streets and jails of Philadelphia," while St. Clair's adjutant general, the astute Colonel Winthrop Sargent, wrote in his diary that they were "recruited from the offscourings of large towns and cities; enervated by idleness, debaucheries and every species of vice." This main force was to be joined on the march by some 350 boisterous Kentucky militia, most of whom were motivated by revenge or hope of profits from Indian scalps. Experienced backwoodsmen were few, and even those knew not a thing about the country to be invaded.

Quartermaster services were a shambles, and the expedition was long postponed while, explained St. Clair, "a great number of axes, camp-kettles, knapsacks, kegs for musket cartridges and spare cannon balls, and boxes of ammunition had to be made." The impatient governor was also less than enthused when he met his Congress-appointed second-in-command, (brevet) Maj. Gen. Richard Butler, a moody, taciturn, egotistical martinet with little frontier experience. Sparks flew between the two generals from the start.

At long last, on September 17, the expedition lumbered out of Fort Washington, ax-men hacking down trees to make a road wide enough for the carts, guns and caissons. Some 2,350 men set forth at the somnolent pace of the road cutters, with St. Clair writing whiningly that "both the geography and the topography were totally unknown" to him. There was no excuse for that, because many of the men of the 1st Regiment had been over the same terrain with Harmar the preceding year. In fact, if one were to accept St. Clair's protestations of ignorance, then his failure to send large numbers of scouts far in advance of his main column is incomprehensible, if not also criminal.

A few days' march from Fort Washington, a halt was called, and two entire weeks were spent building Fort Hamilton (today's Hamilton, Ohio). Only on October 4 did the advance resume, the vanguard strung out for more than a mile and averaging a mere four miles of progress daily—no blitzkrieg this! On October 14, 44 miles from Fort Hamilton, with hundreds reporting sick, the column again lurched to a halt, and for 10 more days the grumbling men were put to work, building Fort Jefferson (just south of today's Greenville).

These were bad days; atrocious weather (rain and hail), deteriorating food in short supply. (Colonel Sargent laconically noted in his diary on October 17 a real crisis: "Liquor there is but [only] sufficient for tomorrow's issue.") In addition, there was hard work, endemic illness, collapsing discipline and the visible presence of Delaware and Miami scouts.

Some of the levies, their enlistment terms expiring, marched home, a volunteer was hanged for murder, two regulars were executed for desertion "to the enemy," and another given 500 lashes for contemplating the same. Morale had evaporated. On the 19th, Adjutant Sargent recorded nonchalantly that six men had "disappeared...whether by desertion, or to the enemy is uncertain."

St. Clair, marveling that morale had sunk so low that some of his men preferred service with the hostiles, was by this time all but immobilized by illness. In one dispatch to Knox, he wrote with obvious pleasure of his afflictions, noting that "a bilious cholic, and sometimes a rheumatic asthma, to my great satisfaction changed to a gout in the left arm and hand." He was hardly an inspiration to his disheartened host!

General Butler, something less than a confidant of the governor and frustrated by the continual delays, proposed (some say demanded) that he take 1,000 selected men, make a forced march to the Miami heartland and finish the business. St. Clair, enraged, harshly rebuffed Butler, and the subordinate retreated into himself, sulking in stony silence.

On October 24, the march was resumed with 100 sick left behind as garrison for the new fort, but in the afternoon of the following day a five-day halt was ordered for rest and pasturage for the horses. On the 28th, Colonel Sargent wrote blandly in his diary: "We had a soldier killed and scalped this morning three miles from camp. He was hunting." The presence of hostiles did not, however, stop desertion or exit of the levies, and a worried St. Clair admitted that "the Virginia battalion is melting down very fast." In fact, with the garrisons of Forts Hamilton and Jefferson, desertions, enlistment expirations and large-scale illness, the entire army was fast dissolving.

A record seven miles was covered on October 30, for the army was now marching along an old and broad Indian "road," but camp was made that night in a spongy bog in the mist of violent, chilling thunderstorms. Unable to move out the next day because the soggy morass would not support the wagons, St. Clair saw discontent in the ranks boil over. In addition to much brawling and general insubordination, 60 Kentucky militia men marched angrily out of camp for home, bitterly promising to loot the supply train they expected to meet en route from Fort Washington.

Unsure of himself as usual, but anxious to maintain some semblance of discipline lest his entire expedition come apart, St. Clair bestirred himself and ordered the whole of Major John Hamtramck's 1st Regiment (300 men of that unit were then with him) to pursue the deserters, capture them, and escort the supply wagons back to the main force. Those men, described as "the flower of the Army," soon lost their way. They would fulfill neither of their assignments and would be absent from the coming battle—a battle in which they alone might have made a crucial difference.

St. Clair, in ignorance of the whereabouts of his 1st Regiment, moved out of the bog on November 2, his army now reduced to less than 1,400 sniffling, coughing malcontents. Watched, but not attacked, by increasing numbers of Indians of assorted tribes, he pitched camp that evening on the bank of the Mississinewa Creek, well within Miami country. Next day, the expedition moved out. St. Clair neglected to send scouts more than a few hundred yards from his main column despite the fact that Sargent recorded seeing "an immense number of old and new Indian camps" along the well-worn track they were following.

On the afternoon of November 3, the governor bivouacked his men on elevated terrain on a branch of the East Fork of the Wabash, only a few miles from a large cluster of Miami villages. Unfortunately for his men, he thought he was still several days' march from the Miami heartland, a notion that a few scouts could have promptly dispelled. He had also chosen poor ground for his camp. He was on the proverbial "high ground," but surrounded by thickets and forests through which he could not observe movement, but from which his camp was perfectly visible from any point on the compass. Refusing to learn from the Harmar/Wyllys experience, he posted his men where they offered perfect targets for Indian marksmen. Almost all the Indians were adept at firearms, were armed with them and would prove themselves natural snipers.

What remained of the militia, under Colonel William Oldham, made camp across the 12-yard-wide stream near the forest; most of the levies were posted in the woods to the rear (out of sight of St. Clair); and the main body, with the artillery, was stationed on the highest ground in a rectangle between the two. Just after dark, 30 volunteers, under Captain Jacob Slough, slipped out of camp to reconnoiter, but the governor and most of his men went to sleep.

Near midnight, Slough returned with important news, relating it to Butler, who was still awake. The captain reported that his scouts had fired on a small party of skulking Indians nearby and had later observed a very large body of warriors close to the camp. Butler thanked and dismissed the captain and then, incredibly, went to sleep without warning St. Clair or taking any further precautions! As he dozed off, militiamen on the other bank of the stream were kept nervously awake by sounds of Indians scuttling through the underbrush a short distance away.

On November 4, about five in the morning, the usual parade of troops was held. No further scouting parties were sent afield, and Butler continued his silence concerning Slough's reconnaissance. As the soldiers squatted around their breakfast campfires in the pre-dawn chill and gloom, a ragged burst of musketry spurted from the trees across the stream, followed by blood-curdling war cries as a swarm of painted Indians rushed the militia. The Kentuckians, surprised, horrified and outnumbered, broke and ran, most throwing away rifles, muskets and any other impediment to speed. Many were shot in the back as they sprinted, but most scrambled across the shallow waters and dashed wildly into the main camp, their panic sowing confusion, fear and disorder among the men there. A congressional inquiry later charged them with fleeing "without firing a gun."

Only rapid and well-aimed artillery fire prevented the pursuing Miami and their friends from crashing into the camp, and they were driven back into the trees, giving the regulars a moment to regain order.

As St. Clair painfully mounted up and rode through the camp giving calm orders, long-range Indian musket fire erupted on all sides. The soft-lead balls buzzed through the camp, and men began to fall—it became obvious that the almost unseen enemy had the soldiers surrounded. The governor's men fired back at will, but the Indians, concealed and protected by the trees, were (unlike the whites) elusive targets.

Several times lulls in the firing heralded screaming, mass attacks toward the artillery. The hordes of determined Indians rushed boldly up with tomahawks to the very mouths of the cannon, but they were repeatedly thrown back to the cover of the woods. Still, the intense musketry soon devastated the gun crews.

St. Clair later admitted, almost admiringly, that "the weight of the fire, which was always a most deadly one," caused almost all of his casualties and cost him the battle. Within an hour or so, all eight cannons were silent: all artillery officers and most of the crews were dead or wounded. The levies in the rear, themselves under savage attack, soon moved to join the main body, but found that there was little room to maneuver in the exposed camp, where the ground was almost covered by the fallen.

General Butler, shot in the chest and stomach (probably mortally) had himself propped up in the middle of the camp and continued to issue somewhat incoherent orders, while St. Clair, a prominent and enticing target, avoided the hail of bullets as if by magic. Though he had three horses killed under him and had his uniform pierced by eight musket balls, he remained untouched, calmly directing the battle as best he could, in full view of the enemy. Sargent, though painfully wounded, did the same.

The din was hellish: the gunshots, the tortured screaming of gut-shot horses, the pitiful cries of the badly wounded, the shrieking of the now confident Indians, the angry, piercing whine of musket balls, the harshly, hoarsely screamed orders. Three times, Colonel William Darke of the 2nd Regiment met bounding Indian charges with bayonet charges of his own. Close enough to the howling enemy to ply his saber, Darke three times threw the Indians back with his dwindling regulars.

Each time they were repulsed, however, the Indians renewed their accurate fire, and as more men fell, confusion approaching panic spread. According to a witness, many men—levies and regulars alike—"appeared stupified and bewildered with the danger," some even sitting down and tranquilly eating their interrupted breakfast as their comrades thudded to the earth nearby in death throes.

About 9:30 a.m., after some three hours and more of savage fighting, Colonel Darke's ravaged regulars drove back the Indians in the rear far enough to uncover the approach road, and, with his decimated command holding the "door" open, the remaining, terrified troops "hurried like a drove of bullocks" toward the south.

The retreat was a blind rout. Everything, including many personal weapons, was left behind or thrown away. Luckily for St. Clair (now mounted on a scrawny, almost crippled pack horse) and his fleet-footed men, the Indians pursued only a few miles, picking off relatively few stragglers. The lure of what to them was princely booty took them back to camp for serious looting, "and to mutilate, torture and kill" the many wounded, among whom was the recumbent General Butler. Captain Thomas Morris, who had fought the Miami in the 1760s, had reported with accuracy that "torture is continued often for two or three days, if they can contrive to keep the prisoner alive."

The retreat was far more swift than the approach had been; most of the survivors made Fort Jefferson (30 miles away) by sunset, finding there the "missing" men of the 1st Regiment. As they straggled in, almost half of them wounded, they were a sorry sight, "one being described as scalped and having a tomahawk sticking in his head." If that description is a true one, that tomahawk might be the only weapon lost by the Indians in the Battle Without a Name! Many of the wounded were destined to die over the coming days and weeks.

Leaving the severely wounded at Fort Jefferson, St. Clair and the remnants of his army made a forced march to Fort Hamilton in a day and a half, arriving there exhausted on November 6, and reaching Fort Washington just two days later. It was only there that the general learned of Captain Slough's neglected report to General Butler. On November 9, with shaky hand, he penned official reports of the action to Secretary Knox and President Washington.

Behind him on the field, he had left his dead and badly wounded, some 316 horses, eight cannon and about $30,000 in assorted government property. Strange to say, he did not leave his reputation among the corpses.

A seven-man committee of the House of Representatives investigated the tragedy and St. Clair's alleged culpability in early 1792, but the general was a very influential man. He was exonerated, and with honor, because of the obstacles he had had to overcome, because of his unquestioned personal bravery under fire, and because everyone (except, ironically, St. Clair himself) grossly overestimated the number of Indians involved. The committee's official report ended with the words: "The failure of the late expedition can in no respect be imputed to his conduct." The general nonetheless resigned his army commission later in the year, content to remain for a decade more the governor of the Northwest Territory.

If St. Clair's defeat had been largely due to incompetence and weakness on the U.S. Army's part, it may also be said that those weaknesses were brilliantly exploited by the Miami, Shawnee and Delaware. In a battle never given a name, the three hostile tribes had crushed St. Clair's army with an estimated 1,200 braves and a handful of interested Canadians. Their own losses had totaled 66 dead and nine wounded. It was rumored that the legendary Revolutionary War veteran, Chief Joseph Brant, was present with a select band of his Mohawk warriors. According to an Indian account, General Richard Butler's scalp was carefully dried and preserved so that it could be sent to Brant as a way of chiding him for his failure to commit the Iroquois to Little Turtle's and Bluejacket's successful campaign. American scalps were hawked throughout Eastern Canada. While their women scalped the dead Americans, the Indians also crammed earth into their mouths to mock the insatiable greed for land that had brought them out to fight in that wilderness.

Eighty-five years later, Lt. Col. George Armstrong Custer would fall amidst his 270 or so men in a United States replete with newspapers that vied with one another to shock the nation with tales of his grisly finale. Few Americans in 1791 would read the appendix of the Congressional Record. The screams of St. Clair's men dying near future Fort Wayne, Indiana, were considerably muted by the forest, the distance, and a curious indifference. Their battle had been but one of a string of bloody encounters that soaked the entire Northwest in blood for a half-century.

Reading General St. Clair's action report in New York, the normally imperturbable first president blurted out to his secretary: "O God, he's worse than a murderer," and ordered a congressional investigation. The general had written rather blandly that he had been surprised in hostile territory, and his army had lost an appalling 39 officers, 621 men killed and 21 officers, 271 men wounded. Further, scores of men were "unaccounted for," and 30 of 33 female camp followers had perished. His army, in fact, had been butchered.

By the winter of 1791, the U.S. Army was eviscerated and demoralized, and the young United States as a nation found itself on the defensive. St. Clair's unnamed defeat had cost more American lives than had any one battle of the Revolutionary War and would rank as the worst defeat at the hands of Indians in American history. The victorious tribes, their spirits soaring, promptly put the torch to the Northwest frontier, raiding as far as Pennsylvania and Kentucky and attempting to mold a giant confederation embracing the Iroquois nation, the Wabash tribes, the Wyandot, Ottawa, and the congeries of Illinois tribes. Clearly, the United States as a nation was at risk.

Fortunately for the Americans, their most capable adversary, Little Turtle, did not remain in charge of the Indian confederation for long. Aging and losing confidence in his people's ability to sustain a protracted war with the whites, Little Turtle relinquished his power on December 31, 1793, retaining leadership only of his own Miami tribe. His successor, Bluejacket, had been a brave lieutenant, but proved to be less capable as a commander in chief than Little Turtle had been.

It would remain for General "Mad Anthony" Wayne and an expanded U.S. Army, which he remodeled into the Legion of the United States, to break the back of the hostile confederation at the Battle of Fallen Timbers on August 20, 1794, and establish Fort Wayne in Miami country. On August 7, 1795, 91 chiefs signed the Greenville Treaty, relinquishing territory in the Ohio Valley and ending hostilities. The last to sign it was Little Turtle, who remarked to Wayne, "As I am the last chief to sign this with the Americans, so also will I be the last to break the agreement." A chief of the Seneca, Warhoytonehteh (Cornplanter), later personally returned the medal of the Society of Cincinnati found on General Butler's body to his widow. He swore to her that her brave husband had been neither scalped nor mutilated.

Time for Second Battle

*Apparently having lost one battle,
First Consul Napoleon Bonaparte seized upon
real glory after his General Louis Charles Desaix
noted there was yet time for another to be won.*

By M.C. Robbins

W as it entirely Napoleon Bonaparte's military genius that swept him to everlasting glory, or did extraordinary good fortune—luck—play a part in his extraordinary career? The authorities still argue and, oddly, Bonaparte's conduct in one key campaign and battle supplies students of Bonaparte's military career fuel to argue either side of the question.

In October 1799, the 30-year-old Bonaparte returned to France from a year of campaigning in Egypt, where he had left behind to uncertain fate a band of officers, along with 30,000 French soldiers, all isolated in the Valley of the Nile, and all with two years of suffering ahead of them before they— or the survivors among them—were to return home. The disastrous Egyptian expedition had undermined the great victories in Italy in 1796 and 1797 that the young Bonaparte had achieved as commander-in-chief of the French Army of Italy. While he was failing in Egypt, Austria reconquered almost all of Italy.

As Bonaparte knew from his own recent experience, any campaign against Italy would be extremely difficult because northern Italy was enclosed by a great mountain chain—rough roads through a few passes. Even those were sometimes impassable. Now, he must face an enemy who was familiar with his style and still stung by recent defeat.

Back in France, where shrewd publicity had concealed his defeats in Egypt, Bonaparte received a hero's welcome. He immediately jumped into the serious political fracas of the time. Disorder was rampant, discontent everywhere, finances in a terrible condition, and the government did not know which way to turn. He led a conspiracy to overthrow the incompetent Directory and emerged from the affair as First Consul, with all-inclusive powers, both domestic and foreign. It was the end of the French Revolution and the beginning of dictatorship, with Napoleon Bonaparte the dictator.

As First Consul he wrote to the governments of England and Austria, stating his opinion that continuation of the conflict would be futile and suggesting that the war should cease. His overtures were rejected. He then told his French followers that France, opposed by a powerful coalition, was forced to fight—only by victorious battle could peace be attained.

Bonaparte energetically prepared for war. Throughout the winter of 1799-1800, evidence of his enthusiastic efforts was everywhere. The spirit of the French people was aroused. A French historian wrote that the very magic of Bonaparte's name made them confident France would be victorious.

Before Bonaparte became First Consul, French soldiers were ill-fed and poorly clothed. Supplies were scarce because the treasury was empty. He placed the nation's finances upon a firm basis and arranged that arms should be manufactured and army supplies collected. Some parts of western France were plagued by civil war, which he stamped out. Then, financed by the taxes he had instituted, he ordered and directed the organization of forces that enormously strengthened French military power.

One of the two French armies in the field, the Army of the Rhine, was sent substantial reinforcements. Its command was given to General Jean-Victor Moreau, a strong supporter of the First Consul. The other army, the Army of Italy, half-starved and struggling against overwhelming odds upon the rocks of Genoa in northern Italy, was sent the first small army train of promised supplies—but it took a long time for the supplies to reach the soldiers because the mountain passes were clogged with hazardous snow, ice, avalanches and glaciers. Bonaparte gave command of the Army of Italy to Marshal André Masséna, a veteran of more than seven years of fighting in Italy.

Meanwhile, Bonaparte, delighted to have control of all military operations, had begun collecting, organizing and drilling large bodies of men in several different parts of France. For the planned campaign, all the men, together with already-organized French units, were to unite by early May near Lake Geneva to form a third army of at least 40,000 soldiers—the Army of the Reserve. He himself would lead it into Italy.

In early April of 1800, an Austrian army commanded by Marshal Paul Kray and numbering 120,000 men, guarded the right bank of the Rhine on a line stretching from beyond Strasburg, Germany, far into the Alps, east of Switzerland, with Kray's center occupying the Black Forest and his line of communication running down the Danube to Vienna. Across the Rhine from Kray's army was General Moreau's French Army of the Rhine, about 130,000 soldiers (including forces in French-occupied Switzerland).

Another Austrian army in northwestern Italy, commanded by General Michael von Melas, was being reinforced to about 100,000 foot soldiers and 14,000 cavalry—with the promise of 20,000 more men to be provided by the King of Naples. It was largely concentrated in the vicinity of Genoa; it also guarded the entrances to the passes through the Alps at the army's rear. General Melas, competent but totally conventional, was preparing to pursue his one purpose of driving all French troops back into France. His lines of communications were by roads down the valley of the Po River and thence north across the Brenner Pass into the Danube valley and northeast across the Pontebba Pass to Vienna. Marshal Masséna's Army of Italy, 40,000 strong and opposing Melas' army, was stretched thin in its struggle to hold its ground. A British fleet lay in the Gulf of Genoa, and a British corps of 12,000 holding Port Mahon in Minorca was ready to march inland on call to join the Austrians.

When hostilities began in late April, Bonaparte had several very capable and daring couriers riding back and forth between him and the French armies in the field while he was readying his Reserve Army, by now grown to 58,000. (He personally checked on the collection of ammunition, armament, horses and mules, wagons, food and clothing, including mountain boots and heavy mountain coats.)

About May 1, he learned that Masséna's army had been cut in two while it was dispersed to forage. Masséna and some 10,000 men had been pushed back to Genoa and surrounded there by an Austrian force of about 20,000; the remainder of the Army of Italy had retreated to Nice, there to face a large part of Melas' Austrian army.

The First Consul's immediate message to Masséna, sent by courier, was, "I count on you holding out as long as possible." Then, on May 14: "The Reserve Army is on the way...You are in a tight corner; but what reassures me is that it is you who are in Genoa. It is at times like these that one man can be worth 20,000."

Bonaparte's plan was to slip his Reserve Army through the mountain passes in Switzerland and strike the rear of the Austrian forces in northern Italy. The more experienced French military men couldn't believe that a force the size of the Reserve Army, along with all its necessary equipment, could be successfully moved over the mountains, a logical and conventional view. But that didn't bother Bonaparte, who rarely was conventional in his thinking.

Long before daylight on May 15, a few days after Bonaparte had left Paris, he began the truly massive operation of moving his army over the Alps. Each man had been issued nine days' rations and a supply of cartridges—and was expected to take care of himself on the march. The real difficulty would be to get the guns over, Bonaparte wrote. The steep mountain roads, deep in snow, were impassable to heavy, wheeled vehicles. Several methods, suggested by his generals, were used to move the guns. As one, hollowed-out tree trunks shaped into troughs were used to carry the eight-pounders and the mortars, with 100 men pulling each gun. Also used were sledges on rollers. Gun carriages were taken apart to be carried in pieces, but the bulky mountings of the eight-pounders required 10 men using a sort of stretcher. Wagons were simply emptied, their contents hauled by men or mules. The Reserve Army made remarkably fast progress. Often the First Consul, sometimes astride a mule, rode back and forth, checking the movements.

Bonaparte divided his Reserve Army into five parts and ordered the final advancements through the five separate passes, successfully concealing the strength and location of his main force, which he personally led. Melas believed that only minor diversionary forces, rather than an entire French army, were approaching. And when he learned the truth, he had no idea which of the five rapidly advancing columns was Bonaparte's main battle force. He ordered Austrian divisions from the Mediterranean coast to prepare to go north to meet the advancing French, but there was confusion as to just where they should go.

While Melas was floundering in uncertainty, the main force of the Reserve Army was, wrote Bonaparte later, working its way across the Great Saint Bernard Pass, fighting ice, gales, and avalanches that could bury several battalions in a flash.

The crossing of the Great Saint Bernard by Bonaparte's army was a remarkable feat, accomplished by the remarkable Corsican's specific rules for marching through the mountains. Among them: March at night only when the moon is shining, and in the day only before the sun has melted the surface of the snow; Do not fail to fire guns to bring down all threatening avalanches; Drink the allotted portion of vinegar to offset the bad effects that drinking snow water could have on the digestive system.

At the Hospice of Saint Bernard high in the mountains, the monks gave the French soldiers wine, bread and cheese as the weary columns rested for a short time. The soldiers had to dislodge a few Austrian garrisons en route down the Alpine slopes. That was no great task—until, some distance down the valley of the Aosta River at the small village of Bard, the French ran into trouble in the form of a small Austrian fortress. It occupied the top of a rock formation and came as a surprise to the French. The narrow mountain road went through the village, and there was no other road around it—or the fort.

General Jean Lannes, in charge of Bonaparte's advance guard, decided to attack first the village and then the fort. He and his men found that driving the Austrians out of the village was easy, but even the most desperate attacks on the fort failed.

The fort, garrisoned by 400 Austrian grenadiers with 26 assorted cannons, was practically impregnable. Lannes, forced to find another way to get past the deadly obstacle, finally located a footpath along the mountainside around the fort. After a few repairs, it was passable for the men and horses but not for the artillery. Lannes solved that problem by bamboozling the native Austrians. On a dark night, the village road in front of the fort was spread over with straw and manure to deaden the sound of artillery wheels. These, in turn, were wrapped in straw and tow cloth, and then soldiers, not horses, quietly pulled six guns past the fort. The First Consul later declared that Fort Bard caused him greater anxiety than the Great Saint Bernard and added, "If the passage of the artillery had been delayed until the fort's fall, all hope of a successful campaign would have been gone." (Fort Bard did not fall to the force Bonaparte left surrounding it until some weeks after he passed by, and only then did the rest of his artillery pass through Bard.)

Bonaparte, restless because of the delay at Bard, set off on the downward journey ahead of the bulk of his army and continued at least part of the way in an unconventional manner. According to an official bulletin, the First Consul came down from the top of the Great Saint Bernard Pass sliding, rolling and tumbling in the snow over steep places and mountain torrents. Another account added, "The First Consul's luck held out again—he was not injured."

On May 20, General Lannes arrived at Ivrea, Italy, the gateway to the Po River Valley. He attacked the Austrian garrison there, defeated it and captured the town. By the next day, all five sections of Bonaparte's Reserve Army had completed the soon-to-be-famous Passage of the Alps and reached the valley of the Aosta. By May 24, they were largely gathered into one body and in the valley of the Po. On the 24th, Napoleon Bonaparte wrote his brother Joseph: "We have fallen on the enemy like a thunderbolt. They did not expect it and seem scarcely able to believe it."

The Austrians had the advantage of interior lines, but the major portion of Melas' force was spread in a wide arc around Turin (which Melas apparently thought was Bonaparte's first target), while the French, with the Army of the Reserve head-quartered at Ivrea, were reasonably concentrated.

Bonaparte decided to keep the initiative. He could advance on Turin, which was not far away, or he could march for Genoa, which was quite some distance but under siege, with Masséna anxiously awaiting him. Or Bonaparte could move toward the great city of Milan, some 70 miles to the east. To occupy Milan, in fact, would be entirely unexpected by the enemy! And from there, he could cut Melas' lines of communication along the north banks of the Po. Milan would provide the French Reserve Army with all sorts of supplies from its depots, while its nearness to vital strategic areas might influence Melas to abandon the siege of Genoa.

And so Bonaparte decided on Milan. As he did so, Lannes made a southward swing, winning skirmishes on the way, to strengthen Melas' belief that the French and Austrians would meet in battle near Turin. Soon en route to Milan, meanwhile, Bonaparte and the Reserve Army met, attacked and defeated an Austrian force on the bank of the Ticino River, then continued eastward. They entered Milan on June 2 and were met by huge cheering crowds of Italians, who hated the Austrians. Bonaparte stayed in Milan a week.

Meanwhile, Masséna was struggling desperately in Genoa. He had successfully kept the major Austrian field army occupied while Bonaparte crossed the Alps, but he could hold out no longer. Relatively few men of his original army were still alive. After surviving for some time on a daily ration of a bit of bread (made partially of straw) and a few ounces of horsemeat, they were very weak, many so weak they could hardly stand. On June 4, Masséna surrendered.

During Bonaparte's stay in Milan, he directed forces against Brescia, Lodi and Cremona, pushing back the Austrians in all three locations. He sent a force to Placentia (Placenza) to seize the Po River crossing there. It was June 8 before he heard that Masséna had surrendered Genoa to Melas.

In the interim, the remarkable Lannes had managed to so mask the movements of the Reserve Army that Melas had delayed in taking advantage of the fact that his besieging army was now free to concentrate against Bonaparte's main force. But then the 71-year-old Austrian general became very busy very fast, dispatching parts of his army against his much younger French opponent.

Bonaparte, who seems to have expected miracles of Masséna, apparently was surprised to hear that Genoa had been surrendered. That would, he said, cause him to speed up his plans to move from Milan south and west toward Genoa. But he was far from being discouraged—perhaps too far. Apparently, the First Consul's ego had been so inflated by the lavish praises of the Milanese that he underestimated his elderly Austrian opponent.

On June 8, Bonaparte sent Generals Lannes, Alexandre Berthier and Joachim Murat these instructions: "You will very soon have upon your hands 15,000 or 18,000 Austrians, coming from Genoa. Go meet them and cut them to pieces. It will mean so many less enemies upon our hands on the day of the decisive battle which we are to expect with the entire army of Melas."

Like Lannes, Berthier and Murat were experienced soldiers, both of proven skill and staunchly loyal to Bonaparte. Lannes himself and General Claude Perrin Victor, who had been one of Bonaparte's strong supports in previous campaigns, now turned their columns and headed westward toward Tortona, with Lannes commanding the vanguard and Victor at a distance of about five miles. For their part, Berthier and Murat marched toward the Stradella Pass.

At Montebello the next day, Lannes, with 9,000 men, encountered Austrian General Peter Ott (who had been in command, under Melas, of the Austrians surrounding Genoa and had received Masséna's surrender) with more than 16,000. A furious battle began immediately. The Austrian numerical superiority would have been overwhelming to the ordinary soldier, but Lannes was no ordinary man or general. He encouraged his soldiers to stand firm in the face of deadly fire, and with his own heroic actions inspired them to do so through the repeated onslaughts of the Austrians. Lannes and his men somehow managed to hold off defeat until General Victor and his 6,000 men joined them. Then, the French responded so fiercely as to force an Austrian retreat in complete defeat. The Austrians lost 5,000 killed, wounded and captured; the French, 3,000. By Napoleonic dictate, Lannes thereafter was called the Duke of Montebello.

Bonaparte and some troops arrived at Montebello not long after the battle ended. Austrian General Ott, with the remnants of his corps, had fallen back across the Scrivia River and proceeded to Alessandria. Bonaparte, guessing that Melas was assembling all his forces at Alessandria and would soon advance on the French, quickly began rearranging his army and preparing for battle. As he was deficient in both cavalry and artillery and Melas was well supplied with both, he decided to fall back in front of the Stradella Pass, where his flanks would be protected on one side by the Po and on the other by the spurs of the Apennines. In that strong position, he collected all 29,000 of his forces south of the Po.

Just before Bonaparte started into the mountains with his army, a messenger brought him a letter from his good friend General Louis Charles Desaix, a distinguished military man who had served under him in Egypt—and been left there. Desaix, finally escaping from Egypt after running the British blockade, had arrived in France. Bonaparte immediately sent a reply expressing his delight and adding, "Come, as quickly as you can, to join me wherever I am." On June 11, Desaix arrived at French headquarters south of the Po, and the First Consul promptly gave him command of a corps consisting of two divisions.

The next day Bonaparte, surprised that no Austrians had arrived and fearing they might evade him and march on Milan, decided to advance and find Melas. On the afternoon of June 12, he moved toward Alessandria, leaving a force occupying the entrenched camp at the Stradella Pass. On the 13th he crossed the Scrivia and marched into the plain of Marengo, which lies between the Scrivia and Bormida rivers, without meeting any Austrians. That afternoon he sent Victor and a small force to the town of Marengo, situated near the east bank of the Bormida on the highway from Alessandria. Victor found only a small detachment of Austrians and quickly drove them across the river. He found no force of Austrians near any of the three Bormida bridge crossings.

When Bonaparte heard this—and that there were no Austrians at Pavia or along the Ticino River—he concluded that Melas was no longer at Alessandria. Surely the Austrian general would not have remained there without maintaining strong forces in the surrounding areas. But where had he gone? Was he escaping to Genoa, for the support of the English fleet while he made a stand?

Bonaparte sent Desaix with one division of his corps, numbering 6,000 men, to find out. On the evening of June 13, the French forces were very scattered, with Desaix, Lannes, Victor, Murat and other generals out on the various missions ordered by Bonaparte. That night the First Consul slept in a little town near the edge of the plain, apparently confident that the next day he would have information about the movements and intentions of Melas. Certainly, there was no possibility of a battle on the morrow.

185

All the while, Melas was still in Alessandria, where, according to one early account, he and his generals had been in confusion since General Ott's defeat at Montebello. Melas had lost control of all reasonable escape routes; he could only march to Genoa and there, indeed supported by the English fleet, battle Bonaparte. Or he could cross the Bormida, face the French, and fight to save his army. Melas called a council of war, during which his officers expressed doubt that the first plan would work and advised an all-force attack on the French. Melas agreed, and on June 13 decided to make the attack the next day. At that time, he had 35,000 infantrymen, 200 pieces of artillery and 7,000 cavalry gathered with him at Alessandria.

At daybreak on June 14, 3,000 Austrian soldiers crossed the river, drove back the French outposts and marched toward Marengo. Two more divisions followed. At 8 o'clock these forces opened the attack with heavy artillery fire, then pushed toward Marengo.

Bonaparte, it can only be said, had been taken completely by surprise. He began dispatching his scattered forces to new positions. General Victor, who took up a position in front of the town of Marengo, was the first to receive the attacks of the Austrians. At first he not only held his line but drove the attackers back, but as Austrian reinforcements, including General Ott, poured in, he was forced to gradually retreat. Before 10 o'clock, Lannes, supported by a cavalry brigade, brought his corps into line on the right of Victor. He was followed by Murat and his troops. Still the French line of battle, two miles long and numbering about 15,000 men, faced nearly 30,000 Austrians.

At 10 o'clock Melas' troops attacked the whole French line with determined fury. The fighting was markedly fierce and bloody by the time of Bonaparte's arrival about 11 o'clock, together with the Consular Guard and two regiments of cavalry—in all, nearly 7,000 men. The furious battle lasted until midafternoon, with a pause at midday while the Austrians regrouped for another all-out attack. The French were forced to retreat, at first slowly, then faster, but fighting all the way.

Bonaparte had earlier sent an aide to Desaix with a frantic message: "I had thought to attack Melas. He has attacked me first. For God's sake come if you still can." Desaix, who fortunately had been held up by a swollen river, received the message at 1 p.m. He immediately turned his 6,000 men and started them moving cross-country toward Marengo at a fast pace. Then the general galloped on ahead of them and arrived, mud-splattered and rumpled, at Bonaparte's side shortly before 3 p.m. By that time, the French had largely been driven from the field.

Bonaparte, greatly relieved to see Desaix, asked, "Well, what do you think?" Desaix replied with a famous line, "This battle is completely lost, but there is time to win another!"

Heartened by his friend's support, the First Consul rode among his soldiers, calling out: "We have retreated far enough. We shall fight again today!" Within an hour, French reinforcements began arriving, and within another half-hour all of Desaix's force was there.

Meanwhile, Melas and his Austrians were confident that the battle was over. In their view, he had defeated Bonaparte on the field of Marengo! And truly, more than 6,000 French soldiers had been killed, wounded or captured. The French had been driven nearly four miles beyond Marengo and more than two-thirds of their cannons had been captured.

Slightly wounded and extremely fatigued, Melas had turned over command of the pursuit of the shattered French army to his chief of staff, Colonel Anton Zach, and returned to Alessandria. His subordinate spent considerable time rearranging his troops to follow the French. His tired Austrians needed rest, and he saw no need to rush after soldiers who he believed to be completely routed. Since resistance was not expected, when Zach did begin to advance, well after 4 o'clock, he moved his Austrians in marching order rather than in order of battle.

The strengthened French army, with Desaix and his men in the van, met the Austrians and poured heavy fire on them for 20 minutes before a crack battalion of Austrian grenadiers swung into action. For a few minutes it was a desperate fight for the French. Then, suddenly, an Austrian ammunition wagon exploded, throwing the Austrians into complete confusion. The French seized the opportunity and charged. "It was the great lucky moment for Bonaparte which turned near-defeat into crushing victory," wrote a French officer. "It was perfect timing; a minute earlier it would not have been effective. North Italy was recovered in that moment for France."

Zach and several thousand of his soldiers suddenly found themselves captured; Austrian resistance collapsed, and all those still able joined the flight toward the Bormida, then on to Alessandria. The Austrians had lost 6,000 dead and 8,000 captured. The voices of the French rose in shouts of joy. But General Desaix, who had won the victory, lay dead, shot in the chest.

The next morning, June 15, 1800, while Bonaparte was preparing to cross the Bormida and attack Alessandria, he received a message from Melas proposing terms of surrender. As a result of their agreed armistice, Austria was to evacuate the whole of northern Italy.

On April 17, Bonaparte left his army of the Reserve, reduced a full quarter by its dead and wounded, in the command of General Masséna and departed for Paris by way of Milan. The First Consul was deeply grieved by Desaix's death—but that didn't keep him from taking credit for the army's victory. In one month he had crossed the Alps with an army, won a great battle and recovered Italy for France!

He was received in France as a great hero, and he willingly accepted the praise of the French people. Few at the time dared to point out that, without the heroic deeds of his generals—Masséna, Lannes, Desaix, Berthier, Murat,

Victor and others—and their men, the campaign of Marengo would not have been successful. Napoleon Bonaparte was indeed a military genius, and he repeatedly was blessed with good luck, it may be said. Possibly his greatest gift, though, was his ability to select loyal and able leaders to serve under him. Extraordinarily capable, they were men who willingly gave their utmost efforts, even their lives, to further his victories, and who rarely demanded to share in the glory bestowed upon him.

The Sepoy General's Debut

For an untried sepoy general named
Arthur Wellesley, the Battle of Assaye in 1803
always would loom larger than Waterloo.

By Eric Niderost

Major General Sir Arthur Wellesley cantered over the steaming plains of the Deccan, a region in turbulent central India. It was September 1803, and the fate of British India rested on this as yet obscure officer who would one day become the Duke of Wellington.

The climate was subtropical, and after a few miles a fine sheen of sweat glistened upon his horse's flanks. Gaudy green parrots scolded Wellesley from the safety of gnarled banyan trees, and sharp-eyed kites darted and soared in the sky above. The Anglo-Irish general rode on until he finally drew rein at the banks of the Kaitna, a broad, meandering river on the Deccan Plateau.

Although the torrid temperature caused distant objects to shimmer like a mirage, what Wellesley beheld across the river was all too real and enough to make the blood run cold in spite of the blistering heat. The seething masses of a huge native Mahratta (or Maratha) army filled the plain across from him.

Not only were French-trained infantry and artillery present but also cavalry, thousands upon thousands of swarthy, beturbaned warriors superbly mounted on prancing steeds. From a distance, the army blended into an amorphous horde, a swaying, rippling, pulsating entity that had a collective life of its own, like some giant amoeba.

When his own army came up, Wellesley was faced with some monumental decisions. His Army of the Deccan was composed of three European regiments and the native sepoys of the British East India Company. Both the British troops and their red-coated native comrades in arms were tough and well-trained, but they were vastly outnumbered by the opposing army. If Wellesley chose to fight, he would be outnumbered 6-to-1 in infantry, 20-to-1 in cavalry, and 5-to-1 in artillery.

It was more than serious; it was impossible. If he attacked, he might be annihilated. If he retreated, his baggage train might fall prey to the enemy and he would lose face, always a consideration in the East. Wellesley was a man not given to histrionics, but later he admitted that if he had failed, "I should have made a gallows of my ridge-pole and hanged myself."

189

Wellesley's dilemma had its roots in the recent past. When the 19th century dawned, British power in India was not yet supreme. In fact, British possessions were technically not even controlled by Whitehall, but by a coterie of merchants collectively known as the Honourable East India Company. Beginning with a few trading posts in the 17th century, the Company had built a power base more by accident than by design.

War is bad for business, and whenever threatened by native enemies or European rivals like the French, the Company would launch its private armies against the offenders. Usually a British victory meant either the annexation of the enemy state or its incorporation as an "allied" territory.

By the 1790s, the British government was assuming more control, supervising East India Company territories by means of a governor general who ruled from Calcutta. When Richard Wellesley, Lord Mornington, took office in 1798, Company possessions seemed far-flung and vulnerable. There were Bengal, the dependencies of Bombay and Madras, and one or two other patches of territory, perhaps 30 million people all told. Mornington was obsessed with French influence in India. And well he might have been, for Britain was locked in a titanic struggle with Revolutionary France.

Vigorous action against Tipoo Sultan, the Francophile ruler of Mysore, had resulted in that ruler's disposition and death in 1799. The Gallic flowering in India had been nipped in the bud, but Mornington contemplated the vast Mahratta Confederacy with ever increasing anxiety.

The Mahratta Confederacy lay athwart the Indian subcontinent, occupying an area measuring 970 miles by 900 miles. But geography was only part of the story—the Mahrattas had a military machine that boasted 200,000 cavalry, 100,000 infantry and a huge artillery train. When the Mogul Empire had decayed in the 17th century, the lack of strong government allowed the growth of the Mahrattas, a hard-riding, hard-fighting horde of plunderers who became the scourge of India.

By the end of the 18th century, the Mahrattas themselves were growing suspicious of each other. No less than five Mahratta potentates jealously shared power within the confederacy, each jockeying for position and intriguing against his neighbor. There was no honor among these thieves, and Lord Mornington was right to fear them—at any moment these rapacious pirates might descend on Company territories like a swarm of locusts, stripping everything to the bone.

Mornington soon also had reason to deplore French influence in the Mahratta states. There was evidence that the new French First Consul, Napoleon Bonaparte, had dispatched emissaries to Pondicherry with secret offers of men and arms for the expulsion of the British from India.

Even if Bonaparte's promises proved worthless, a French adventurer named General Pierre Perron (among others) had succeeded in bringing the Mahratta infantry and artillery up to contemporary European standards.

While the Mahratta cavalry retained its freebooting dash, the infantry and artillery were now as well trained and equipped as any European force. It was a threat Mornington could hardly afford to ignore. Still, the British governor had a few assets of his own, not the least of which was his brother, Maj. Gen. Arthur Wellesley. Although Wellesley had not yet fought a major battle with his own independent command, he was, by 1802, beginning to be noticed as an officer of great potential.

Just when Mornington needed to find a crack in the united Mahratta front—something he could exploit to bring the whole confederacy down—fate beckoned. Late in 1802, *Peshwa* Baji Rao of Poona was attacked by a fellow Mahratta, Jeswant Rao Holkar of Indore, and forced to flee his capital. Here, at last, was a chink in the Mahratta armor that the British might exploit. The routed *peshwa*, or chief minister, appealed to the British for aid, and they responded with alacrity.

According to the Treaty of Bassein, the *peshwa* now became a "subsidiary ally" of Britain and as such would allow British troops and advisers into his territories. First, though, he must be restored to his throne—and that would probably mean war with the rest of the Mahrattas.

General Wellesley had grave doubts about British policies in India, firmly believing the East India Company was already overextended. Nevertheless, he plunged forward without hesitation when he received orders to march on Poona and restore the *peshwa*.

The journey from Wellesley's base at Seringapatam to Poona was in itself a two-month logistical nightmare, but he managed to overcome all obstacles. The general's well-organized bullock-powered supply train performed wonders, marching rapidly without the loss of a single animal. Poona was taken in April 1803, and the *peshwa* was back on his *musnud* (throne) by the middle of May.

Then came a lull in the campaign while peace negotiations started. The Mahrattas began to squabble among themselves. Mornington wisely invested his brother with full powers. Now supreme in local military and political affairs, Arthur Wellesley could fight or talk as events warranted.

Eventually the maharajah of Gwalior, Daulat Rao Scindia, and his colleague Bhonsla, the rajah of Berar, emerged as the chief British enemies. When it became clear these two Mahrattas were only playing for time, negotiations broke down and war began on August 6, 1803.

Maharajah Scindia of Gwalior began the moves on the geopolitical chessboard by massing troops along the borders of territory belonging to the nizam (or native ruler) of Hyderabad. The nizam was doddering and half-senile, but he was a loyal British ally with rich territories ripe for plunder. The British campaign plan that now evolved was simple enough, yet depended on precise coordination of three separate armies. To the north, Colonel John Murray's 4,000-man army would operate in Gaikwar and Baroda. In the east, a colonel named Stevenson would protect the nizam's threatened dominations in Hyderabad. But perhaps the most important member of the trio was Wellesley himself, who with an 11,000-man army would operate out of Poona.

Since Wellesley knew "a long defensive war would ruin [the British position in India]," he invaded Scindia's territory and marched on the latter's main fortress. This was Ahmednuggar, considered the greatest fort in India, a brooding pile bristling with cannons. Nevertheless, it was taken in three days. "These English," declared a dazzled Indian, "are a strange people, and their general is a wonderful man. They came here in the morning, surveyed the wall, walked over it, killed all the garrison, and returned to breakfast!"

Using the newly won—and well-stocked—Ahmednuggar as a forward base, Wellesley plunged ahead. Wars are not won by capturing fixed positions when an enemy army is still in the field. The general knew he had to bring the Mahrattas to battle or his gains would be washed away like soil in a monsoon. Wellesley was an organizational genius, and once again his bullock trains kept his advancing army well supplied. The resourceful general even took a leaf from Julius Caesar's *Commentaries*, the only book besides the Bible he took on campaign. Since most Indian rivers were bridgeless, Wellesley copied Caesar and had basket boats constructed out of bamboo, thorn and leather. Although the 1803 monsoon season was abnormally dry, there was still enough rain to turn the Godavari River into a swollen torrent. But thanks to Caesar's basket boats, the British army crossed without difficulty.

Wellesley's crossing of the Godavari prompted Scindia to abandon his massing movement near Hyderabad and turn abruptly northward. With the long-sought battle perhaps in the offing, it was now time to pull all the pieces of the strategic picture together.

Since he was hundreds of miles to the north, Colonel Murray was pretty much out of the picture, so far as Wellesley was concerned. Colonel Stevenson was much nearer, but Wellesley was having trouble with his lethargic subordinate. Time and speed were everything, yet the tardy Stevenson plodded along at a snail's pace. Eventually Wellesley and Stevenson linked up, only to discover the need to part once again.

When a low range of hills confronted them, Wellesley dispatched Stevenson to cross them through a valley about 14 miles west of his own line of march. That way, hopefully, the passage would be that much quicker. Once through those defiles, the two men were to rendezvous at Bokerdun. But before this juncture could take place, fate again intervened.

Wellesley threaded through the hills without difficulty, then paused to wait for the ever-tardy Stevenson. On September 23, Wellesley's native spy-scouts, called *hircarrahs*, gave him some important intelligence: the Mahratta infantry and artillery were less than six miles away, preparing to join their elusive cavalry at some unknown point.

Here was a golden opportunity: if he could catch the Mahratta infantry alone, perhaps even strung out along a line of march, it might be destroyed. Knowing the god of war rarely bestows second chances, Wellesley decided to gamble and attack without Stevenson.

But when he made his personal reconnoitering visit to the Kaitna River, he found his scouts were wrong—terribly wrong. Scindia and Bhonsla had not divided their forces. Instead, the entire combined Mahratta army paraded and wheeled before Wellesley's telescope. The mere sight of such a juggernaut might have wilted another general's courage, but not this man of iron.

Wellesley had between 6,000 and 7,000 men under his command and 22 guns, mostly of light caliber. Opposing him were 50,000 Mahrattas with 100 or more guns. If he fought, he risked annihilation; if he retreated, he risked piecemeal dismemberment.

Even nature itself conspired against Wellesley. The Mahrattas had chosen their positions well. Their army, a veritable horde, was drawn up behind the Kaitna River, extending along a six-mile front. Actually, it occupied a wedge of land that was sandwiched between the Kaitna and a neighboring stream, the Juah. The two muddy ribbons eventually merged, forming a wiggly "V" as they drew together. The village of Assaye, sheltered in an arm of the Juah, would give the coming battle its name.

Audacity, not caution, was the right tactic here—Wellesley needed a plan that would keep the enemy off balance. His blue eyes flashed as he contemplated his options. The general decided his army would march along the enemy's front, ford the Kaitna on the Mahratta left, and then attack the great host in flank before the Mahrattas could react.

The Mahratta army was formidable but was like a lumbering beast, and perhaps it could not maneuver as rapidly as Wellesley's redcoats. Once its left was crushed in flank, the rest of the line might crumble as well.

But first the Kaitna must be crossed—and the native guides insisted there was no ford. Wellesley and a small cavalry escort galloped up to a little brown rise near the river, and from there the general scanned the horizon. He noticed a village on the far shore and another village directly opposite, on the British side. Coincidence? Wellesley didn't think so.

The general reasoned the villages must mark the end points of a ford, and investigation proved him right. The redcoats began to cross at once, but were harried by Mahratta artillery fire. Cannonballs skipped across the water, sending up white geysers when they broke the surface of the Kaitna. Casualties, while relatively few, were horrific; Wellesley's mounted dragoon orderly had the top of his head carried off by a hurtling ball.

The terrible sight only made the men push forward with redoubled effort. Soon Wellesley's army had crossed the river, dripping but triumphant and ready to take the Mahrattas in flank, but no such luck—their leaders had taken their French lessons in military science to heart and easily wheeled the great host about to meet the new threat.

The rules of the game were changing, but Wellesley still had a good hand. He formed his meager forces into three lines: two infantry lines in front and a cavalry line in reserve. And he could not be turned, because the Kaitna and Juah rivers secured his flanks. The British situation was still serious, but Wellesley had confidence in his troops.

Out of his 7,000 men, barely 1,800 were European, including the 74th and the 78th Highlanders, the 19th Light Dragoons and a few artillerymen—all of whom had been marching since dawn under a sweltering sun. Their scarlet tunics, stained with sweat and caked with mud from the river crossing, were now covered in a fine brown dust, yet the men behaved as if parading before the king himself. Those tough Scots were a long way from the heather-covered valleys of their homeland, but they were ready and eager to fight anywhere.

The East India Company's sepoys of the Native Infantry regiments were also in fine fettle and ready to fight. Their uniforms were a combination of native and European dress, with jaunty caps, scarlet tunics and short white pants that left their muscular legs bare. They wore sandals instead of boots, but could march with the best of European units. Just now, they were busy looking after their India Pattern "Brown Bess" smoothbore muskets.

The Mahratta artillery opened up, spewing a hail of iron that grew in intensity with each passing moment. Wellesley decided to attack at once. An immediate strong assault on the Mahrattas' right, rather than the left—personally supervised by the general himself—would capture their forward batteries and push the center and left toward Assaye and the Juah river.

But there was a danger that Wellesley's own lines, stretched almost to the breaking point, might snap and unravel. In particular, Wellesley cautioned his pickets on the British right not to go too far toward Assaye before the moment was ripe. Assaye and its immediate environs were studded with cannons, and any unsupported attack would be cut to ribbons.

On the British left, meanwhile, the 78th Highlanders went forward, oblivious to the iron hail that shredded their ranks. Drums beat a throbbing tattoo, and the skirl of bagpipes, the rattle of musketry and the roar of cannons assaulted the eardrums of the participants.

The Mahratta guns were well served, their fingers of flame appearing through billows of swirling muzzle smoke to mark each salvo. Cannonballs mowed down men like bowling pins, dismembering, flaying, killing and maiming.

But the 74th Highlanders would not be denied. Soon, very soon, hot iron would be replaced by cold steel, as bayonets and the officers' basket-hilted swords glistened in the late afternoon sun.

A final volcanic eruption of metal and then the cannons fell silent as the surging red-coated infantry reached them. The fierce Celts swarmed in and around the Mahratta batteries, thrusting their 17-inch bayonets and impaling the turbaned gunners. The guns taken, the Highlanders swept on toward the impassive masses of Mahratta infantry just ahead. Seemingly unnerved by the slaughter of their artillery comrades, the Mahratta foot soldiers began to give way.

But then some of the "dead" clustered around the guns in bloody ruin sprang to life again and began to pour fire into the Highlanders' rear. Some of the Mahratta gunners had apparently feigned death to pull off just such a surprise. The Scots then returned and made short work of the reanimated artillerymen.

Overall, the battle was going according to plan—British plan. The Mahratta right and center were folding, neatly rolling up like an oriental rug. But trouble was looming on Wellesley's right. Mahratta batteries were intact in that sector and were belching death with clockwork regularity. Heavy cannon smoke shrouded the field in a literal "fog of war" that blinded even as the thunderous reports deafened. Under heavy fire, benumbed and confused, the 74th Highlanders plunged right into the gaping maw of the massed batteries around Assaye.

The 74th was subjected to a punishing fire, as more and more cannons added their booming voices to the swelling chorus of destruction. Mahratta infantry chimed in, pouring musket volleys into the reeling, yet still advancing red-coated ranks.

When their lacerated lines were disordered by a cactus hedge, the men of the 74th briefly halted, a magnet for every Mahratta musket and artillery piece that could be brought to bear. All semblance of order dissolved into bloody ruin as the stoic Scots fell back around their colors. The king's and regimental colors were more than mere flags; they were the heart and soul of the regiment, something to defend to the death.

Exhausted, bloody, begrimed by smoke and stained with sweat, the men of the fast-dwindling 74th awaited the end. And sure enough, swarms of Mahratta cavalry appeared, a pack of "wolves" scenting a kill. Scimitars raised, the swarthy, bearded warriors charged, but even now well-placed volleys tumbled scores from their saddles. Still, it was only a matter of time before the regiment would be destroyed.

Luckily, the 19th Light Dragoons could respond to the 74th's predicament and led a charge to relieve the pressure. The 19th took the lead, followed by the 4th, 5th and 7th Madras Native Cavalry in support. The Mahrattas' cavalrymen, intent on slaughtering the Highlanders, were caught off guard and scattered.

In the meantime, the British left and center under Wellesley's personal direction were pushing the Mahrattas toward the Juah. After much fighting and confusion, the Mahrattas formed a second "last stand" line, with the Juah at their backs and the supporting artillery fire of Assaye to their left.

Wellesley, sensing victory to be within his grasp, refused to let up the pressure. In fact, he put himself in the thick of the fighting. During the last stages of the battle, Wellesley led a wild charge, and his beautiful Arabian horse, Diomed, was speared by a Mahratta pike. Spurting blood, the noble creature collapsed in a heap, spilling the general to the ground. Fortunately, the general was not hurt by his fall. Soon after that, though the Mahrattas still outnumbered the British, they had had enough. Quickly, their formations melted away, their men plunging into the Juah to reach the far bank and safety. Only a few of the formations kept their discipline.

No one could doubt that the outcome of the battle was a major British victory, though it was a victory dearly bought. Various estimates have been given, but Wellesley lost around 1,584 dead, wounded and missing out of some 7,000 engaged; the Mahrattas lost perhaps 6,000 of their original 50,000-man horde.

General Wellesley had won an impossible victory against all odds, but unlike some commanders, he was able to recognize that his men deserved their full share of the credit. When one *havildar* (sergeant) of the Native Cavalry brought a captured Mahratta standard to him, Wellesley declared, "*Acha havildar, jemadar.*" ("You are promoted from sergeant to lieutenant.")

After giving orders that the wounded should be cared for, Wellesley sank down onto the brown earth, utterly exhausted in mind and spirit. He sat in a kind of fetal position, his head buried between his knees. The dead and dying lay all about, and the day's carnage tormented him. Sleep finally came, but it brought nightmares instead of oblivion. When Wellesley first awoke from his fitful rest, he had a momentary impression that his whole army had been killed. In fact, the Battle of Assaye—and his own generalship—had broken the back of Mahratta power. Two more years of hard fighting remained, but there was little doubt that Britain's star was in ascendancy over central India. And Assaye was the first major victory for one of Britain's finest soldiers. More victories would follow, a roll call of honor that would culminate on June 18, 1815, with the Duke of Wellington's triumph over Napoleon at Waterloo.

Many years later, when Wellesley was lionized as the Iron Duke, an old sepoy said his general would always be "Wellesley *Bahadur*"—Wellesley the Conqueror. When the duke himself, after a long and successful career, was asked the best thing he had ever done in battle, he replied without a moment's hesitation, "Assaye."

Field Swept by Lance

*On the plains of Carabobo, a final battle
for Simon Bolivar would determine
the political fate of Venezuela.*

By John Galey

As the early fog lifted from the plains ahead, the rebel general peered through a spyglass at the royalist army a mile distant from his vantage point on the hills. Five monarchist infantry columns totaling 3,500 men and 1,500 more in three cavalry regiments were deployed in a roughly linear battle formation along a narrow, main road leading through the plains. Wearing brilliant white uniforms, the elite infantry units drew up in tight columns while mounted officers galloped back and forth giving last-minute instructions. Two royalist cannons flanked the road. The monarchists were ready to block the patriot advance on the nearby city of Valencia, gateway to the capital city 100 miles away.

Surveying the panorama before him on June 24, 1821, the rebel pondered the enemy's strengths and weak points. His opponent, Spanish Field Marshal Miguel de la Torre, had disciplined peninsular infantrymen at his disposal, but some of his troops were unenthusiastic Venezuelans. La Torre had deployed most of his professional Spanish battalions near the main road's exit from the hills. With little forward room for maneuver, la Torre now must adopt defensive tactics. He had located his unreliable Venezuelan cavalry far behind. Only several squadrons of King Ferdinand VII's mounted hussars closely supported the infantry.

Simon Bolivar easily could guess la Torre's numerous other weaknesses. In general, royalist military morale had declined. Instead of being rotated back to Spain, the peninsular troops had been forced to remain in primitive Venezuela for the past six years, often without pay and subsisting on scarce, miserable food. Though la Torre had camped at nearby Carabobo for three weeks, he failed to reconnoiter the surrounding hills—incredibly, he left them unprotected. La Torre's longstanding rivalry with his cavalry leader, Spanish General Francisco Morales, had distracted both men from more pressing concerns. Worse, la Torre was an unimaginative, plodding commander haunted by forebodings of a Spanish debacle. His forces constantly were reduced by native desertions, and the royalists controlled only an ever-shrinking segment of coastal Venezuela. He, himself, may well have secretly harbored some sympathy for the patriot cause. La Torre would make a stand at Carabobo only because honor demanded it.

But Bolivar had his own troubles. In the months before, he had seized the offensive initiative with a daring union of three widely dispersed patriot armies for a final battle to defeat Spain in Venezuela. While planning the risky confrontation, he was plagued by critical food shortages and epidemics in his armies.

Nine years of revolution and civil war had exhausted Venezuela. Livestock and crops were destroyed. The soldiers had suffered extreme privations. General Francisco Bermudez's patriot Army of the East had been decimated by malnutrition and a smallpox epidemic. With good reason, one of Bolivar's generals once remarked, "The patriot ranks constantly have more strength in the hospitals than at the front." Bolivar himself had said, "The army is a sack with no bottom."

Lacking food and horses, Bolivar had considered abandoning the entire offensive, until he received word that patriot General Jose Antonio Paez's Army of Apure would drive livestock north from Venezuela's remote southern plains area.

Near Carabobo, Bolivar planned to unite his own forces with Paez's army and General Rafael Urdaneta's Army of the West as the latter force made its way to him from Maracaibo.

The patriots won the first round with a successful diversionary attack on Caracas. Bolivar ordered Bermudez to invade the city and thus draw off some of la Torre's forces. After a short battle on May 14, Bermudez "occupied" a startled Caracas with but 1,200 soldiers. To save the prestigious seat of the viceroyalty, la Torre dispatched his rival, General Morales, with a full division, including the crack, 1,000-man 2nd Valencey Battalion, which recaptured the city. Retiring quickly before those superior forces, Bermudez and his Army of the East escaped but remained in the Province of Caracas, where he harassed the royalists. Because of deficient intelligence, Bolivar was wracked with doubts about la Torre's further movements and intentions. But Bolivar's ruse at Caracas had worked, for it kept a distracted la Torre from isolating each patriot army. The diversion also enabled the patriots to occupy more enemy territory in the Caracas Province, which at that time contained over half of Venezuela's population.

Bolivar then toyed with la Torre a second time. General Urdaneta's Maracaibo Battalion, composed of raw recruits, together with a guerrilla unit and a cavalry squadron attacked a royalist column west of Valencia and then advanced on the city. Again, la Torre overreacted to a weak force—he dispatched the strong Tello Division to stop the advance. Thus, Bolivar further whittled down the royalist forces available to defend his goal of Carabobo.

And it was fortunate, since Bolivar's own divisions were so depleted. He should have had 10,000 troops with him on the hills of Buena Vista; thanks to disease and malnutrition he instead commanded 6,400 soldiers in three divisions.

Jose Antonio Paez, a headstrong 31-year-old general, commanded the 1st Division, which included the disciplined British Battalion, composed of various European legionaries. Also in the 1st Division were the *Bravos de Apure* (Brave Ones of Apure) Battalion and 12 squadrons of fierce but undisciplined plainsmen cavalry. General Manuel Cedeno's 2nd Division consisted of the *Tiradores* (Skirmishers), Boyaca and Vargas battalions, as well as Bolivar's Sacred Squadron and the 2nd Brigade of the Guard, which once had mutinied for lack of pay. Colonel Ambrosio Plaza's 3rd Division united several units—the 1st Cavalry Regiment of the Guard, along with one hussar and one dragoon squadron; the Rifles, 1st Brigade of the Guard, the *Vencedor en Boyaca* (Conqueror at Boyaca); the Anzoategui and Granaderos battalions. The latter unit included Hanoverians who had fought for the Duke of Wellington at Waterloo. Trained rigorously by German professionals, the stoic grenadier battalion reputedly was the only patriot unit that had never failed in discipline.

Four military bands were scattered among the various battalions. For the first time in the long war for independence, the entire patriot army, except for Paez's rustic cavalrymen, was outfitted in resplendent dress uniforms.

The tips of their 12-foot lances flashed in the sunlight as Bolivar ordered Paez's centaurs forward. With a roundabout flanking maneuver, the 1st Division would attack the royalists' weak right wing—that would avoid initial engagement with la Torre's strong center and left flank. Paez's opening maneuver could decide the battle's outcome. At stake could be Venezuela's political future.

Bolivar himself was convinced that South America's independence was preordained by fate. Despite catastrophic defeats in the continent's independence struggle from 1811 to 1826, his optimism not only endured but in the most dire adversity gained in moral strength and resolve. La Torre once grudgingly admitted that Bolivar was more terrible in defeat than in victory.

The Venezuelan rebellion against Spain sprang from all-too-familiar sociopolitical grievances and economic inequity. Strict laws and customs had frozen the colony's society into different classes and castes based partly on race but also, more importantly, on birthplace. Indians and black slaves ranked the lowest, followed by people of mixed races. Creole (native-born) white aristocrats like Bolivar himself constituted a higher order as land owners and captains of commerce, but they remained second-class citizens because the top colonial administrative posts were reserved for the Spanish-born. The Creole elite would lead the rebellion, while a large percentage of the population had no firm convictions and readily would join whichever side had the best prospects of winning.

When Napoleon Bonaparte had placed his brother Joseph on the Spanish throne in 1808, Venezuelan municipalities indignantly proclaimed their loyalty to Ferdinand VII, the hereditary Bourbon claimant. By the time Venezuela's Congress proclaimed national independence on July 5, 1811, ostensible fidelity to Ferdinand had changed into a full-blown demand for separation from Spain.

Venezuela thus became the first American colony to rebel against Spain. With a central geographic location in a colonial domain extending from California to Chile, Venezuela occupied a strategic geopolitical location for spreading rebellion to the entire string of colonies. Spain reacted by sending far larger military forces to Venezuela than to any other colony during the independence wars.

Venezuela's fragile and utopian First Republic brought Bolivar into political-military prominence at the age of 28. At the beginning of the Second Republic in 1814, Bolivar received the title of Liberator of Venezuela and became captain general of the patriot forces. During the rest of his career, he served as military commander and intermittently as congressionally elected president or as a reluctant dictator of the patriot republic. A huge region, it included the future countries of Colombia, Peru, Equador, even Panama, and naturally Bolivia, along with Venezuela.

In 1814, Bolivar instituted the controversial "war to the death" in which all Spaniards who remained neutral or continued to fight for the royalists would be executed when taken prisoner. Spaniards and Venezuelan royalists would receive amnesty if they joined the republican side. With this draconian measure, Bolivar reacted to a brutal royalist counterrevolution against independence.

A new breed of independent royalist guerrilla leaders soon emerged in the region's chaos. As the taciturn General Urdaneta described it: "Any dissident felt authorized to raise a [guerrilla] band and shout, 'Long live the king!' Robbing and killing, he assumed, would win Spanish approval."

The most important of those was Jose Tomas Boves, the notorious commander of the "Legion of Hell." He was a short, stocky Spaniard with reddish-blond hair and beard. He briefly joined the patriot side, but then was imprisoned for misconduct. Gaining an inexorable hatred of the republicans, he sought revenge in fire and blood.

In Venezuela's southern plains region he conceived the sinister idea of encouraging a race and class war to exterminate the patriot Caucasian elite and thus destroy the republican cause. He offered black slaves their freedom while he also enticed various soldiers of mixed race with promises of plunder. Boves promoted blacks, zambos (offspring of a black and an Indian) and mulattos to senior commands in his campaign army of about 7,500, in which fewer than 125 were Caucasians. Ironically, this cunning, sadistic *caudillo*, known as "the whip of Heaven," was a gifted amateur tactician; he became the unwitting tutor of patriot commanders, who learned much from his startling and innovative cavalry maneuvers.

Boves' rugged *llanero* (plainsman) cavalry was well suited for combat, since its men operated with great mobility and few needs. The product of a primitive lifestyle, the plainsman was inured to hardships. He lived almost exclusively on meat, sometimes eaten raw. Well accustomed to improvisation, this expert horseman often rode barefoot and bareback. If he couldn't find clothes, he advanced into battle naked except for a loin cloth. If he had no lance, he ripped the iron bars with sharp tipped points from village windows and used those to skewer the enemy.

Flying a black pirate flag, Boves' demonic hordes crushed patriot resistance and committed bestial atrocities to terrorize Venezuela's cities. His role in the apocalyptic counterrevolution ended in late 1814, when he was killed by an anonymous patriot lance. After the death of their revered *caudillo*, many of his plainsmen switched to the patriot side. And they later would fight at Carabobo.

By then a very different breed of monarchist soldier had arrived in Venezuela. Lieutenant General Pablo Morillo landed at Caracas with the largest army ever sent by his nation to America, 11,000 seasoned veterans of the Napoleonic Wars who represented the cream of the Spanish infantry. Morillo himself was a battle-hardened hero of the war against Napoleon's French.

Spain sent the so-called "Army of Pacification" to Venezuela after Ferdinand's assumption of the Spanish throne and his restoration of royal absolutism. He vowed to punish the insolent Venezuelan rebels, and Morillo boasted that he would soon dictate the orders of his king from California to Chile.

In fact, he never fought outside New Grenada (today's Colombia) and Venezuela, but rather became mired in a seemingly endless civil war. His professional soldiers nurtured no racial-class hatreds like those of Boves' Legion of Hell, nor did they want to plunge into a civil war to the death. But eventually they, too, descended into the maelstrom of horrifying atrocities.

After a period of exile in Haiti, Bolivar returned in 1817 to resume the struggle by winning control over the Orinoco River and establishing patriot headquarters at the river port of Angostura (today's Ciudad Bolivar). The year marked an important turning point in patriot planning and strategy. Bolivar used the republican stronghold of Margarita Island and the Orinoco for importing aid from abroad. The plains of the Guayana and Apure regions, bisected by the river, became an isolated refuge for the patriots and an ideal sphere for their hit-and-run guerrillas.

From that environment, a striking new personality joined the republican cause. Jose Antonio Paez was a poor, illiterate cattle herder before he began his ambitious, meteoric rise in the patriot ranks. In his early career as a general, he still didn't know how to use a knife and fork, but he was a superb horseman. A 12-hour ride through the rugged plains and across rivers teeming with carnivorous piranha fish was an endurance test for the European cavalryman, but Paez regarded it as a normal day's work. Orienting himself by the stars, he marched at night to avoid the daytime heat and to hide the telltale dust clouds from enemy view. In one night, his cavalry could cover 100 kilometers.

Like Boves, Paez used deception and trickery in tactics. He was a master of defensive warfare, in which he lured European royalist forces into the unfamiliar ground of the plains and then ambushed them. He often set fire to the plains grasslands and stampeded riderless horses into monarchist ranks in order to confuse them. He launched repeated cavalry attacks with little semblance of order; Paez rode in no less than 14 of these assaults in one battle alone. An epileptic, he sometimes rode into battle foaming at the mouth. Though the seizures momentarily disabled him, Paez' superstitious, awestruck plainsmen regarded them as a sign of supernatural powers.

Here was a plainsman *caudillo* to inherit the dreaded mantle of Boves, but Paez fought for the patriots. Nor was Paez a sadist, though he had the plainsmen's deprecation of human life. His magnanimous freeing of prisoners was calculated to attract former royalists to his cause. Paez also permitted looting. And in Venezuela, by 1817 only the monarchists had anything worth plundering.

Among the former royalist cavalrymen who flocked to Paez's army was a robust, black ex-slave named Pedro Camejo. An expert lancer, he led the vanguard in patriot cavalry attacks; thus he became known as the "First Negro," and Paez commissioned him as a lieutenant. Camejo became Paez's personal bodyguard and rescued his commander from death many times. When Bolivar once asked Camejo why he had fought for the royalists, the former slave answered with disarming frankness: "For greed. I noticed that everyone went to war without a shirt and a single peseta, and they returned with a beautiful uniform and money in their pockets. So I also went to seek my fortune."

Paez followed Boves' precedent by encouraging a rough, frontier sense of equality among his racially mixed soldiers. His soldiers called him "Uncle Antonio," but in battle they generally obeyed his orders out of fear that if they didn't, they might commit fatal errors. Paez intimately knew their psychology of intense personal loyalty. His maxim was, "The plainsmen obey only the master of the plains."

In many respects, Simon Bolivar was his opposite. He had enjoyed a privileged background in education and travel, and he came from a wealthy, aristocratic family. As a convinced republican, he stood for equal representation but within the limits of a strong, centralized government led by a well-educated, enlightened elite. Bolivar knew some of his fellow white Creoles were uncomfortable with the idea of a racial democracy; as he once wrote, "We have democracy on our lips and aristocracy in our hearts." Bolivar also knew he couldn't win the war without the aid of native soldiers from all races. He stubbornly advocated legal equality for all and the abolition of slavery.

Unlike the provincial-minded Paez, Bolivar had a far-sighted political vision of union among the future nations of South America. Under his guidance in 1821, Venezuela's Congress created the Republic of Grand Colombia, including Venezuela, Cuindinamarca (Colombia) and Quito (Ecuador), which was still under royalist control.

Only 5 feet 6 inches tall, Bolivar was small but well proportioned, with an amazing endurance of both hunger and fatigue. Expert in the use of various arms, he was also a skillful, daring horseman. Even the plainsmen were impressed with his riding stamina (among themselves they called him "Iron Ass").

Bolivar seldom complained about campaign hardships. The man who would liberate half a continent helped in the menial tasks of loading or unloading supplies during his epic campaign marches. With boundless generosity, he went deeply into personal debt to help his soldiers and their families.

The Liberator learned military tactics the hard way, through mistakes. Because of his changeable, fiery disposition, he made rash moves in battle. But he was an expert improviser, and his impetuous tactics were improved by his gifted protege and chief of staff, Antonio Jose de Sucre.

When their imported European legionaries first arrived in Angostura in 1818, they found the patriot army in shocking condition. Bolivar's own forces totaled only about 2,000. Many were untrained, unarmed adolescents, and 600 were Indians with bows and arrows. Malaria scourged their ranks. The "soldiers" had no uniforms and no pay.

Among other results, British colonels were reduced to marching barefoot. When Colonel James Rooke, a future hero of the British Battalion, attended a military banquet in Angostura, he appeared in a buttonless coat held together by thorns, his way of hiding the fact that he had no shirt. Bolivar asked his servant to give the colonel one of his own shirts, but the servant replied, "My General, you have only two shirts, the one you're wearing and the one in the wash."

Bolivar concentrated on strengthening the patriot forces with newly arriving supplies, foreign legionaries and Paez's army. After a staggering trek over the Andes mountains into New Grenada, Bolivar won that region for the patriots.

By early 1820, political and military upheaval in Spain favored the establishment of an armistice. The Spanish people were war weary and estranged by the despotic absolutism of King Ferdinand. A new expeditionary corps of more than 24,000 soldiers, bound for Venezuela, mutinied; its liberal-minded officers refused to help restore in South America a tyrannical rule that they hated at home. Spain then made peace overtures to the Venezuelan patriots, who gained a temporary respite from combat.

At the tiny village of Santa Ana in western Venezuela, the two opposing commanders met after the armistice of November 25th was signed. In the bitter civil war, this unprecedented scene resembled a vignette from the era of medieval chivalry. General Morillo arrived in full uniform with all his decorations. Initially wary of the patriots, he came with a hussar squadron and 50 senior officers, including his General la Torre. When he learned of the tiny patriot contingent, Morillo sent away the hussars and some of his staff. The Spanish commander did not recognize Bolivar in civilian clothes. "What?" Morillo murmured after learning his identity. "That little man in the blue coat and campaign hat, sitting on a mule...that is Bolivar?"

The enemy commanders embraced cordially and toasted the valor of each other's armies. That night they slept in the same hut as a token of their mutual trust. From that very hut, Simon Bolivar had once proclaimed the war to the death.

The Liberator summoned all his impressive eloquence and diplomacy in trying to win further concessions from the Spaniards. Morillo's second-in-command, la Torre, seemed sympathetic toward the patriot cause. The future Spanish commander at Carabobo even offered an ambiguous toast seemingly directed against Ferdinand VII: "To the Colombians and to the Spaniards," he said, "who side by side will march to Hell itself, if necessary, against despots and tyrants!"

The five-month armistice issued in a radically different era for the independence struggle. Spain treated the new republic on an equal footing as a legitimate opponent. Under new rules of war, both sides agreed to protect all prisoners. And so by the time of the Battle of Carabobo, the savage war to the death was over, although the civil war's underlying malaise still remained.

For his part, Morillo had welcomed the armistice because he felt Spain's cause was doomed. By 1820, less than one third of the original "Army of Pacification" had survived. Morillo knew that Spain would send no more soldiers to his aid, and he feared the government would even refuse to send ships for evacuating the remaining army in case of defeat. The Spanish commander also realized that the war of independence had dragged on for so long because it also was a civil war. Without her South American soldiers, Spain might have suffered a decisive defeat much earlier in the conflict. But Morillo had never felt comfortable with his native, dark-skinned soldiers either. Though he needed them desperately, he suspected that they would one day turn against the Spaniards—by late 1820, the desertions of his native soldiers had increased dramatically.

Caught in this equivocal quandary, Morillo felt tremendously relieved when Spanish authorities finally accepted his 10th attempt to resign. The monarchist cause thus lost its most able commander. Morillo recommended the plodding la Torre as his successor, because at least la Torre was honorable. Morillo passed over the more talented and aggressive cavalry leader Francisco Morales, a former Boves associate whose notorious atrocities in Venezuela had made him unacceptable as commander in chief. Furious over that apparent slight, Morales immediately tried to resign.

The patriots broke the armistice with an uprising at Maracaibo, and Bolivar united his armies for the showdown at Carabobo. There, he displayed a cautious tactical expertise that marked his maturity as a commander.

Bolivar feinted by moving his main forces slightly forward to deceive la Torre into expecting a frontal assault. Moving off to the left of the main road, meanwhile, Paez's 1st Division ran a gauntlet of artillery fire and then disappeared along a rough, seldom-used path behind some hills, out of the enemy's sight. Forging ahead through a narrow defile, Paez's sappers hacked with machetes at dense foliage. In the intense heat, locusts clamored for rain, and already hungry vultures circled overhead. The *Bravos de Apure* reached the top of a hill, exposed to royalist view. Paez's soldiers would have to descend a slope and cross a stream bed through another defile so narrow that only one could pass at a time. Then they would have to rush another hill to a crest of the Carabobo plain. To stop them, royalist General la Torre hurriedly formed a strong skirmish line with units of his Burgos, Hostalrich and Barbastro Battalions.

The *Bravos* first dashed down the slope, but murderous Spanish fire struck them at the stream-bed crossing, and eventually they retreated. Bolivar's British Battalion then rushed through the crossing in single file and deployed below the crest. To the beat of the battalion's drummers, veterans of Waterloo now advanced with parade-ground precision up the hill toward the enemy skirmishers. They carried full packs with all their equipment as they pushed upward, panting for breath. Lieutenant Charles Ashdown hugged the flag staff of the republican colors to his breast.

As the battalion soldiers knelt and fired and then reloaded, the royalist skirmishers found perfect targets. The British commander, Colonel Thomas Ferrier, fell mortally wounded. Seventeen officers fell in as many minutes. Though wounded, Captain James Minchin then ordered a bayonet charge. The remainder of the battalion gained the crest and formed a hollow square to resist an oncoming attack by the hussars of King Ferdinand VII.

The British Battalion's assault enabled the *Bravos* to reform and charge up the hill while two skirmisher companies, sent by Bolivar, advanced upward at a different position nearby. Paez ordered a cavalry charge by 34 of his staff officers and a company of the Honor Guard; they mounted the hill at a less steep incline and clashed with the hussars.

On the field itself, Paez saw his Lieutenant Camejo riding erratically toward him and away from the battle. "Are you afraid?" Paez shouted angrily, "Go and die bravely!" On his meandering horse, Camejo came closer. He had two chest wounds and was bleeding down his scarlet British Dragoon's jacket and onto the horse's neck. The horse was also wounded. "General," Camejo finally replied, "I came to tell you goodbye. I can't die because I'm already dead." Slipping from his horse, the "First Negro" fell dead next to his commander.

But the battle went on—with his cavalry, Paez charged the Barbastro Battalion, which quickly surrendered. In the midst of a subsequent cavalry clash with the Valencey Battalion, Paez suffered an epileptic seizure. In a bizarre turn of events, a royalist cavalry commander, Antonio Martinez, formerly one of Boves' lancers, rescued him.

On the main road, meanwhile, Bolivar had held back most of his army while awaiting the outcome of Paez's enveloping movement. So successful was it, however, that in less than one hour, the battle was all but won, with no more than one-fifth of the patriot forces engaged. On a wounded horse, General la Torre exhorted his soldiers with shouts of encouragement, threats and insults, but to no avail. They refused to obey his orders to stand fast. The Burgos Battalion was destroyed and the Hostalrich dispersed. Probably to further embarrass la Torre, his rival Morales simply withdrew his cavalry (most of the horsemen later deserted). The 900-man Valencey, its former commander Morillo's most prized and beloved battalion, now stood alone on the battlefield to face the entire patriot army.

The disciplined Valencey formed a hollow square with three staggered ranks of bristling bayonets. Inside, with the general staff and the artillery, Spain's gold and crimson banner fluttered defiantly. The Valencey then began a stubborn and valiant retreat.

Bolivar ordered his army to pursue the monarchist units streaming backward across the plain. Impatient at holding back for so long, Bolivar's General Manuel Cedeño charged alone against the whole Valencey Battalion and was shot from his horse. As the Liberator worried that the royalists might suddenly rally with fresh forces he hadn't counted on, the pursuit around him had turned into a wild melee. Colonel Ambrosio Plaza rode forward alone to take the retreating Infante Battalion's surrender. He was shot through the heart. "Order!" Bolivar shouted at his troops. "Discipline!"

Fighting off patriot attacks, the Valencey tenaciously held its square but abandoned the artillery to speed its retreat. Halfway back to Valencia, Bolivar ordered his Rifles and Granaderos infantrymen to mount up behind the rebel cavalrymen so they could overtake the Valencey. But a torrential downpour turned the ground into slimy mud. Each weighted down with two riders, the cavalry horses had to slow their pace so they wouldn't slip and fall. Delayed, the patriot forces nonetheless hounded the Valencey Battalion into Valencia itself, where street fighting briefly erupted. Some of the brave battalion escaped when darkness fell—nearly 400 Spanish soldiers found refuge in the nearby fortified port city of Puerto Cabello.

The patriots lost only about 200 soldiers at Carabobo; of those, more than half were in the British Battalion. Bolivar decorated every remaining battalion member with the Order of the Liberators. Paez received from Bolivar a battlefield promotion to General-in-Chief of the Army.

Unopposed, Bolivar took the city of Caracas, but the last royalist strong-hold of Puerto Cabello did not surrender until November 10, 1823, when 1,539 soldiers and 56 officers capitulated to Paez.

Militarily, the patriot victory at Carabobo broke forever Spain's power in Venezuela. Politically, the victory ushered in the figure of Paez, who twice became president of his country and in 1830 led its separation from Bolivar's cherished Grand Colombia.

With his prophetic vision, Bolivar knew even before Carabobo that the new country's peasant-soldiers would rebel against the state if they did not benefit from it with measures such as land distribution. And Paez would lead them.

"These are not the soldiers you know," Bolivar wrote to Grand Colombia's minister of foreign affairs in May 1821. "These are men who have fought long and hard and who, believing that they deserve much, feel thoroughly humiliated and miserable. They have no hope of gathering the fruit of what they have won by the lance."

Bolivar concluded, "I fear peace more than war."

Among the many ironies of the South American wars for independence was Bolivar's eventual death in exile from his native country. Impoverished and deserted by most of his followers, he would be reviled in 1830 by his compatriots who now followed Paez, his hopes for real peace shattered by countless military mutinies and mini-civil wars in the newly liberated nations. Bolivar found his own image in a famous Spaniard when he re-read Don Quixote during his last days. And the Liberator's despairing statement that "those who have served the Revolution have plowed the seas" tended to belittle his achievements—but unfairly so. He had freed half a continent.

Sam Houston's Revenge

*Avenging the Alamo and Goliad would be one goal as
Sam Houston and his Texans turned from apparent retreat
onto the road leading to certain battle.*

By Allen Lee Hamilton

On February 17, 1836, General Don Antonio Lopez de Santa Anna y Perez de Lebron, president of Mexico and self-styled "Napoleon of the West," crossed the Rio Grande River near the town of Matamoros. He had come furiously marching north from Mexico City at the head of some 6,000 troops to crush a revolution that had broken out among the 30,000 or so settlers (two-thirds of whom were Anglo-Americans) in Mexico's easternmost province, Texas.

It was not the first uprising *El Presidente* had faced since abolishing Mexico's democratic constitution and assuming dictatorial powers three years before. In 1835, the rich and beautiful province of Zacatecas had rebelled, and had paid the price. Santa Anna swiftly descended upon the province, defeated the rebel militia, executed hundreds of prisoners and loosed his troops upon the countryside to rape and pillage. As he liked to say, "If you execute your enemies, it saves you the trouble of having to forgive them."

Now it was the Texans' turn to feel His Excellency's wrath. It was his intention (officially approved by the Mexican Congress) to execute every colonist who was in rebellion, drive all the Anglo-Americans out of Texas, and to make certain that no more of their kind ever returned. General Martin Cos (Santa Anna's brother-in-law) wrote: "The government has ordered to take up line of march...troops which were in Zacatecas. These Texans will be ground down."

For the next eight weeks, Cos' boast seemed anything but empty. Santa Anna and his men overwhelmed all opposition. On February 23, they invested a ramshackle fortress called the Alamo on the outskirts of San Antonio de Bexar. Inside, 186 Texans and Americans led by Colonel William B. Travis and two frontier legends, James Bowie and David Crockett, knew they faced certain death when Santa Anna hoisted a blood-red battle flag and ordered his regimental bands to play the *Dugeullo*, signs that no quarter would be given.

On March 6, the Mexicans launched a mass assault against the place and, despite all that courage and ferocity born of desperation could do, the Alamo fell and all its defenders were slain (a few, some accounts claim, were taken alive and then, over the vehement objections of many staff officers, executed at *El Presidente's* orders). Only Mrs. Suzanna Dickenson, wife of one of the defenders, her 18-month-old daughter, and Travis' black servant were spared. Santa Anna gave them a mule and sent them east, hoping that the terrible news they bore would spread panic and despair among the rebels.

On March 19, General Jose Urrea, leading a hard-riding column of heavy cavalry and lancers, caught Colonel James Fannin and some 400 men, mostly volunteers from the United States, on the open prairie near Goliad. Surrounded, cut off from water and pounded by grape shot and canister from Urrea's light artillery, Fannin surrendered the next day. Urrea, who was an honorable man and a professional soldier, seems to have promised Fannin good treatment, perhaps even the "Honors of War," as some survivors claimed. But Santa Anna demanded that his standing orders regarding traitors be carried out. Urrea refused, and rode on eastward with most of his men, leaving a Lt Col. José Nicholás de la Porilla in charge of the prisoners at Goliad. On Palm Sunday, March 27, Porilla, at Santa Anna's insistence, marched the prisoners out onto the prairie, lined them up and shot them— 390 died; only 27 Texans managed to escape.

Thus, by the end of March, Santa Anna felt positive that the rebellion had been broken up. He organized his army into several columns of pursuit and began a drive to the Sabine River, the boundary between Texas and the United States. His commanders had orders to burn every town and farm in their path and to push all the Anglo-American settlers out of the state. Despite the advent of unusually heavy spring rains that frequently mired his columns in seas of mud and made every river a major obstacle, *El Presidente* believed that the rest of the campaign was merely a mopping-up exercise.

While Santa Anna was sweeping all opposition before him, however, the alarmed Texans had been organizing a government. On March 1, 59 delegates attended a convention at the town of Washington-on-the-Brazos. The next day they approved and signed a Declaration of Independence from the tyranny and despotism of Mexican rule and, to preserve that independence, elected Sam Houston commander in chief of all the militia, volunteer, and regular forces which together constituted the "Army of Texas."

It would be difficult to imagine a more perfect choice for this position of destiny than Sam Houston. At 43, 6 feet, 2 inches tall, ruggedly handsome with dark hair and iron-hard eyes, Houston was just what Texas needed—a leader. By the time he arrived in Texas in 1832, he had already led a remarkable life, and his booming voice, towering personality, and colorful reputation brought him instant attention from the most prominent citizens of the state. As one admiring observer said, "Old Sam was a man commissioned for leadership by God."

Houston was one of those rare individuals who seemed capable of mastering any task, but his adopted land was asking a truly Herculean labor of him—to find some way to defeat Santa Anna and save the new republic. The delegates at Washington-on-the Brazos would find that, in the end, they chose wisely and very well.

Houston left the convention on March 6 with only three aides and rode into Gonzales, some 60 miles due east of San Antonio de Bexar, on March 11. There he found the "Army of Texas" waiting for him, all of 374 effectives, mostly dressed in buckskin and homespun, wearing everything from coonskin to stovepipe hats, and armed with every sort of firearm imaginable. Houston described them as "half-fed, half-clad, half-armed, and unorganized."

They were not soldiers, but they were first-rate fighters and superb blasphemers (the Mexicans nicknamed them *"Soldados God Dammes"* because of their steady stream of curses).

It was Houston's formidable chore to turn that rabble into an army capable of stopping Santa Anna. He began by organizing those on hand into the First Texas Volunteer Regiment and naming Edward Burleson as their colonel. Two days later, the first of many morale setbacks exploded upon the Texans—the scouts brought in Mrs. Dickenson and her daughter. Her tale of the Alamo's fall rocked the town, for 32 of Gonzales' men had heeded Travis' call from the Alamo for reinforcements and marched to his aid. Now the widows and orphans of those gallant men wailed and mourned, even in the streets. That night, Houston ordered a general retreat, knowing full well his pitiful force, untrained and badly outnumbered, just then stood no chance against the victorious Mexican army. Time and distance might change the odds, might alter the situation in some unforeseeable fashion; but for now, retreat, hard and bitter though it might be, was the only chance for survival. As the soldiers marched away, the cries of the women and children of Gonzales echoed in their ears and burned in their memories.

By March 17, Houston and the army had reached the Colorado River, only to find the crossing choked with refugees fleeing the advancing Mexican columns. For three days the soldiers stood, backs to the river, shielding the civilians as they struggled to ford the rain-swollen river; then they, too, crossed. The next day, General Joachin Ramirez y Sesma arrived with some 800 cavalry and infantry. Houston's force had swelled to around 800 (within a week it would peak at around 1,200 men), and most of them wanted to recross the river and attack Ramirez, but their own general refused. When the time came, he would allow his men to fight. But now was not the time, and Ramirez was not the Mexican Houston wanted.

For six days the two armies lay with the flooding river between them, while the Texans grumbled and cursed and grew more discontented with their commander. On March 26, Houston, to the dismay of his men, ordered another retreat.

Two days later, Houston reached San Felipe on the Brazos River. From there he intended to march northeast to a place called Groce's Plantation, a huge, well-stocked farm surrounded by rivers where the army could rest and train. But two of the company commanders, Wily Martin and Mosely Baker, tired of drill and spoiling for a fight, refused to retreat any farther. Houston, fed up with malcontents, ordered Martin and Baker and their men to remain behind to guard the Brazos river crossings. He then marched on to Groce's Plantation with fewer than 900 men.

Meanwhile, the entire countryside was in a state of alarm. The news of the Alamo and Goliad tragedies spread like a prairie fire among the settlements. The older men, women and children gathered what they could and fled before Santa Anna's rampaging columns while the younger men grimly marched off to find General Houston and join his army. This mass exodus became known as the "Runaway Scrape," and its progress eastward was marked by the black smoke from scores of burning towns and ranches.

On April 7, Santa Anna rode into the smoldering ruins of San Felipe, to find the Brazos River crossing blocked by Mosely Baker and his men, who were dug in on the east bank. Santa Anna sent orders for two of his columns to consolidate at San Felipe, while he pivoted south with a flying column composed of some 500 grenadiers and 50 cavalry, searching for another ford. On April 12, *El Presidente* forced an alternate crossing guarded by Wily Martin and his company, and, on information gathered from local sympathizers, raced for the town of Harrisburg, hoping to catch the fleeing Texan government there.

He entered Harrisburg on April 15, only to find that the President of Texas, David G. Burnet, and most of his cabinet had left just hours before. Santa Anna burned the town and pushed on to the port of New Washington on Galveston Bay, arriving just in time to see Burnet and his party board a schooner and sail away. Furious at being deprived of the pleasure of hanging Burnet and his cabinet, Santa Anna now turned his attention to Houston. He ordered New Washington burned and, on April 20, turned northwest to rendezvous with reinforcements and then hunt down the pitiful little force of *Soldados God Dammes* that so grandly called itself the Army of Texas.

For two weeks, that army camped at Groce's Plantation while Houston tried to instill some discipline and military training into the raw troops, who in turn cursed everything from their commander to the incessant rain. Houston was under great pressure to stop retreating and drilling and to engage the enemy. Some even talked of staging a mutiny and electing a more aggressive leader. Texas Secretary of War Thomas Jefferson Rusk (whose descendant would one day be the United States secretary of state) brought a letter to Houston from President Burnet that said: "The enemy is laughing you to scorn. You must retreat no more. The country expects you to fight. The salvation of the country depends on your doing so."

To Burnet, Houston replied that the president and the cabinet, all able-bodied men, had retreated a great deal faster than the army, and had little room to criticize. To his men, Houston promised to hang anyone attempting a coup. And to Rusk, Houston said he was keeping no one's counsel except his own, and that whatever mistakes might be made, the blame would be his alone. Rusk agreed to back Houston no matter what.

In truth, Houston had no real grand strategy. Like Quintus Fabius Maximus did before Hannibal Barca's Carthaginian invaders, Houston simply had traded territory for time, waiting for the enemy to make some great mistake. Time, however, was rapidly running out as desertions quickly began to outnumber reinforcements, and the threat of mutiny hung heavy in the damp air. Houston needed a stroke of luck, and he needed it soon. On April 12, it came.

A colonist named Joseph Powell reported that on April 10, Santa Anna had spent the evening at the Powell family's inn on the lower Brazos, and had boasted that he would personally capture Burnet and his cabinet at Harrisburg. Houston knew that Santa Anna was fond of raiding ahead of his main forces with a modest personal guard, and here he saw an opportunity to isolate *El Presidente* and possibly defeat him before his support columns could intervene. It was a slim chance, but Houston grabbed at it.

On April 12 and 13, the army crossed the Brazos River and on April 14 marched east. Along the way, Mosely Baker and his men rejoined the army. So, too, did Wily Martin, but he came alone, as his company had disbanded rather than serve under Houston again. There were now slightly more than 1,000 men in the army.

On the morning of April 16, the road they followed forked, the left-hand path leading to the Sabine River and the United States, and the right-hand south to Harrisburg. Since Houston had confided his plans to only Secretary of War Rusk there was great concern among the troops that their commander intended to keep retreating. The officers and men held their breath as they neared the fork, and then loosed "loud and joyous shouts" as Houston and the advance guard swung down the right-hand road to Harrisburg. They knew at last they were going to fight.

On April 18, Houston received his second great stroke of luck. Two of his far-ranging scouts, Erastus "Deaf" Smith and Henry Wax Karnes, intercepted a Mexican courier with dispatches from General Vincente Filisola, one of the Mexican column commanders, to Santa Anna. The letters revealed that the Mexican dictator was even farther ahead of his army than Houston had dared dream, that as of that day he was at New Washington with about 1,000 men, and that reinforcements of 500 more were on their way from Filisola's column to join him. Houston now knew his enemy's whereabouts and his strength. On that day, the hunted became the hunter.

On April 19, Houston established a camp for his baggage and for his sick and ailing outside the smoldering ruins of Harrisburg, and then set out with some 800 effectives. They crossed swollen Vince's Bayou and marched east along the southern bank of a flooded tributary of the San Jacinto River called

Buffalo Bayou. The next day, Houston's and Santa Anna's forces found each other and fought a light skirmish on a spot of open prairie in a bend of the fast-flowing San Jacinto. The sparring was inconclusive, and neither side tried to press the matter. Since Houston seemed to be trapped between two raging rivers and the Mexican force, Santa Anna was content to retire about three quarters of a mile, hastily construct a semifortified camp of brush, packs and saddlebags, and sit down to await his reinforcements.

There was no possible escape for the Texans, so there was no hurry. The *coup de grâce* could be administered when Filisola came up. Meanwhile, Santa Anna was careful to place his camp just over a slight rise in the prairie so that it was protected from Houston's two 6-pounder cannon, gifts from the citizens of Cincinnati, Ohio, that were called "Twin Sisters" by the Texans. He then ordered that his men should sleep on their weapons in battle formation, and that a watch be kept. Then, satisfied with his dispositions, the supremely confident "Napoleon of the West" retired for the evening.

At 9 the next morning, April 21, General Cos rode into camp with the 500 reinforcements, bringing the total Mexican strength to more than 1,500. The Mexican president's optimism soared. He outnumbered Houston's rabble nearly two to one, and was in an easily defensible position. Today he would rest his men, and tomorrow he would successfully conclude his most satisfying campaign ever. Santa Anna sent orders to his men to stand down, and he retired to his tent for an afternoon of siesta. His officers lounged under the trees sipping champagne and dozing. By 4 in the afternoon the Mexican camp was silent.

By contrast, the Texan encampment was alive with furious, but relatively quiet, activity. Rifles were checked and loaded, Bowie knives and tomahawks were honed, and the horsemen saw to their mounts and sabers. The army readied itself to fight, and their commander at last was ready to let them.

When Houston arose that morning, he is supposed to have said, "This is going to be a damned good day to fight a battle." He then made the final preparation for that battle. Unknown to his men, he dispatched the dependable Deaf Smith and six other scouts to destroy Vince's bridge, the only span over Vince's Bayou and the only practical access to their present location. That was done to prevent any further reinforcements from reaching Santa Anna, but it also cut off any realistic avenue of retreat for the Texans. Many times the soldiers had used the brave words "victory or death," had even embroidered the sentiment on their only battle flag; but when Vince's bridge collapsed into the bayou's swirling waters, the phrase literally became their destiny.

At 3 p.m., Houston formed his men. The dirty, cold, hungry soldiers of the Army of Texas ranged from Mirabeau Lamar's cavalry on the right flank, through Burleson's First Texas in the middle, to Colonel Sidney Sherman's

213

Second Texas (formed at Groce's Plantation) on the left, with Mosely Baker's malcontents and several smaller units arrayed between. Altogether there were 783 effectives in a line two ranks deep and more than 900 yards long. In the center floated their white-and-blue battle flag, and beside it rode General Houston, mounted on a great, white stallion named Saracen.

At 4 p.m. Houston slowly trotted out so that all in the line could see him. He made no speech; the time for brave words was past, and few of the men could have heard him anyway. For weeks they had hated him and cursed him, and some had even threatened to kill him, but now all looked to him. For a long moment Houston was still, gazing intently at the rise which hid the Mexican camp from view. Then he drew his sword, pointed the way, and the army followed.

In deadly silence the long line advanced, rifles leveled, while the Twin Sisters were manhandled up the slope with quiet curses. The crest neared— 800 yards, then 500, then the army was almost to it; and still there were no sounds of alarm from the Mexican camp. Incredibly, in what would prove to be one of the most fateful mistakes in military history, Santa Anna and his officers had neglected to throw out pickets or scouts. Not until the Texans reached the crest and stood a scant 200 yards away were they noticed by the sentries, and by then it was far too late.

The Mexican artillery boomed, but the shots sailed harmlessly high. The Texans' band, three fifers and a drummer, screeched into life, and the long line descended at a trot upon the enemy, the Twin Sisters careening along in front. From out of nowhere Deaf Smith appeared, galloping along the battle line shouting: "Vince's bridge is down! Fight for your lives! Vince's bridge is down!"

Those who heard him realized that little hope of retreat now remained, and they drove grimly on. Then, at 80 yards or so, it was first heard—what has become one of the most famous battle cries in history. From the left of the line, Colonel Sidney Sherman bellowed at the top of his lungs, "Remember the Alamo!" And how could any Texan ever forget it?

Among the attackers were seven survivors of the Goliad massacre and they added, "Remember Goliad!" The Spanish-speaking solders took up the cry, *"Recuerden el Alamo!"* And then all semblance of order dissolved. The Texans fired a great volley that swept clear the brush and saddle-bag wall, and the Twin Sisters, firing at point-blank range, blew it apart. Then the savage, screaming, unstoppable *"Soldados God Dammes"* threw themselves upon their disorganized enemies—literally with a vengeance.

The Mexican soldiers had desperately tried to form ranks to fight, but the Texans were too close and it all happened too fast. Their officers shouted frantic, conflicting orders at them; form line, fire, fall back. Santa Anna was seen "running about in the utmost excitement, wringing his hands and unable to give an order." And then came the terrible, accusing cry again:

"Remember the Alamo!" *"Recuerdan el Alamo!"*

It broke Mexican morale like a dry twig. As the Texans tore into them, many of the Mexican soldiers threw down their weapons and begged for mercy. They died. Most of the rest fled. Colonel Pedro Delgado, a staff officer, wrote: "I saw our men flying in small groups, terrified, and sheltering themselves behind large trees. I endeavored to force some of them to fight, but all efforts were in vain...."

The actual battle was over in less than 18 minutes. The shooting, clubbing and stabbing went on for at least an hour, or until the Texans' thirst for vengeance and blood was sated. Houston rode among his men roaring for them to parade, to form ranks, but he was mostly ignored. To one group that did stop momentarily to listen, he shouted: "Gentlemen, I applaud your bravery. But damn your manners!" Finally, he gave up and rode off in disgust.

Though most of the Mexicans ran, there was no escape. Lamar's cavalry cut down those who fled across the open prairie, while the vast majority of fugitives found themselves driven back against the San Jacinto. Many drowned trying to swim the muddy river, but most were methodically slaughtered by riflemen who poured a relentless fire into the milling, helpless mob. Not until late in the day were surrenders accepted.

By the next morning the extent of the Texans' victory had become apparent. They had lost two killed, and another seven would soon die of their wounds. There was a total of 23 wounded, including Sam Houston. He had had two horses killed under him, and had taken a musket ball in his ankle.

Mexican losses were staggering—630 lay dead on the field, including one general, four colonels, two lieutenant colonels, five captains and 12 lieutenants. Another 208 were wounded, and 730 were prisoners. The Mexican force had literally been erased. But the one man Houston wanted most had eluded death or capture. Santa Anna had fled just before his camp was overrun, and since nightfall Houston's scouts had been scouring the countryside for him. Unless he could be caught, the great victory would mean little, for the Mexican army in Texas still outnumbered Houston's force by four to one.

One last time Houston's luck held. On April 22, a Texan patrol brought in what they thought was just another dusty Mexican private, but when he was put with the other prisoners, some of the soldiers imprudently cried, *"Est El Presidente!"* Their officers tried to hush them, but it was too late. Closer inspection revealed the private's shirt was held together with diamond studs. It was indeed General Santa Anna, president of Mexico.

Houston was at that moment lying under an oak tree, cursing his wounded ankle. But when he looked up and saw a prisoner being herded into his presence by what seemed to be half the camp, his mood brightened considerably.

"Ah, General Santa Anna, have a seat," said Houston, motioning to an ammunition box. Ignoring shouts of "Shoot him!" and "Hang him!" Santa Anna bravely said, "That man may consider himself born to no common destiny who has conquered The Napoleon of the West. And now it remains for him to be generous to the vanquished."

After a long silence, Houston softly replied, "You should have remembered that at the Alamo." Within a month, however, Santa Anna would sign a treaty with the Republic of Texas that would end hostilities and withdraw the Mexican army south of the Rio Grande. Texas would have her independence. But for now it was enough that the men of the Alamo and Goliad were avenged, and that the Texas refugees toiling along the muddy roads to the United States were overtaken by hat-waving, wildly delirious riders who shouted at them the joyous words: "Hallelujah! Hallelujah! San Jacinto! San Jacinto!"

Race to the Capital

*For American General Winfield Scott, standing at
Mexico City's doorstep, everything was wrong. His army was
outnumbered. He had no supply line to the rear. He was surrounded
by hostile territory on all sides...and so he advanced!*

By G. P. Stokes

In the early dawn of August 7, 1847, a column of blue-coated dragoons trotted out of the sleeping Mexican city of Puebla and turned westward, toward the distant, snowcapped peaks of Popocatépetl and Iztaccihuatl. It was the vanguard of an American army that, since landing at Veracruz in March, had marched and fought its way to within 70 miles of Mexico City.

Now deep in enemy country, his army outnumbered almost 3-to-1 by the forces that General Antonio López de Santa Anna had gathered to defend the Mexican capital against the hated Yankees, was America's venerable Maj. Gen. Winfield Scott. His lines of communication to the rear abandoned, like those of Hernando Cortés three centuries earlier, Scott had to win every battle lying ahead or face annihilation.

At the outset of the Mexican War in May of 1846, Maj. Gen. Zachary Taylor, campaigning along the Rio Grande, had decisively defeated the Mexicans at Palo Alto and Resaca de la Palma. Following those victories, he invaded the northern Mexican province of Nuevo Léon and, after overcoming a stubbornly resisting garrison, captured the fortress city of Monterey on September 25, 1846.

Taylor's victories, plus successful American operations in New Mexico and California, raised President James K. Polk's expectations that the Mexican government would soon sue for peace. But instead, General Santa Anna rallied his scattered forces and Mexican resistance stiffened.

Reluctantly, President Polk concluded that the only way to end the increasingly unpopular war was to invade the heart of Mexico and seize the capital. With 800 miles of rugged terrain lying between Taylor's army and Mexico City, however, invasion from the north clearly would be impractical. After several weeks of delay, President Polk approved the plan proposed by the U.S. Army's commander, Maj. Gen. Winfield Scott, for an amphibious landing on the Gulf of Mexico at Veracruz, to be followed by an advance on Mexico City.

On March 9, 1847, Scott landed, unopposed, near Veracruz with 10,000 men. After a prolonged artillery bombardment, the port with its harbor fortress fell on March 29 with the loss of only 67 Americans killed or wounded. The next day Scott's vanguard, following the route once taken by Cortés, began its 260-mile march inland on the Mexican capital.

As they climbed out of the fever-ridden coastal plain, the Americans encountered their first serious resistance at Cerro Gordo. By April 18, after acting on information gathered during a daring scouting mission by Captain Robert E. Lee, Scott's men outflanked the Mexican left and rear positions. A diversionary demonstration on the Mexican frontal positions, led by Maj. Gen. Gideon J. Pillow, advanced in a disorderly manner along a route that exposed it to fire from three Mexican batteries—on top of which Pillow blurted out an exclamation loud enough to alert the Mexicans to his presence. Caught in a point-blank volley of muskets and cannons, the frontal assault was thrown back with 80 casualties, including Pillow, who said he was "all shot to pieces," but turned out only to have suffered a flesh wound in the arm.

Despite Pillow's failure, the flank attacks, led by Colonels William S. Harney, Bennet Riley and James Shields, succeeded brilliantly. Taken by surprise, Santa Anna fled after losing 1,200 dead or wounded, and some 3,000 troops taken prisoner. Jalapa surrendered on April 20, and the great fortress at Perote fell two days later.

Although the one-sided battle of Cerro Gordo cost the Americans only 63 dead and 368 wounded, their losses mounted as Scott moved deeper into Mexico. Elusive guerrillas plundered the lightly defended American supply trains and made life hazardous for any Yankee unwise enough to stray beyond the sentry line.

Late in April, more than 3,000 men from seven volunteer regiments, their 12-month enlistments about to expire, ignored the entreaties of their officers to re-enlist and marched back to Veracruz for transportation back to the United States.

Scott was forced to halt at Puebla on May 15. He was only 70 miles from the Mexican capital. But mounting losses, mainly from malaria and diarrhea, had reduced his force to only 5,000 effectives. Uncertain of when, or even if, reinforcements would arrive, he decided to augment his army by ordering the garrisons he had left behind at Perote and Jalapa to march to Puebla. While waiting for their arrival, the force with Scott exacted food and supplies from the local countryside. Reinforcements finally arrived during July and early August, bringing the army up to a paper strength of 14,000.

On August 7, the Americans resumed their advance as 10,783 men marched out of their camp at Puebla, leaving behind 3,000 invalids in the care of a small garrison. Scott, in his usual flamboyant manner, was to write to William Marcy, Polk's secretary of war, "We had to throw away the scabbard and to advance with naked sword in hand."

Observers of the war in Mexico were unanimous in their criticism of

Scott's daring (or foolhardy) decision to cut loose from his line of communications. Polk called it "a great military error," and a more qualified observer, the British general and statesman Arthur Wellesley, the Duke of Wellington, exclaimed to a friend: "Scott is lost! He cannot capture the city and he cannot fall back on his base!"

The army that left Puebla in faded and patched uniforms was largely the creation of the tall, stern-faced man who commanded it. A soldier since 1808, Scott personally knew most of the officers and long-service sergeants in the minuscule Regular Army. Although he had earned the nickname "Old Fuss and Feathers" because of his fondness for showy uniforms and pomp and ceremony, Scott was a meticulous planner and a sound tactician.

For the advance into the Valley of Mexico he had organized his army into four divisions, giving commands to Brig. Gens. William J. Worth and David E. Twiggs, Regular Army veterans who had served under Zachary Taylor along the border, and to Maj. Gens. Pillow and John A. Quitman, both militia generals. Quitman, who had acquired combat experience under Taylor, handled his division well. But Pillow, Polk's former law partner and generally regarded as the president's eyes and ears in the army, was a military novice who had demonstrated his ineptitude as a tactician at Cerro Gordo.

Sixteen understrength infantry regiments—13 regular and three volunteer—and a battalion of U.S. Marines formed the core of the little army. Regular artillerymen, most drawn from forts along the Atlantic seaboard, manned the big guns and howitzers of the siege train. Others served the quick-firing 6-pounder batteries commanded by young West Pointers like Captains Simon Drum and James Duncan.

While hundreds of Mexican lancers and mounted guerrillas hovered on his army's flanks, Scott was deficient in cavalry, having only one small brigade made up of detachments from three dragoon regiments. Several squadrons disembarked at Veracruz without mounts and served as infantry until remounted on horses bought or captured from the Mexicans.

During its stay at Puebla, the army had drilled seven days a week. Their ability to maneuver—to outflank static defenses—honed by long hours on the parade ground, enabled the Americans to engage larger Mexican forces on equal terms.

On August 10, the American vanguard crossed the high pass between Popocatépetl and Iztaccihuatl and descended into the Valley of Mexico. In its center, Mexico City was screened to the east by three large lakes and shielded around much of its perimeter by marshes and irrigated fields.

Access to the city was largely limited to causeways—elevated roads running along the lake shores and over the low, wet land. A *garita*, a fortified building complex holding a police barracks and customs office, was located at the head of each causeway to control entry into the city. Mexico City's 25,000 defenders varied from veteran regiments to hastily recruited militia.

Mexican gunners were well-trained and well-led, but their batteries, laboriously drawn into position by oxen, lacked the mobility of the American horse-drawn 6-pounders.

Anticipating a direct American advance on the city from the east, Santa Anna established his headquarters on El Peñón, a 450-foot hill commanding the highway, and garrisoned it with 7,000 men and 30 guns. But Scott, after receiving a report on the strength of the Mexican position from Captain Lee, sent his other divisions by forced march over a waterlogged road from Ayutla to San Augustín, 10 miles south of the city.

Santa Anna reacted quickly, fortifying San Antonio, two miles north of the American army, and directing his Maj. Gen. Gabriel Valencia, with 4,000 men, to occupy a hill west of the Contreras Road. Between those strongpoints lay the Pedregal, a lava bed with razor-sharp rocks and deep fissures that was regarded as impassable for artillery and cavalry. But Lee and Lieutenant Pierre G.T. Beauregard, scouting for a way around Valencia's left, discovered a narrow track through the southern edge of the Pedregal. Engineers, assisted by infantry, marked and widened it, and by the afternoon of August 19, three brigades led by Brig. Gen. Persifor F. Smith crossed the Contreras Road north of Valencia's camp. Early the next morning, Smith's men groped their way down a ravine to the rear of Valencia's camp. At dawn, while the Mexicans were distracted by a feint from the front by Brig. Gen. Franklin Pierce's brigade, Smith's force fired one volley and charged. It was all over in 17 minutes. With more than 1,500 of his men casualties or prisoners, Valencia and what remained of his command fled.

Realizing that his first line of defense was broken, Santa Anna sent orders for the garrison at San Antonio to fall back to Churubusco. But Worth, coming up from San Augustín, sent a brigade through the edge of the Pedregal around the Mexican left and cut the road between San Antonio and Churubusco. The Mexican retreat became a rout.

Scott, from his observation post in the Coyoacan church tower, then ordered an attack on Churubusco, and the Americans overconfidently advanced through high cornfields that obscured the true strength of the Mexican position.

The Mexican left rested on the San Mateo Convent and its walled garden, defended by 1,800 troops under Maj. Gen. Manuel Rincon, one of Santa Anna's best generals. Three hundred yards to the east, a regiment manned a redoubt protecting the southern approach to the bridge, while two more regiments lined the north bank of the Churubusco to protect the Mexican right, east of the bridgehead. Serving in the Mexican batteries on the walls of the convent garden and at the bridgehead were men of the "San Patricio Battalion." Induced earlier to desert Taylor's army by appeals to shared Catholic faith and offers of land, the 260 San Patricios, many of them recent Irish immigrants to the United States, faced severe punishment if captured.

Twiggs' division had come within musket range of the convent when Rincon's batteries suddenly opened fire, sending the surprised Americans reeling back. General Worth, attacking the Mexican redoubt at the bridgehead, fared no better. The 6th Infantry, one of his best regiments, was twice beaten back.

Seeking to move around the convent, Scott sent two brigades across the Churubusco north of Coyoacan, but Santa Anna had anticipated him and deployed his reserves along a ditch paralleling the road. As the Americans neared the road, accurate fire sent them back in disorder as well.

At that point, however, Santa Anna, reacting to the threat against the road leading to Mexico City, withdrew troops from his regiments lining the river. Worth's men were then able to cross the Churubusco and circle behind the shortened line of defenders. Fearing that they were about to be cut off, the defenders of the bridgehead abandoned the redoubt to the U.S. 8th Infantry.

With the batteries at the bridgehead silenced, the Americans were able to force their way into the convent and drive the San Patricios from their guns. The garrison personnel fell back to the massive convent for a last stand. The Mexicans wished to surrender, but three times the desperate San Patricios pulled down the white flag raised by their comrades until the slaughter finally was halted by a white handkerchief that stayed on display.

The Mexican defenders lost 3,200 captured and 4,000 killed and wounded during the engagements of August 20, while the Americans counted 112 killed and 865 wounded. Confident that the Mexicans would soon ask for an armistice, Scott had his siege guns brought up and ordered his men to camp on the ground they had just taken.

The next morning, Scott and Nicholas P. Trist, Polk's diplomatic representative, began discussions with a Mexican delegation which led to an armistice on the 23rd that included the proviso that neither side would seek to improve its position while peace terms were being negotiated. At the same time that Santa Anna was protracting the negotiations with extravagant demands for the unconditional return of all New Mexico and California, however, he was rallying his scattered forces and strengthening the city's defenses. On September 6, Scott denounced the armistice and, with too few troops for a siege, laid plans to take Mexico City by assault.

That night the American headquarters at Tacubaya received intelligence that church bells were being melted down and cast into cannons in the foundry of El Molino del Rey. Scott ordered Worth to destroy the foundry and the cannon barrels.

The buildings of El Molino occupied the western end of a walled park that extended westward for 1,000 yards from the Hill of Chapultepec. Since El Molino and the nearby magazine at the Casa Mata were extensions of the Chapultepec defensive complex, they held large garrisons.

At dawn on September 8, after a scout reported that El Molino had been abandoned, Worth ordered his division advanced in three columns: Lt. Col. John Garland's brigade to attack the south and east sides of El Molino; a picked command of 600 under Major George Wright to storm the west wall of the foundry; and Lt. Col. James S. McIntosh's brigade to seize the Casa Mata.

Wright's column had closed to within point-blank range when the batteries in El Molino opened a devastating fire, the first volley cutting down 11 of the 14 officers at the head of the column. Despite scores of casualties, the Americans pressed on and overran the batteries, but faltered when the Mexicans held fast at the *Molino's* parapet. A spirited Mexican counterattack, launched from Chapultepec, reoccupied the battery and drove Wright's men back in confusion.

McIntosh's brigade was checked 30 yards short of the Casa Mata by heavy fire, but Major Edwin Summers, with only 250 dragoons, rode directly at the Mexican irregulars, bluffing them to a halt before they could counterattack. Duncan then renewed his bombardment of the Casa Mata.

Action now centered on El Molino, where Garland's brigade battered in the gates and, fighting from room to room, drove the Mexicans from the foundry. Francis Perez, commanding the garrison in the Casa Mata, had no artillery to reply to the punishment meted out by Duncan's battery and ordered his men to retire. Shortly afterward, the powder magazine blew up, killing six Americans who had entered the ruined building. By 1 p.m. the engagement was over, and Scott's army was back in its old position.

Although the Mexicans had lost 2,000 men and El Molino was in ruins, it had been a Pyrrhic victory for the Americans. Scott's sources in Mexico City had misinformed him. No guns, only a few unused molds, were found in El Molino.

At a conference on the 11th, most of the American generals favored an attack on San Antonio Garita. But Scott, arguing that the marshy soil between the causeways would make maneuvering difficult, ordered an attack on Chapultepec. This, he argued, would open up the western causeways leading to Belén Garita and the lightly fortified San Cosmé Garita. To mask his intentions, he ordered Twiggs to demonstrate against the southern *garitas* with only one brigade while he moved his real attack into position.

The defenses of Chapultepec were centered on top of the 200-foot hill at El Castillo, a massive building complex in which the nation's military college was located. It was a strong position; the north and south faces of the hill were too steep to climb. The southern road to the gate of the *Colegio Militar* was protected by one redan at the entrance and another at a bend in the road halfway up the hill. The western walls were protected by a ditch and a minefield at their bases, while halfway down the hill, breastworks had been erected to slow any attack from the ruins of El Molino.

On the 12th, four batteries of heavy howitzers, mortars and 24-pounder siege guns opened fire on the Chapultepec defenses. When Santa Anna arrived at the *Colegio Militar* during the bombardment, his General Nicholás Bravo, commander of the 1,000-man garrison, asked for more troops to man the 15-foot walls that extended for more than a mile around the buildings on the crest. But Santa Anna refused, still misled by Twiggs' movements into believing that the main attack would be against the Niño Perdido Garita.

Scott had hoped that the bombardment would drive Bravo's men off the hill, for El Castillo had been built not as a fort but as a residence for the Spanish viceroy. But, inspired by the resolute example of the 100 cadets of the *Colegio Militar*, its garrison was still holding out when night fell.

That evening Pillow was ordered to make the main attack against the west wall of the citadel. Supporting his right flank, Quitman kept the Mexicans from reinforcing Chapultepec and made a feint at Belén Garita while Worth forced his way past San Cosmé Garita.

Early the next morning, the siege batteries resumed their pounding with solid shot, shifting to canister after two hours to clear snipers from the cypress grove that lay between El Molino and the western slope of Chapultepec. Promptly at 8 o'clock, the heavy batteries checked fire, and Pillow's infantry surged out of the ruins of El Molino. Dodging from tree to tree, the 9th and 15th Infantries, flanked to the south by four companies of the Voltigeurs, an elite light-infantry regiment dressed in gray, cleared the cypress stand of its last snipers and, quickly overrunning the breastworks at the base of the hill, surged up the slopes.

Pillow, however, had entrusted the scaling ladders to raw men who, burdened with them, could not keep pace with the rapid advance of the infantry against the western wall. For 15 long minutes his men, jammed into the ditch below the wall, endured the fire pouring down from the parapets above.

Finally, the ladders arrived—to a chorus of curses from the impatient infantry massed at the base of the wall. The first few ladders were toppled backward by Bravo's men, but then, as first one and then another remained upright, the Americans swarmed up and over the parapet, driving the outnumbered garrison before them.

Coming up from Tacubaya, Quitman sent a brigade off to the left to join the assault on Chapultepec. The brigade reached the south wall just in time to join Pillow's men as they fought their way through the citadel, room by room. Most of the garrison surrendered, but the cadets, some only 13 years old, fought to the last. Six of them who died were immortalized in Mexican history as *Los Niños Heroicos*.

Two miles away at Mixcoac, 26 San Patricios condemned to die stood with nooses around their necks—and cheered loudly when they saw the American flag hoisted over Chapultepec. Then the wagons under their feet lurched forward and they dropped to their deaths. An officer on Santa Anna's staff shook his head and groaned, "God is a *yanqui*."

Now, Worth's division, plus two additional brigades and a battery of siege guns, moved northward from Chapultepec against light opposition and turned eastward onto the San Cosmé causeway. Under continuous fire from the *garita* and snipers on his left, Garland's brigade inched forward underneath the elevated viaduct that ran down the center of the causeway. North of the causeway, sappers in the van of Colonel Newman S. Clarke's brigade battered a hole in the wall of the first house they reached, then burrowed from one building to the next with pickaxes and crowbars, while the infantry cleared out the snipers with bayonets. Lieutenant Ulysses S. Grant, with men of the 4th Infantry, placed a mountain howitzer in a church tower and took the redoubt under fire. By 5 o'clock the defenders of the redoubt had abandoned it and retreated behind the ruined walls of the *garita*.

Within an hour, Worth's division had entered the northwestern section of the city. Judging that it was too late to continue his advance, he ordered his men to bivouac in the houses they had just taken, but at midnight, he had a 10-inch mortar lob five shells at the presidential palace.

While Worth was advancing on San Cosme, Quitman, without orders, turned what was to have been a feint against Belén Garita into a personal race to beat Worth into the city. Collecting the regiments that had just stormed Chapultepec, he personally led them down the Belén causeway. Greatly outnumbered, the *garita's* 180-man garrison fought bravely until, their ammunition exhausted, the survivors retreated to the *Ciudadela*, a large, fortified barracks 300 yards north of the *garita*.

Using three captured cannons and their own battery, Quitman's gunners spent the rest of the afternoon fighting an unequal duel (in which every American artillery officer was killed or wounded) with the 18-gun battery of the *Ciudadela*. After they ran low on ammunition while fighting off counterattacks from the *Ciudadela*, Quitman's men spent an uneasy night in the ruined *garita*.

Although the city's defenses were now broken, Scott's army had suffered almost 1,000 casualties. Now down to less than 7,000, it faced days of savage street fighting. But the city's leaders had had enough. Perhaps persuaded by Worth's midnight mortar shells, the city council prevailed upon Santa Anna to withdraw from the city and retire to Guadalupe Hidalgo with what remained of his army. Just before dawn, the mayor and three aldermen waited on Scott in his headquarters at Chapultepec and surrendered the city.

The next morning, the American soldiers, looking like scarecrows in their ragged uniforms, marched into the Grand Plaza. There, while Colonel William Selby Harney's mounted dragoon band played "Yankee Doodle," they cheered themselves hoarse as their old general, resplendent in gleaming epaulets and an abundance of gold lace, raised his white-plumed hat in acknowledgment. There would be more fighting before the Treaty of Guadalupe Hidalgo ended the war on February 2, 1848, but Mexican resistance was effectively finished.

For sheer audacity crowned by success, Scott's landing at Veracruz and subsequent capture of Mexico City is today regarded as the equal of Mac-Arthur's 1950 Inchon–Seoul campaign. Even the Duke of Wellington later wrote: "His campaign was unsurpassed in military annals. He is the greatest living soldier."

Command Shift Dictated

Taking over for the stricken Stonewall Jackson at Chancellorsville, cavalryman Jeb Stuart faced his greatest challenge. Now he had to think in terms of the infantry.

By Philip L. Bolté

When nervous, battle-weary troops of the 18th North Carolina Infantry fired at what they thought were Federal cavalrymen approaching their position the evening of May 2, 1863, they caused one of the greatest tragedies to befall their Army of Northern Virginia. One of the men approaching was their corps commander Lt. Gen. Thomas J. Jackson! The mighty Stonewall Jackson was shot, severely wounded by his own troops as he returned from a reconnaissance.

Moments later, Jackson's senior lieutenant, Maj. Gen. Ambrose Powell Hill, was wounded by artillery fire, and although remaining on the battlefield for a time, he was unable to continue in command.

The situation was critical. In Jackson's corps of three divisions, the next senior officer, Brig. Gen. Robert E. Rodes, had only that day commanded a division in action for the first time. The one staff officer who probably knew Jackson's plans for continuing the operation, Captain J.K. Boswell, was killed in the same volley that wounded his commander. Until that moment, Jackson's orders to Hill, whose division had taken over the lead in the attack as darkness was falling, had been: "Press them, Hill! Cut them off from United States Ford. Press them!"

After turning command of his division over to Brig. Gen. Henry Heth in order to assume command of Jackson's II Corps, Hill soon realized his own condition and passed word to Rodes to assume command of the corps. There is some confusion at this point as to exactly how the decision was made, but made it was—to send for James Ewell Brown Stuart, the senior officer and the only major general in the vicinity, to take command of the corps. Either Hill made the decision in conjunction with Rodes, or Rodes simply had to acquiesce, regardless.

In his after-action report, Rodes stated that on the one hand he did not feel cavalryman Stuart was entitled to command because Stuart was from a different service. But Rodes, on the other hand, was concerned that if the troops of the II Corps heard that he, unknown except to his own brigade, was in command, it would "in their shaken condition, increase the demoralization of the corps." In short, Rodes said he "yielded because...the good of the service demanded it."

Stuart, who was five or six miles away at Ely's Ford, was sent for and reported to Hill, who formally turned over command of the corps to him. By the time Stuart arrived, late in the evening, Rodes had met with the other division commanders; they had agreed that further attack should be left until morning.

Stuart was aware of General Robert E. Lee's overall strategy of attacking Union Maj. Gen. Joseph Hooker on the west flank and either destroying his force south of the Rappahannock or at least forcing it back across the river. But now he was in command, the battle was only half won, and the responsibility for continuing the attack the next day was his. It was a formidable task even for the self-confident cavalier.

An 1854 graduate of the U.S. Military Academy, at West Point, N. Y., Stuart had served as a cavalryman on the Texas frontier, in Kansas, and against the Cheyenne Indians before the war. He resigned in 1861 to serve the Confederacy and was commissioned in the Virginia cavalry. He had distinguished himself at the First Battle of Manassas on July 21, 1861, by charging a Federal force threatening Jackson's flank and was promoted to brigadier general. By 1863, he had risen to command all the cavalry of the Army of Northern Virginia, and Lee had come to rely on him for his ability to accurately determine and report enemy dispositions.

Others also recognized his able nature. For one, General Joseph E. Johnston had written to President Jefferson Davis of Stuart: "He is a rare man, wonderfully endowed by nature with the qualities necessary for an officer of light cavalry. Calm, firm, acute, active and enterprising, I know of no one more competent than he to estimate the occurrences before him in their true value."

As a fighter, Stuart was superb. A commanding officer once wrote that Stuart was "gallant, always prompt in the execution of orders, and reckless of danger and exposure." An officer of his staff wrote of Stuart after the war: "I have spoken of his reckless exposure in battle. It would convey a better idea of his demeanor under fire to say that he seemed unaware of the presence of danger. This air of indifference was unmistakable."

Thus, Stuart brought to his new challenge expertise in quickly assessing a tactical situation and unsurpassed battlefield bravery. But now, for the first time, he was faced with the command of a large force of infantry already engaged in a major battle.

In order to understand the challenge faced by Stuart, it is necessary to retrace the events of the preceding few days.

After the failure of Union Maj. Gen. Ambrose Burnside to lead the Army of the Potomac to success in its attack on Fredericksburg in December 1862, President Abraham Lincoln had continued his search for a commander who could match the talents of Lee. His choice fell on Maj. Gen. Joseph "Fighting

Joe" Hooker. A good combat commander who had demonstrated no lack of self-confidence to date, Hooker devised a sound plan for defeating Lee. With Lt. Gen. James Longstreet and two of his divisions gone, Lee's strength of 60,000 at Fredericksburg was arrayed against Hooker's 130,000. Leaving one-third of his army to hold Lee at Fredericksburg, Hooker marched two-thirds of it up the Rappahannock River, crossed the river and advanced on Lee's left flank.

Hooker was so confident of having Lee in a trap that on April 30 he issued a general order stating, "Our enemy must either ingloriously fly, or come out from behind his defenses and give battle on our own ground, where certain destruction awaits him." Outgeneraling Robert E. Lee, though, was not so easy a matter.

Based on his analysis of intelligence provided by Stuart concerning the enemy's movements, Lee realized that the main attack would come from his left and set about taking appropriate action. He first moved Maj. Gen. Richard H. Anderson's division to his left flank, ordering the construction of field fortifications to bolster Rebel defenses in that sector.

In spite of the relative strength of the armies and the tactical situation, Lee decided the advantages of staying on the Rappahannock warranted taking a risk to maintain his position. Loss of the Rappahannock line could uncover his railroad communications, and the loss of Fredericksburg would threaten his right flank and rear. He decided to attack rather than withdraw.

Leaving a small force under Maj. Gen. Jubal A. Early to hold at Fredericksburg, Lee would take the bulk of his army and attack Hooker's force south of the river. He reinforced Anderson with Maj. Gen. Lafayette McLaws' division early on the morning of May 1 and moved Stonewall Jackson's II Corps westward toward Hooker.

At that point, Hooker, through his own actions, made one of several unintended contributions to the ultimate success of Lee. Instead of capitalizing on his turning movement and attacking Anderson and McLaws vigorously, Hooker abandoned his advance and ordered his troops to withdraw to good defensive positions.

Now Lee needed to revise his attack plan. Stuart arrived and informed him that Brig. Gen. Fitzhugh Lee, operating with his cavalry beyond the Confederate left, had discovered that Hooker's right flank appeared to be open. At the same time, reconnaissance to the front of Anderson and McLaws determined the Federals had prepared strong defensive positions there. Lee concluded he must attack from the west. Jackson was trusted with the flanking movement, and a concealed route was found. Stuart would screen the march of Jackson's force.

When, at their historic last meeting, Lee asked Jackson what force he would take, he replied, "My whole corps"—leaving Lee with only Anderson and McLaws' divisions from Longstreet's divided I Corps to hold Hooker.

Lee's reply, "Well, go on," was indicative of his own boldness and his faith in Jackson. Jackson was on the road by 7 o'clock the morning of May 2.

Another factor that contributed to Lee's ultimate success occurred when Maj. Gen. Daniel E. Sickles' II Corps detected Jackson's movement and, in fact, attacked his rear guard. When Jackson's force disengaged and moved south, Hooker concluded from the reports he received that Lee was retreating. Hooker was not alone in such "contributions" to Lee, for his orders to Maj. Gen. Oliver O. Howard, commanding the XI Corps on his right flank, to strengthen his flank in case Lee attacked were, for the most part, ignored.

Originally planning to attack Hooker along the Orange Plank Road, Jackson was convinced by Fitz Lee's showing him the wide-open enemy flank along the Orange Courthouse Turnpike to move farther north and use that approach. By the time Jackson had his troops in position to attack the unsuspecting Federals, though, it was about 5 o'clock in the evening, with only two hours of daylight left. The corps was arrayed for the attack in three parallel lines—first came the division commanded by Rodes, followed at a distance of 200 yards by Brig. Gen. Raleigh Colston's division, and then by A.P. Hill's division another 200 yards back. Satisfied that all was ready, Jackson ordered Rodes to attack.

Howard's XI Corps was caught by surprise and routed completely. Jackson, the light of battle in his eyes, spurred his forces on, apparently determined to drive the Federal forces from south of the Rappahannock or destroy them before they could withdraw. But it was not to be. The Federals eventually were able to establish a defensive line, and the Confederates of Rodes' and Colston's divisions became intermingled because the heavily wooded terrain brought disorder to their charging ranks. And finally darkness fell.

Not to be turned from his objective, Jackson brought Hill's division through those of Rodes and Colston, and it was then that Jackson urged Hill to "Press them!" When Hill complained that his staff did not know the area through which he was to attack, Jackson brushed his objection aside and provided his own engineer to assist.

With a small party of staff and couriers, Jackson rode beyond the forward positions of his troops; he was convinced the enemy was beaten and withdrawing and wanted to reconnoiter the area to the front. He was returning from his reconnaissance when the North Carolinians fired on his party, and not long after that, A. P. Hill was struck in both legs by a fragment or a Minié bullet. It was after 9 p.m. by then.

Now, late at night, perhaps as late as midnight, Stuart arrived on the scene and assumed command. Informed by Rodes of the decision to postpone any further attack until morning, Stuart agreed. He had little choice at that point, for it was late, many troops were still sorting themselves out from the attack through the heavy woods, and others were sleeping where they had stopped.

Stuart had no experience commanding an infantry formation, but, never shy, he set about with confidence to build on the preparations initiated by Rodes to renew the attack in the morning. In an attempt to learn more of Jackson's plans, Stuart sent a staff officer to the wounded general asking for guidance. The only response from Jackson was, "I don't know—I can't tell; say to General Stuart he must do what he thinks best."

To add to the challenges Stuart faced, Jackson's senior artilleryman, Colonel Stapleton Crutchfield, had been wounded. One of Stuart's first actions was to send for Lt. Col. E. Porter Alexander, the senior artillery battalion commander present. Stuart had already demonstrated an appreciation for artillery in forming the horse artillery of his cavalry division; his actions now reflected that appreciation. Directing Alexander to assume command of all the artillery of the II Corps, Stuart ordered him to be prepared to attack at daybreak along the entire line. Alexander, a West Point graduate and experienced artilleryman, spent most of the night reconnoitering suitable positions and getting the artillery in position for the morning. Having positioned his own battalion earlier behind the southern end of the corps line, Alexander had observed the Federal position on the high ground known as Hazel Grove. Recognizing it as a critical terrain feature, Alexander was able to site a battery in a position to fire on that location in the morning. He also located his artillery on the Plank Road in a position to fire down the road.

While Stuart was conducting his own reconnaissance and developing his plan, he received a dispatch from General Lee, who had been informed of Jackson's wounds and the passage of command to Hill, to Rodes and then to Stuart. It was written at 3 a.m., and it must have taken at least an hour to reach Stuart because of the circuitous route that had to be followed between the two wings of the army. In the message, Lee urged Stuart to press the enemy and give him no time to rally, and to "endeavor, therefore to dispossess them of Chancellorsville, which will permit the union of the whole army." Shortly after sending that message, Lee provided further guidance to Stuart, emphasizing the importance of attacking on his right to turn the enemy and unite the two parts of the Confederate army. Lee assured Stuart that he would press the enemy from his side.

It was clear that Jackson earlier, and Lee now, considered that, after the success of the flanking movement and attack, they were dealing with a beaten enemy. In fact, Hooker was in better shape for the battle on May 3 than he had been the day before. Howard's corps had rallied, and the right flank of Hooker's force now faced the enemy. He had the bulk of his men between the two wings of Lee's army. More troops had joined Hooker from Fredericksburg, and the Union army spent much of the night preparing strong defensive positions. There would be no sudden surprise attack this day.

Stuart's first move of his newly acquired infantry was to swing the right flank brigades—from right to left, those of Brig. Gens. James J. Archer, Samuel McGowan and James H. Lane—more into line with the main front. At about 5:30 a.m., Lane started to execute a partial left wheel to bring his brigade in line with those on the left. Archer and McGowan moved forward. Archer then lost contact with McGowan's brigade, but soon made contact with the enemy at Hazel Grove.

Hooker, in a tactical error, had ordered Sickles to abandon the Hazel Grove position. And so, driving the Federal infantry back with little trouble, Archer seized the high ground, capturing four guns and 100 men. Without realizing it, he had captured a most strategic position. As soon as Stuart was told of the capture of Hazel Grove, he ordered Alexander to immediately move 30 guns onto the site. Alexander duly obeyed, placing the six batteries on the hill under the command of Major Frank Huger.

There was some confusion along the line when Lane's brigade started its movement to realign; some elements misunderstood the movement as the start of the attack. Realizing the situation, at about 6 a.m. Stuart ordered the entire first line of the corps to attack and the second and third to follow. Hill's division, now commanded by Henry Heth, was in the lead—its men charged forward on a front of about a mile and a quarter, overcoming the first Federal line and pressing on to the second.

Now the battle began in earnest, with fighting as hard as either army had experienced. Brigades attacked and were counterattacked. Formations became entangled and separated in the woods. Brigades successful in advancing found themselves subjected to flanking fire. Gaps between brigades were exploited by aggressive commanders on both sides.

Based on Alexander's reconnaissance the night before, as well as his own assessment, Stuart recognized the high ground of Hazel Grove as the critical point of the battlefield—it was there that he spent part of the morning. But Stuart also seemed to be everywhere, particularly at the key points at critical times. When Confederate infantry was forced back along the Plank Road, Stuart directed Alexander to place artillery in the road. It was Stuart, though, who led the guns into position. In the words of a Confederate colonel at the scene, Stuart committed "the bravest act I ever saw," leading in person several batteries down the road.

Initially, there was heavy fighting on the north; then the critical fighting was along and to the south of the Plank Road. Stuart was at the critical points, moving brigades as required and exhorting those who hesitated to attack.

When Brig. Gen. Alfred Iverson's brigade was threatened from the left, Stuart moved Brig. Gen. Alfred H. Colquitt's brigade to support him. When Maj. Gen. Stephen Ramseur reported to Stuart that he had bumped up against the brigades of Brig. Gens. E.F. Paxton and John R. Jones, neither of whom would advance, and asked to attack through them, Stuart quite easily gave permission. When told that some units were out of ammunition and would have to withdraw, Stuart was tough—they would have to hold their position with the bayonet.

The battle was touch-and-go during the morning hours. Shortly after 9 o'clock, Ramseur reported to Rodes that, unless the enemy was driven from his right, he would have to fall back. Rodes tried to bring up troops from the rear, but none would follow him. Even the veteran Stonewall Brigade faltered and refused to attack into the maelstrom. Stuart, though, "rode forward in his usual happy manner, and ordered a charge, which was executed by the brigade with its accustomed gallantry and enthusiasm," according to a 19th-century account.

Stuart's horse was shot from under him during the first half hour of the battle, but he quickly mounted another. One observer called him "Prince Rupert reincarnated," likening him to the high-spirited and daring Royalist cavalry officer of the English Civil War. He was even singing his song for the day: "Now, Joe Hooker, won't you come out of the Wilderness?"

The lines were forced back and forth, but the Confederate fire from the guns now positioned at Hazel Grove was too much for the Federal troops. As Alexander later wrote, "We opened on the fugitives, infantry, artillery, wagons—everything—swarming about the Chancellorsville house, and down the broad road leading to the river."

Meanwhile, Lee had been attacking Hooker's forces from the southeast with the divisions of Anderson and McLaws. By about 10 o'clock, Archer's brigade, attacking from Hazel Grove, had made contact with the left flank of Anderson's division, so that now the two wings of the Confederate army were united.

The Federal forces soon abandoned their positions around Chancellorsville and withdrew to the north. By 10:30 a.m., Lee was at Chancellorsville. About 1 o'clock, Lee ordered Colston to advance along the U.S. Ford Road to feel out the enemy and keep him in check. The Federal position proved to be strong enough to discourage further Confederate action.

Furthermore, Lee now received word that Union Maj. Gen. John Sedgwick's VI Corps had overrun Fredericksburg and had advanced west to Salem Church, where they were being engaged by five regiments of Alabama infantry, led by Brig. Gen. Cadmus Wilcox. Deciding to leave Stuart to hold Hooker while he attacked Sedgwick, Lee sent first McLaws' division, and then Anderson's to meet that threat to his rear. Although he had hopes of destroying Sedgwick, with the aid of Early's division—which, after being driven from Fredericksburg, he had kept to the south, ready to strike Sedgwick in flank if the opportunity presented itself—Lee was unable to meet that objective, primarily because the battle-weary troops were unable to get into position soon enough to execute his plan. Sedgwick was able to extract his corps from Lee's trap and recross the river.

On Stuart's front, all remained quiet on May 4. Lee was ready to turn his attention once again to Hooker on May 5, but Hooker had had enough and quietly had withdrawn his troops across the river. The Battle of Chancellorsville was over.

The price had been high. Hooker's army of 130,000 had lost 1,606 killed, 9,762 wounded and 5,919 captured or missing; Lee's army of 60,000 had 1,649 killed, 9,106 wounded and 1,708 captured or missing. Although the Federal forces had suffered more heavily than those of the South, the Confederate losses were irreplaceable in terms of manpower.

The battle had a major impact on the long-term conduct of the war. It gave Lee an opportunity to invade the North again, but it was an invasion, that would lead, in that summer of 1863, to Gettysburg. Lee and the South also had lost one of their greatest resources: Stonewall Jackson.

On another note, historians and strategists generally and justifiably have praised Lee and Jackson in most reviews of the Battle of Chancellorsville. Perhaps Stuart, though, has not received all the credit that should have been his.

Clearly, Jackson planned to continue the assault on May 2 into the night, although night attacks were seldom conducted during the Civil War. Had he not been wounded, he probably would have pushed Hill on. Considering, though, the condition of his troops by this time and the fact that a major part of Hooker's force lay before him, still uncommitted, it is doubtful that Jackson could have cut Hooker off from U.S. Ford Road and destroyed him. As General Colston put it later, "The halt at that time was not a mistake, but a necessity." Lee and Jackson were probably overly optimistic at the time. Thus, the decision to postpone attacking until morning made by Rodes with the advice of others, a decision supported by Stuart when he arrived, was probably the correct one.

Stuart gained a quick and accurate appreciation of the situation and the critical terrain after arriving on the scene, no doubt in part because of the advice of the artilleryman Alexander. Guided by his own judgment, as well as direction received from Lee early in the morning, Stuart planned and conducted the battle on May 3 in a sound manner. The prompt placement of 30 guns on the Hazel Grove heights was perhaps the key action of the battle that morning.

In the terrible fighting in the morning, with even the most reliable Confederate troops faltering, battlefield leadership of the highest order was required. Stuart provided it. His sound tactical commitment of reinforcements was matched by his personal bravery, which supplied the inspiration so important to even the best soldiers under fire.

About the only criticism found of Stuart during the battle is that he might have driven the troops too hard. The alternative, though, might well have been failure. Although Hooker had completely forfeited the initiative, any battlefield success for his troops might have returned the momentum to the Federal forces and resulted in commitment of the many still-available Northern troops.

Thus, after the brilliant generalship demonstrated by Lee and Jackson in conceiving and executing the strategy of attacking Hooker on May 2, it was Stuart—albeit assisted by Hooker's lack of aggressiveness—who was largely responsible for the successful Confederate attack on May 3.

It is understandable that in the aftermath of the battle the citizens of the Confederacy were shaken by the loss of Jackson and impressed by the successful strategy of Lee, so that the role played by Stuart went largely unnoticed. In the years since, the Battle of Chancellorsville has attracted the attention of historians and military strategists primarily because of the planning and execution of the first day of the battle, so that again the part played by Stuart has been largely ignored.

Lee himself, though, recognized the challenges faced by Stuart and the manner in which he met them. In his report of the battle, he wrote: "[Stuart] ably discharged the difficult and responsible duties he was unexpectedly called to perform. Assuming command late in the night, at the close of a fierce engagement, and in the immediate presence of the enemy, necessarily ignorant in a great measure of the disposition of the troops and of the plans of those who had preceded him, General Stuart exhibited great energy, promptness and intelligence. During the continuance of the engagement the next day, he conducted the operations on the left with distinguished capacity and vigor, stimulating and cheering the troops by the example of his own coolness and daring."

Chancellorsville was a great tribute to the military genius of Lee and Jackson, but without Stuart, the battle might have ended far less successfully than it did.

Fatal Delayed Response

With one battle, in one day, the Prussian war machine of Helmuth von Moltke shifted the seat of power in Central Europe. The effects would last well into the 20th century.

By G.J. Morris

It is not difficult to understand why the Battle of Königgrätz in 1866 still is considered one of the decisive battles of the modern era. It has been suggested that the rise of Adolf Hitler could not be explained without the events of 1866. While that may be a debatable supposition, the battle and campaign demonstrated the power of Prussian science and military art.

The Seven Weeks' War, as the campaign in Bohemia became popularly known, was the first war in Europe in which the steel rifled cannon and the breech-loading rifle were put to the test. Likewise, the uses made of the electric telegraph and the railway pointed to the future importance of communication and transport. As a battle alone, no modern frills attached, Königgrätz (sometimes called Sadowa) was by far the largest fought in Europe during the 19th century. Well over 450,000 men were on the field in an area of less than eight square miles. And within that space, the Austrian artillery maintained a rate of fire seldom witnessed before, portending the massed barrage fire of World War I. The Austrian cavalry, meanwhile, despite the fearful toll exacted by the enemy's Dreyse needle gun (named for its needle-shaped firing pin), did indeed prove itself a most disciplined and able force in delaying the advance of the victorious Prussian infantry; but the days of the horse soldier were clearly numbered when set against rapid rifle fire.

Prussia had emerged from the Napoleonic wars in 1815 as the weakest of the five great European powers (England, France, Austria, Russia and Prussia). She seemed far inferior to Austria both in military strength and in total population. By 1859, however, the squeaking cogs of the Austrian military machine had been heard by the Prussian general staff in Berlin. Perhaps what the small monarchy of Piedmont recently had done for a unified Italian cause might also be achieved by a German confederation under Prussian control.

To that end, *Graf* Otto von Bismarck, first minister of Prussia, addressed all his efforts. From the moment he came to power in 1862 until the outbreak of hostilities in 1866, Bismarck pursued a course whose main objective was securing Prussian domination over Austria and the smaller German states. His policy of aggrandizement was based largely on a strong military program. For Bismarck, as it had been for military theorist Karl von Clausewitz, war was an extension of state policy by other means. And the crushing of domestic Prussian liberalism in 1862 had left the way clear for confrontation with Austria.

A situation now arose that gave Bismarck his chance to inaugurate a series of diplomatic maneuvers that would nudge Austria along the road to war. For some years, the two duchies of Schleswig and Holstein had been a thorn in the side of both Austria and Prussia, with the kingdom of Denmark claiming sovereignty over both. In 1864, Austrian and Prussian troops under the overall command of Austria invaded the duchies. By October of that year, the Danes were defeated and their king, Christian IX, was compelled to sue for peace. By the terms of the Treaty of Vienna, signed on October 30, the Danes ceded their rights over both Schleswig and Holstein. The two duchies were placed under the control of Prussia and Austria, Holstein going to Austria and Prussia administering Schleswig.

Such a condominium between Austria and Prussia could not be expected to work without friction. In fact, the allotment of the two duchies had been part of Bismarck's devious plan to provoke a confrontation with the Austrians, since Holstein was geographically a tenuous prize, easily isolated by the Prussian presence in Schleswig. British Prime Minister H. J. Temple, Lord Palmerston, once remarked: "Only three men understood the complexities of the problem. One of them has died, another has gone crazy, and I myself have forgotten it all." Nevertheless, the bellicose forces exploited by Bismarck in the Schleswig-Holstein Question proved to be inexorable.

By the summer of 1865, the two powers were on the brink of war, but Bismarck was not ready to enter into a conflict at that time—a convention of sorts was signed at Gastein, Austria, to paper over the cracks and allow a breathing space, during which both sides began to organize their military forces for the showdown that was bound to come.

Bismarck made full use of the lull to win over Prussian King Wilhelm I and his advisers. He also managed to talk round Prussian Chief of Staff Helmuth *Graf* von Moltke, who was cool toward any proposition of an all-out war with Austria, by promising him an alliance with Italy that should divert some of the Austrian forces. The Italians agreed to an alliance provided that, in the event of a Prussian victory, the former Roman province of Venetia would be handed over to them, and that the war would commence within three months after April 1866. The Mexican war of 1865 had been such a disappointment to Napoleon III, meanwhile, that French neutrality was won over by a shadowy assurance of compensation from Bismarck when he met the French emperor at Biarritz. Bismarck also used his diplomatic skills to neutralize Russia. At last, he could set his sights on the confrontation he had so long desired and so artfully delayed.

On June 1, 1866, Austria announced that the settlement of Schleswig and Holstein should be entrusted to the Germanic Confederation, within which

Austria held control. Whereupon Prussia declared that Austria had broken the Convention of Gastein, and she in turn claimed control over both duchies. On the 7th, *General* Edwin Rochus *Freiherr* von Manteuffel led a Prussian force of 12,000 men into Holstein, forcing a much weaker Austrian contingent to retire before him. Austria promptly demanded from the various states of Germany a declaration against Prussia. On the 14th, the motion was carried by nine votes to six—the war was on.

The conflict that followed would show how little the Austrian high command had learned from the catalog of mistakes made during the 1859 Italian campaign. Although Austria by now had endeavored to remedy the discrepancy between her paper army and the numbers of trained men actually available for a war on two fronts, in tactics and troop control Austria persisted in the archaic methods of a bygone age.

Theoretically, the Austrian army, which was made up of conscripts, had 10 corps of 83,000 troops each. That mass of manpower was, however, a long time in forming from its cadres onto the battlefield. Further problems arose with the Italian regiments in Austrian service, as they had to be moved away from their own recruiting areas for fear of desertions. Moreover, while Prussia had the *Landwehr*, Austria had no militia to provide a backup service in functional or fortress duties. Worse yet, certain professions within Austrian society were exempt from military service—a substitute could be hired to serve in another man's place.

Because of those problems, plus deductions for the sick, laborers and security forces, Austria could place only 320,000 men in the field; of those, only 240,000 would be able to operate against Prussia, while 80,000 were needed on the Italian front. Three of the army's 10 corps were assigned to northern Italy. Austria had no divisional system except in the cavalry, the infantry being formed into brigades of two regiments and a *Jäger* battalion. A corps had four such brigades, plus a regiment of light cavalry. The brigades maneuvered in dense battalion columns of some 1,000 men each, relying on mass attacks with the bayonet.

Prussia had nine army corps, each comprised of two infantry divisions and an artillery reserve. Each division had four infantry regiments, four batteries of artillery and four squadrons of cavalry; in all, some 15,000 men, 600 horses and 24 guns. Unlike the Austrians, whose infantry was armed with the Lorenze muzzleloading rifle, the Prussians enjoyed the benefit of the breech-loading Dreyse needle gun, which could fire five rounds per minute and could even be fired from the prone position, thus reducing the enemy's target. When advancing to the attack, battalions moved in parallel columns, by companies.

Both Prussia's cavalry and artillery failed to play a major role in the campaign. The artillery suffered from a combined lack of funds and bad administration; the cavalry was simply neglected, being used in the main for duties behind the lines instead of for intelligence work.

At the outbreak of hostilities Prussia could muster more than 350,000 men, of which 250,000 were set against Austria. Prussia could also call upon large numbers of reserves if the need arose, an element totally lacking in the Austrian system.

Prussia's Chief of Staff, Moltke, was placed in command on June 2, 1866. With only the king to answer to, he was well aware of the Austrian lead in mobilization, but he made good use of Prussia's railway system to mass his troops well forward in an arc extending from Silesia to Saxony, a distance of some 275 miles. When that concentration was complete, the three Prussian armies stood as follows: the Army of the Elbe under *General* Karl Eberhard Herwarth von Bittenfeld, approximately 45,000 strong, around Halle and Zeitz on the Saxon border; the First Army, 94,000 men commanded by Prince Friedrich Karl, at Torgau and Kottbus; the Second Army, including the Guard Corps, in all some 120,000 men commanded by the crown prince of Prussia, Friedrich Wilhelm, at Landshut and Reichenbach, Silesia.

The Italian War of 1859 had shown the Emperor Franz Josef that he was not the man to take charge of Austrian troops at the front. He therefore chose the popular *Feldzeugmeister* (General of Infantry) Ludwig August von Benedek, who was considered by many, after his exploits during the Battle of Solferino (1859), to be Austria's best commander since Josef Radetzky. The only person who did not agree with that view was Benedek himself. He knew his limitations and was quite out of his depth fighting a war in Bohemia, far from his old campaign grounds in Italy. Try though Benedek did to decline the post, the emperor was adamant. Benedek reluctantly accepted his fate.

Not wishing to be seen as the aggressor in the eyes of Europe, Austria adopted a plan based on a defensive attitude in both diplomatic and military terms. The memorandum for war was therefore prepared by a former chief of the topographical bureau, *Generalmajor* (Brig. Gen.) Gideon *Ritter* von Krismanić, for no other reason than that he apparently had some knowledge of the geographic defensibility of Bohemia. That supposition not only proved to be quite unfounded but also something of a joke, since all maps of the region supplied to the Austrian general staff were out of date. Krismanić's plan was based on a defensive position that was centered around the fortified town of Olmutz in Moravia and was intended to protect Vienna. Unfortunately for Austria, the decision to go straight onto the defensive was tantamount to throwing away any initiative gained by advanced mobilization.

Even so, the position of the Austrian corps around Olmutz still could have proved favorable under other leadership. But Benedek showed he had no idea how to use that central position, unlike a certain Corsican-born general some 60 years before who used central positions so effectively.

On June 15, secondary forces under the Prussian *General* Vogel von Falkenstein cut off the Hannoverian state's army and isolated Bavaria, effectively knocking two of Austria's allies out of the war. On the 16th, the Prussian *General* von Bittenfeld's Army of the Elbe crossed into Saxony. Upon its approach, the Saxon crown prince, Albrecht, withdrew his army of some 25,000 men across the Iser River, there linking forces with the Austrian I Corps under *General* Eduard Clam-Gallas. Benedek now placed Crown Prince Albrecht in command of the same I Corps, as well as his own Saxons, and ordered a defensive position taken up in front of the town of Gitschin. The Austrian commander in chief would concentrate his forces at Josefstadt and march to their aid. By June 29, however, no other Austrian forces had arrived, and the Saxon prince had to fight a very heavy engagement against Friedrich Karl, from which he managed to extricate himself with great skill but heavy losses.

Meanwhile, Benedek still believed that the Prussian Second Army was moving northward and was therefore not a problem. After border battles at Nachod, Trautenau and Eypel, however, the chance to catch Crown Prince Friedrich Wilhelm's army as it debouched through the mountain passes only emphasized earlier opportunities Benedek had let slip by.

As the official Austrian account of the war says: "If, instead of waiting until the last moment, the IV and VIII Corps had been sent off a day or two earlier, and the II Corps, which was nearest to Josefstadt, had led the march instead of bringing up the rear, the concentration round that town could have been effected far more rapidly. Even if a few brigades of infantry had been sent into Bohemia by rail with orders to observe and close the frontier defiles, they could have delayed, even had they been unable to check, the advance of the Prussian Second Army. In doing so, they would have made it possible for the principal Austrian forces to have fallen upon the army of Prince Friedrich Karl and crushed it with superior numbers."

Indeed, at Trautenau, Austrian *Feldmarschalleutnant* (Major General) Ludwig *Freiherr* von Gablenz's X Corps attacked the Prussian I Corps with such spirit that it drove the Prussians back across the mountains. However, Gablenz alone could not repeat his success and was in turn defeated at Prausnitz by the Prussian Guard Corps. Only on June 30 did Benedek realize the full error of his dispositions and telegraph his emperor to sue for peace. Franz Josef had no such intention. He told Benedek that he had every confidence in Benedek's ability and that he had sent one of his personal officers to the front to view the situation.

The result was that Clam-Gallas was removed from his command for his failure at Gitschin, and *Feldmarschalleutnant* Alfred *Freiherr* von Henikstein, Benedek's chief of staff, was replaced by *General* Baumgarten. He did not arrive at headquarters until the very day of the Battle of Königgrätz, a delay confusing the situation still further by giving Austria two commanders in the field during the battle. Still, Benedek saw the possibility of a defensive battle on the high ground between the Bistritz and Elbe rivers. His confidence began to return as he regrouped his army for the decisive battle that was to come.

The Bistritz River is no more than a small tributary of the Elbe. On its east bank the ground rises in a series of slopes and undulations that soon form a small chain of hills that overlook the approaches to the river from the west. Those hills had been strongly fortified with abatis and earthworks and ran from Problus northward to the villages of Lipa and Chlum. From there the ground dipped and then rose again to the hills of Maslowed and Hore-nowes, falling away again to the Trotina River, on Benedek's right flank. Two thick woods of approximately 1,800 square yards each, the Holawald and the Sweipwald, stood in front of the villages of Lipa and Maslowed to the north; and in the south, at Neu Prim and Problus, two more dense clusters of trees, the Steziek wood and the Briza wood, abutted from the main Austro-Saxon position itself.

For two days before the battle, Benedek's inspector-general of artillery, Archduke Wilhelm of Austria, had reconnoitered the area, positioning his artillery so that it had a clear field of fire and marking the ranges for his excellent rifled cannon. On the high ground at Lipa and Chlum, many batteries were placed in tiers overlooking the approaches from Sadowa and the Bistritz Valley. There, on July 3, 1866, the fate of Germany was to be decided.

Benedek's forces were divided into four groups. In the center, at Chlum-Lipa, III Corps and X Corps held the line—in all, some 44,000 men and 134 guns. Both corps had units well forward near the Sadowa bridge to dispute the crossing. On the left, the Saxons and VIII Corps, comprised of 40,000 men and 140 guns, held the sector composed of Techlowitz, Neu Prim, Ober Prim, Nieder Prim and Problus. On the right—by far the weakest position on the field—stood IV Corps and II Corps with 55,000 men and 176 guns between Chlum and Nedelist. Entrenchments had been dug and massive gun emplacements constructed along the ridge that ran between these two villages, but they were themselves overlooked a little farther north by the heights of Maslowed and Horenowes. Each flank was covered by a cavalry division. Between Rosberitz and Wsestar, I Corps and VII Corps, together with the heavy cavalry and artillery, formed a reserve mass of 47,000 men, 11,435 cavalry and 320 guns.

The weakness in Benedek's position, a rough semicircle with both flanks resting on the Elbe, was the fact that it would be difficult to meet an enveloping attack, since the Austrian main line of retreat ran along the Sadowa-Königgrätz highway and was therefore susceptible to being cut. Quite possibly the Austrian commander did not expect that the Prussian Second Army would be able to join the battle, thinking that he would be confronted by only the two other Prussian armies in a frontal attack against his prepared positions.

Owing to a total lack of reconnaissance on their part, the Prussians did not know the whereabouts of the Austrian army, and there was some consternation at headquarters as to whether Crown Prince Friedrich Wilhelm would arrive in time, should Benedek make a stand. Even so, Moltke managed to keep a cool head. He sent out patrols, which on July 2 discovered the Austrian position. Then, orders were dispatched to the Second Army urging all possible speed in descending upon the Austrian right flank. The Prussian VI Corps and Guard Corps divisions, which were nearest to the Austrians, still had no hope of reaching the battlefield until midday; the other units of the crown prince's army would not arrive until some time later. It appeared that the Prussian Elbe and First armies would have to fight alone for at least four or five hours against the full weight of Benedek's army.

The morning of July 3 dawned gray and damp as the Prussian units moved forward toward the Bistritz River line. The principal objective, as far as Friedrich Karl was concerned, was to drive in the Austrian outposts and, after establishing a firm hold on the right bank, to push on into the heart of Benedek's position. Only after great difficulty did Moltke persuade Friedrich Karl that his task was limited to pinning down the enemy until the Second Army came in against the Austrian flank. To that end, at 7 a.m., Moltke ordered the 8th Division to move forward toward Sadowa while the 3rd and 4th divisions, keeping in line with the 8th, advanced to the south of the main highway, against Unter-Dohalitz and Mokrowous. The 5th and 6th divisions followed in the wake of the 8th. Between those forces, the combined cavalry corps kept in contact with the Army of the Elbe. Out on the left, *Generalleutnant* Eduard Friedrich von Fransecky's 7th Division moved against the village of Benatek, using a single cavalry division to keep in touch with the rest of the First Army. A good deal of discretion was given to the commander of the 7th Division, an enormous responsibility really, since he had to contain the Austrian right until the crown prince arrived on the field.

On the Prussian right, Bittenfeld's Army of the Elbe reached Alt Nechanitz at about 8 a.m., marching in a cold mist and drizzling rain that had been falling since dawn. During that time, the Austrian and Prussian artillery had been exchanging shot for shot, with neither as yet doing any great damage. At Nechanitz, the Saxon and Austrian outposts fell back in good order to their main positions around Problus. From there they poured a destructive fire into the Prussian ranks as the latter emerged from the smoke of battle. Bittenfeld showed no great hurry in getting his troops across the river, believing that he would be isolated should the Austrians mount an offensive against the Prussian center. Therefore, by 10 a.m. *Generalleutnant* von Schöler's advance guard of some seven battalions, finding itself without support, was forced back by a spirited counterattack from Nieder Prim to the Hradek-Lubno ridge, led by the Saxon Life Brigade.

In the center, the 8th Division cleared Sadowa of its defenders at 8:30 a.m., while on the right the 4th Division attacked Unter-Dohalitz, and the 3rd

Division pushed into Mokrowous. Like the Saxons, the Austrians fell back in an orderly manner to the high ground. Almost all the villages along the Bistritz were now on fire—the smoke and haze made it impossible for the Prussians to see their enemy clearly, while the defending *Jäger* battalions poured a continuous fire at the mere sound of the advancing columns. The 3rd Division also now came under fire from part of the massive battery of guns ranged from Langenhof to Lipa, halting the Prussians for almost four hours. The 3rd Division's troops were ordered to find cover until the enemy battery could be outflanked.

The 8th and 4th divisions, after advancing from the river line, found that they, too, were prey to a good number of the Austrian guns. Forced to use the trees of the Holawald and the crumbling ruins of Ober-Dohalitz for protection, they received such a pounding that some units made desperate yet futile attacks against the bristling ridge of cannon. Whole battalions dashed forward, only to be cut down in swaths by the measured range of Austrian fire.

The royal headquarters had by this time moved to the Roskosberg to the rear of Sadowa. From that vantage point the king of Prussia had a good view of the punishment his two divisions were receiving in the Holawald. Seeing some bloodied battalions retiring, he rode forward, shouting that he was going to lead them back again so that they could "fight like brave Prussians." Staff officers tactfully managed to restrain their monarch, but by 10:30 a.m. the losses incurred by the 8th and 4th divisions were mounting significantly, without any obvious relaxation in the Austrian barrage. The 7th Division, too, was receiving a tremendous hammering on the left.

The dilatory behavior of the commander of the Army of the Elbe found no counterpart in Fransecky's make-up. His 7th Division was to perform prodigies of valor and improvisation as it took on almost one-quarter of the Austrian army. As already mentioned, the Austrian IV Corps and II Corps were overlooked from the north by the heights of Horenowes. Both corps commanders had decided, with the approval of their respective chiefs of staff, to move their front 90 degrees to the west, taking station along a line extending from Chlum and Maslowed, and leaving only five battalions and a cavalry division to guard the approaches from the north.

After he sent out couriers to the crown prince's Second Army requesting urgent assistance for his right flank, Fransecky's troops took the village of Benatek at 8 a.m. After consolidating that position, they then debouched from the village in the direction of Maslowed. They suddenly came under a heavy fire from the Sweipwald, which had been presumed clear of enemy units. The advance guard under *Oberst* (Colonel) von Zychlinski now halted its forward movement until the 26th and 66th regiments came up to join it. Then, at 8:30 a.m., Zychlinski threw the combined force, some 5,000 men, into the Sweipwald, pushing the defenders back up the wooded hillside toward Cistowes. There, *Generalleutnant* Tassilo *Graf* Festitics' IV Austrian Corps had recently come into line after moving from the right flank. In a series of counterattacks, Festitics' battalions suffered appalling casualties as they advanced in column formation against the rapid fire of the Prussian needle guns. By 9:30 a.m., three full brigades had been used up, to hardly any avail. Festitics himself was wounded, but his second-in-command, *Generalleutnant* Anton von Mollinary, rather than forming a defensive line at Maslowed, was even more determined to evict the Prussians from the wood. Calling on the assistance of *Generalleutnant* Carl *Graf* Thun von Hohenstein's II Corps, Mollinary threw still more troops into the corpse-littered wood.

At 10 a.m., *Generalleutnant* Emerich Fleischacker's Austrian brigade went in with the bayonet, drums beating and flags unfurled. By now, all the 7th Division's reserves had been used up in holding back those suicidal attacks, and Fransecky sent for help from the 8th Division on his right. The fresh troops arrived just in time to pour a hail of bullets into the tightly packed Austrians, driving them back once again to the edge of the wood.

Waving his sword like a dervish, Mollinary sent in yet another full brigade. These fresh troops, under *Oberst* Carl von Pöckh, drove into the Prussian front and left flank, forcing them, in turn, to fall back to the farthest outskirts of the wood. It now seemed as if one final push would unhinge the entire Prussian left flank and send it back across the Bistritz in rout.

But it was not to be. At 11 a.m., the right flank of Pöckh's brigade came under a tremendous fire from the direction of Wrchownitz. In a matter of minutes the brigade commander was dead and more than 2,000 of his men were killed or wounded. The Prussian Second Army had arrived on the field.

The Prussian 1st Guard Division had marched from Dobrawitz as soon as its officers received Fransecky's appeal for help. They were now descending the low hills in front of Wrchownitz, catching the Austrians in flank as they attacked the Sweipwald. Not far to their rear came the 2nd Guard Division, its advance guard already near Zizelowes.

Away to the east, the Prussian VI Corps under *General* von Mutius was heading straight for Racitz, the 11th Division on the right of the Trotina River and the 12th Division on the left. Both divisions were as yet unblooded in battle, but their men were eager to prove themselves in action before the arrival of their more experienced brothers in V Corps, which was still some distance to the rear.

With the annihilation of Pöckh's brigade as a fighting force, and the imminent arrival of the entire Prussian Second Army, Benedek realized the full implication of the errors made by Mollinary and Thun in moving their corps from their prepared positions. True that during the fighting in the Sweipwald he had been preoccupied with the vision of a counterattack against the whole front of the Prussian First Army, but he should not have canceled an order to *Feldmarschalleutnant* Wilhelm *Freiherr* von Ramming's VI Corps to fill the gap on the right. It was now too late. All he could do was order his IV and II corps to fall back to their original positions between Chlum and Nedelist. That proved not only difficult, owing to the amount of commitments given to the fighting in the Sweipwald, but also fatal to the morale of the troops who had been under the impression they were winning the battle. The result was that the whole force fell back in great disorder, taking a good part of Thun's corps along too. Thun himself seems to have given up the battle as lost and marched two full brigades toward the Elbe bridges.

In the south, the Army of the Elbe was, at last, making some headway against the Saxons. At 3 p.m. the Prussian 14th and 15th divisions captured Problus and Nieder Prim. The Saxon crown prince, seeing his position about to crumble, sent in a strong counterattack to gain time for the retreat of his remaining forces. Once again Bittenfeld fell into a torpor, and after driving back the Saxon attack, the Army of the Elbe halted. Bittenfeld still had the fresh 16th Division at hand, but was content to consolidate his position around Problus. Thus, the chance of a double envelopment of Benedek's army was lost.

The right flank of Benedek's position was about to fall apart in any case. His troops had been forced out of Maslowed, and most of the high ground to the north was in Prussian hands. Along the lower Trotina River, the five battalions of Henriquez's brigade were driven back, while the Austrian gun line had also retired to a position between Langenhof and Wsestar. There the Austrians formed a line containing more than 120 cannons.

The commander of the Prussian 1st Guard Division, *Generalleutnant* Friedrich Hiller von Gärtringen, now saw that the hinge of the whole Austrian position rested on the village of Chlum and its high ground. In the village itself, the Austrian brigade of *Generalleutnant* Carl von Appiano had, as yet, not become aware of the tide that was about the break over it. Then, when it did, his troops were forced out of the village and streamed back toward the rear, taking their reserves along with them. One lone cavalry battery, under *Hauptmann* (Captain) August von der Groeben, endeavored to stem the Prussian advance. Its first salvos were answered by such a crippling enemy fire from all sides that within the space of five minutes he was killed, together with 53 men and 68 horses. Groeben is little remembered today. A crude monument erected on the spot bears the inscription "The Battery of the Dead."

By 3 p.m. all Benedek could do was order a general retreat. Mollinary and the Austrian VI Corps commander, Ramming, both begged their chief to counterattack, but he had by now lost all control over the battle. At 3:15 p.m., without a direct order, Ramming took it upon himself to send forward two fresh brigades to retake Rosberitz and Chlum. At the same time, the Austrian guns at Langenhof redoubled their fire to cover the attacks.

In a fierce fight, the Prussian 1st Guard Division was forced out of Rosberitz and back to Chlum, pursued by the blood-stained battalions of *General-leutnant* Ferdinand Rosenzweig von Dreuwehr's Austrian brigade. Three guns were captured, but the only other thing their valiant counterstroke achieved was to bring still more Prussian units to the assistance of the 1st Guard Division. The 2nd Guard Division now came into action, together with elements of the Prussian I Corps. Those units, joined in a well-timed attack by the 11th Division (from the direction of Nedelist), smashed into Rosenzweig's brigade and sent it reeling back in turn toward Rosberitz. There, the Austrian I Corps and VI Corps made a gallant effort to contain the Prussian masses, and only after suffering immense losses were they gradually forced back.

The battle was now firmly in Moltke's pocket. Only the fire from the Austrian artillery delayed the victorious Prussians as they moved ever nearer to cutting the Sadowa-Königgrätz road. It was now, too, that Benedek played his last cards by sending in the cavalry divisions of *Generalleutnant* Carl *Graf* Condenove and the prince of Holstein to attack westward and break up any pursuit by Friedrich Karl's First Army.

In the charges and countercharges that followed, the Austrian cuirassiers, uhlans and dragoons not only threw the Prussia cavalry into disarray and made pursuit by them very unlikely, they also held back the Prussian infantry for more than half an hour. The cost, however, was terrible: 64 officers, 1,984 men and 1,681 horses.

The cavalry attacks, plus the bloody attacks sent in by I Corps, were successful in containing the Prussian advance and allowed the retreating Austrians to reach the Elbe. At 9 p.m., the last shot was fired by their horse artillery. Moltke now halted the carnage, and in the gathering dusk his men sank to the ground, exhausted.

Panic reigned in Königgrätz, where the Austrians became jammed together in one chaotic mass of men, wagons and horses. The only good fortune that Benedek had had at all during the day was that no Prussian pursuit was forthcoming.

The losses incurred by the Austrians and Saxons amounted to 1,372 officers and 43,500 men killed, wounded or missing, of whom almost 20,000 were taken prisoner. The Prussian losses were much lower: 360 officers, 8,812 men killed, wounded or missing, more than half of whom came from the First Army. Moreover, the disproportionate difference in the wounded and missing between the two antagonists was increased by the Austrians, who had never signed the Geneva Convention. Consequently, their medical personnel, who were unprotected by the Red Cross and classified as combatants, withdrew with the rest of the Austrian army, thus leaving many men on the field who could otherwise have been administered to rather than being left to bleed to death or to be captured.

The Austrians now decided that to carry on the struggle would be futile, and a five-day armistice was arranged, subsequently extended to August 2.

The final peace terms were signed at the Blue Star Hotel in Prague on August 23. From that time until the outbreak of World War I, Prussia would be the undisputed head of the German confederacy—and one of the most awesome military powers in the world.

Imperial Interest Protected

The press and even Sir Garnet Wolseley's
own staff were led to believe the British landing would
be at Aboukir. Britain's 'only general,' however,
had his own strategy to pursue.

By Peter Harrington

If India at one time could be called the jewel of the crown for the British Empire, then surely it was Egypt that provided the golden thread linking the great jewel to Britain—the Suez Canal.

From the moment Ferdinand de Lesseps' engineering marvel opened to the strains of Verdi's "Aida" in 1869, the security of the Suez had been imperative to the future of India. The overland route via the canal immediately became vital as a lifeline for the commerce of the empire—a link that avoided the three-month voyage around South Africa's Cape of Good Hope.

By the operative year of 1882, more than seven million tons of shipping passed through the Suez annually, four-fifths of it British. In addition to that commerce, the canal provided enormous revenues for London, since Britain had invested 4 million pounds sterling to acquire a controlling share of the Suez Canal Company. In short, the Suez had become absolutely indispensable to England, and England was by then committed to an active interest in the fortunes of Egypt.

France, too, had strong interest in affairs Egyptian, an affinity dating to Napoleon Bonaparte's frustrated Egyptian campaign at the turn of the 19th century. Culturally and commercially, French influence had remained a force in Egypt. Further, one of her sons (de Lesseps) having built the canal, France was joint proprietor with Britain of the Suez passageway. The French also had a stake of their own in the North African colonial empire they were building in the region around Egypt.

Then there was Turkey, another ingredient of the Egyptian political stew late in the 19th century. Egypt was a semi-autonomous part of the crumbling Ottoman Empire. Her army and senior positions in the Cairo government were controlled by Turks under their puppet head of state, the khedive. In 1882, as the stew reached a boil, the khedive was Mohammed Tewfik, who had been appointed by the government in Constantinople to succeed his wastrel father Ismail after Ismail's attempts at the Westernization of Egypt left the country bankrupt. Under Tewfik's administration, corruption was rife throughout the civil service, and the country was still in financial ruin.

247

To compound the problem, army pay had been cut back. Despite all, meanwhile, larger British policy was aimed at preserving the Ottoman Empire as a shield against Russia.

The native populations of the area did not share the same sympathies as their European masters. Spurred by the nationalist sentiments displayed in India during the Mutiny of 1857 and by the Boers in the Transvaal more recently, a movement was underway in Egypt to deny any further interference and exploitations by foreign governments. The growing fervor among Egyptians found a voice in Ahmed Arabi Bey, a man of the people whose father was a fellahin or peasant. Arabi had risen by his ability and force of character to a prominent role in the Egyptian Army as a colonel and would probably have achieved even greater status had it not been for the deliberate Ottoman policy of keeping Egyptians from positions of command.

Arabi fomented enthusiasm with his cry of "Egypt for the Egyptians," and his call was answered by the fellahin. He called for an end to the corruptions of the Turkish upper classes in Egypt and for a halt to foreign interference in the affairs of his impoverished country. Arabi was arrested and brought before a council of ministers for censure, but at his hearing, peasant troops and fellow officers burst in, throwing inkpots at the council, and forced the weak khedive to appoint Arabi to a ministry in the government.

To the British, Arabi was an upstart, a mutineer and a blood-thirsty fanatic who would have to be dealt with. In a state of panic, Prime Minister William E. Gladstone's government and the French pledged their support to the khedive and requested that the sultan of Turkey send a force into Egyptian waters as a warning to any further ambitions Arabi might have.

Not to be intimidated, Arabi set about reinforcing the defenses along the Mediterranean coastline, placing heavy artillery within the forts around the port of Alexandria, despite the arrival of several French and British ships in the port on May 19, 1882. Turkey failed to comply with the Franco-British request—it was becoming clear that they would have to do the dirty work themselves—but it was the Egyptian nationalists who made the next move.

On June 11 and 12, there were large anti-European riots in Alexandria, which left 50 Europeans dead. It was now the turn of France to panic. The French Chamber voted to refuse any credit for the suppression of disorder in Egypt, and it used the excuse of a change in government in Paris to withdraw its ships, thus leaving Britain alone.

Undaunted, although still reluctant, London went ahead with plans for a military strike against the nationalists. On July 3, Admiral Sir Frederick Seymour was given authority to destroy the Alexandria batteries if work on them continued. Seymour, whose patience by then was wearing thin, sent an ultimatum on July 5, demanding the Egyptians evacuate and dismantle the forts immediately, but the demand was flatly rejected by Arabi. That was exactly what the British wanted; they had now been given a pretext to open fire on the Egyptian defenses. Meanwhile, plans moved forward in Britain to prepare an expeditionary force; orders were sent out from the war office to 61 towns to prepare for the immediate calling out of reserves, while out in India, another expeditionary force was preparing to sail. Also, on their way from Malta, were four ironclads, a torpedo ship and a well-packed troopship.

The British ironclads steamed out of the inner harbor of Alexandria on July 10 and, joining up with the reinforcements from Malta, took up a position opposite the forts surrounding the city. At 7 a.m. the next day, the fleet of 14 ships opened a crashing bombardment on the city and port. The ironclads *Monarch*, *Invincible* and *Thetis* began firing at point-blank range. The Egyptian batteries returned the fire, but by 8:30, Forts Marsa-el-Kanat and Meks to the west of the town had nearly been silenced. At 1:30 p.m., a shell from the warship *Superb* blew up the magazine of Fort Ada and killed about 900 Egyptians.

In spite of losing about 40 men itself, the Royal Navy kept up the attack all day, with the result that the forts were totally demolished and 2,000 of their defenders were reported killed. The damage would have been more severe had it not been for the failure of many of the naval shells to explode.

But Arabi's nationalists were unmoved and continued to reject Seymour's terms. The Egyptian and his force of 60,000 men now evacuated the city and retreated to a strongly entrenched position at Kafr Dowar in the desert, 16 miles toward Cairo, as a challenge to the British to try and destroy him in conditions that favored his troops. A landing party from the fleet occupied Alexandria, but not before the city had been set on fire and looted by convicts who had been released from the prisons.

There was no turning back now. With the spread of nationalist sentiment fueled by Arabi's claim that Islam was in danger and that all good Moslems should rally to the champion of faith, the rebel would have to be dealt with swiftly. Egypt must serve as an example to other colonies—anti-British attitudes would not be tolerated and would be dealt with severely. On July 28, the House of Commons passed a vote of credit for 2,300,000 pounds sterling to pay for the expedition, and upon the cry of "send out Wolseley," the country turned to her "only general," Sir Garnet Wolseley, to lead it.

At 49, Wolseley was the bright light in an army that had suffered major setbacks throughout the world. The failures in the Crimea and India were heightened by recent setbacks in Afghanistan and in South Africa (both the Zulus and the Boers). The popularity of the army in Britain was at a low ebb despite recent reforms, and Wolseley was the shining exception.

Whenever he had taken to the field, he had returned victorious. Commissioned as a second lieutenant in 1852, he left for India, and it is oddly symbolic that on his arrival in Calcutta he heard the salute honoring the Duke of Wellington, who had just died. Perhaps it was his destiny to succeed the great duke. After distinguishing himself in Burma and the Crimea, Wolseley returned to India and its mutiny, to participate in Sir Colin Campbell's first relief of Lucknow. In 1860, he saw action in the China War. Two years thereafter, he visited the civil war-torn America, where he met Confederate generals Robert E. Lee and Thomas J. "Stonewall" Jackson. But it was his leadership in the Red River Expedition in Canada in 1870 and the successful war against the Ashantis in 1873-74 that thrust Wolseley into the limelight.

Surrounding himself with trustworthy officers from "the Ring" (a circle of specially favored officers who had served with Sir Garnet in most of his campaigns), Wolseley set about planning the Egyptian expedition. The general plan of operations was to forward two infantry divisions from England to Alexandria, while a mixed division of British and native troops was to be directed from India to Suez. He saw the campaign as a problem in logistics rather than in strategy or tactics, and while his plan of campaign was simple, he was concerned over possible Egyptian interference with the water supply. Strict secrecy was maintained about the outline of the campaign, with the press duped into thinking that Aboukir, west of the Nile, was to be the objective. This was a deliberate ploy on the part of Wolseley, and even his staff was fed the ruse. It was a diversionary move to deceive the enemy, who no doubt had access to the British newspapers.

Large steam transports arrived daily at Alexandria from August 10 onwards — 16,400 troops came from England and a further 14,400 arrived from India and the Mediterranean. Wolseley himself reached Alexandria on the 15th to great excitement, but the questions abounded. What was the plan of campaign? A landing at Aboukir? An assault on Arabi's position at Kafr Dowar? If the last were the objective, what about the eastward entrenched position at Tel-el-Kebir, which covered the approach to Cairo from the direction of the Suez Canal?

On the afternoon of August 19, the fleet of transports, with the 1st Division on board, 6,000 men in all, anchored in Aboukir Bay with the apparent intention of forcing a landing in the vicinity. As night fell, however, the ships got under way again — the Suez Canal itself was to be utilized as a base of invasion. The commander in chief's plan had been successfully kept secret. On the 21st, disembarkation from the landing transports took place at Ismailia at midcanal, and on the following day the Indian contingent landed at Suez, at the bottom of the canal. It was now apparent to everyone that Sir Garnet was concentrating his forces for an attack on the works at Tel-el-Kebir, which lay across the Sweetwater Canal connecting the Nile at Cairo with the Suez Canal at Ismailia.

Wolseley's first concern was the fate of this secondary canal upon which the whole outcome of the campaign hinged, as it was the only source of fresh water available. Arabi had the same thought and made several attempts to dam the canal, as well as to destroy the railway that ran parallel with it. Wolseley moved quickly to thwart those Egyptian hopes. The British advance guard under Maj. Gen. Drury Lowe led the way across the desert from Ismailia on the Suez, following along the line of the Sweetwater and the railway with rapidity so as to prevent, as far as possible, irreparable damage being done to the water supply. At Tel-el-Mahuta on August 24, they were exposed to a blistering fire from 12 Egyptian guns, but most of the shells were fitted only with percussion fuses and buried themselves harmlessly in the soft sand.

In fact, it was the burning hours of the midday sun and the parching glare of the desert sand, more than anything, that took its toll on the British troops, who were dressed in their traditional red-serge jackets, thick flannel shirts and blue-woolen trousers. Many collapsed with severe sunstroke. Throughout the rest of the campaign, the troops were ordered to march in the cool hours of the early morning, or the late afternoon and evening. Sun goggles and face veils were also issued to alleviate the problems. Some observers noted that the scarlet coats were less conspicuous in the desert at a distance than the white uniforms of the Egyptian army, although the grimy, sweat-stained scarlet was far less favorable than the cool, practical khaki worn by the contingent from India.

By the 25th, the main force had come up to Tel-el-Mahuta, only to find that the enemy works had been abandoned. Moving on, the British cavalry found the enemy occupying a position at Masama Station, and following a short skirmish, they dislodged the Egyptians and captured their camp, which was well-supplied with food, ammunition and seven Krupp guns. Next day, the troops set to demolishing the Egyptian dams across the Sweetwater and a large embankment that had been hastily erected over the railway lines.

Two days later, the British 2nd Division of 2,000 men under General Gerald Graham reached Kassassin Lock on the canal, and it was there that Wolseley's plan was put to the test. Already the supply situation was beginning to break down and there was a serious shortage of mules; further supplies could not be brought up the track, as 200 yards of rail had been torn up.

Arabi had been closely following the movements of Graham's force and, realizing that his force outnumbered the British by five to one, decided to gamble on an attack. He had about 8,000 infantry, 1,000 cavalry and his 12 guns, two of which were brought up on railway trucks to within 4,000 yards of the British camp.

The cavalry under General Lowe was called out of the camp at Masama to assist Graham, but returned at 4:30 p.m. believing that the situation was well in hand. An hour later, a heliograph message arrived to the effect that the enemy was now advancing in force upon the position at Kassassin. A young lieutenant of the 4th Dragoon Guards was also dispatched to confirm the message. In the excitement of the moment, the ground officer gave the erroneous impression that Graham was in a desperate situation and was only just able to hold his own. In reality, the fanatical nationalists in white uniforms and red fezes had been successfully withstood by a small British force armed with only two guns and a captured Krupp gun.

By now, the British cavalry—composed of the Household Cavalry, two regiments of Dragoon Guards and four guns—had departed along the four miles of difficult terrain to Kassassin, and at about 7:15 p.m., the troopers found themselves standing out on a ridge, clear-cut against the skyline of a fine moonlit night, with the shot and shell of the alarmed Egyptians raining down upon them. The order to dismount was given immediately by Colonel Sir Baker Russell, in command of a cavalry brigade, but Lowe, riding up, shouted, "Mount, form line, charge!" On this order, Baker Russell, after having his horse shot from under him, remounted a second charger and led his tired and weary troopers in a brilliant charge against the Egyptians. Coming out of the dark from the northwest like an unexpected avalanche, the Household Cavalry and the Dragoon Guards, their flashing sabers glinting in the moonlight, cut down astonished soldiers who vainly tried to flee the hoofs of the mounts. Momentarily, the Egyptian fire emptied a few saddles. Many of the soldiers fell on their faces after the troopers passed, only to get up and and start firing at the British, who turned about and summarily dispatched them. The pressure was too much for Arabi's men, who broke and fled.

On September 9, Arabi made his last attempt to rush Kassassin before the whole weight of Wolseley's force came down upon him, but he was repulsed and solemnly retreated to Tel-el-Kebir to await the inevitable onslaught. There he had gathered 25,000 troops, including fierce Sudanese fighters, and a large number of field guns, some of which were the latest Krupp breechloaders.

The campaign now reached its critical juncture. The position at Tel-el-Kabir had been well prepared. Lines of solid entrenchments extended some four miles from flank to flank, divided at intervals by bastions mounting 75 guns and protected in front by successive series of deep trenches. At right angles to the extreme left of the position, a deep trench extended for two miles. Behind was another trench to serve as a defense for the front line from a flank attack. British reconnaissance, however, had failed to locate an isolated earthwork mounting four guns 1,000 yards in front of the trenches.

Wolseley entertained no doubts in his mind: the position must be carried. His plan, in fact, was his only possible option, due to the weakness of his force. Nevertheless, he felt that his soldiers were superior to the Egyptians. The reconnoitering of Arabi's position continued in an effort to find a weakness in the defenses, and finally the Achilles' heel was discovered: The enemy did not man its outposts at night.

The British force now numbered 634 officers and 16,767 men, and the commander in chief determined that in order to prevent a heavy loss of men, the march of just over six miles from Kassissin to Tel-el-Kebir would be covered at night, arriving just before daybreak to attack. That could create problems, especially if the troops became separated from their officers. But with pluck and nerve, Wolseley was confident that his divisional officers would come through. There could be no room for maneuvering, no afterthought, no rectification. Everything would have to run like a well-oiled machine, or disaster would be facing him squarely. The main attack was to be made north of the canal and railway, while the Indian division would advance on the south side. Accordingly, the two divisions forming the main attack moved out of camp and bivouacked at 11 p.m. on the 12th.

The troops sat in silence on the sand while comrades moving about appeared as black figures coming out of the darkness. Secrecy was vital, and the men were ordered to advance without yet loading their weapons. One hundred rounds and two days' rations were issued to each man.

At 1:30 a.m., the main body arose and in absolute silence moved forward. This force was divided into two distinct bodies, separated from each other by an interval of 1,200 yards. The soldiers, tired and cold, their joints tightening, must have had pangs of anxiety, but they had confidence in the commander. As the cockney soldiers said, it was "all Sir Garnet"—in other words, all was correct! The stillness was eerie as the feet of thousands passed softly over the sand. With no moon, the night was dark and silent. Without landmarks, it proved difficult to keep the desired formation, despite the guides taking observations from the stars. Progress was slow, and there were the inevitable delays. Unknown to the guides, the British line began to veer toward the right and passed within 1,100 yards of the unforeseen forward redoubt without being discovered. It was a stroke of luck, but then Wolseley always seemed to have luck on his side.

A streak of light appeared in the sky at 4:50 a.m. If this were dawn, the attack had arrived too late and would be discovered. The light did not develop, however, and the advance continued swiftly and silently. In fact, at that very moment, a comet had passed over Cairo!

Shortly before dawn, the left of the advance line stood within 350 yards of the entrenchments. No word was spoken. The tension was mounting among the troops, who could just make out the silhouetted rise in the ground that indicated the Egyptian defenses. Ahead, in the "safety" of their earthen defenses, lay the sleeping Egyptians unaware of the pending violence. Among the British, there was an acute air of nervous anticipation as the order was passed around at a whisper. The men were to reserve their fire until closeup, and then at 200 yards' distance, to cheer and carry the position at the point of the bayonet.

Quiet suddenly, the all-pervading silence of the desert was broken by four signal shots fired from a picket, followed shortly thereafter by a rattling of musketry that burst along the Egyptian line. An enemy cavalry patrol had blundered into the right of the British line. And now, trumpets rang out. The time was 4:55 a.m.

At that moment, the bugles sounded the charge. As the pipers struck up, the Highlanders on the left, under Sir Archibald Wilson, fixed bayonets and, with a lusty cheer, charged madly in two waves toward the parapet just as the light was coming up. Climbing the embankments presented some difficulties, as the sand was loose, and the first line dissolved into groups with each man helping his comrade up the parapet. Others fell headlong into the deep Egyptian trenches.

The wave of redcoats with their kilts swaying was too much for some of the Egyptians, who fled, but many of their comrades put up a fierce resistance. The left of the British line was driven back. The troops then were rallied and, joining up with the second line, drove the enemy out of the front trench. Soon after, the right of the British line, including the Irish Brigade, was also over the embankments and fighting man-to-man in the trenches.

Meanwhile, the British cavalry was sweeping around the enemy's line. Even the artillery got into the thick of things, moving five guns over the trench and parapet before going into action. The redoubt in front of the British lines opened fire, but was soon silenced by a salvo that blew up the magazine.

The death struggle was enacted many times over the next few minutes as Egyptian and Sudanese troops grappled with the British Tommies. Arabi's men were a formidable foe, and in some places along the line they managed to counterattack and to drive the assault troops back over the embankment. But the iron discipline of the British regiments held, and after half an hour's severe fighting, both the fortified position and the camp were in the hands of Wolseley's troops. By 6 in the morning, the fighting was over. The Egyptians were in full retreat, pursued by the cavalry. Cairo, 39 miles away, was captured on the 14th. Arabi himself escaped on horseback and then took a train to Cairo, where he was captured soon after.

The Egyptian army dissolved completely after Tel-el-Kebir. Inside the works were strewn the bodies of 2,000 dead and wounded Egyptians lying alongside their dead horses and camels; the losses on the British side were a mere 58 killed and 22 missing. The sun was high in the sky as the British columns reformed and moved off across the canal bridge in the direction of Cairo. Continuing south, Wolseley entered the Egyptian capital on September 15. Shortly afterward, the khedive Tewfik was reinstated as head of Egypt, which now became a British protectorate, but as one newspaper ruefully observed, Tewfik was "without a friend among the people he nominally ruled."

In 25 days, the army had effected a disembarkation at Ismailia, had occupied the capital of Egypt and after a bold and daring night march had soundly defeated the enemy. It had been a brilliant campaign. Wolseley had left home at the beginning of August and was back at the end of October. Upon his arrival, he was received by Queen Victoria, who conferred a peerage on the man to whom W. S. Gilbert and Arthur Sullivan had alluded five years earlier in their operetta, "The Pirates of Penzance," as "the very model of a modern major general."

The same cannot be said of Arabi, who ended his days in solitary exile on the island of Ceylon. But if he reflected on his vain attempt to overthrow the British, he could console himself with the knowledge that his brave troops had been an even match for the might of Britain, and had luck been on his side, the outcome might have been different.

So ended another episode in British colonial history, as perhaps the first purely imperialist British military expedition. What to Britain had seemed yet another terrorist uprising, however, was to the Egyptians, purely and simply put, a struggle for national freedom. In the world of 1882, such natural yearnings were not allowed to surface, and might made right. After Egypt regained full independence in the next century, however, Colonel Arabi would be resurrected as a national hero.

Day of the Storm Trooper

In March 1918, the Germans tried to break years of deadlocked trench warfare with new, devastating tactics developed by an old soldier, Colonel Georg Bruchmüller. One after another, the Allied front lines crumbled under their onslaught. But success brought new problems....

By Thomas Fleming

At 4:40 a.m. on March 21, 1918, 6,000 guns opened a stupendous bombardment on the 34 divisions of the British Third and Fifth Armies along their 42-mile front south of Arras. In the center of the Fifth Army's lines, an officer called it "more like a convulsion of nature than the work of man." The noise was so stupendous it was impossible to hear an order beyond a few yards, even when it was shouted through a megaphone.

Unlike previous bombardments on the Western Front, the German guns were on target from the first round. Thanks to ingenious artillerymen and painstaking mapmakers, the Germans had figured out how to fire their big guns accurately without registration. The rain of steel was under the direction of a master of destruction, Colonel Georg Bruchmüller, whom the black humorists among the high command nicknamed *"Durchbruchmüller"* ("Breakthrough-Müller"). After four years of studying his murderous subject, he had composed a kind of symphony that combined precise combinations of poison gas and high explosives, carefully orchestrated to wreak specific havoc on different sections of the battlefield.

Yellow-cross shells, containing mustard gas, were confined to the flanks of the selected target because mustard tended to disperse slowly and could hinder attackers as well as defenders. Green-cross shells contained deadly, odorless phosgene gas, which dispersed quickly. These were used on the forward trenches, the immediate target of attack. Huge quantities were also fired into the enemy rear to immobilize the artillery. They then were mixed with blue-cross shells, containing diphenyl chloramine, which fouled gas masks and caused men to expose themselves to the phosgene.

With a 3-to-2 advantage in manpower on the Western Front, thanks to the collapse of Russia, the German general staff had decided by early 1918 to strike for victory while the sluggish Americans were still spectators. Twelve months after Woodrow Wilson's declaration of war, the American Expeditionary Forces (AEF) consisted of four half-trained divisions—about 120,000 men. Their commander in chief, General John J. Pershing, had spent

256

most of his nine months in France fending off British and French attempts to break up his army into fragments to be absorbed into their own decimated divisions. Such amalgamation would render Pershing and every officer above the rank of colonel superfluous.

Not satisfied with their overall manpower advantage, the Germans had managed to concentrate 67 divisions opposite the British on the Arras front, undetected by spies, patrols or aircraft—giving them the 2-to-1 advantage the textbooks said the attacker required. For a final touch, the high command unveiled a new book of tactics, one that would profoundly affect infantry battles for the rest of the century. Certain units had been designated *Angriffs-divisionen* ("attack divisions"), and they had been trained as *Sturmtruppen* ("storm troopers") with a radically different approach to the battlefield.

Instead of being told to seize certain objectives, the standard form of orders issued to infantry for the previous two centuries, the storm troopers were given what are now called mission-oriented orders. Equipped with light machine guns and mortars, they were to break through the weakened British defenses in small squads and companies, leaving to the rest of the army the job of mopping up any holdouts in the enemy's forward battle line. The tactical orders were especially strong on that point. "The inclination of leaders to assemble their troops and get them in hand after a certain objective has been reached must be suppressed," the high command insisted.

Storm troopers were not a new idea, but previously they had been relatively small, elite units, trained mainly to execute trench raids or attacks on limited objectives. The Germans now were betting they could imbue whole divisions with their reckless ardor. Originally developed by several junior officers, the tactics had been tested on the Russian Front by General Oskar von Hutier, who now commanded the Eighteenth German Army as it attacked the British Fifth Army's center and right flank in Operation Michael.

At 9:30 a.m., after five hours of constant, merciless artillery pounding, out of the heavy ground fog loomed the storm troopers. Their rifles strapped to their backs, they relied almost totally on their favorite weapon, the hand grenade. Typical was Lieutenant Ernest Junger, commander of a company, who urged his men forward with frenzied impatience. "We had gone over the edge of the world into superhuman perspectives," he later wrote. A rage to kill squeezed "bitter tears from my eyes."

He and other company officers like him rolled up trench after British trench, capturing prisoners by the hundreds, sending thousands of other Tommies into headlong flight. So swiftly did they advance that in several cases the storm troopers reached abandoned mess halls with bacon sizzling on the stove and, in one case, "half a cow on the table." They ate, stuffed their haversacks with cigarettes and food, and kept going until they found themselves in danger of being killed by their own artillery, which was shelling batteries deep in the enemy rear. In less than 10 hours, von Hutier's Eighteenth

Army storm troopers had burst through the center of the Fifth Army and reached open country.

In 1916, in the Battle of the Somme, the British and French had lost 500,000 men fighting across those same woods and fields, gaining a grand total of 98 square miles in six, blood-soaked months. On March 21, 1918, south of Arras, the Germans gained 140 square miles in 24 hours, at a cost of 39,329 casualties. Von Hutier and his friends had invented a whole new type of warfare.

The desperate British threw in every available airplane—but the Germans had outconcentrated them in the sky, too, mustering 730 aircraft to their 579. The British threw in 25 tanks to save the key road junction of Bapaume. Only nine returned, and the personnel casualty rate was 70 percent. Panic began seeping through all ranks. In the hospital at Trouville, well behind the lines, a wounded sergeant called over his favorite nurse, displayed a pistol he somehow had smuggled into his bed, and told her not to worry—he would shoot her rather than let the Germans capture her.

Bluff, Irish-born General Hubert Gough realized his Fifth Army was in imminent danger of rout; he pleaded for reinforcements. Field Marshal Sir Douglas Haig, jittery about the rest of his battle line, would only spare him one division, which took two days to arrive. But Gough had reason to hope for help from the French who were manning the front on his right flank. It was understood, when the British extended their lines south to Saint-Quentin at French urging, that the *quid pro quo* was a guarantee that the French *poilus* would come to their aid if needed.

Alas, the Germans had tricked the cautious French commander, General Henri Pétain. The day before the attack the Germans had arranged for one of their observation balloons to "tear loose" and float into the French lines. In its gondola were plans for a massive assault on the French army around Reims. Convinced that the information was authentic, Pétain declined to send Gough more than a handful of riflemen, and husbanded his reserve of 50 divisions for the defense of Paris.

By the third day of the offensive, the British Third Army, commanded by General Sir Julian Byng, began to crumble. Byng had ignored Haig's orders to man his forward trenches lightly and keep the bulk of his army farther back for a defense in depth. Although the advance of the German Second and Seventeenth Armies was slow at first, once they broke through the densely packed forward areas, there was little to stop them. An appalled Haig realized there was no alternative to a general withdrawal south of the Somme River.

It was a devastating experience for the British army. Having paid 500,000 men to win that part of France, they had presumed they would stay. Huge fuel and ammunition dumps had to be destroyed, entire hospitals and airfields evacuated. Soon, on the road between Bapaume and Peronne, Gough's fear of rout became reality. As thousands of infantrymen trudged south in a disorganized mob, without officers, walking wounded mingling with the well, a cry went up: "German cavalry!" Panic swept along the line of march like an electric charge. In seconds the Tommies stampeded down the road, flinging wounded men into the ditch, throwing away packs, rifles and gas masks.

Ironically, that headlong retreat was probably the best tactic the harried British could have devised. It kept at least part of the disintegrating Fifth Army and the crumbling Third out of the grasp of the oncoming Germans. General Erich Ludendorff, the German commander, narrowed the focus of the attack to two objectives. He ordered von Hutier to continue to advance along the Fifth Army's right flank, hoping to drive a wedge between the French and the British. He ordered the Seventeenth Army to concentrate on seizing Amiens, the crucial rail center for bringing French reinforcements to battle.

Then, inexplicably, the German drive began to run out of steam. One reason was glimpsed by a German junior officer, Lieutenant Rudolf Binding. On March 28, he wrote in his diary: "Today the advance of our infantry suddenly stopped near Albert. Nobody could understand why. Our armies had reported no enemy between Albert and Amiens....When I got near the town I began to see curious sights...men driving cows...others who carried a hen under one arm and a box of notepaper under the other. Men carrying a bottle of wine under their arms and another one open in their hands...."

Binding described the English back areas as a "land flowing with milk and honey." Along with seeking refreshments, liquid and solid, thousands of German infantrymen had stopped to equip themselves with English boots, jackets, raincoats. They fed their half-starved horses on "masses of oats and gorgeous foodcake."

But those were not the only factors in the sudden loss of momentum. By the end of March, von Hutier's men had advanced more than 40 miles. Their artillery units could not get their guns across the devastated battlefield to continue to support them. The German *Luftstreitskräfte* (air service) complained that the staff was giving pilots only haphazard guesses about the location of the forward troops. Burdened with loot, in addition to the ordinary load an infantryman carries into battle, the storm troopers—and the less elite units that followed them—became exhausted. On April 4, after bringing Amiens within artillery range, Ludendorff called off the offensive.

He had captured 90,000 prisoners and more than 1,300 guns, and inflicted 212,000 casualties on the British. His armies had acquired another 1,200 square miles of France. The price was high—239,800 officers and men killed or seriously wounded. But the magical new tactics cried out for another attempt to achieve Ludendorff's original goal—to crack the British front and isolate Haig's troops from the Channel ports, leaving them no alternative but surrender.

Ludendorff and the general staff considered the British Expeditionary Forces (BEF) their only obstacle to victory. In April 1917, the French army, staggered by the failure of a massive offensive in Champagne, had mutinied and come within a whisker of collapsing. Pétain had managed to glue the *poilus* back together with a hasty combination of firing squads and promises of better treatment, but the army's morale still hovered near zero.

At 4:15 a.m. on April 9, 1918—which happened to be Ludendorff's birthday—Colonel Bruchmüller went to work again. This time his rain of steel and gas descended on a mere 11 miles of front, but in a far more crucial sector—Flanders. Little more than 15 miles behind the enemy lines lay Hazebrouck, another key rail center. Without it, the British army would become a marooned whale, bereft of food and ammunition.

Four attack divisions of General Ferdinand Quast's Sixth Army converged on a single Portuguese division holding a center piece of that 11-mile front. Their uniforms stained yellow with gas, the men from the Iberian Peninsula sprinted for the rear at a pace that made the soldiers of the British Fifth Army look like slowpokes. Not a few of them stole the bicycles of a British cycle corps that pushed forward to support them. Another 6,000 surrendered on the spot.

Storm troopers poured through the gap and assaulted British divisions on the Portuguese flanks, producing more panic and a less-rapid, but no less ominous, retreat. The British First Army fell back five miles, while General Sir Herbert Plumer's Second Army was thrown back from Messines Ridge. On April 11, Quast's Sixth Army linked up with General Friedrich von Arnim's Fourth Army, which had joined the offensive north of Armentières. By April 12, the breach was 30 miles wide and 10 miles deep. Hazebrouck was only five miles away. A desperate Haig issued an order that had the trumpet of doom in it: "There is no other course open to us but to fight it out! Every position must be held to the last man: there must be no retirement. With our backs to the wall, and believing in the justice of our cause, each of us must fight to the end. The safety of our homes and the freedom of mankind alike depend on the conduct of each one of us in this crucial moment."

Haig did more than write apocalyptic orders. He put Plumer, his best general, in charge of the battle and rushed Australian reinforcements from the Amiens sector. Every available airplane was thrown into the struggle, the aerial casualties of which included *Rittmeister* Manfred *Freiherr* von Richthofen, leader of *Jagdgeschwader* I and, with 80 victories, the leading fighter ace of the war. Killed on April 21, the "Red Baron" left behind instructions bequeathing command of his wing to *Hauptmann* Wilhelm Reinhard, who continued to fight for local air superiority.

Fighting stubbornly and ferociously, the British began making the storm troopers pay for every foot of ground. The French also moved several divisions to Flanders. Although they did not go into action, they threatened the

Germans' left flank, forcing Ludendorff to divert troops from the drive on Hazebrouck. Slowly, as the month of April dwindled, the storm troopers ran out of steam again. Many of the attack divisions were still weary from the original assault on the Third and Fifth Armies. On April 29, Ludendorff called off the offensive.

The German commander sensed the British army was like a boxer who had taken two terrific punches. One more could finish him off. But the swelling number of French reinforcements made Ludendorff think twice about trying to land an immediate knockout punch—even though, with a final chop, he had driven a French division headlong from Mount Kemmel, one of the key heights in the monotonously flat Flanders plain. He decided to strike a blow at the French lines in the south, to panic them into withdrawing their forces from Flanders. Then he and Bruchmüller would swing north to throw the final haymaker at the BEF.

Once more concealing his movements with astonishing success, Ludendorff moved his attack divisions south by night and concentrated them around the town of Laon, opposite the French Sixth Army north of Soissons. The front line ran along a commanding ridge, the Chemin des Dames, named for a carriage road hacked out of the limestone escarpment and used for outings by the ladies of the *ancien régime*. The French had captured it during the previous autumn in a limited offensive and proudly christened it the outer rampart of Paris. It was rugged country, pocked with small, deep valleys and steep hills.

By May 27, Ludendorff had 41 divisions in and around Laon. Facing him were 11 understrength French and British divisions, all decidedly second or third class. The four British divisions had been mauled in the March and April offensives and sent to the Chemin des Dames for a rest. There had scarcely been a shot fired in the sector for a year. It was known as the sanitarium of the Western Front. Among the French divisions was one that had been especially mutinous in the 1917 upheaval—its men had never forgiven the commander of the Sixth Army, General Denis Duchêne, for his ruthless use of firing squads to restore order.

Pétain, still the commander of the French field army, had issued orders for a defense in depth. But Marshal Ferdinand Foch, appointed generalissimo of the Allied forces in a hasty conference during the first German offensive, had canceled the order and insisted the front lines be fully manned, to make sure not a millimeter of France's sacred soil was surrendered. The result had almost every man in the Sixth Army packed into a three-mile wedge between the Chemin des Dames and the Aisne River—perfect targets for Bruchmüller and his murderous musicians.

Ironically, an American intelligence officer, Captain Samuel T. Hubbard, with nothing better to do—since the semitrained American divisions had yet to be given a sector of the front—predicted that the next German offensive would hit the Chemin des Dames. The French loftily ignored his warning. General Duchêne, known as "The Tiger" to his admirers, spent the night of May 27 in Paris with his mistress.

At 1 a.m. multicolored Very lights soared into the sky, signals for Bruch-müller's gunners. In seconds, the orchestra was at full crescendo, with 3,719 guns pouring destruction on the hapless *poilus* and Tommies trapped by Duchêne's overconfidence. At dawn, the storm troopers swept forward, their ranks bolstered by mountain troops to handle the difficult terrain. On the Chemin des Dames, they found little but corpses and dazed survivors eager to surrender. The mutinous French division evaporated, and others swiftly imitated it. Only the British did any serious fighting, and they were soon driven over the Aisne.

So swift was the German advance that scarcely a bridge over the Aisne was blown. A French army corps thrown in to restore the front found itself outflanked by hundreds of surging storm companies and was itself swiftly routed, causing its commander, General Jean Degoutte, to break down in tears. In 12 hours, all the objectives originally designated by Ludendorff as the limits of the offensive had been taken. But the storm troopers, ablaze with victory, kept going. They crossed the swift and narrow Vesle River on the 28th and headed south for the Marne, chewing up division after French division as they debouched on the chaotic battlefield.

Soon, Fére-en-Tardenois, a key road junction in the center of Champagne, was in German hands. Then Soissons, a vital rail center, fell. Only around Reims, where the French had built a network of fortifications, did the *poilus* hold. By May 30, the storm troopers were on the Marne, having captured 50,000 men and 800 guns.

Suddenly, Paris, the original goal of the invasion in 1914, was only 40 miles away. Ludendorff postponed his plan for a knockout blow in Flanders. He summoned every available soldier from other parts of the front to exploit this colossal breakthrough. But once more the Allies, by headlong flight, had given themselves time to muster more reserves and throw up a new, if shaky, defense line. When a German battalion crossed the Marne on May 30, its men found themselves isolated by a rain of shells that made reinforcement a form of suicide.

East of Soissons, the *poilus* and a British division also successfully resisted a German attempt to link the huge salient created by this third offensive with the bulge von Hutier and his storm troopers had carved in March. By hanging onto the hinges of the new salient, the Allies narrowed the focus of the German advance. Meanwhile, the French and British at last had reached an accommodation with Pershing. He was willing to let his divisions fight under French commanders temporarily—with a guarantee they would not be cannibalized and swallowed piecemeal. At that point, an American division of 28,000 men equaled four French divisions—it was the equivalent of a corps. General Omar Bundy's 2nd Division, half Marines and half regular infantry, went into position west of Château Thierry, while General Joseph Dickman's 3rd Division manned the banks of the Marne east of that strategic town. The 42nd (Rainbow) Division became part of the French Fourth Army, closer to Reims. Past them streamed thousands of beaten *poilus* shouting "fini la guerre."

General Degoutte, having replaced Duchêne as the commander of the French Sixth Army, authorized the American 2nd Division to launch a spoiling attack on Belleau Wood, with the main burden falling to the Marine brigade commanded by General James Harbord, assisted by General Edward Lewis' 3rd Infantry Brigade. Using the outmoded tactics of the Civil War, the Americans were mowed down by the thousands to capture a piece of real estate that had no value whatsoever. The wood was not finally cleared until July 1, with Vaux also being recaptured—at a cost of 9,777 American casualties, including 1,811 dead.

Except for this exercise in futility, the front along the Marne subsided into minor skirmishing. The storm troopers had again reached their physical limit. On June 6, Ludendorff called off the offensive and began reorganizing for a massive thrust toward Paris. He called this final drive *Friedensturm*— "peace offensive."

If Ludendorff had stuck to his original plan and switched Bruchmüller and his attack divisions north to Flanders at that point, he might have won the war. But he was mesmerized by memories of success in 1914, by the Marne and Paris. He was so convinced of his storm troopers' invincibility that he all but sacrificed the crucial element in their previous successes— surprise. The Allies knew where the blow would fall—the only question was when. It was difficult, if not impossible, to keep a secret shared by hundreds of thousands of men. Trench raids soon brought in prisoners who revealed that the offensive was scheduled to begin at 10 minutes past midnight on July 15. The German high command was hoping that the *poilus* would still be sleeping off their celebration of Bastille Day, the principal French national holiday, on the 14th.

Although some French generals still took Foch's advice and jammed their men in the forward trenches, others, like the Fourth Army's General Henri Gouraud, decided Pétain's defense in depth made better sense. They left only suicide squads up front and targeted their artillery on their own lines. The rest of their men went underground, into sandbagged dugouts. Precisely at 12:10, Bruchmüller's orchestra went to work, hurling destruction across 42 miles of front. Four hours later, the storm troopers went forward— to disaster.

French and American gunners poured concentrated fire into their ranks. After overrunning the sparsely defended first-line trenches of Gouraud's Fourth Army, the Germans were stopped in their tracks by grimly determined *poilus*, tough colonial troops and black New York National Guardsmen of the 369th Infantry Regiment. In the east, around Reims, by the time the Germans reached the main defense line, their attacks were scattered, uncoordinated. "Their legs are broken!" exulted Colonel Douglas MacArthur, chief of staff of the Rainbow Division. Along the Marne, machine gunners and riflemen of the 3rd Division took a terrible toll on the attackers as they paddled through fog and gunsmoke in rubber boats.

On the 3rd Division's right flank, however, a half-dozen French divisions evaporated, abandoning a battalion of the 28th Division, planted in their midst to stiffen them. But the 3rd Division, with the 38th Regiment as its centerpiece, stood firm, leaving the 20,000 Germans who had gotten across the river east of them exposed to entrapment. By the end of the first day, the Germans knew the offensive had failed. Lieutenant Binding now wrote in his diary, "I have lived through the most disheartening day of the whole war."

A discouraged Ludendorff tried to tell himself and others that the effort was a success. They had pinned down almost the entire French army and most of the American army to defend Paris. And now was the time to launch his knockout blow in Flanders. On July 16, after calling off further attacks, he took a train north to make the attempt. He had scarcely arrived when frantic telephone calls informed him of a totally unexpected development.

On the morning of July 18, out of the Forest of the Retz, east of Soissons, had stormed two American divisions, the 1st and 2nd, and the French Fourth Army's Moroccan division, in a ferocious counteroffensive that was biting deep into the flank of the Marne salient, threatening to trap a half-million Germans along the river. A dismayed Ludendorff had to abandon his knockout dreams and rush reinforcements south to blunt the threat.

The 2nd Division, already bled white by Belleau Wood, collapsed after two days, and the 1st Division and the Moroccans did not last much longer. But the Soissons offensive took the initiative away from the Germans—and they never regained it. Foch, buoyed by hundreds of thousands of Americans finally pouring into France, went over to the offensive all around the Marne salient. On August 8, led by hundreds of tanks, the British struck a hammer blow into the flank of the salient along the Somme. Three months later, the war was over.

The day of the storm trooper had come—and gone. But the lessons he taught the German high command were not forgotten. Young officers such as Captain Erwin Rommel never forgot the value of mission-oriented orders and the impact of a breakthrough to the enemy rear. Pondering the German defeat, they saw the fatal flaw in the storm trooper concept: the tendency to reach the limit of human endurance too quickly. The Germans found the answer to the problem in the machine the British had invented—the tank.

While the British, French and Americans continued to see the tank as the infantryman's helper, the Germans saw it as a weapon unto itself, with infinite possibilities—if it was manned by men with the storm troopers' elan and daring, operating on mission-oriented orders. Storm troopers on treads would not get tired, and they could penetrate 20, 30, 40 miles into the enemy's rear in a day. The result was the *panzer* division, the *blitzkrieg*—and another war that the German army almost won.

Allenby and the Last Crusade

*With Christmas only weeks away, the British
under Sir Edmund H.H. Allenby stood on the threshold
of a prize that no European army had held in 730 years—
the Holy City of Jerusalem.*

By John Thom Spach

The first rays of dawn on November 26, 1917, found Major Vivian Gilbert, commander of a machine-gun company in Britain's Egyptian Expeditionary Force (EEF), standing at the base of the mosque on top of Nebi Samwil, the highest point in Judea at 3,000 feet. His veteran troops of the 180th Brigade, 60th (London) Division, XX Corps, had wrestled the point and its surrounding heights from the Turks in a fierce firefight the day before. From that vantage point, he could see the white ribbon of the Jaffa Road as it wound westward through the craggy hills and terraces to the Mediterranean Sea. To the southeast as the early sun burned away the morning mist he could see the glistening spires and domes of Jerusalem just five miles away.

Nebi Samwil, the holy place and burial site of the prophet Samuel, known as Mizpah in the Old Testament, is the pinnacle from which King Richard *Coeur de Lion* refused to look upon Jerusalem—the city he could not deliver from the Saracens during the Third Crusade (1189-1192). Now Major Gilbert was a member of another British armed force seeking to wrest Jerusalem from Moslem rule—the last 400 years of which had been under the Ottoman regime. He had no qualms about looking at Jerusalem, because he believed that, having broken the Gaza–Beersheba fortified line the month before, this final crusade under General Sir Edmund H.H. Allenby would succeed where the others had failed.

With its towering position, the mosque and its minaret would have made an excellent observation post, but the British soldiers did not occupy the holy shrine. They hoped to protect it from hostile fire. When the Turks launched three counterattacks to retake Nebi Samwil on December 1, however, their initial assault destroyed the mosque with shellfire. As its crumbling walls fell, an entire company of British infantry was buried in the trenches and machine-gun posts dug in the slopes below the shrine. Joined by reinforcements from the flanking 75th Division and rushing in its reserves after the Turkish barrage ceased, the 180th Brigade was able to repulse the Turks in a daylong battle. They retained possession of the "Key to Jerusalem," and after darkness fell, the brigade buried 500 dead Turks at the foot of Nebi Samwil.

On December 5, the 74th Division took over the Nebi Samwil area, and the 60th Division moved westward on the Jaffa Road to Beit Nakula, where it set up a temporary camp. Then the torrential winter rains began to fall and filled the parched wadis with deep streams of icy water. They also turned the dusty footpaths and trails into quagmires that contested every step of the British Tommies and their horses and mules.

In order to spare Jerusalem from damage, General Allenby deployed his troops in encircling movements that forced the Turks into defensive positions in the surrounding hills. Under his strictest orders, no fighting was to take place in the Holy City itself, nor were any shots to be fired in its vicinity—and none were. He also left the Nablus Road to the north open as an avenue of retreat for the Turks. They could also avail themselves of the open area to the east into the Jordan Valley as a means of escape, but that was not so much by his design as by their own.

At dawn on December 8, a concerted attack began against the Turkish fortifications. The 180th Brigade attacked across the valley before Kustul and advanced up the steep hills where they overran the Deir Yesin line of entrenchments, taking the last two with bayonet charges. At the same time, the 53rd Division advanced from the south up the Hebron Road and captured the village of Lifta. The troops of the 53rd continued on for about a mile and a half beyond the village to link up with the 60th Division on their left. It was the usual practice of the Turks, when evacuating, to destroy a village and kill all the inhabitants—including women and children. But the sudden advance on Lifta caught them off guard, and in their haste to retreat they left the village intact and the villagers unharmed.

As the troops bedded down for the night, exhausted from the day's fighting, they were startled to hear clocks striking the hour. Then they realized how close they were to Jerusalem, for the clocks they heard were located within its city walls. Major Gilbert looked at the luminous dial on his wristwatch and noted that it was a few minutes fast.

During the night in his wet and dripping tent, the second-in-command of the 20th London Regiment, 180th Brigade, a Major Oxenham, got the brilliant idea of sending the headquarters cook out to the village of Lifta to buy some eggs for breakfast. He had heard a rooster crow, and where there was a rooster there had to be hens and eggs. He also knew that if he had heard the rooster, so had others, and he wanted his cook to have a head start before anyone else got the same idea.

It was 4 a.m. on December 9 when he ordered the cook, a Private Murch, to buy as many eggs as he could with the 60 piasters he gave him. "Don't come back without the eggs," he ordered.

The just-roused cook's uniform was dirty and covered with grease, and the rolls of his puttees, loosened for sleep, still dangled around his calves.

Donning his misshapen pith helmet, which he apparently had used for a pillow and which was a size too small for his head, he started out on his journey with only a vague idea of where the village was. In his trek through the rainy darkness, he had to bypass many enemy entrenchments as well as those of his own troops, and although he always kept going east, he lost his way. At the break of dawn, he discovered a well-constructed road to his left, and he decided to travel on it instead of the rocky footpath he had been following—the rocks had injured his exposed toes, which were sticking out of the fronts of his battered brogans.

As it got lighter and he passed many huts, Murch began to think that the village was larger than had been described to him, but he scratched the stubble on his unshaven face and kept going east. Eventually, he met up with a large, wildly cheering delegation that had come out on the road to greet him. The municipal officials, arriving in an open touring automobile, were obviously delighted to see him. "Al Nebi," the Arabic name for General Allenby, was shouted over and over.

The bewildered soldier tried to explain that all he wanted was to buy some eggs for his officers, but no one would listen. Private Murch, a headquarters cook, was probably the most disreputable-looking soldier in the entire British EEF, but he was offered the surrender and keys to the city of Jerusalem. He refused to accept the surrender, and as quickly as he could he returned to the regimental headquarters of the 20th London and reported what had happened—the Turks had fled, and Jerusalem was an open city.

Immediately, Major Oxenham and Colonel Warde-Aldham, commanding officer of the 20th, reported this development to the brigadier, General C.F. Watson. Since he was the general nearest to the city, Watson excitedly mounted his horse and, followed by a groom on a mule, rode to the Holy City to receive the surrender and keys to the city. He, in turn, reported it to his divisional commander, Maj. Gen. John Shea, who informed him that he would take the surrender himself and to return the keys to the mayor to await his arrival. As ordered, Watson returned to Jerusalem, gave the keys back to the Muslim mayor, and they awaited the arrival of General Shea.

At 11 o'clock on the same morning, Shea arrived in his staff car via the Hebron Road, followed by his entourage of headquarters officers, and accepted the surrender from the mayor. His first duty upon returning to his headquarters at Kuryet et Enab (Mount of Grapes) was to send a telegram to his commander in chief at Ramleh, through XX Corps: "I have the honor to report that I have this day accepted the surrender of Jerusalem." By return wire came the message: "General Allenby will himself accept the surrender of Jerusalem on the 11th inst; make all arrangements."

On December 11, Allenby, followed by representatives of the Allies, made his formal entry on foot into Jerusalem by the Jaffa Gate and received the surrender of the city on the steps of the Tower of David. Representing the first Christian army to control the city since its fall to Sultan Saladin in October 1187, Allenby issued his proclamation, read in English, French, Arabic, Hebrew, Greek, Russian and Italian, in which he declared that order would be maintained in all the hallowed sites of the three great religions, which were to be guarded and preserved for the free use of worshipers. He did not allow the Union Jack to be flown over the conquered city, nor the flag of any of the Allies, and thus gave a clear indication of England's intentions toward Palestine. The only flag allowed was that of the Red Cross, which flew over the American Hospital in Jerusalem.

On December 24, the 60th Division took up positions at Shafat and Tel el Ful, astride the Nablus Road north of Palestine; on their right flank, in the plains leading east to the Jordan Valley, were the defensive positions of the Jewish Legion. The Legion consisted of three battalions: the 38th, 39th and 40th Royal Fusiliers. After the Balfour Declaration of November 2, in which the Jews were promised a "National Home" in Palestine, Jews were recruited from England, America and Palestine itself. Among their ranks was David Ben Gurion, who later (in 1948) became the first prime minister of Israel. The Legion had acquitted itself well in the remaining battles to oust the Turks.

Before dawn on December 26, the Turks launched their expected attempt to recapture Jerusalem. Eight times they hurled themselves against the 60th Division holding the critical road. Forewarned and massed in depth on a narrow front, the British troops were able to withstand the assaults and throw the Turks back into the Jordan Valley. The British had opened fire with every gun in the corps area and chewed up the exposed Turks in the open fields that the enemy had to cross. The defeat drove them well beyond Ram Allah to the north and out of artillery range of Jerusalem to the east. It also opened the way for the British to advance against Jericho.

On February 13, 1918, the 60th Division took over the Deir Ibu Obed-Ras es Suffa-Hizmeh Line from the 53rd Division, and on the next day, operational orders were issued for an attack on Jericho, with the object of driving the enemy across the Jordan River. Before the main attack could take place, it was necessary to straighten out the British line by capturing a small village in the hands of the Turks and directly in front of the 180th Brigade. The village was named Mukhmas, or Michmash.

A frontal assault was decided upon. Supported by artillery and machine guns, the brigade was to move down into the valley separating two lines, and at dawn it would storm up the other side, in the face of enemy fire. The plan would entail some casualties, but those were deemed unavoidable. All orders were issued, then the troops got what rest they could.

In his bivouac, by the light of a candle, Major Gilbert read his Bible. When the raid was first discussed, the name Michmash had sounded vaguely familiar, although he could not quite place it. Just as he was about to put out his candle, he thought he would try one more time to find the name. At last he found what he was searching for in I Samuel, Chapters 13 and 14: "And Saul and Jonathan, his son, and the people that were present with them, abode in Gibeah: but the Philistines encamped in Michmash.

"Now it came to pass upon a day that Jonathan, the son of Saul, said unto the young man that bare his armour, 'Come and let us go over to the Philistines' garrison, that is on the other side,' but he told not his father....And the people knew not that Jonathan was gone.

"And between the passages, by which Jonathan sought to go over to the Philistine garrison, there was a sharp rock on the one side, and a sharp rock on the other side: the name of one was Bozez, and the name of the other Seneh. The forefront of one was situated northward over against Michmash, and the other southward over against Gibeah. And Jonathan said to the young man that bare his armour..., 'It may be that the Lord will work for us; for there is no restraint to the Lord to save by many or by few.' "

The major read on how Jonathan went through the pass of Michmash, between Bozez and Seneh, and climbed the hill with his armor-bearer following behind, until they came to a place high up, about "a half acre of land, which a yoke of oxen might plow," and the Philistines who were sleeping awoke, thought they were surrounded by the armies of Saul, and "the multitudes melted away" as they fled in disorder. Saul then attacked with his whole force of 600 men. It was a great victory for him, and "so the Lord saved Israel that day and the battle passed over unto Bethaven."

"This pass, these rocky headlands and flat piece of ground are probably still there," Gilbert told himself. "Very little has changed in Palestine throughout the centuries." He woke General Watson and informed him of what he had found in the Bible. Together they read the story over again. Then Watson sent out scouts, who came back and reported finding the pass, thinly guarded by the Turks, with rocky crags on either side—obviously Bozez and Seneh. Up in Michmash, the moonlight shone on a flat piece of ground just big enough for a team to plough.

Immediately, Watson decided to change the plan of attack. Instead of the whole brigade, one infantry company advanced in the dead of night along the pass of Michmash. The few Turks they met were quickly and silently dealt with. They passed between Bozez and Seneh, climbed the hillside and, just before dawn, found themselves on the flat piece of ground. When the Turkish soldiers awoke, they thought they were surrounded by several British armies and fled in disorder.

Every enemy soldier who had slept that night in Michmash was either killed or captured. After thousands of years, the tactics of Jonathan and Saul had again met with success.

The attack on Jericho that followed was turned into a cavalry victory by the Anzac Mounted Division, under the command of Lt. Gen. Sir Harry Chauvel. Their sweeping assault on the flanks caught the defending Turks unaware. The Australian and New Zealand horsemen had moved east from Bethlehem, and using the corridors of the Dead Sea, they had reached the plains in the Jordan Valley undetected. They accomplished in a few hours what it had taken Joshua and his army of Israelites a week to do—the fall of Jericho. But the Turkish soldier was a formidable foe, and with his back to the Jordan River, he fought even harder. To the 180th Brigade was given the task of storming the Talaat el Dumm, the rocky hill above the Good Samaritan's Inn, and in terms of casualties, it was one of their most costly in the entire campaign. The fortifications were taken at 7:15 a.m. on February 20. Now the battle would move into the plains of Moab, but first the Jordan River had to be crossed, and the retreating Turks had blown up or burned all the bridges across it.

Normally, the Jordan River is easy to cross, even by swimming, but not during the rainy season. Unfortunately, that was the exact time in March 1918 when Allenby was directing his rapid drive. During and immediately after the rains, the Jordan becomes flooded and swollen to twice its usual width—a great, brown torrent choked with trunks of trees and other refuse spinning toward the placid waters of the Dead Sea.

Volunteers were called for to swim the river and fasten rope lines to trees on the opposite shore, to establish a link by which troops might be ferried over on rafts. After that, the engineers could begin constructing temporary pontoon bridges. An enormous number of men stepped forward, and from them eight of the strongest and best swimmers were selected to make the attempt. In the darkness of night they stripped down to shorts, and with ropes tied around their waists, they entered the flooded river to fight their way to the other side.

The Turks, anticipating the actions of the British, lit huge fires of reed and brushwood along the eastern banks and commenced firing wildly with rifles and machine guns into the dark, swirling river. Gilbert was concealed in the scrub on the western bank with two sections of his company, and he watched helplessly as all eight of the swimmers were hit and killed. More volunteers came forward and tried to make the crossing; all failed except one young officer—a 2nd Lt. Jones of the 19th London Regiment. He was a champion swimmer who had once said, "I am always lucky in water!" He confirmed that by managing to reach the other shore and fix his rope to a stunted tree trunk. The first flat-bottomed raft was then sent into the river with 32 officers and men, but in midstream it took a direct hit from Turkish fire. All the men on board the raft became casualties.

The raft was retrieved and reloaded for another crossing. Two more swimmers, an officer and a corporal, managed to join Lieutenant Jones, and they succeeded in attaching steel chains to various trees. With those lines, the first temporary bridges were constructed. The 180th Brigade was one of the first units to make it safely to the eastern bank of the Jordan. By daylight the Turks had fled, and the beachhead was established. The size of the British force quickly grew to divisional strength.

On March 24, the British advance began in earnest, and they took the foothills at Shunet Mimrin and forced the pass leading up the steep mountain to the Armenian village of Es Salt. The objective of the advance was to take the fortifications at Amman, 10 miles to the southeast, and the arduous capture of Es Salt was a harbinger of the awesome task before them. It proved impossible to haul the heavy artillery across the desert from Jericho to Amman; without the big guns, the British could not breach the walls of Amman, 3,500 feet above the Jordan Valley. Also, the Aleppo–Medina railroad ran through Amman, and the Turks could receive reinforcements and supplies from Damascus. To make matters worse, the weather turned bitterly cold and took its toll on the British soldiers, who had been fighting continuously since October 1917.

On March 28, the attack on Amman was launched, but the firepower of the horse artillery proved insufficient to support the infantry climbing up the rugged slopes of the impregnable stronghold. Allenby ordered a halt to the attack and began a withdrawal to the Jordan Valley. With the 180th Brigade acting as rear guard, all the wounded were evacuated by March 31, and the special "Shea Group" retired across the Jordan. The failed attack against Amman was regarded as Allenby's one great failure in the Palestine campaign, but the unpredictable "Bull" (the troops' nickname for their commander in chief) would turn the failure to his advantage in subsequent operations.

It was at that time that Allenby found himself facing a new adversary in the person of General Otto Liman von Sanders. From his role in the tenacious defense at Gallipoli, Sanders had gained a reputation as one of the best defensive minds in the German army. As of March 1, he had taken over the command of all Turkish and German forces in Palestine. Like Allenby, Sanders was a cavalry officer and was well-acquainted with the Turkish military organization, since he had been sent to Constantinople as head of a military mission to rejuvenate Turkish forces in 1913.

The fateful month of March 1918 also saw the launching of the last great German offensive in France. General Douglas Haig soon had his back against the wall, and the decision was made by the British high command to send him reinforcements from all fronts. Two complete divisions, the 52nd and 74th, were transferred to Europe from Palestine, and other divisions were depleted of battalions, 24 going by the end of May. In addition, nine yeomanry regiments, 5½ heavy batteries and five machine-gun companies were withdrawn to join them. In all, Allenby lost 60,000 troops from his command.

The two divisions were replaced by two from Mesopotamia, and the 24 British infantry battalions were replaced with unseasoned and ill-equipped troops from India. The raw recruits had to be trained and integrated into the ranks before any new offensive operations could begin in Palestine. What normally took two years to teach had to be accomplished in two months. Needless to say, the summer was spent in reorganization and training.

During that time, the British army's remarkable liaison officer, Major T.E. Lawrence, who had succeeded in uniting the Arabian tribes and stirring them into an uprising against their hated Ottoman rulers, continued his raids against the Hejaz railroad. An archaeologist turned intelligence officer turned revolutionary leader, Lawrence was a unique individual whom destiny seemed to have prepared for his role in defeating the Turks. The capture of the port of Aqaba on the Hejaz was the first real success of his campaign, and it was accomplished with Bedouin warriors, not British soldiers. That victory occurred at the same time General Allenby took command in Cairo—June 1917—and it greatly impressed the new commander in chief. The cavalry general, fresh from the static, slaughterhouse warfare in the trenches in France, was quick to grasp the significant part Lawrence and his mobile Arabic tribesmen could perform outside the immediate theater of operations.

Providing arms, ammunition, "tulip bombs," armored cars and airplanes with crews, Allenby did his best to support "El Aurens" (the Arabs' name for Lawrence), even to the extent of putting 1 million pounds in gold at his disposal. Lawrence used the gold to bribe and pay the leaders of the various tribes, and to keep them from going over to the service of the Turks. Allenby sent British officers to train the Bedouin tribesmen under Emir Feisal, son of the Sherif of Mecca, but Lawrence convinced him that they could not fight a standard, pitched battle and should only be used in hit-and-run raids, at which they were superb. He also convinced Allenby of the wisdom of bypassing the Turkish garrison at Medina and in keeping the Hejaz railroad open. The Turks had an absurd obsession with their railroad, which they considered a modern engineering marvel. Moreover, the railroad connected Constantinople with Mecca, the holiest of all holy places to the followers of Mohammed, thus supporting the claim of the Sublime Porte (the Ottoman Turkish government) to be the religious and political leader of the Moslem world.

Defending the railroad, however, kept approximately 20,000 Turkish soldiers away from the armies that Allenby's forces faced west of the Jordan River. About 15,000 were isolated in the garrison at Medina, and another 5,000 to 6,000 were occupied in guarding the railroad and repairing those stretches of track that Lawrence and his raiders kept blowing up. Allenby, however, made Emir Feisal a lieutenant general and designated his Arab hosts as the "Arab Army of the North," which brought them under his control. He planned to put them to good use in his final drive to oust the Turks.

Deciding not to wait for developments in France to release troops for his EEF, Allenby conceived an offensive operation that he named "Armageddon." It was the work of a commander with supreme self-confidence. After a massed infantry assault, the cavalry corps would ride through the breach across the Plain of Sharon, some 40 miles behind the enemy lines, cut the Turkish lines of communications and, after forcing the Turkish army to capitulate, move on to Damascus. It was a simple but audacious plan involving the largest concentration of cavalry to be hurled against a still-organized enemy force in the annals of modern warfare. Machine guns and mortars had eliminated massed attacks by mounted horse soldiers in the minds of most military thinkers.

The initial infantry assault on the enemy's right was to be undertaken by the XXI Corps, under Lt. Gen. E.S. Bulfin, while XX Corps, under Lt. Gen. Philip Chetwode, would be drastically reduced but would launch a mock offensive on the enemy's left. The British force on the far left of the Turks, in the Jordan Valley, would cooperate with Lawrence and the Arab Army of the North to take Deraa—a vital rail junction 20 miles behind the enemy's main line of defense.

The 60th Division, always a favorite of Allenby's for obtaining decisive results, was given the post of honor on the far left of the British line in the Maritime Plain. It was loaned to the XXI Corps and was moved secretly from its position before Jericho to the west. Its assignment was to break through the three lines of Turkish entrenchments and create the gap for the entire cavalry corps.

The constant raids in the Moab Mountains and the failed assaults on Amman finally paid dividends for the British. The Turks were convinced that the main effort would be launched against their left. For that reason, a large force of infantry was kept there, and the positions were strengthened with massed batteries of artillery. Armageddon called for the exact opposite of what Allenby had done in his operations against the Gaza–Beersheba Line in October 1917—there, feints had been made on the enemy's right while the main attack was launched 30 miles away at Beersheba, on the enemy's left.

The deception had to be total and constantly maintained, and Allenby used many imaginative and elaborate schemes to carry it off: the construction of camouflage camps and ration dumps; the erection of 15,000 dummy horses made of army blankets and tent poles; the construction of additional bridges over the Jordan River; a dummy general headquarters in the eastern area, with telephone lines strung to it; and additional dummy airfields. As another distraction, empty trucks traveled constantly between Jerusalem and Jericho. Every day, too, West Indian battalions, like extras in a film, marched toward the left of the Turkish line, and every night they secretly returned in trucks to their starting points to do it over again the next day. Lastly, sand sleds and tree limbs were dragged across the ground by trucks and mules to create huge clouds of dust. The reconnaissance planes of the Turkish air force reported all of that activity to headquarters.

As if that were not enough, Lawrence and his Arabs spread false rumors about the coming offensive in the east. Later, captured communiqués between the various Turkish commands showed that General Sanders and the Turkish commanders swallowed the deception hook, line and sinker.

In order to concentrate his troops on the left, opposing the Seventh and Eighth Turkish armies, Allenby had them march by night; during the day, they hid in the olive and almond groves. No activity was allowed during the daylight hours, and that kept the Turks ignorant of the movement of troops toward the west. Using the same method, many batteries of guns were transferred by tractors from the Jordan front to the Maritime Plain. By September 18, everything was in place and the troops were anxiously awaiting the opening of the battle. At 4:40 a.m. on September 19, a thunderous 15-minute barrage by 300 British guns was let loose on the Turkish lines. By 4:45, the first of the three Turkish trench lines was in the hands of the British infantry. Attacking on a one-brigade front, the 180th Regiment of the 60th Division achieved the breach and widened it on the flanks. Within 30 minutes, the gap in the three enemy lines was sufficient for the cavalry to pass. Nine thousand horsemen, with their guidons flying and their sabers clanging, came pounding across open ground and raced to the north.

The objective of the 60th Division was to seize the foothills south of Jiljulieh on the Hableh–Tul Keram Line, and then advance to the northeast. The XXI Corps was to swing on a 16-mile front from Rafat to the sea, driving the Turks into the hills of Samaria, where they would find all avenues of retreat cut off by the British cavalry. The Turks' remaining line of retreat would then be the Messudieh–Jenin Road, at the end of which they would run into the cavalry at El Afule. Meanwhile, British bombers had destroyed all telephone and telegraph lines leading out of Nazareth, where the headquarters of Sanders and his Turkish staff were located, leaving them completely in the dark as to what was developing at the front.

The Arab Army of the North, under Emir Feisal and Lawrence, had blown up all the rail lines leading out of Deraa—west at Muzeirib, south at Nisib and north at Tell Arar. No reinforcements could reach the Turkish armies from any direction.

Within 36 hours, the greater part of the Turkish Eighth Army had been overwhelmed, and the Seventh Army was in full retreat through the hills of Samaria. Shortly after those developments, the coastal cities of Haifa and Acre were captured.

The desperate Turkish Fourth Army below Besian, with its right flank exposed and the situation deteriorating all around it, pulled out of its lines and retreated toward Deraa. British aircraft then moved in to bomb and strafe the retreating Turks of the Fourth Army, and by the time they finally reached Deraa, they were thoroughly disorganized. Then began the wild dash to Damascus, with the Arab Army of the North on the right flank and the Desert Cavalry Corps on the left.

Operation Armageddon was a complete and astounding success. On October 1, Feisal's army occupied Damascus, and on the 26th, Aleppo was occupied by the British. By that time, more than 70,000 prisoners had been taken, 4,000 of whom were German or Austrian soldiers. On October 31, Turkey requested an armistice, the terms of which amounted to an unconditional surrender.

In all the crusades organized and mounted to take the Holy City of Jerusalem, only two were successful: the first led by Godfrey de Bouillon, Duke of Lower Lorraine, in 1095; the last under General Sir Edmund Allenby, commander of the EEF, in 1917.

While stationed in Palestine, Major Gilbert learned of a 200-year-old Arabic prophecy concerning the capture of Jerusalem. It read, "When the Nile flows into Palestine, then shall the prophet from the west drive the Turk from Jerusalem."

When the prophecy was made, it must have seemed an utter impossibility that the water of the River Nile should ever flow over 200 miles of arid desert into Palestine. But the pipeline the British laid across the Sinai Peninsula brought the Nile water from Kantara; and just before the capture of Jerusalem, that water from Egypt was being pumped into Palestine, north of Gaza, at the rate of thousands of gallons a day. *Fanatis* (copper cisterns) were filled with it, placed on the backs of camels and taken up to the troops fighting in the line to take Jerusalem.

Then too, "the prophet" in Arabic is "Al Nebi"—and General Allenby was called Al Nebi by practically the entire native population. Thus, the ancient prophecy was fulfilled to the letter; the waters of the Nile flowed into Palestine, and the prophet, Al Nebi, came from the west and drove the Turk from Jerusalem.

Bolshevik Wave
Breaks at Warsaw

Commanding 160,000 troops, Mikhail N. Tukhachevsky
was said to be the most brilliant general in the Red Army.
If the newly resurrected Polish nation was to survive,
Marshal Jozef Pilsudski would have to be even smarter.

By Robert Szymczak

One of the most easily overlooked, yet momentous short wars of the 20th century was the swift-moving clash between the post-World War I Polish Republic and Russia's brand-new Bolshevik regime of Vladimir Ilyich Lenin. Reaching a climax during the summer of 1920, the Russo-Polish War is often regarded as the final episode of the Russian Civil War. In fact, it was much more—at once a reflection of the age-old enmity between two Slavic neighbors, and a Marxist crusade bent on carrying the torch of revolution into the heart of Europe. The campaign featured a remarkable cast of characters on both sides and mixed ferocious cavalry charges with early blitzkrieg tactics in quest of exceptional objectives.

The roots of the war ran deep. For a century and a quarter, the once-formidable Polish nation was a political nonentity, having been dismembered by Prussia, Austria and Russia in the infamous partitions of 1772, 1793 and 1795. Three national insurrections had failed to dislodge the occupying powers; severe Germanization and Russification efforts, aimed at the destruction of the Polish language and culture, were imposed upon the population during the 19th century. Although such campaigns had little effect, by the turn of the century only the most optimistic of Polish patriots could still dream of independence.

Yet World War I provided exactly the right set of circumstances for the Poles. On November 6, 1916, Austro-Hungary and Germany, in a desperate bid to ensure the loyalty of their Polish populations, jointly agreed to the formation of a semi-autonomous "Kingdom of Poland." In Paris, France, Polish spokesmen beat the ears of Allied statesmen on behalf of an independent Poland, but none of the Western powers cared to antagonize their Imperial Russian ally, which opposed such a move. In 1917, however, Russia had dropped into a violent vortex of chaos and revolution. Partly in consequence to that development, the Fourteen Points for peace drafted by United States President Woodrow Wilson included the creation of an independent Poland

and its recognition as "an allied belligerent nation" as of June 3, 1918. On October 7, 1918, with the Central Powers clearly on the brink of defeat, the Regency Council in Warsaw declared Polish independence. After the guns of war fell silent on November 11, 1918, the three torn pieces of the Polish nation were triumphantly reunited.

The representatives of France, Great Britain, Italy and the United States met in the mirrored halls of Versailles in 1919 to dismember the German and Austro-Hungarian empires and to set the world right. Russia, the erstwhile ally that in November 1917 had established the world's first Communist government, was shunned by the Western Allies; Lenin's decision to make a separate peace with Germany at Brest-Litovsk in the spring of 1918 would not be forgiven just then. Moscow's absence from the Versailles conference later proved to be a costly blunder. While the Allies were able to produce a tentative settlement for Poland's western frontiers, they had no means of establishing any agreed-upon border between the new Polish state and the Russian colossus.

The resurgent Poles, meanwhile, quickly established a Western-style parliamentary government and chose a 51-year-old romantic, a conspiratorial and avidly Russophobic military hero named Jozef Klemens Pilsudski as chief of state. Pilsudski, a longtime member of the Polish Socialist Party's right wing, had always placed the achievement of Polish independence ahead of the social reforms advocated by some of his more ideological comrades. As a young man he had felt the brutality of czarist justice, spending five years in Siberian exile for revolutionary activity. During World War I, he organized and commanded a Polish legion under Austrian auspices on the Eastern Front, convinced that Russia was the chief enemy of his country's independence. But he soon became disillusioned with vague Austrian promises in favor of Polish independence and refused to take an oath of allegiance to the Central Powers. Arrested and imprisoned in Magdeburg for two years, he was released on November 10, 1918, and returned home to be acclaimed a national hero.

Pilsudski possessed an iron will and a quick mind. He clearly regarded the new Polish army as his special province, and himself as the guarantor of independence. The republic's forces, still motley and ill-equipped, would soon be put to the test as the commander in chief turned his attention eastward.

The re-establishment of Poland's pre-partition 1772 frontiers, which included substantial parts of the Ukraine and Belorussia (White Russia), was a matter of top priority for Pilsudski. To accomplish that goal, the veteran revolutionary resurrected the old Polish idea of federalism, first championed in the Middle Ages by the kings of the Jagiellonian dynasty. Put simply, the plan called for an East European Federation consisting of the independent republics of the Ukraine, Belorussia and Lithuania, bound together with Poland. The latter nation would, according to the Pilsudski scheme,

278

play the leading role.

This incredibly ambitious design was destined to disintegrate almost immediately. The Lithuanians, former partners in the old Polish kingdom, were intensely nationalistic after their long submergence in the Russian Empire, and they zealously sought to protect their own newly proclaimed independence made possible by the fall of the czar. They wanted no part of Pilsudski's federalist notions. The Ukrainians, while keenly desiring independence, were naturally suspicious of the Polish leader's motives, realizing how much of the Ukraine was intended for incorporation in the resurrected Polish state. The Belorussians, for centuries caught at the crossroads of Roman Catholic Poland and Orthodox Russia, had no outstanding national consciousness yet and were frankly interested neither in independence nor in Pilsudski's proposals of union. The Polish argument that none of those three nations could stand next to Russia alone fell on deaf ears. To all three of the potential federal members, it appeared that they might be exchanging the former Russian yoke for a Polish one.

The Western Allies, too, were decidedly against Pilsudski's plans. Both Great Britain and France accused the Polish chief of state of imperialism at the expense of Russia, and they urged Poland to limit its eastern frontiers to the farthest extent of clear-cut Polish ethnicity. As for Russian Bolshevism, London and Paris saw that not as a threat, but as a temporary disease, soon to be destroyed by the anti-Communist White forces, which the Allies supported in the then raging Russian civil war.

But it made no difference to General Pilsudski whether the new Russian rulers wore red stars on their collars or the double-headed Romanov eagle. He regarded any Russian government as the sworn enemy of Polish independence. Whether under the guise of revolutionary socialism or the gilded banners of the czars, Russia had always sought the destruction of the Polish nation. Steeped in the glory of Polish history, the chief of state would heed neither the advice of the Allies nor the warnings of his domestic political foes. Poland must be reconstituted just as she had been before the ignominious partitions of the 18th century.

The new Bolshevik government, besieged by armies commanded by aristocratic, conservative czarist generals who hoped to restore the old order, had its hands full at the time. The White forces of Generals Anton Denikin, Nikolai Yudenich and Pyotr Wrangel and Admiral Alexander Kolchak, supported by Western arms and funds, had to be stopped. There was little time in 1918 and 1919 to worry about Polish schemes to expand on Russia's western periphery.

Lenin's dynamic associate Leon Trotsky organized the Red Army to meet the White threat. By using the powerful idealism awakened in the revolution, and invoking fears that the landowning aristocrats might return to power, Trotsky built a formidable force of workers, peasants and ex-soldiers of the old czarist army, complete with a tough cavalry corps, to protect the Bolshevik government. Throughout 1918 and 1919, the Reds turned the tables on their foes, one by one.

At that moment of chaos and civil war in Russia, the Poles struck. In February 1919, Pilsudski sent his troops northeast, occupying as much territory as possible for the purpose of presenting a *fait accompli* to the Allied Supreme Council. That body then would be forced to recognize Poland's expanded eastern boundaries.

The Polish forces encountered little resistance and advanced rapidly, soon capturing Wilno (Vilnius), a historically Polish city, from the Lithuanians, who had proclaimed it the capital of their new republic. By the autumn of 1919, the Polish red-and-white banner was flying over large sections of Belorussia and the western Galicia part of the Ukraine as well.

Pilsudski ordered a halt at that point, his intelligence service having informed him that the Whites under General Denikin were pressuring Moscow from the south and could possibly capture the seat of the Bolshevik regime. The Poles surmised that a White government bent on the reconstruction of the old empire would prove more recalcitrant than the hard-pressed Bolsheviks. Denikin was willing to allow Poland to exist up to the borders of Privislanski Kraj, a former Russian province carved from Poland, in exchange for Polish participation in an anti-Communist crusade, but since those terms would deprive Poland of half the territory Pilsudski wanted, the Polish commander in chief rejected that and other White offers. Although Pilsudski secretly negotiated with the Reds for an acceptable eastern frontier, he was by no means convinced of Lenin's sincerity.

In December, the British foreign minister, George Nathaniel Lord Curzon, proposed a frontier that roughly corresponded to the ethnic limits of Poland but failed to include the two predominantly Polish cities of Lwow and Wilno; ironically, the "Curzon Line," as it was later dubbed, was to become the eastern border of post-World War II Poland. The frontier proposed by the British, although never meant to be a final frontier, was rejected by the Poles, for they had already pushed beyond it.

When it became evident to Pilsudski that the Bolsheviks had turned the tide in the civil war and the Whites appeared doomed, Polish-Soviet negotiations were broken off, and the Poles prepared for another thrust into Belorussia and the Ukraine. Such an action, the Poles knew, would be tantamount to a full-blown anti-Soviet war.

Before pressing forward, Pilsudski shopped around for an ally and found one in the anti-Bolshevik Ukrainian *Ataman* Semyon Petlyura, whose bedraggled troops had fought both Denikin's Whites and Trotsky's Reds for possession of Kiev, the Ukrainian capital. Nothing less than complete Ukrainian independence was Petlyura's goal, but he concluded the Poles were decidedly less evil than the Whites or Reds. Overcoming the severe objections of several of his nationalist associates, the Ukrainian leader came to Poland to ask Pilsudski's help and, on December 2, 1919, signed a treaty granting eastern Galicia and western Volhynia to Poland in return for Polish support of Petlyura's efforts to recapture Kiev and extend the Ukraine's borders to the western bank of the Dnieper River.

Immediately after the collapse of the Polish-Soviet negotiations, Pilsudski ordered several Polish divisions to move north and assist Latvian troops in dislodging the Bolsheviks from the banks of the Dvina River. The campaign resulted in the capture of the crucial fortress of Dvinsk on January 3, 1920, and frightened the Soviets into resuming negotiations with the Poles.

Pilsudski rejected Lenin's offer of a frontier settlement that corresponded somewhat to the existing front line; he deliberately dragged his feet, convinced that the Red offer was insincere, a ploy masking Moscow's real intentions—a transfer of troops from the crumbling White fronts to the Polish line. As proof of Soviet sincerity, Pilsudski insisted that the peace talks should be conducted at Borissov, a small Belorussian town near the front. The Soviets' consistent rejection of this demand apparently convinced the Polish leader that an attack on his position was imminent.

While playing the Bolshevik negotiating game throughout the winter months, Pilsudski prepared for battle. Determined to strike first, he managed to station 100,000 Polish troops on the front, but they were spread out on a line more than 600 miles long. Meanwhile, Warsaw's intelligence service kept Pilsudski informed of every detail of Soviet troop movements toward the front while the negotiations continued.

By that time, London and Paris had received reports of the Polish war preparations; the Allied governments were greatly alarmed. British Foreign Secretary Curzon fired a sharply worded telegram to Pilsudski on February 9, warning him that Poland should expect "neither help nor support" from Great Britain. The Allied Supreme Council followed suit two weeks later with a stern admonition. Pilsudski ignored both messages.

Polish spies reported to Warsaw that more Red troops, fresh from victory over the Whites, were transferring west to the front every day. By spring, Pilsudski could wait no longer. On April 21, 1920, the Polish chief of state signed a military agreement with Petlyura and his Ukrainian National Council for a preemptive expedition against the Bolsheviks. Should the campaign prove successful, the Ukrainians were pledged to enter a federal union with Poland. Four days after the pact was signed, Jozef Pilsudski launched a daring offensive deep into the Ukraine.

The Western Allies were as dumbfounded as the Reds by the Polish commander's aggressive action. How could newly restored Poland, whose population had suffered terribly during World War I and whose economy was virtually nonexistent, even contemplate—let alone mount—a full-scale attack on Russia? Undeterred by the protestations of the Western Allies, Pilsudski pushed his forces all the way to the Dnieper in less than a fortnight. On the tips of their lances, the Polish cavalry carried a proclamation written by the chief of state that promised "all inhabitants of Ukraine, without distinction of class, race, or religion" the brotherly protection of Poland; it exhorted the Ukraine to drive out the Bolshevik intruders "to win freedom for itself with the help of the Polish Republic."

By May 7, Kiev had fallen to the Poles without resistance. For the fourth time since 1918, the Ukrainian Soviet government under Christian Rakovsky was forced to flee the Ukrainian capital; once again, the anti-Bolshevik regime of Petlyura ensconced itself in the city and announced the end of Russian domination of the Ukraine. The capture of Kiev boosted Pilsudski's popularity at home. Even his political enemies, the National Democrats, changed their minds about the "Ukrainian adventure" and ceased their verbal attacks. The Polish parliament passed a resolution of praise for Pilsudski on May 18, and a *Te Deum* Mass was sung in his honor in every Polish church. Portraits of the bushy-browed, heavily mustachioed old revolutionary were hung in all public buildings. Hardly an honor remained unbestowed on him, for he had already been promoted to the rank of marshal in March.

The celebrations would be short-lived. Red Army Commissar Trotsky, no longer concerned about the White threat, was able to muster a sizable and battle-tested Soviet force for action against the Poles. Pilsudski's swift drive to Kiev had severely overextended his supply lines, and his troops found little comfort in the Ukraine, whose population, although anti-Russian, was also historically anti-Polish.

The initial Bolshevik response came in late May, with the appearance of the most famous unit of the civil war—the First Red Cavalry Army, or *Konarmiya*. Consisting of 16,000 sword-swinging horse soldiers replete with five armored trains, it was commanded by the 37-year-old General Semyon Mikhailovich Budyonny (often spelled "Budënny" by Westerners), described by a British military historian as a "hard-riding, spectacular savage of great personal courage." On June 5, the Red Cavalry crashed through the rear of the Polish lines south of Kiev, pausing to burn down a Polish military hospital filled with hundreds of wounded men. The thinly stretched Polish forces could not sustain the Soviet counterattack and immediately retreated westward toward Volhynia and Podolia. Kiev was abandoned on June 11.

The rapid Bolshevik advance forced the hapless Petlyura and his Ukrainian National Council to flee the city for the last time. The fierce Soviet counterattack was part of a two-pronged strategy. While Budyonny's horsemen of the Southern Front pushed the Poles out of the Ukraine, a northern attempt at evicting the Poles from Lithuanian and Belorussian areas was underway. Five Bolshevik armies, estimated at 160,000 troops under the command of the "Demon of the Civil War," General Mikhail Nikolaevich Tukhachevsky, opened a massive campaign at the beginning of July.

The commander of this Northern Front was a 27-year-old former czarist lieutenant who had joined Lenin's cause shortly after the Bolshevik triumph in 1917. Considered something of a military genius, Tukhachevsky had rendered invaluable service to the Communists throughout the civil war; it was he who brutally suppressed the Kronstadt sailors' rebellion in St. Petersburg. Now the "Demon" would turn his considerable talents against the Poles. On July 5, Tukhachevsky opened his campaign in the north, his right flank led by another remarkable character, the Armenian cavalry general Chaia Dmitryevich Ghai, whose hard-riding Caucasian Third Cavalry Corps consistently outflanked the Poles, driving them toward Warsaw.

Undersupplied, outgunned, outnumbered and outmaneuvered, the Poles fought hard but could not stop the Russians' northern drive. On July 12, Minsk, the Belorussian capital, fell to the Reds, followed by Wilno on the 14th and Grodno on the 19th. In his order of the day for July 20, Tukhachevsky sounded an ominous note: "The fate of the world revolution is being decided in the west; the way leads over the corpse of Poland to a universal conflagration...To Warsaw!"

Western military observers were quite surprised by the speed of the Bolshevik advance. The flames of World War I had been extinguished not two years, and memories of the long months of preparation necessary to advance a few yards at a time from the trenches were still keen. Yet here was a conflict of swift movement spearheaded by cavalry—a branch of military that had long since been pronounced useless. The question was, where and when would the Bolsheviks stop their advance?

The Soviet government at first had met the serious Polish challenge by appealing to the Russian people, not for the sake of Bolshevism, but for nationalist reasons. Even the aristocratic old czarist General Aleksei Brusilov, the last Imperial Army commander, responded to this approach and joined in the anti-Polish campaign; many other patriotic former czarist officers followed his example.

But now that the Poles had been evicted from Belorussia and the Ukraine, ideology overwhelmed nationalism. The intoxicating success of Budyonny and Tukhachevsky against the Poles revived in Lenin's mind an old Bolshevik dream: the Red Army breaking through Poland to Germany, where it would assist the strong and well-organized German Communist Party in establishing a Soviet Republic in the homeland of Karl Marx.

Several key members of the Bolshevik Central Committee, including Trotsky and Josef Stalin, strenuously objected to Lenin's plans to reach Germany. Karol Radek, the Soviet expert on foreign policy, opined that the Polish and German people were not prepared to accept communism. Why not make peace with the Poles on the basis of the British-proposed Curzon Line of 1919? In the heated arguments that followed, Lenin vehemently and repeatedly insisted that the time was right to spread the revolution westward. Supported by Lev Kamenev and Grigori Zinoviev, the Bolshevik leader's point of view held sway; Stalin and several others changed their minds when the crucial vote was taken, giving Lenin the victory.

The Soviet plans became readily apparent when Tukhachevsky's troops reached ethnically Polish territory. In the city of Bialystok, the Russians installed a "Polish Revolutionary Committee," headed by Felix Dzerzhinski, Julian Marchlewski and Felix Kon, longtime Communists known for their opposition to Polish independence. It was obvious that this group was to become the nucleus of a Polish Bolshevik government pending the capture of Warsaw. On August 3, the committee issued a "Manifesto to the Polish Working People of Town and Country," proclaiming a revolutionary socialist government.

To Lenin's great surprise,the promulgations of this Moscow-organized regime fell on deaf ears. None of the committee's members had the remotest link to the Polish working class; indeed, one of the Bialystok group's most important members, Dzerzhinski, was Lenin's close associate and the head of the Cheka, the Soviet secret police. The mere mention of the "Polish Revolutionary Committee" was enough to send thousands of Polish workers flocking to the national colors to defend the capital. Still, the uncharacteristically impatient Lenin disregarded those ominous signs and insisted on the immediate capture of Warsaw. The Bolshevik leader's political advisers warned him not to count on a proletarian insurrection anywhere in Poland. Bitter, century-long memories of Russian oppression could not be erased by raising the red flag of revolution in Warsaw. Trotsky, who seconded that gloomy appraisal, also warned Lenin that the speedy capture of the Polish capital could only be achieved by stretching the Red Army's supply lines to precariously thin limits. Again, Lenin rejected the opinions of the doubters in his midst.

Meanwhile, panic had struck in Warsaw; the rapid Soviet advance caused a serious political crisis that resulted in the collapse of the Polish Cabinet. After 15 days of haggling, Prime Minister Wladyslaw Grabski finally managed to form a crisis government, and then he immediately beseeched the Western Allies for help in the defense of Warsaw. Hat in hand, the prime minister appeared before the Allied Supreme Council at Spa, Belgium, where he was subjected to bitter criticism of Pilsudski's eastern policy. If the Poles expected the Supreme Council to help arrange a truce with the angered Bolsheviks, the price would be high. On July 10, Grabski, having little choice, signed the Protocol of Spa, in which Poland agreed to accept the council's recommendations on the disputed Polish-Czechoslovak and Polish-Lithuanian frontiers; to return Wilno to Lithuanian control; to respect the Allies' solution for the Polish use of the port of Danzig; to abide by any future decision on the status of Ukrainian-inhabited eastern Galicia; and, finally, to pull all Polish troops behind the Curzon Line of 1919 until an armistice could be arranged.

The severity of those terms masked the actual alarm felt by the Allies as Tukhachevsky's forces crossed the Bug River and headed for Warsaw. Frantic appeals from the Polish capital for arms and ammunition underscored the urgency of the situation. Torn between saying "you made your bed, now sleep in it" and providing the requested assistance, the Western Allies decided they had no alternative but to render aid to the beleaguered Poles, lest the Red Army thrust its way into the heart of Europe.

Accordingly, the French and British sent high-powered civilian and military missions to Warsaw. The combined Allied mission reached the city on July 25. The French contingent featured the prominent General Maxime Weygand, Marshal Ferdinand Foch's chief of staff during World War I. The celebrated Frenchman brought along his young aide-de-camp, a trim and proper junior officer named Charles de Gaulle. The British were represented by Viscount d'Abernon and Maj. Gen. Percy de B. Radcliffe, an old-time cavalryman with a reputation for logical thinking.

The Western military experts swiftly proceeded to show the battered Poles how the Red Army could be stopped. Fed information on the existing situation by French officers attached as advisers to the Polish Army, the Allied mission came to believe that Marshal Pilsudski had seriously underestimated the gravity of the Soviet threat. The British felt it necessary under these circumstances to force the Poles to accept General Weygand as de facto commander of the Polish forces. The Poles steadfastly refused, although they feigned deference to the great French general's advice rather than jeopardize their source of supplies. In reality, Weygand was excluded from the decision making whenever possible.

By July 22, the day Tukhachevsky's troops crossed the Bug into indisputably Polish territory, the defenders' resistance had stiffened considerably. Pilsudski was reported to have been quite surprised that the Soviets had dared traverse the Curzon Line, the truce frontier suggested by the British. By August 1, the Polish leader realized that the Bolsheviks' intended destination was Warsaw. On that day, the fortress town of Brest-Litovsk fell to the invaders; the capital lay only 130 miles west.

Pilsudski knew that a drastic counteroffensive was the only possible way to save the capital. But where, he wondered, could he muster the forces necessary for such a move? The entire Polish army was committed to the defense of the country. Despite the more pressing threat posed by Tukhachevsky in the north, the Poles were reluctant to pull out their troops facing Budyonny on the Southern Front—the Galician region that had never been under Russian control even temporarily. They preferred to build their military strength by conscription and volunteers.

Time was obviously of the essence. Pilsudski finally decided that the war would be decided in the north. But for effective resistance, the Poles were in desperate need of Allied war supplies, which became increasingly difficult to obtain. The problem came from pro-Bolshevik German and Czech railroad workers, and even some British dockworkers, who refused to load the Polish-bound equipment in their countries. Some of the materiel could reach Poland only through the Baltic port of Danzig, the Free City under League of Nations administration. There, too, German dockworkers—convinced by Bolshevik and German propaganda that a Soviet victory would reunite Danzig with Germany—obstructed delivery. French marine infantry had to be sent to Danzig to expedite the unloading of munitions.

On August 8, Tukhachevsky, confident the Poles were on the verge of collapse, issued his orders for the capture of Warsaw. He intended to bypass the city's northern defenses, move on to the lower Vistula River, and attack from the northwest. The Sixteenth Red Army was to proceed from the east, while its flank was to be protected only by the 8,000-man Mozyr Group. Although Moscow had detached Budyonny's cavalry from General Alexander Yegorov's Southern Front and assigned the horsemen to Tukhachevsky, the latter appears not to have planned to use these additional forces for the protection of his flank. The Bolshevik commander apparently believed that the Poles posed no danger to his exposed periphery. Additionally, Lenin wanted Warsaw delivered as soon as possible.

As Tukhachevsky planned his strategy, the Polish forces had grown much stronger than his 150,000 men. Pilsudski's army had grown to 185,000 by August 12, and in two more weeks the Poles would count 370,000 hastily trained, poorly equipped soldiers on their rolls, including almost 30,000 cavalry. Included in this force was General Jozef Haller's army of Polish-Americans, which had seen Western Front service in World War I, and a squadron of daring young American volunteer pilots. The capital's defense was augmented by a motley but enthusiastic force of 80,000 workers and peasants. The crisis government of Prime Minister Wincenty Witos, which had replaced the Grabski Cabinet on July 24, had done its job well.

Despite the progress of the Polish defense plans, the situation remained grave. Marshal Pilsudski, having little time left, issued his orders for a bold and imaginative counterattack on August 6, several days before he learned of Tukhachevsky's plans to encircle Warsaw. The Polish commander had finally brought several key units up from the south. A 20,000-man strike force, commanded by General Edward Smigly-Rydz, was to smash through Tukhachevsky's Mozyr Group and begin a sweeping, encircling movement to cut off the Soviet northern forces. The Polish Fifth Army under the able General Wladyslaw Sikorski was to hold the crucial Wkra River line north of the capital. The city itself was defended by a 46,000-man garrison aided by the worker-peasant volunteer brigades, while the Third and Fourth armies were to support the strike force.

By August 12, it was apparent to the Allied military mission in Warsaw that Tukhachevsky intended to attack the city from the northwest. Weygand expressed grave reservations about the ability of the Poles to defend the Wkra River line, where they were severely outnumbered. The Allied commission even recommended that a more effective Polish defense might be mounted west of the Vistula River, though that would mean abandoning Warsaw. The following morning, Bolshevik infantry units broke through Polish lines and captured Radzymin, only 15 miles from the capital. Bloody hand-to-hand combat ensued until the arrival of reinforcements enabled the Poles to recapture the town on the 15th.

Meanwhile, General Sikorski's Fifth Army attacked the Soviet Fourth Army northeast of Warsaw and broke through, seriously exposing the Polish flank in the process. The Russian failure to capitalize on such an opportunity was a result of a lack of communications—disrupted by the Poles—and a lack of cooperation among the Bolshevik commanders. In addition to poor coordination among Tukhachevsky's army commanders around Warsaw, the headstrong Budyonny (possibly on the advice of Stalin) had ignored the Soviet commander's call to join him, instead remaining in the Lwow area to the southeast.

Sikorski, quick to take advantage of the chaos among the Reds, continued his advance, raiding the Red Fourth Army headquarters at Ciechanow and capturing its plans and ciphers. Using tanks, trucks, armored cars and mobile columns, the Polish general has been credited with employing the first blitzkrieg tactics of the 20th century. Instead of attacking Sikorski's vulnerable left flank, Red Cavalry commander Ghai, who refused to support the Fourth Army, busied himself cutting Polish railway lines some 40 miles west.

In those desperate days of mid-August, more Allied supplies finally arrived. At Warsaw's Mokotow Airfield, Polish mechanics labored day and night assembling former British Royal Air Force fighter planes in order to deny the Soviets any aerial reconnaissance. On the 16th, when Budyonny's Cossacks finally crossed the Bug River and began their advance on the city of Lwow, aircraft of the III Dyon (air division), comprised of the 5th, 6th, 7th and 15th *Eskadri*, began three days of bombing and strafing in an effort to stem the onslaught. Flying a total of 190 sorties, dropping nine tons of bombs, the Polish and American airmen managed to slow Budyonny's advance to only a few miles a day, buying precious time for Polish land forces to move to counter the southern threat.

On August 16, too, Marshal Pilsudski ordered his strike force into action. Covering roughly 70 miles in three days, the Polish northward movement encountered almost no resistance. Breaking through the gap in the Bolshevik ranks, the Polish Fourth Army, supported by 12 French-built Renault M-17FT light tanks, reached Brest-Litovsk and in the process cut off and trapped the Red Sixteenth Army. While Sikorski's troops kept the Bolsheviks in a state of confusion, Pilsudski, who traveled in the back of a truck with his forward units, pushed his forces farther north.

The Allies, meanwhile, had arranged for another round of Polish-Soviet peace negotiations, apparently believing that only a truce could save Warsaw now. On August 17, delegates from both sides met at Minsk, where Moscow presented its conditions for a cease-fire: the Polish Army was to be dismantled, and the Allied military mission was to be sent packing. The Curzon Line was the only acceptable frontier, declared the Soviet delegates, with some small alterations in favor of the Poles.

News from the front, where Pilsudski's success astonished everyone, including the marshal himself, made the Bolshevik peace terms sound ludicrous. By August 18, Tukhachevsky realized that he had been completely outflanked and ordered what amounted to a general retreat—it was, in reality, a rout. Those Red units in a position to do so immediately bolted for the East Prussian border before the Poles could close the ring. Some groups, such as Ghai's cavalry and the Red Fourth Army, were locked in battle with Sikorski's troops and were trapped. Although badly mauled by ferocious encounters with pursuing Polish units, Ghai's battered horsemen managed to reach East Prussia, where they were immediately interned by the German authorities. The Fourth Army could not escape and was forced to surrender in Poland.

By August 24, it was virtually over. Tukhachevsky's forces had left behind more than 200 artillery pieces, more than 1,000 machine guns, 10,000 vehicles of every kind and nearly 66,000 prisoners of war. Total Russian casualties were in the vicinity of 100,000; the Polish victory cost 238 officers and 4,124 enlisted men killed, as well as 562 officers and 21,189 soldiers wounded.

There remained only the threat of Budyonny, whose cavalry had committed atrocities the Poles would not soon forget. Placing General Sikorski in command of the Third Army on August 27, Pilsudski then ordered him to oust Budyonny's force from the Southern Front. On August 29, Sikorski's vanguard Operation Group, consisting of the 13th Infantry Division and 1st Cavalry Division under the overall command of General Stanislaw Haller, confronted Budyonny's Cossacks at Zamarsc. In an unusual battle by 20th-century standards, Polish lancers rode at full gallop into the Red cavalry and tore the Russians to pieces. After a second engagement with Sikorski's forces that evening at Komarov, Budyonny quickly ordered a rear-guard action and fled homeward, barely avoiding the complete annihilation of his army.

While Sikorski gave chase to Budyonny in the south, Pilsudski pursued Tukhachevsky's battered legions into Belorussia. Catching up with the Reds on the Niemen River on September 26, the Poles smashed the Soviet defensive lines and inflicted another humiliating defeat upon them, destroying their Third Army in the process. Pilsudski's troops entered Grodno on the same day. Following up on September 27, the Poles pummeled Tukhachevsky's beaten and demoralized troops yet again at the Szczara River, sending them scurrying back to Minsk. In the Battle of the Niemen River, the Russians lost another 50,000 prisoners and 160 cannons.

The rout now complete, Poland rejoiced in her hour of victory; Marshal Pilsudski's prestige soared, and the Allies breathed a sigh of relief. The Red Army had been solidly trounced, suffering its most disastrous defeat of the entire civil war period. An armistice was officially declared on October 12, followed by a protracted series of negotiations to formally end hostilities and settle the Polish-Soviet border question.

The result was the Treaty of Riga, signed on March 18, 1921, in the Latvian capital. Poland received a significant portion of her pre-partition frontiers, including the city of Lwow, and took possession of territories inhabited by about 12 million Lithuanians, White Russians and Ukrainians.

Little remembered in the West, the Battle of Warsaw was in fact one of the most significant land engagements of the 20th century. Strategically, it reversed an ideological onslaught that might otherwise have carried Communism into Western Europe in 1920—an eventuality the consequences of which can only be imagined by posterity. Militarily, the sudden counterattack by which Pilsudski and his lieutenants split and routed the Bolshevik forces—themselves led by one of the enemy's most brilliant generals—deserves a place among the tactical masterpieces of history.

Sabotaging the Soviet Steamroller

*Facing what looked like overwhelming odds
in the winter of 1939, the Finns, led by officers like
Colonel Hjalmar J. Siilasvuo, made skillful use of their
terrain to cut the Russian armies down to size.*

By Eloise Engle

The November wind sweeping the Karelian Isthmus above Leningrad was cold and no happy omen to the thousands of Russian troops massing at the Finnish border in their summer uniforms. Still, General Kirill Meretskov, 42-year-old commander of four Russian armies poised for invasion, would not be issued winter clothing for his troops, since the campaign was not expected to last more than a few days.

It was 1939, and in Moscow's Kremlin, Josef Stalin and his henchmen expected little trouble from neighboring Finland, a miniscule David to the Soviet Goliath. "All we had to do was raise our voices a little bit and the Finns would obey," wrote Nikita Khrushchov many years later. "If that didn't work, we could fire one shot and the Finns would put up their hands and surrender. Or so we thought."

Behind that thinking was the projected onslaught against 120,000 Finnish men-at-arms by up to 600,000 well-armed Russian troops supported by hundreds of tanks and aircraft. The strategy was one of simply bludgeoning the weak Finns by sheer numbers—and with the new engines of war.

Indeed, Stalin himself only recently had proclaimed, "Modern warfare will be a war of engines—engines on land, engines in the air, engines on water and under water." The winners would be those having "the greater number and more powerful engines." If the Finns would not agree to Soviet Russia's recent demand for territorial concessions (for the defense of Leningrad, basically), then Russia would walk in and take what she wanted.

And so the Russian tanks were lined up on the Karelian Isthmus that blocks the Gulf of Finland at its far eastern end. And there Meretskov's Seventh Army would smash through the Finns' 90-mile Mannerheim Line, seize Viipuri, Finland's second largest city, and then march on to the capital Helsinki, halfway toward the western end of the Gulf of Finland.

With an 800-mile frontier separating the two countries northward, far into the Arctic Circle, however, there was more to the Soviet invasion plan.

Meretskov's Eighth Army would sap Finnish defense of the Isthmus by attacking along the shores of Lake Ladoga, on the eastern side of the isthmus but still in the region known as Karelia.

Another major force, the Ninth Army, would cross the Finn border at the small country's narrow midwaist and strike for Oulu on Finland's west coast fronting the Gulf of Bothnia. The Ninth would cinch a tight belt cutting Finland in half.

Then, too, in the storied Lapland far to the north, the Fourteenth Red Army would drive for Petsamo, the ice-free port on an inlet of the Barents Sea in Arctic Finland that could, in the wrong hands, threaten the nearby Russian port of Murmansk.

Independent Finland had known that trouble was on its way, despite its nonaggression pact with Russia. The Baltic states below Finland already had been forced to grant Stalin air and naval bases on their territory; in August 1939 he had signed a nonaggression pact with German Chancellor Adolf Hitler, and by the end of September, Germany and the Soviet Union were both carving up Poland to suit themselves. Stalin in the autumn of 1939 warned Finland that the great powers would not "allow" her to remain neutral in the world war already started, but the Finns had refused his demand for territorial concessions. "All the best," Stalin had called out to the Finn negotiators at the end of the last fruitless bargaining session in Moscow early in November. Toward the end of the month, the Russians staged a border "incident" and then declared the nonaggression pact no longer binding. Tiny Finland now could only await its severe fate.

At 7:57 a.m. on November 30, 1939, the Karelian fields and forests celebrated in the music of Jan Sibelius lay silent in the frozen dark of winter in the northland. At Finland's intermittent frontier outposts, however, her soldiers clustered around radios listening for any further news—only that night had they learned the nonaggression pact had been broken.

Then, at the stroke of 8 o'clock on the Karelian Isthmus, the air suddenly was filled with the whistle of shells, the echoes of their bursts, the muffled boom of their distant artillery pieces. From Kronstadt, the Russian sea fortification on the Gulf of Finland, came the muted additional roar of its great fortress guns.

In 30 seconds, the horizon became a sheet of flames; the entire frontier seemed ablaze. Snow-laden trees flew through the air; boulders, dirt, slush and pieces of farm houses were silhouetted against the blue-red sky of dawn. Winding country roads disappeared in chunks.

Then began the rattle of Russian machine guns, answered by those of the Finns, competing refrains of the Finns' rapid-fire Lahti-Saloranta automatic rifles with the Russians' slower-firing, light machine guns. The Russian artillery barrage continued for 30 minutes, to be followed by green rockets fired into the air as a signal for the Red infantry to attack—they surged for-

291

ward, shouting their battle cry, "Ura!"

Many first had to plunge into the icy waters of the Rajajoki River at the border itself, where they immediately began assembling pontoon bridges. At 9:15, sections of the first battalion had crossed the new bridges—and the frontier—to enter Finnish Karelia.

Farther north, the forests so silent an hour before the attack now were assailed by the cough of tank engines, the clank of their treads and the sound of their sirens along the snow-covered roads. Here, too, fields and woods shook with exploding bomb and shell, as the Finns found themselves under attack at virtually every road leading to the 800-mile border between the two countries. Even at the tiny village of Myllyjärvi, north of Lake Ladoga in the Karelia region, a narrow path became a conduit for a strong Russian unit rushing forward under cover of artillery.

Up and down the combat zone, Soviet aircraft roared low over the tree-tops to strafe and drop bombs. Although the Finns had gone through a civil war in 1918 (their German-aided White Guard overcoming a Russian-aided Red Guard), there was no nightmare in their collective experience to compare with the Soviet assault that day in 1939. Surely the small light that was an independent Finland was about to be extinguished.

But not, it would seem, right away. As Russian tanks clattered along the icy, narrow roads, followed by hordes of infantry in tight formation, there were only meager contingents of Finnish border guards as targets. Both on the Karelian Isthmus and along the lengthy battle line to the north, the initial Finnish response was to fight long enough to delay, then fall back to a new line or to refuge in the surrounding snowy wilderness, only to emerge and strike back again.

Winter, the harshest in some years, was the Finns' ally against the massed Russian troops, many of the latter untrained, poorly clothed for such severe climate and poorly led, due to Stalin's recent purges of his own Red Army's officer corps. On the Karelian Isthmus, a more or less "normal" situation prevailed as the Soviet Seventh Army advanced upon the stationary Mannerheim line of small fortifications and machine-gun emplacements.

To the north, however, the Russians faced a mobile army on skis, "invisible" in snow-white parkas and perfectly suited for hit-and-run tactics against the unwieldy Russian columns. The Finns were experts at such tactics and quite at home in temperatures of 50 degrees below zero. Nearly all were Home Guards and reservists who had grown up together, gone to school and trained together. They were fine physical specimens. They knew what they were defending—their homes and farms—and their fighting was fierce, determined, almost fanatic. They were shrewd hunters and sharpshooters. No one needed to tell them when to pull the trigger or in which direction to aim.

The guerrilla fighting began in earnest almost from the moment of the

Russian onslaught, as white-clad ski patrols raced up and down to harass the enemy columns. Most of those northerners had their own homemade cross-country skis with leather toe-bindings. Their handmade *pieksu* boots with turned-up toes fitted neatly into the toe-bindings so that they could be in and out of their skis in seconds. When they crawled along the snow, shooting, they had their skis beside them, attached to a leather belt. Using their quick-firing Suomi submachine guns, the skiers appeared out of nowhere, poured a deluge of fire into the massed Russians, and then disappeared into the whiteness again.

At Petsamo in Arctic Finland, the Soviet 104th and 52nd Divisions, supported by the coastal artillery guns of their own Arctic Ocean ports, began garnering a harvest of towns, villages and industrial property. Their plan was to push through to Rovaniemi, capital of Lapland, by December 12, and they expected little opposition from the local forces. The odds here were 42 Russians against each defending Finn.

In the Salla-Savukoski area, 300 miles south of Petsamo, a double-headed spear of the Russian 88th Division, together with the 122nd, rumbled into the small Lapland village of Salla, anticipating a quick victory and a reunion with the forces from Petsamo at Rovaniemi.

Suomussalmi was at Finland's waistline and offered the shortest distance to Oulu on the western coast. There, the Murmansk railroad could carry supplies to the invading Red Army. Moreover, the road system on the Finnish side was good. As the Soviet troops stormed over the border, they brought their own heavy road-building equipment, along with tanks, trucks, artillery, horses, field kitchens, propaganda leaflets, gifts, brass bands and the troops of the 163nd Division, some 17,000 strong.

At Kuhmo, 65 miles south of Suomussalmi, the Russian 54th Division advanced along the Repa-Hukkajärvi road with 12,800 men, more than 120 artillery pieces and 35 tanks. A Finnish lieutenant's 1,200 reservists attacked and counterattacked this force before withdrawing from the un-even battle.

Elsewhere on the northern frontier, the Russian 139th Division rumbled along all available roads leading to Tolvajärvi, a 10-mile frozen lake boasting a small village, church and co-op store. The 20,000 Reds brought with them 147 artillery pieces and 45 tanks to use against 42,000 home-town Finns.

Finnish Reserve Lieutenant Toiviainen was celebrating his 45th birthday that morning at a border post near Artahuhta in northern Karelia. His men had come to congratulate him and present him with a new pen. The commander had just made his thank-you speech when sounds of heavy guns echoed from the direction of tiny Myllyjärvi. The awed silence was broken finally by Toiviainen saying: "Comrade Molotov must have ordered gunfire in my honor. Let's get going!"

At Lieksa farther north, 6,400 Russians with 40 artillery pieces and 12 tanks screamed "Ura!" as they attacked the Finns' 12th and 13th Detached

Battalions, the latter's combined strength only consisting of 3,200 men and four cannon.

If the Soviet tanks, artillery and masses of men on the ground had been wantonly rammed into Finland's icy forests, often to face wholesale slaughter, so had the crews of 3,000 Russian bombers and fighter planes been dispatched to their own kind of hell. These hastily trained Soviet pilots were no match for their well-schooled adversaries—they soon learned that the Finnish fighter pilot was as much a killer in the air as was his counterpart the ski-patrol guerrilla on the ground. Although the Russians had their superior "engines in the air," as Stalin called them, to use against the Finns' 162 antiquated aircraft, it was clear from the beginning that the Russians would suffer strangely disproportionate losses. The Finnish anti-aircraft fire was alarmingly accurate, but far worse were Finland's fighter planes. Entire squadrons of Tupolev SB-2 or Ilyushin DB-3 bombers disappeared while on missions over Finland, and those personnel waiting for their return to base at Tallinn, Estonia, could only guess at what had happened. (In one notable instance later, on January 6, 1940, Finnish ace Jorma Sarvanto flew his Fokker D-XXI fighter into a formation of seven Russian DB-3s at 12:03 p.m. By 12:07, the Finn had shot down six of them. He used 2,000 rounds in this incredible feat, while another Finnish pilot, Lieutenant Per Sovelius, downed the seventh Russian bomber in the same formation.)

By the final count of the 105-day Winter War, the Finnish Fokker D-XXI fighters alone had shot down 120 Russian bombers, while losing 12 of their own planes and only eight men. In all, fighter pilots on the side of Finland could claim 240 Russian aircraft as confirmed kills. The total known Russian aircraft loss, including those brought down by anti-aircraft fire, was 684 and perhaps as many as 1,000. The total Finnish losses were 62.

In early December, such grim statistics were not yet known to the confident invaders, of course. But it soon was clear they would not be conquering little Finland by their original schedule of just a few days. Their vast armies, in fact, were stymied and bogged down on just about every major front. They had failed thus far to storm the Mannerheim Line, named for Finland's military commander, Marshal Carl Gustav Mannerheim. North of the Karelian Isthmus, stalled Russian columns, stretching sometimes for 18 to 20 miles in all, soon were cut off from resupply and were being chopped into small pieces by the aroused Finns.

Aside from poor training and leadership, the Russians suffered now from a variety of strategic errors. First, the Finnish populace showed no inclination to welcome the Red "liberation." Indeed, Russian bombing of Helsinki and other civilian targets infuriated the Finns and provoked worldwide sympathy for them; the League of Nations went so far as to eject Soviet Russia from its otherwise ineffectual ranks.

Further, the invaders failed to coordinate their massive artillery with their incursions by ground forces. In the frozen northland, they committed their superior forces to the few roads available and thus exposed the strung-out columns to constant harassment by small but punishing Finnish units. Finally, the Russians simply were not prepared for an extended Winter War.

Outfitted in their lightweight uniforms, thousands of Red Army soldiers froze to death in the northland. Others fell prey to illnesses such as pneumonia, while to be wounded in such isolation and severe climate was a death sentence in itself. If the Russians gathered around campfires for solace and warmth in the terrifying night, they often were picked off by Finnish sharpshooters. Even in daylight they feared the "White Death" that awaited anyone foolhardy enough to penetrate the deep forests along the invasion routes, that also ventured into the open and struck at them unexpectedly from those same sanctuaries.

A vital part of Finnish strategy, in the big battles and in countless small ones all up and down the 800-mile border, was the *motti* concept. For years, a *motti* in Finland had meant a half cord of wood chopped and stacked in the Finn's great northern wilderness to be picked up and used later. Like the wily woodsman, the Finn soldier chopped off Russian units from their supplies, then left them floundering in the snow and ice to deal with later, when it was more convenient.

In the Battle of Lapland, the Russian 104th and 52nd Divisions fell 250 miles short of reaching the capital city of Rovaniemi, while in the Salla-Savukoski area, 40 miles into Finland territory, the Russian 88th and 122nd Divisions also were halted far short of the planned link-up at Rovaniemi.

At Tolvajärvi, the 10-mile frozen lake, the Finns at first were scattered in confusion by the powerful thrust of two Russian divisions, the 139th and the 75th, with total manpower of 45,000, plus 90 tanks, 50 armored vehicles and 335 artillery pieces. Reeling, but lightly reinforced, the Finns rounded up their scattered men and in desperation jabbed back with light punches of their own. A company and a half struck an enemy campsite the night of December 8, and left the Russians so confused that two of their battalions fought each other for two hours.

Soon exhausted and desperately thin in strength, the Finns on skis kept moving and jabbing at the Russian 139th in effort to gain the initiative. In one major engagement, 1,000 Russians were counted dead.

The same Finnish forces then had to engage the fresh 75th Division, pressing and pressing the invaders until they had been forced into the wilderness. From December 12 to December 23, a few Finnish battalions managed to push some 36,000 Russians 25 miles back toward their own borders. The Finns had suffered 630 killed, and the Russians 4,000.

It was perhaps at Suomussalmi, first stop in the march across Finland's waistline, that the Finns employed their *motti* tactics with greatest effectiveness. Here the enemy consisted of the 163rd Division, composed mostly

of tough but poorly trained Mongols, and the proud 44th Division of Ukrainian troops from the Moscow Military District, complete with military band
and smart uniforms for display in the anticipated victory parade at Oulu, 150
miles to the west. The two divisions combined would total 48,000 men, plus
100 tanks, 50 armored cars and 335 artillery pieces.

With the 163rd already in the Finnish lake district and the 44th cumber-
somely moving along the Raate Road for their planned link-up at Suomussalmi, the outnumbered (17,000) Finns knew they had to keep the two
divisions from joining forces for the march west. While jabbing at the 163rd,
Finnish Colonel Hjalmar J. Siilasvuo sent two Finnish infantry companies
(350 men) detached from his 27th Infantry Regiment to block the entire 44th
Division at a narrow isthmus in the lake country. With the lake waters frozen, the Russians might have considered leaving their road—but on the
same flat plain of ice any such movement would have invited slaughter by
even a lone machine-gunner.

It was a gamble, but it worked: the paralyzed 44th was locked into place
on the road, bumper-to-bumper, until such time as the Finns were ready to
descend in force. They turned, meanwhile, on the still attacking 163rd, six
miles north of Suomussalmi village.

What happened there was a tangle of small-unit actions, even hand-to-
hand fighting in the incredible cold, the Finns' objective to harass and to
wear down, while also preventing any supplies from reaching the 163rd. In
time, the Russians gave up on pushing the Finns farther west and settled
into the village to await the 44th's arrival. At that point, the Finns felt strong
enough to launch a counteroffensive that lasted 17 days and covered a 50-
mile line of battle before it was over.

Then, one by one, the Russians began leaving their positions; soon hundreds were gathered on a frozen lake. Weapons thrown away, they formed
columns for their trudging retreat across the ice and through the deep
snow. Along the roadsides, in shelters and dugouts, bodies frozen solid
remained glued in place by winter.

After Suomussalmi, the 163rd Division was finished as a fighting force—
5,000 left dead on the battlefield, untold others scattered in the frozen wilderness. And now, as the exultant Finns turned their skis south again, it
would be the turn of the blocked 44th Division on the Raate Road.

The division's main forces were bunched in a five-mile stretch between
Kuivasjärvi and Kikkojärvi, but other units of the 44th extended all 15 miles
back to the Russian border. The Russians had "secured" their road at strong
points every eighth of a mile, with tanks endlessly patrolling in between. The
first Finnish action now was to "interrupt" the tanks with barriers of barbed-
wire and fallen trees, then turn their few anti-tank cannons on the big
machines crunching through.

Two battalions (or about 800 men) then attacked the head of the long

Russian "snake." As Colonel Siilasvuo anticipated, the enemy began to fortify, dig in, turn passive—a phenomenon observed throughout the Soviet campaign in Finland thus far. That gave the Finns time to regroup and seriously begin to chop the "snake" into smaller and smaller bits, with much of the fighting hand to hand in the dark of the night.

Soon, Soviet aircraft circling above could only watch while 17,000 of their troops packed into the five-mile stretch at the head of the column simply milled about. Mad with hunger after five days without food in temperatures 30 and 40 degrees below zero, many panicked and ran; others simply gave up. Most of the men of the 44th Division were killed or frozen (1,300 did become prisoners of war).

Thus, by mid- to late December, the Finns had stopped the Russian juggernaut—*blitzkrieg*, some called it—at almost every major front. Concerted anti-tank attacks by Finnish squads and exaggerated Russian fear of the Mannerheim Line had combined to slow down the offensive on the Karelian Isthmus, while reports of the twin debacles at Tolvajärvi and Suomussalmi had sapped any remaining Russian initiative in the hard-fought Lapland region to the far north.

But the Winter War was not yet over. As the new year of 1940 began, the situation for the Russians in Finland certainly was bleak. Most of their operations along the eastern front had ground to a halt. Their unwilling, wondering troops clearly had been used as cannon-fodder—stories abound of Russian soldiers advancing over minefields, their arms linked together, the guns of their political commissars at their backs to egg them on. Even the Karelian Isthmus was holding. The Russians were suffering heavy casualties against the Mannerheim Line, and the coldest period of winter was yet to be faced.

With the Red Army suddenly held up to ridicule around the world, Stalin, of course, was furious. As he "rearranged" the entire leadership of his armies in the field, some commanders were shot, among them the leader of the 44th Division. One-time factory-worker Meretskov was fortunate only to be demoted, to command of a single Soviet army in Finland. In one angry scene at the Kremlin, Stalin jumped up in a rage and began to berate his defense commissar, Marshal Klimenti E. Voroshilov.

Hot-tempered himself, Voroshilov also leaped to his feet, Nikita Khrushchov later wrote. Voroshov hurled Stalin's accusations back in his face. "You have yourself to blame for all this! You're the one who had our best generals killed (in the purges)."

When Stalin hotly answered in kind, Voroshilov picked up a platter containing a roast suckling pig and smashed it down on the table before them.

After such "conferences," new plans were made. Marshal Semyon Konstatinovich Timoshenko, freshly returned from the Soviet occupation of Poland, replaced Voroshilov as commissar for defense and was also made commander in chief of Soviet forces on the all-important Karelian Isthmus.

Once a noncommissioned officer in the Czar's army, he very practically won assurances he would not be held liable for any great Russian losses. A thorough, meticulous planner, Timoshenko spent much of the month of January 1940 reorganizing the forces at his disposal and lending an overdue measure of coordination to the next offensive.

On February 1, 1940, a blanket bombing of the Finnish rear forces by the Soviet Air Force heralded the new Timoshenko offensive against the stubborn Finns. Massed for the attack were some 600,000 fresh Soviet personnel, among them Timoshenko's own well-seasoned Ukrainian troops (he had been commander of the North Caucasian, Kharkov and Kiev Military Districts). Masses of Russian cannon, lined up hub to hub, now rained fire and steel on the Mannerheim Line. In a single 24-hour period, no less than 300,000 shells fell on the Finns at Summa, 20 miles southeast of Viipuri, the most massive artillery barrage since the German shelling of the French at Verdun in World War I. At Summa and nearby Lahde, the Soviet artillery was so heavy that the Russians resorted to the seldom-used tactic of the rolling barrage. They simply increased and decreased their range without shifting the fire.

The Winter War was an intensely personal one for the Finns, their country so small and underpopulated that people tended to know one another's business, eccentricities, problems, and fortunes—good and bad. The Western press had a difficult time reporting the war because almost no outsider knew the complex language, few could ski into the forests in 40-below temperatures and, besides, Marshal Mannerheim didn't want to be responsible for them, under the circumstances. "This is war, not Hollywood," he declared. Thus, visiting reporters were holed up at the Kamp Hotel in Helsinki, to file their stories from press releases issued by the Finns. Some excellent reporting was done by Finnish newsmen—one in particular, Erkki Palolampi, fought alongside the defenders and later described "The Miracle of Kollaa," a microcosm of those last days.

At Kollaa, 20 miles north of Lake Ladoga, the loneliness and exhaustion for the soldiers strewn across the wilderness were so dominating that they were aware of little of the world's happenings. They only knew that Kollaa must hold. And against the Russians' great new offensive, the numbed Finns became almost fanatical in their defense—they would fight to the last man. During those last days there were no fewer than 12 Russian divisions with 160,000 troops in the 100-square-mile area north of Ladoga. Opposing them were men like Captain Carl von Haartman, battalion commander attached to the 34th Infantry Regiment: handsome, monocled, debonair German soldier-of-fortune who recently had fought with Franco in Spain. With one leg shorter than the other because of an old wound, he was more a gourmet than a skier. His command post was famous for its heavy aroma of spaghetti sauce and garlic. Under von Haartman was hard-drinking, flamboyant Lieutenant Aarne Juutilainen, otherwise known as the "Terror of Morocco," because of his earlier exploits with the French Foreign Legion.

And then there were men like Simo Häyhä, master shot of the 6th Company, who went out to "hunt Russians" each day. In civilian life, Simo was a smalltime farmer who had cabinets filled with trophies for marksmanship. In war, he became the best-known sniper in the Finnish army. In the evenings he quietly cleaned his rifle and seldom said a word, but that one man personally killed more than 500 Russians before he was seriously wounded.

Now, as the Russian regiments advanced toward Tsuhmeikka and Kontro to attack the rear of the Kollaa defenders, other Russian tank divisions were pressuring the Finns at the Ulismainen swamps, trying to slash the road between Saarijärvi and Uumaa. The threat of being surrounded increased by the minute. Kollaa was weakening.

But the division commander, Antero Svensson, a stout, blond optimist, never lost his Kollaa defenders and blindly believed that Kollaa would not fall. When the situation had seemed hopeless so many times in the past, the Finns somehow had managed to get some sort of help, so that by evening the lines were still intact. But by now the men were few; reinforcements consisted of older troops who were unable to hold out as tenaciously as the younger defenders had. And under the murderous artillery fire from the Reds, these older men were swallowed up almost daily, sometimes even before they reached the line. For Kollaa, for Finland, the uneven conflict was winding down to its inevitable end.

On March 13, 1940, Finland was the saddest country in the world. As the men skied home from the battlefields, many of them wept at the appalling peace terms just concluded. They were tired from the strain, but they still considered themselves an unbeaten army. In Russia, one general is said to have commented, "We have won enough ground to bury our dead...."

For the Finns, there were 25,000 dead and 55,000 wounded—for the United States in 1940, with a population of 130 million, that would have meant 2.6 million Americans dead or wounded in just 105 days.

For the Russians, it was not until Khrushchov published his memoirs in 1970 that the world learned that a million Russian lives had been lost in the Finnish campaign. It also cost the Soviets a possible 1,000 airplanes and 2,300 tanks. If, as Khrushchov also said, the Germans watched the Soviet drubbing with "undisguised glee," the Winter War against Finland ultimately served Russia well—it revealed shortcomings of the Red Army that largely were repaired in time to greet Hitler's onslaught against former "ally" Stalin in 1941.

Following the Winter War, Russia took Finland's second biggest city, Viipuri (now Vyborg), her largest Arctic Ocean port, Petsamo (now Pechenga); the strategic area of Hanko; her largest lake and the entire Karelian Isthmus, home for 12 percent of Finland's population. Finland relinquished a total of 22,000 square miles of land to the Russians.

The Finns took up arms again during World War II, the so-called Continuation War, in which as a nominal ally to Germany—though more of a co-belligerent in practice—they fought the Russians solely to regain their lost territory. Most soldiers lost their enthusiasm once their old borders were regained. At one point, the Finns formed a line north of Leningrad, and there was considerable pressure for them to occupy the city. Marshal Mannerheim, however, wisely decided not to send troops there because the war obviously was lost by the Germans, and, in the end, the Russians would never forgive the disgrace of occupation.

In September 1944, the war with the USSR came to an end. The Finns rid themselves of the Germans on their soil in Lapland but lost Karelia and Petsamo forever.

Reparations to Russia for both the Winter War and the Continuation War were enormous ($300 million), but the Finns paid them.

Of all the small countries in the Soviet vicinity in the postwar years, Finland alone remained an independent republic, decidedly pro-West while also dealing delicately with the Soviets. Perhaps that small country's fierce struggle in the Winter War persuaded the Soviets that business with Finland was better carried out on a peaceful basis.

Bastogne Belatedly Besieged

*"Nuts," was Brig. Gen. Anthony C. McAuliffe's response
when asked to surrender at Bastogne. "This is war," said
the Germans....And the Battle of the Bulge continued.*

By David H. Lippman

Brigadier General Kenneth Strong held a captured German sword over the map on the floor and tapped a road junction on the map. "There is a place here called Bastogne which looks all right," Strong said. General Walter Bedell Smith nodded assent. And with that, the U.S. 101st Airborne Division was sent to defend Bastogne.

By December 1944, the Allies were on the border of Nazi Germany. But Adolf Hitler aimed to reverse his fortunes with a massive offensive that he hoped would split the Allies both militarily and politically. To do so, he hurled three armies through the Ardennes on December 16, driving to the Meuse through light American defenses. One U.S. division was destroyed; another was surrounded and forced to surrender.

The situation was increasingly desperate. General Dwight D. Eisenhower tapped his two reserve outfits, the 82nd and 101st Airborne divisions, to halt the German drive. Where to send the airborne was decided by Strong. The 82nd, closer to Saint Vith, would go there. The 101st, by default, drew Bastogne.

The 101st was an elite outfit, but its veteran paratroops were tired. One fourth of the "Screaming Eagles" had been killed or wounded in Holland during Operation Market Garden the previous September, and replacements were either unavailable or not yet fully trained. Officers were new to their commands. The division staff had been reorganized after Holland and was still coming together. And worse, the division's commanding general (CG), Maj. Gen. Maxwell Taylor, was in Washington. The acting CG was the quiet, self-effacing Brig. Gen. Anthony C. McAuliffe, who normally commanded the division's artillery. On Monday morning, December 18, 1944, the division moved out of its old French army base at Mourmelon-le-Grand, most of the men having to ride in the open beds of cattle trucks. Some paratroopers lacked ammunition, others wore Class A uniforms, not combat gear. McAuliffe rolled northeast, past Werbomont to Bastogne, VIII Corps' headquarters.

Bastogne and her 3,700 citizens were strung along a north-south railway for three-quarters of a mile surrounding a tall church steeple. The Belgian city was the junction of five main and three secondary highways. On the evening of the 17th, her citizens had seen flashes of light to the east, artillery duels.

Gradually, elements of the 101st entered the town. Sergeant Schuyler Jackson of the 502nd Parachute Regiment noted the temperature was 46 degrees. It fell to zero in three days. Captain Wallace Swanson, who commanded 502nd's A Company, worried about rifles and machine guns freezing up.

There were already American troops in Bastogne, mostly fleeing remnants of the divisions shattered on the 16th. In addition, Combat Command B (CCB) of the 10th Armored Division, a brigade-sized outfit under Colonel William L. Roberts, had also been assigned to Bastogne. CCB deployed into three, 500-man combat teams serving as roadblocks east of the town while the 101st moved in. All of that took some time, with VIII Corps personnel retreating and jamming roads. Panicked GIs created more chaos. Intelligence was sketchy.

Still, the advancing Germans were having their own trouble. Spearheading part of the Nazi advance was the Panzer Lehr Division, made up of demonstration troops from all of Germany's training schools. Lehr's CG, *Generalleutnant* (Maj. Gen.) Fritz Bayerlein, was an old *Afrika Korps* hand, but no great thinker. To find his way, Bayerlein asked Belgian civilians which road led to Bastogne. The Belgians naturally sent Panzer Lehr down the wrong roads. The four-mile drive to Mageret took four hours.

On the 18th, one of the CCB units, Team Desobry—named for its boss, Major William R. Desobry—moved into Noville, a village northeast of Bastogne. At 10:30, the fog abruptly lifted, revealing more than 30 approaching German tanks from the 2nd Panzer Division. The Americans opened fire, and the Germans answered with heavy artillery and surrounded the village.

Desobry asked for permission to withdraw. Instead, he received reinforcements, the 1st Battalion, 506th Parachute Regiment, under Colonel James L. LaPrade. Desobry and LaPrade attacked at 2 p.m., just as the Germans were doing the same. A wild firefight ensued, and the Americans were forced to pull back. That night, a German shell exploded near Desobry's command post, wounding him and killing LaPrade. Desobry was subsequently captured when the ambulance in which he was being evacuated to Bastogne ran into a German road ambush.

On the morning of the 19th, Allied leader Eisenhower summoned his senior commanders to confer at Verdun. The German offensive was growing more serious—it was already gaining the name "Battle of the Bulge." On situation maps, the black grease-pencil arrows pointed the Germans directly at Bastogne. Ike needed Lt. Gen. George S. Patton's U.S. Third Army to halt its attack into the Saar, make a 90-degree turn and drive north to Bastogne. "When will you be able to attack?" Ike asked Patton.

"The morning of the 21st, with three divisions," Patton replied.

"Don't be fatuous, George," Ike retorted. "If you go that early, you won't have all three divisions ready, and you'll go piecemeal. You will attack on the 22nd." Then Eisenhower added, "The present situation is to be regarded as an opportunity for us and not a disaster."

That same day, Lt. Col. Julian Ewell's 501st Parachute Regiment of 1,200 men took position outside around Bastogne. McAuliffe had ordered Ewell to "make contact, attack, and clear up the situation." That situation was highly confused. The 1st Battalion of the 501st Regiment (1/501) headed east to Neffe and came under German fire amid heavy fog. One German reconnaissance unit came in close to Bastogne, just ahead of the 101st. The unit's commanding officer (CO) saw only a lone American military policeman, and he radioed his headquarters recommending that Panzer Lehr drive immediately into the town. Instead, the German was scolded for leaving his assigned area. The Nazi unit pulled back, and the 101st streamed in.

At his Mageret HQ, Bayerlein tried to figure out what was in front of him. *Luftwaffe* reconnaissance planes were grounded by bad weather. A Belgian civilian told Bayerlein there were 50 American tanks ahead, an exaggeration. When his troops finally entered Neffe, they came under heavy American artillery fire. Bayerlein was forced to hide in a cave. After the bombardment abated, an irritated Bayerlein radioed his boss, Lt. Gen. Heinrich von Lüttwitz, commander of the XLVII Panzer Corps, saying, "We should attack Bastogne with the whole corps."

Lüttwitz, a veteran commander, figured it made sense to attack Bastogne at once in force. But he passed the buck to his own boss, the Fifth Panzer Army's commander, General Hasso von Manteuffel.

Manteuffel was reluctant to tie down two whole armored divisions in a siege. And his supply lines were snarled. He gave Lüttwitz permission to make one hard attack. If that failed, Bastogne would be encircled.

As the 101st set up shop in Bastogne, the airborne troops got some ad hoc reinforcements. In the town were retreating American units of all sorts, and McAuliffe was given permission to add them to his assets. Among the outfits were artillery batteries with plenty of ammunition. Two of them, the 696th and 333rd field artilleries, were all-black units. The 695th Tank Destroyer Battalion turned up as well. McAuliffe rounded up survivors of shattered formations and created "Team Snafu."

Then the roof fell in. The 10th Armored troops in town weren't taking orders from McAuliffe. Company I of the 501st lost 85 men and five officers in a skirmish with German tanks. The 506th took heavy casualties relieving Noville, and intelligence identified the enemy forces closing on Bastogne as the XLVII Panzer Corps. The 101st had clearly reached Bastogne just a step ahead of the German army.

Late on Tuesday night, the 101st gained more help, as the 705th Tank Destroyer Battalion came rumbling into town. The unit's Lt. Col. Clifford

Templeton had to walk into Bastogne, as German troops had ambushed his party and destroyed his jeep. Meanwhile, the 101st's hospital was not so lucky; German troops captured it.

The 705th's tank destroyers, along with some 501st troops, were sent to Bizory and were hit by the 26th Volksgrenadier Division. The paratroopers, backed by division artillery, held their fire until the German infantrymen closed in, then opened up with a 20-minute hail of gunfire. The Germans fled.

That was good news at division base in Bastogne, but Noville was still surrounded, the 506th could not relieve it, and the other two 10th Armored teams were still menaced. German troops were attacking from the northeast at Noville, and the southeast at Marvie. There, Lt. Col. Joseph H. "Bud" Harper's 327th Glider Infantry Regiment, along with some 10th Armored tanks, were facing Panzer Lehr. Harper's men fought hard, killing 30 Germans and capturing 20, with a loss of five dead and 15 wounded.

Marvie was holding, but Noville could not. On the morning of Wednesday the 20th, Team Desobry began pulling out, down the road to Bastogne, under heavy fire. Of 15 tanks originally sent to Noville, only four returned, and the 506th lost more than 200 men.

McAuliffe knew his men were better fighters than his German opponents, but Bastogne itself would soon be surrounded. Should the 101st pull out? McAuliffe's officers broke things down for him—the men were in good shape, and there were enough to hold a pocket. Artillery ammunition and medical supplies were short, but if the fog lifted, they could be resupplied by air.

McAuliffe walked away, into the middle of the HQ's operations room, and stood alone. Then he faced his staff and announced, "I am staying."

With that decision made, McAuliffe drove to see Maj. Gen. Troy H. Middleton in his new digs at Neufch,teau. The VIII Corps commander had bad news—the Germans were sending a third panzer division to attack Bastogne, the 116th. McAuliffe said, "I think we can take care of them." Middleton promised to send help.

Middleton had one piece of good news for McAuliffe—he was given full command of all units in Bastogne, including the 10th Armored's troops. As McAuliffe left, Middleton had one more comment, "Now don't get yourself surrounded, Tony."

As McAuliffe had set out in search of Middleton, their enemy counterparts were also conferring at Mageret. Lüttwitz told Bayerlein to take the town on Thursday.

McAuliffe returned to Bastogne by night without difficulty. That evening seven German tanks and an infantry company hit the seam between the 501st and 506th, along railroad tracks leading into Bastogne. The Germans were spotted by a 501st patrol, but the nearest Americans were 600 yards from the track.

A platoon from A Company, 1/501, dashed into position for an ambush at the back of a swamp. When the Germans appeared 40 feet off, the Americans opened fire. The Germans counterattacked, and the firefight raged into the foggy night. Finally, after several hours of gunfire, the Germans withdrew.

Meanwhile, at 7 p.m., German tanks and self-propelled guns attacked the 1/501 and 3/501 on the Longvilly Road, south of the rail line. McAuliffe concentrated 11 battalions of artillery and brought down a curtain of fire on the enemy.

The 705th Tank Destroyers rumbled into fog and mist, found German self-propelled guns in a railroad cut, and destroyed three. Sergeant George N. Schmidt poured thousands of rounds of .50-caliber machine-gun fire down a hillside against German infantry. By midnight the Germans had withdrawn, leaving their dead heaped on the barbed wire.

Dawn of Thursday, the 21st, bought falling temperatures and heavy fog. In Bastogne, four American infantry regiments, 11 artillery battalions and a worn-out tank brigade still held an oval-shaped area 5 miles in diameter.

Meanwhile, the Germans made changes. The 2nd Panzer Division and part of Panzer Lehr were pulled off Bastogne and sent west to resume the drive to the Meuse. The tough 5th *Fallschirmjäger* (airborne) Division replaced them.

As 2nd Panzer moved out, McAuliffe ordered his troops and artillery to hit its columns, hoping to shake the division's nerve. The attacks slowed 2nd Panzer down. It advanced cautiously on the Meuse—so slowly that Lüttwitz would court-martial a regimental commander for cowardice.

Sometime after midnight, 2 inches of snow tumbled down. Supplies were so low that McAuliffe had to limit his artillery to 10 rounds per gun. But the Germans did not attack. Their failure to take Bastogne had forced them to send supply and troop columns down narrow secondary roads, snarling traffic for miles.

McAuliffe received two messages early on Friday, the 22nd: the promise of a supply airdrop at dusk, and word of Patton's drive from the south. McAuliffe, who spoke French, appealed to Bastogne's citizens to part with their bed sheets and tablecloths for his soldiers to use as camouflage snowsuits. The Belgians responded.

Faced with continuing American defiance, Lüttwitz was running out of patience and ideas. He could not use his armor on the sometimes soft ground, and supplies were snarled. Like many senior Germans, however, he believed the Americans were a weak foe and could be induced to surrender.

At 11:30 a.m., two German officers and two enlisted men, carrying a white bedspread appropriated from a nearby farm, arrived at F Company of the 327th with a message. The officers were blindfolded and taken to F Company's CP (command post), while rumors spread among the GIs they passed that they had come to ask McAuliffe for surrender terms. The 327th's CO, Lt.

Col. Bud Harper, passed the Germans' missive to division headquarters.

The message, typed in both German and English, demanded "the honorable surrender of the encircled town," and warned that "one German artillery corps and six heavy flak battalions" were ready to annihilate the 101st. "All the serious civilian losses caused by this artillery fire would not correspond with the well-known American humanity," it concluded. The Americans had two hours to reply. It was ambiguously signed, "*Der Deutscher Befehlshaber* (the German commander)," but it had been drafted in Lüttwitz's headquarters.

McAuliffe's aide, Lt. Col. Ned D. Moore, scanned the document.

"What does it say, Ned?" McAuliffe asked.

"They want you to surrender," Moore answered.

More amused than angry, McAuliffe laughed and said, "Aw, Nuts! We're giving them one hell of a beating. This ultimatum is way out of line." (According to some accounts, McAuliffe's response began with a more vulgar exclamation, and "nuts" was substituted shortly thereafter by his G-3, or operations officer, Lt. Col. Harry W.O. Kinnard.)

With the two German officers still waiting, blindfolded, at the F Company CP, McAuliffe, pencil in hand, pondered over a formal reply to the ultimatum for a few minutes. Finally, he said, "Well, I don't know what to tell them," and asked his staff for suggestions.

"That first remark of yours would be hard to beat," said Kinnard.

"What was that?" asked McAuliffe, who had genuinely forgotten.

"You said "Nuts!'" Kinnard answered.

McAuliffe, delighted, wrote, "To the German commander: Nuts! The American commander."

Harper returned to the blindfolded Germans. "I have the American commander's reply," he told them.

Leutnant Hellmuth Henke, a member of Panzer Lehr who spoke fluent English, asked, "Is it written or verbal?".

"It is written. I will stick it in your hand," Harper said.

Henke puzzled over the note, then asked, "Is that reply negative or affirmative? If it is the latter, I will negotiate further."

"The reply is decidedly not affirmative," Harper snapped. "If you continue this foolish attack, your losses will be tremendous." Harper took the Germans back to the front line, where he removed their blindfolds, and said, "If you don't understand what 'Nuts!' means, in plain English it is the same as 'Go to hell!' And I will tell you something else: if you continue to attack, we will kill every goddamn German that tries to break into this city."

The Germans saluted and Henke said, "We will kill many Americans. This is war."

"On your way, Bud," Harper said, then thoughtlessly added, "And good luck to you." As the German jeep disappeared down the road, Harper mentally kicked himself for inadvertently concluding his bellicose remarks with such a benign non-sequitur.

McAuliffe's terse note was not quite the act of defiance in the face of impossible odds that posterity has made of it. Lüttwitz's threat was a bluff—he did not have the massed artillery he described in his ultimatum—and McAuliffe had simply called it. When word of Lüttwitz's stunt and McAuliffe's reply reached Manteuffel, the diminutive Prussian gave Lüttwitz a furious tongue-lashing.

McAuliffe announced the whole surrender offer and his response to his troops, and American morale soared. But that evening's supply drop was canceled, because heavy weather and ice grounded the U.S. Army Air Force's Douglas C-47 Dakota transports in France and Britain. A 60-plane resupply mission was promised for the first clear day. During the night, however, the *Luftwaffe* came over to bomb Bastogne.

The temperature stood at 10 degrees above zero at dawn on Saturday, December 23, and a bright winter sun shone down. Manteuffel, fed up with Bastogne's resistance and Lüttwitz's antics, drove down with orders for the 26th Volksgrenadier to attack. Fifth Panzer Army's two best divisions, Panzer Lehr and 2nd Panzer, were lapping at the Meuse, but they could not maintain the pace of the offensive without supplies, which were piling up behind Bastogne. Manteuffel told *Oberst* Heinz Kokott, "Bastogne must be taken at all costs."

Kokott was happy to oblige. Before midday, he attacked the 327th four miles west of Bastogne at Mande-St. Étienne. Twelve German tanks hit the 327th's C Company and ran smack into McAuliffe's artillery and tank destroyers. Both sides lost two vehicles, but Kokott's advance had been stopped.

At 10:00 that morning, the first of 241 C-47s flew in from England. The lead planes dropped a pathfinder team, led by Lieutenant Gordon Rothwell. Once on the ground, the pathfinders marked off drop zones on the plain just west of Bastogne for the rest of the C-47s, which parachuted 144 tons of materiel in 1,446 packages. The Screaming Eagles recovered 95 percent of the bundles but found that some contained artillery shells for guns the 101st did not possess.

Even so, the massive airlift had its impact, boosting American morale and irritating Kokott. This time Kokott opted for a night assault, dashing past Mande-St. Étienne with tanks and snowsuit-clad infantry of the 39th Grenadier Regiment.

The Germans overran the American roadblock at Flamièrge, held by the 3/327. Kokott's men destroyed a company aid station and exploded a pile of mortar rounds, scattering the defenders. The glider infantry pulled back, and McAuliffe came down to check on things. "This is our last withdrawal," he told Harper. "Live or die, this is it."

Elated by success, Lüttwitz reinforced Kokott with the 901st Panzergrenadier Regiment of Panzer Lehr Division. Their tanks and half-tracks crashed in at dusk, headed for a hillock southwest of Marvie called Hill 500. Only 98 men under Lieutenant Stanley Morrison held that high ground.

Harper rushed in a 10th Armored anti-tank gun. As the gun's half-track rumbled in, American troops misidentified it as German and destroyed it. That turned out to be a blessing in disguise—the wrecked vehicle now blocked the narrow road.

But the Germans surrounded Hill 500 and whittled down its defenders. Soon Panzer Lehr was driving on Bastogne from the south. Team O'Hara (for Lt. Col. James O'Hara), one of the 10th Armored units, and 2/327 moved to intercept it. The Germans moved in with infantry and 12 Mark IV tanks, and came under heavy bazooka and tank fire. The Germans withdrew to mortar range, then shelled the Americans in the moonlight.

All night McAuliffe regrouped the 327th's line, deploying 10th Armored tanks and guns. The Germans were moving in on Bastogne on the Wiltz and Arlon roads, so McAuliffe set up his artillery to intersect those thoroughfares.

At Marvie, German and American infantry fought to control a village burning down around them. Two American tanks battered attacking German vehicles, and the 101st held.

At his headquarters, Kokott learned early on Sunday, the 24th, that he had made limited gains. While he flipped through messages, he had a visitor, Manteuffel, who gave Kokott an order direct from Hitler: take Bastogne at all costs.

Manteuffel pointed out that the U.S. Third Army was driving hard on Bastogne against the German 5th *Fallschirmjäger* Division. More important, *Luftwaffe* weather forecasters were warning that the fog was due to break. Allied aircraft would fill the skies. If Bastogne didn't fall, the German tanks on the Meuse would be starved of supplies. Manteuffel had some good news for Kokott—the 9th Panzer and 15th Panzergrenadier divisions had just arrived from Italy, and although the divisions themselves were being committed to the offensive to the west , *Oberst* Wolfgang Maucke's 115th Panzergrenadier Regiment and some supporting tanks and *Sturmgeschütze* (assault guns) had been detached, formed into a unit called *Kampfgruppe* Maucke, and placed at Kokott's disposal. Kokott resolved to attack Bastogne from the northeast early on the 25th.

At dusk, McAuliffe radioed Middleton, "The finest Christmas present the 101st could get would be relief tomorrow." More than 100 Catholic paratroopers celebrated Christmas Mass, singing carols by candlelight. The division chaplain told his men, "Do not plan, for God's plan will prevail."

After the service, the *Luftwaffe* broke up the Christmas Eve quiet, bombarding the town and damaging the aid station. Among the victims were Renée Lemaire, a female Belgian Red Cross worker, and her 20 American patients.

Before dawn the *Luftwaffe* was back, along with German artillery, shelling and bombing Bastogne. The barrage was the overture for Kokott's attack, and at 3:30 a.m. Elements from the 77th Panzergrenadier Regiment, clad in snowsuits, attacked the 502nd Parachute Infantry Regiment at the village of Champs. Two thousand yards to the southwest, 18 Mark IV tanks and *Sturmgeschütze* of *Kampfgruppe* Maucke's Panzer *Abteilung* 115, each with about a dozen troops aboard, crashed through the line held by 3/327th at 7:10, destroyed or drove off tank destroyers of the 705th Tank Destroyer Battalion, and then fanned out for 1/502's CP at Hemroulle and the 502nd's regimental CP at Château Rolle. Some of the Germans also headed for Champs.

German shelling cut the 502nd's phone lines, leaving the CO, Lt. Col. Steve A. Chappuis, out of touch. But he knew the attack was serious. Up the line, Captain Wallace A. Swanson, CO of A Company, 1/502, sat through "the strongest, most extensive, continuous barrage" he had ever been in. Company B reinforced A Company, and soon Chappuis sent in his cooks, clerks, even his walking wounded, to stem the Germans. Hemroulle was only two miles from the 101st Division's headquarters, and McAuliffe was in danger of being overrun. He rounded up his own HQ troops, passed out bazookas, and braced for the worst.

The paratroopers opened up on the Germans who were riding tanks and cut them down. But the panzers closed to 150 yards and opened fire. Shells roared over the 502nd. The Germans broke through and headed for the 463rd Field Artillery.

The Americans formed a skirmish line, joined by the 502nd's C Company, the headquarters "paper chasers" and Chappuis himself. The 502nd's CO arrived in time to see German troops charging at him from 600 yards off.

As the Germans closed, so did two American M-10 tank destroyers. They destroyed two German tanks before being knocked out themselves. The Germans plunged in among the Americans, exposing their flank to two more M-10s and B Company. Those Americans opened up, wrecking three German tanks. The headquarters men knocked out another German tank with a bazooka. Only one German Mark IV tank entered Champs, but it was then wrecked by American guns and bazookas. Company C rounded up 35 prisoners and counted 67 enemy dead.

More attacks came in at the southwest on the Mande-St. Étienne highway, at Savy. M-10 tank destroyers wrecked three more German tanks. Sergeant Michael E. Griffith fired a bazooka round into a German tank. The wrecked vehicle blocked a key road.

Chappuis ordered his men to counterattack at Hemroulle, and the exhausted Germans surrendered. One Panzer IV was captured intact in the town.

All around the Bastogne perimeter the battle raged. The Americans sent in their last reserves, 10th Armored's tanks, and halted the German drive. By 8 a.m., Republic P-47 Thunderbolt fighter-bombers had arrived over Bastogne and were strafing the German troops. Kokott's attack was finished. He had suffered about 1,000 casualties.

Luftwaffe aircraft made a daylight appearance over Bastogne to help cover Kokott's retreat. After the German aircraft departed, 160 C-47s rained more supplies on the 101st. The *Luftwaffe* returned that evening, too, scattering bombs across the 101st's perimeter.

On the following morning, December 26, Kokott made what he called "the last desperate effort" to break through to Bastogne, sending an assault group comprised of troops of the 26th Volksgrenadier Division and four *Jagdpanzers* (tank destroyers) northward toward Hemroulle. Artillery fire halted the German infantry, and the *Jagdpanzers* found their way blocked by a large ditch, after which they were destroyed by a deluge of American artillery and tank destroyer shells. In mid-afternoon, Kokott received a radio message from the commander of the 39th Panzergrenadier Regiment: American tanks had broken through the German cordon near Assenois. At that point, Kokott knew it was all over—time had run out on his attempt to take Bastogne before it could be relieved.

Later in the day, American gliders landed just west of Bastogne, bringing in doctors and nurses to replace the 101st's captured hospital.

Late that afternoon, McAuliffe took stock. His division had captured 649 POWs, destroyed 148 tanks and 25 halftracks, and stopped the German offensive cold. Hitler's trucks could not deliver gasoline to his tanks at the Meuse, thus ending the last great Nazi offensive in the West. Soon Hitler's troops would be in full retreat. McAuliffe, staring at his maps, told his officers, "This is without a doubt the war's most important single engagement involving a small force."

More important, the "Battered Bastards of the Bastion of Bastogne" had become an American legend—an Alamo with a happy ending.

Late that afternoon, Combat Command R of the 4th Armored Division drove north up the Arlon Road, leading Patton's drive on Bastogne. The lead element was 37th Tank Battalion, under Lt. Col. Creighton W. Abrams, Jr., who later would command U.S. troops in Vietnam. His vehicles drove to the village of Assenois and encountered resistance. The 4th Armored's artillery shelled the village, and the Germans ran, leaving behind a scattering of hastily laid mines.

Abrams' infantry dismounted and removed the mines. Then Abrams sent on a company of tanks under Lieutenant Charles P. Boggess to Bastogne.

At 4:45 p.m., Boggess peered out of his tank and saw American uniforms ahead, crouched in foxholes along the road. "Come on out," Boggess yelled. "It's all right. It's the 4th Armored."

One of the shapes in a foxhole rose. It was Lieutenant Duane J. Webster, 326th Airborne Engineers. He advanced carefully, keeping Boggess covered with his carbine. "I'm Lieutenant Webster," he said solemnly. "Do you guys have any water?"

Boggess' tankers produced three canteens. The engineers emerged from their holes and drank thirstily. The only water the paratroopers had had throughout the siege had come from melting snow.

Webster sent a message up to Division CP, and McAuliffe soon arrived to meet Boggess' boss, Captain William A. Dwight, and to ceremonially end the siege of Bastogne. McAuliffe was characteristically low-key. "Gee, I am mighty glad to see you," he said to Captain Dwight.

Pivotal Struggle for Pusan

*Korea had its "Battle of the Bulge"—two in fact.
In the First Battle of the Naktong Bulge, the
North Korean offensive threatened to overwhelm
Maj. Gen. John Huston Church's 24th Infantry Division.*

By Uzal E. Ent

With soft "pops," red and yellow flares shot up and glowed briefly and eerily in the warm night. At one minute after midnight, on August 6, 1950, 800 men of the 3rd Battalion, 16th Infantry Regiment, 4th Infantry Division, of the North Korean Peoples Army (NKPA), began crossing the Naktong River near the Ohang ferry site.

The troops carried no heavy weapons or mortars. After crossing, they formed up quietly in a column of platoons and moved stealthily through a draw leading into American lines. Their objective was the town of Yongsan, about eight miles behind the lines of the U.S. 24th Infantry Division.

And so began the First Battle of the Naktong Bulge, a key part of the general North Korean offensive against the U.S. and South Korean defenders of the Pusan perimeter at the tip of the Korean peninsula.

Before North Korea invaded South Korea on June 25, 1950, few U.S. troops were stationed in the South—and the four U.S. Army divisions in nearby Japan were woefully below strength and undertrained. Indeed, assignment to the U.S. 1st Cavalry (actually, infantry) and the 7th, 24th and 25th Infantry divisions had meant fairly easy occupation duty. After June 1949, some serious training was begun, but only on a limited scale.

Worse, the 24th and her sister divisions also lacked one-third of their authorized infantry and artillery commands and two-thirds of their anti-aircraft complement. They had only 15 to 20 tanks per division, instead of the 142 authorized. The tanks were often M-24 light tanks, no match for the Russian-made T-34/85 mediums that supported the North Korean drive southward.

Instead of their authorized strength of 18,804 officers and men, the divisions in Japan were allocated only 12,500. As the closest division to Korea—and the easiest to send—the 24th was the first command deployed. It was brought up from a strength of 12,197 men to 15,965 from the commands in Japan just before departing for Korea.

By the time it fell back to defensive positions on the South Korean peninsula, east of the Naktong River, on August 2, savage fighting had reduced the 24th to 9,882 men. The attachment of 486 U.S. troops and operational control of the 2,000-man Republic of Korea (ROK) 17th Infantry Regiment brought the aggregate strength to 12,368. Major General John Huston Church, a veteran of both world wars and recipient of the Distinguished Service Cross, was now division commander. He replaced Maj. Gen. William F. Dean, who was a prisoner of the North Koreans.

Forming a lengthy, serpentine moat along two-thirds of the Pusan perimeter, the twisting Naktong flowed through a valley that averaged 1,000 yards wide, although the river itself averaged no more than 385 yards across and was from 1 to 3½ yards deep.

The 24th Division occupied a sector 34 miles long, extending northward along the Naktong from its junction with the Nam River. The river frontage was extended by the many loops in the Naktong's course. Hill masses on both sides of the river rose an average of 220 yards, with some reaching 330 yards. The terrain was of equal elevation on either side of the river, except in the far north. There, Hill 409 on the east bank dominated the terrain to the west.

The three battalions of Colonel Kim Hi Chun's ROK 17th Regiment were deployed along the northern 30,000 yards of front, regarded as the most difficult sector to defend and reinforce because of the poor road network. General Church surmised that the North Koreans would strike there.

When the NKPA 4th Division instead attacked to the south, it was unexpected and came sooner than Church thought it would. The U.S. 21st Infantry Regiment, commanded by Colonel Richard W. Stephens, was south of the ROK 17th. The 3rd Battalion (Lt. Col. John McConnell commanding), consisting of K and M companies, plus part of the regimental Heavy Mortar Company serving as a rifle unit, manned the 12,000-yard regimental front. The 1st Battalion, led by Lt. Col. Charles B. Smith, was deployed in separate company positions several thousand yards to the rear of the 3rd. The 14th Engineer Combat Battalion reinforced the 21st Infantry Regiment.

The Heavy Mortar Company was on the 21st Regiment's left flank, just north of a boundary with the 34th Regiment. The company established outposts of four to six men on a line of several thousand yards. A lone halftrack, armed with four .50-caliber machine guns (called a quad .50 by the troops), happened to be close by. Lieutenant Planter Wilson from the Heavy Mortar Company positioned the halftrack so that the four guns could fire all along the company front.

Company K was dug in about a mile from the mortar men, also on an extended frontage. Across the Naktong, a road ran parallel to the river. When the North Koreans tried to use the road on August 5, the men of Lieutenant Elmer J. Gainok's Company K fired at the enemy's vehicles with 3.5-inch rocket launchers, but the range was too great. Company K was a mixed infantry-heavy weapons unit, without regular organizational equipment, but it had two 81mm mortars. Just before dusk, the NKPA force tried to move a truck convoy along the road. Gainok's mortars hit one of the lead trucks, which then blocked the road. The mortars were then systematically fired at the stalled vehicles, inflicting heavy casualties.

South of the 21st was Colonel Charles E. Beauchamp's 34th Infantry Regiment on a 16,000-yard front, guarding what would become known as the Naktong Bulge. Lieutenant Colonel Gines Perez's 3rd Battalion was assigned the river line, with I Company in the north, L Company in the heart of the bulge and K Company in the south.

The somewhat scattered 21st could form a fair defense line, but Perez had to employ platoon-sized strongpoints overlooking the river. The 34th Regimental Intelligence and Reconnaissance Platoon held two observation posts between L and K companies. Some men from Battery A, 26th Anti-Aircraft Artillery (Automatic Weapons) Battalion, employed as infantry, reinforced I Company. The fact that men from a heavy mortar company and an anti-aircraft artillery unit were deployed as infantry on the front lines of the division, and that an engineer battalion reinforced an infantry regiment, shows how understrength the 24th Division was.

The undermanned division's frontage suffered accordingly, with two vulnerable gaps developing—one of two miles between I and L companies and another of three miles between L and K. The front-line troops tried to strengthen their positions with anti-personnel mines and trip flares (both in short supply), and improvised booby traps. Patrols attempted to cover the gaps in the lines, while a regimental reserve (1st Battalion, assembled near the town of Kang-ni) and a division reserve (the two-battalion 19th Infantry Regiment) stood ready to offer emergency support.

One morning, a couple of houses in a village across the Naktong moved slightly. Looking through field glasses, the men of L Company could see a tank's gun barrel sticking out of one house. The enemy had simply driven tanks into the mud-and-stick houses.

On the night of August 5, L Company of the 34th's 3rd Battalion, about 50 men under Captain Douglas W. Syverson, and a 10-man platoon under Lieutenant Leonard Korgie were across from the Ohang ferry on a 300-yard front. About dark, the platoon was moved across the river to establish a listening post.

At about 10:30 that night, Corporal Ed Metowski and Korgie heard slight noises to their front. Frank Pollock and Eugene Singleton, on their left, were also alert. To their right was Alvin Ginn. The men opened fire. Almost at once, the five men were set upon from all sides by enemy soldiers, who quickly overwhelmed and disarmed the Americans. Determined not to be captured, Korgie threw his helmet into the midst of the North Koreans and yelled, "Let's go, Ed!" Ed didn't escape, but Korgie did. He reached the platoon command post (CP) with the enemy now firing flares and noisily crossing the river. As platoon personnel called for mortar fire over their phone, figures were scrambling up the hill toward the CP. Korgie yelled, "Halt!" and 15 or so North Koreans jumped up about 40 yards away, yelling, *"Manzai!*

Manzai!" and spraying the area with burp-gun fire. Korgie and a companion fired into them. When Korgie's rifle was empty, he fell back, fumbling for another clip. As he ran, he noted that he was running parallel to a group of North Koreans advancing in a skirmish line. He knew they were North Koreans, but they thought he was one of them. After running up and down two hills, Korgie collapsed at the top of the third (a victim of bloody dysentery, fatigue and heat), pitched head first over the crest, and rolled about 40 yards down the slope. Just then, the enemy realized who he was, and some began to fire at him. He was able to slip another clip into his rifle, figuring he would shoot as many as he could before they killed him. For some reason, they left. The next morning, Korgie joined about 40 other men of the 34th farther north along the riverbank.

Robert Bayless, a machine-gunner with L Company, had been on the extreme right of the company line. The enemy thrust behind L Company and cut it off. A lieutenant led Bayless and some others north to join I Company, but I Company, with the few men from L, lost its hill. A counterattack was unsuccessful. I Company's old position was then hit by friendly mortar fire. Bayless and his group wandered into the sector of the 21st Infantry. There, he and some of his comrades fell, exhausted, into a roadside ditch, and Bayless dozed off. He was awakened by a column of men coming up the road in the dark. They proved to be the 24th Reconnaissance Company, preparing to counterattack along the southern flank of the 21st Infantry.

Colonel Beauchamp of the 34th Infantry reported the situation in his front line 3rd Battalion to General Church and committed the regimental reserve to counterattack. Mounting 1st Battalion's C Company (about 100 men) on trucks, with A and B companies following on foot, Lt. Col. Harold B. Ayres moved at 7 a.m. to counter the enemy. As Ayres and C Company arrived at Colonel Perez's now abandoned 3rd Battalion CP, they were hit by heavy fire from the nearby hills.

The company commander, Captain Clyde M. Akbridge, was hit three times and had to be evacuated. Ayres was able to escape and go back for the remainder of his battalion. Lieutenant Charles E. Payne took over the company, which was being swept by fire from nearby higher ground. The unit did get a 60mm mortar into action, but the assistant gunner was soon killed as he rose to observe where the rounds were striking. Robert Witzig fired the remaining mortar ammunition, then helped drag the wounded to a culvert. His platoon leader, Lieutenant McDonald Martin, was shot in the stomach. Surviving members of the company took shelter in a nearby grist mill. The defenders also used the .50-caliber machine gun taken from an abandoned personnel carrier to fight off the enemy. In spite of this, the North Koreans often came within grenade range of the mill. Early in the fight, Battery B, 13th Field Artillery, which was deployed nearby, was also attacked. Battery personnel abandoned four howitzers and hastily withdrew with about 50 men and one howitzer.

The fight at the grist mill went on for several hours. Finally, C Company's Lieutenant Payne asked for volunteers to go for help. Witzig and another man volunteered, but intense fire drove Witzig's companion back into the mill. Witzig managed to crawl about 40 yards before being blown up into the air and knocked unconscious. He had three wounds in the back. Coming to, he looked up to see a North Korean soldier reaching for his belt and grenades. Witzig killed him with his .45-caliber automatic pistol. Then he was hit again, his helmet spinning off. At first he thought he had been shot in the head, but he then realized the blood and flesh on his hands were from the back wounds he had patched up with his aid packet. Retrieving his helmet, he saw that its whole right side had been blown away.

Corporals John Nearhood and Harold Tucker, braving heavy enemy fire, dragged Witzig back into the grist mill. Every man who could handle a weapon helped to fend off the determined enemy assault. The wounded Witzig manned a Browning Automatic Rifle. The situation was now desperate. Nearhood volunteered to go for help and was quickly killed by enemy fire.

Soon after, Captain A.F. Alfonso's A Company, led by a tank, came to the rescue. Unfortunately, a tank round went through the grist mill, mortally wounding three of the men and injuring several more, all members of C Company.

After seeing that the dead and wounded of C Company were evacuated, Alfonso's company continued the attack, eventually reaching L Company on the river. The combined force numbered 90 men, including the wounded.

In the meantime, Company B had been stalled on Cloverleaf Hill (Hill 165) by the enemy.

By then, General Church, thoroughly alarmed, had ordered the 24th Reconnaissance Company and the 19th Infantry forward. That alleviated the pressure, but the enemy was across the river and on high ground. Throughout the night, American artillery fired into all known or suspected river-crossing sites, but the North Koreans still reinforced their bridgehead.

The main attack, it now could be seen, had come through the gap between the 34th Infantry's I and L companies. By 3 a.m. on August 6, the North Koreans had penetrated to the village of Kogong-ni, overrunning 3rd Battalion's CP and a detachment of the regiment's Heavy Mortar Company. On the next night, August 6–7, the ROK 17th Infantry repulsed enemy attempts to cross the Naktong in the northern sector. By prior plan, the ROK unit then traded off with fresh American troops while the U.S. 21st Infantry halted the enemy after they developed a lodgement in the village of Sadung near the river. Three companies of the 34th also held to their riverside positions for the moment.

Now, too, the 19th and elements of the 34th were poised for a counterattack against the northern shoulder of the enemy penetration. Local counterattacks had gained time for the 19th and, later, the 9th Infantry—a new and untried regiment from the freshly arriving 2nd Infantry Division—to move against the North Koreans.

But on August 7, the 19th and 34th regiments failed to dislodge the North Koreans, who seized most of Cloverleaf Hill and part of Obong-ni Ridge. From that critical terrain astride the main east-west road in the bulge area, the enemy could see all the way to Yongsan, five miles to the east.

Cloverleaf, as its name implies, was shaped like a four-leaf clover, with the stem pointing north. It was somewhat higher than Obong-ni Ridge, across the pass to the south. Obong-ni Ridge (or No-Name Ridge to some Marines) was a mile and a half long, curving somewhat southeast in a series of knobs known as Hills 102, 109, 117, 143, 147 and 153. The village of Tugok lay at the southern base of Cloverleaf, north of the road between it and Obong-ni Ridge. Obong-ni village was at the eastern base of the ridge a half mile south of the road.

On the nights of August 6-7 and 7-8, the enemy reinforced its bridgehead. At least two battalions crossed on August 7-8, and the NKPA 4th Division completed its crossing on August 10, using an underwater bridge and rafts. Trucks, heavy mortars, about 12 artillery pieces and possibly some tanks were moved into the bulge.

Commitment of the fresh 9th Infantry did not appreciably help the American situation. On the night of August 8-9, Captain Alfonso's force of A and L companies was ordered back from its exposed position along the Naktong. One platoon kept close to the road instead of moving south around Obong-ni, and suffered heavy casualties. The rest of the group entered U.S. lines well after daylight.

On August 10, the 9th Infantry lost 2,000 yards of critical terrain. The enemy also set up a roadblock on the Namji-ri–Yongsan road. Only along the Naktong were the Americans successful. The 19th took Ohang Hill, but its 2nd Battalion was reduced to about 100 effectives in each rifle company.

Church ordered the 1st Battalion, 21st Infantry, to Yongsan and told his operations officer, Lt. Col. James Snee, to seek whatever aid he could. Snee asked Eighth Army for the use of the 27th Infantry Regiment, 25th Infantry Division. Church also ordered a reconnaissance company sent to Yongsan.

As Lt. Col. Gordon E. Murch's 2nd Battalion, 27th Infantry, attacked north from Namji-ri, its F Company seized a bridgehead across the Naktong. Company personnel had to push through throngs of supposed refugees. At one point, a "refugee" cart tipped over, spilling rifles and ammunition to the ground, and about a dozen enemy soldiers, disguised as civilians, began to flee across a field. Staff Sergeant Glenn Ellison and his comrades shot down eight of them.

The 2nd Battalion's attack progressed the next day, supported by artillery, mortars and airstrikes. And on August 10, Church created Task Force

Hill, giving command of the 9th Regiment (less the 3rd Battalion), 19th and 34th regiments, and the 1st Battalion, 21st Infantry, to Colonel John G. Hill of the 9th. But the 19th and 34th were mere shadows of regiments, both reduced by casualties to about 1,100 men each. The entire 24th Division now totaled 9,755 men, with 5,401 more being attached, including elements of the 2nd and 25th Infantry divisions. The addition of 247 replacements and weapons manned by the replacement crew helped minimally.

Task Force Hill was supposed to drive the enemy across the Naktong on the 11th by a general counterattack, driven ahead by the 9th and 19th regiments. But the North Koreans launched a surprise attack against the 1st Battalion, 21st Infantry, while in its assembly area at about 9 a.m. Although few casualties resulted, the attack was disconcerting. Task Force Hill's general attack failed.

The situation around Yongsan by now had so deteriorated that one regimental commander was moved to remark: "There are dozens of enemy and American forces all over the area. And they are surrounding each other."

In response to a call for help from Church, a composite company of men from A Company, 14th Engineers, plus cooks and staff from its headquarters, was sent to Yongsan. Their force numbering fewer than 100 men, the engineers set up four separate positions at about 800-yard intervals along the road from Yongsan. Another ad hoc force, under Captain George Hafeman (commander, 24th Division Headquarters Company), was deployed at the Simgong-ni and Wonjon passes, farther east. Known as Task Force Hafeman, it consisted of clerks and bakers from Hafeman's unit, military police personnel, men from the 24th Recon Company and others from eight different units, all supported by two tanks. Throughout August 12, the engineers and Hafeman battled North Korean infiltrators. Hafeman's two posts held, but two of the smaller engineer positions fell to the NKPA. Three times, U.S. armored vehicles dashed into the Wonjon enclave with food, water and ammunition. Hafeman reinforced his group with an 81mm mortar and continued to hold.

As one highlight well worth noting here, K and L companies of the 34th Infantry at last were ordered to withdraw from their exposed positions along the Naktong. There has been a persistent, and erroneous, impression in the minds of many that the Army ran when the North Koreans attacked across the Naktong in August and, later, in September 1950. This is false. In August, the bulge, a front covering 16,000 yards, was manned by three understrength rifle companies. Two of those units remained in position, although completely cut off. One of the two was reinforced by a counterattacking unit, and the combined force then dug in and held. Only the most northern company was displaced. Men from that unit moved north into the sector of the 21st Infantry. The frontage was far too great for the force available to even outpost, let alone defend. The men of those units have been wrongly, even cruelly, reviled for too long. They stayed in their defensive positions until ordered out by higher authority. They performed their duty with honor. Meanwhile, shortly after midnight on the 15th, the North Koreans attacked across a wide front. Lieutenant General Walton H. Walker, the Eighth Army commander, was upset. "I am going to give you the Marine Brigade," he told Church. "I want this situation cleared up, and quick!"

Although the U.S. 24th Division's situation was grim, prisoners reported that the opposing NKPA 4th Division was also in poor condition, low on ammunition and supplies, and suffering in morale. Hurting or not, the enemy continued to attack on August 16, while on the United Nations side, both the U.S. Army and the U.S. Marine Corps were preparing for a new attack of their own on the 17th. It would be led by Brig. Gen. Edward Craig's 1st Provisional Marine Brigade, consisting of the 5th Marine Regiment (three battalions with only two rifle companies each), supported by a 105mm howitzer battalion from the 11th Marines and a tank company. The Marines also had their own air support—the 1st Marine Air Wing's gull-winged Vought F4U-5 Corsair fighters.

With Obong-ni Ridge ranked as objective No. 1, the plan of attack for August 17 called for the Marines to go first, with the Army's 9th Infantry providing supporting fire from Hill 125. The Marines then would support the 9th when it launched its own attack on the ridge west of Tugok. Unfortunately, the Marine preparatory artillery fire fell beyond the objective for the most part and was ineffective. The planned airstrike was so late the Corsairs had time for just one pass at Obong-ni before the infantry moved out.

After some problems in communications—and tough fighting—massed 24th Division artillery raked Cloverleaf late in the afternoon with airbursts. The 2nd Battalion, 9th Infantry, then took both Cloverleaf and Tugok without difficulty, as surviving enemy soldiers fled. The 9th now could protect and support the Marine right flank. The day ended with Marines on Hills 102 and 109 and in the gully between 109 and 117. On the 24th Division's right flank, the 34th and 19th Infantry regiments had taken Ohang Hill that afternoon. About 8 p.m., four enemy tanks clanked forward toward the Marines north of Obong-ni. They were met by 75mm recoilless rifles, 3.5-inch rocket launchers and fire from two Marine tanks. Three enemy tanks were quickly destroyed. While retreating, the fourth tank was destroyed by a rocket-launcher team from Company F, 9th Infantry.

A North Korean attack that night on F Company, west of Tugok, netted 100 yards. On Obong-ni, the enemy attacked down Hill 117, splitting Marine A Company, shattering its center platoon and driving it to the bottom of the ridge. The enemy assault then sputtered and receded. They made no attempt to flank the company position, nor to attack one of its platoons that was dug in by itself. Some officers believed that the attack was designed to conceal an enemy withdrawal.

319

On the morning of the 18th, the Marines continued their attack along Obong-ni, and by 9 a.m., they had taken Hills 117 and 143. Enemy soldiers retreated, in full view, to the hills beyond. Before morning's end, all of Obong-ni was in Marine hands—but A and B companies now totaled only 216 men, about half their original combined strength.

Once Obong-ni Ridge had been taken, artillery, mortar and tank fire blasted away; Corsairs dove to the attack, and the enemy retreat became a rout.

While the Marines cleared the North Koreans from the ridge and nearby Hill 207, the Army's 19th and 34th regiments still struggled. But by noon on August 18, they, too, had taken their objectives, Hills 240 and 223, and sent masses of enemy soldiers fleeing toward the river. Late in that afternoon Marine and Army attacks resumed, the Marines supported by an awesome array of mortars, artillery, recoilless rifles and tanks. By the end of August 18, most of the North Korean bridgehead had been eliminated, with a fearful slaughter of the enemy.

On the 19th, the 3rd Battalion, 5th Marines, launched the final assault; at 8:45 a.m., the Marines and 34th Infantry linked up with each other.

The price had been high. The Americans lost 137 killed, 763 wounded, 564 missing, and at least 161 non-battle casualties. Of the total, Marine casualties were 66 killed, 278 wounded and 1 missing. Many of the Army missing were later classified as dead. For example, the surgeon of the 3rd Battalion, 5th Marines, discovered the bodies of 30 soldiers in an overrun aid station. All had been murdered by the North Koreans.

The NKPA 4th Division, however, suffered horrendously. The Americans buried more than 1,200 of their dead. Estimated to have numbered no more than 8,000 men at the beginning of the battle, the North Korean division was reported to now number about 3,500. Only the enemy's lodgement on Hill 409 remained. No effort was made to reduce it.

The U.S. 2nd Infantry Division replaced the 24th along the Naktong. On August 31, the NKPA 2nd and 9th Infantry divisions crossed the Naktong both north of and into the old bulge area, and the struggle started all over again. This time, the North Koreans would not be driven back across the Naktong until the final enemy retreat from the entire Pusan perimeter following the Inchon landing on September 15.

THE NATIONAL
HISTORICAL SOCIETY

The National Historical Society was formed in 1996 as a membership organization dedicated to widespread and easy access to nonpartisan history-related information, products and services. Through it's grants program, the NHS supports nonprofit programs and organizations active in efforst to preserve and interpret America's heritage and to further interest in, and study of, history among the general public and students.

The NHS, through its affiliation with the History Group of Cowles Enthusiast Media, seeks to offer its members a wide variety of opportunities to participate in communities of interest. In addition to magazines, books, videos, tours and television programming, the NHS offers members and nonmembers a global gateway to historical information and forums for interaction with history enthusiasts around the world on the Internet via TheHistoryNet (http://www/the-historynet.com).

Other NHS member benefits include discounts at hundreds of historic sites and museums; Travel Club discounts on airfares and accommodations; special NHS-hosted tour opportunities; a subscription to *Historic Traveler* Magazine; the NHS Newsletter and NHS Collection Catalog; and voting privileges on the annual NHS grants.

For more information about the National Historical Society, call 1-800-849-6148.